The Airwaves of New York

Welcome to New York

The Airwaves of New York

*Illustrated Histories of
156 AM Stations in the
Metropolitan Area, 1921–1996*

by BILL JAKER,
FRANK SULEK, *and* PETER KANZE

WITH A FOREWORD BY
Joe Franklin

McFarland & Company, Inc., Publishers
Jefferson, North Carolina, and London

Cover photographs: Sportscaster Joe D'Urso ca. 1950 on WINS, courtesy the Peter Kanze Collection (*front*); the wooden tower of WEVD standing in the Bossert Lumber Yard in Brooklyn, courtesy David Winter (*back*).

Frontispiece: Welcome to New York — Horace Harding Blvd., Douglaston, Queens. 1938.

British Library Cataloguing-in-Publication data are available

Library of Congress Cataloguing-in-Publication Data

Jaker, Bill, 1939–
The airwaves of New York : illustrated histories of
156 AM stations in the Metropolitan Area,
1921–1996 / by Bill Jaker, Frank Sulek, and
Peter Kanze ; with a foreword by Joe Franklin.
p.   cm.
Includes bibliographical references (p.   ) and index.
ISBN 0-7864-0343-8 (case binding : 50# alkaline paper) ∞
1. Radio stations — New York — New York — History.
2. Radio broadcasting — New York — New York — History.
I. Sulek, Frank, 1945–   . II. Kanze, Peter. III. Title.
TK6548.U6J35 1998   384.54'06'57471— dc21
97-46948 CIP

Manufactured in the United States of America

*McFarland & Company, Inc., Publishers
Box 611, Jefferson, North Carolina 28640*

CONTENTS

FOREWORD

Like many another New York thoroughfare, Memory Lane gets pretty congested. Can you remember picking up a copy of the *New York American* or the *Herald Tribune*, then hopping a bright-red Third Avenue trolley car and riding to an exhibit at the magnificent Grand Central Palace? Or maybe you'd drop in on a six-day bicycle race at Madison Square Garden—not the present arena above Penn Station but a sweaty cavern sixteen blocks to the north.

Even if you do remember all those New York institutions (and if you do, as the old tune goes, "then, dearie, you're much older than I"), can you recall listening to WMSG, whose studios were located in the old Garden, or WGCP at Grand Central Palace? The company that ran the streetcars up and down Third Avenue also operated a little radio station called WEBJ. Those stations may have disappeared into thin air, but WINS is still going strong. It began in 1931 as the radio voice of Hearst's *New York American*. The *Trib* was also on the air with not just one AM station but four, a 1950-era radio network that covered Long Island and the northern suburbs.

New York was the center of big-time network radio, and it is still the home of many of the medium's most talented people. "The March of Time" once brought the nation a theatrical narrative of events around the world, and WMCA's "Five Star Final" did the same with local docudramas. Edward R. Murrow covered Europe in crisis, speaking live from the rubble of London; WOR's Dave Driscoll reported personal reaction to the war from the sidewalks of New York. Major Bowes' "Original Amateur Hour" was originally a local show on station WHN and continued in a New York version even after it became the top-rated national program on CBS (whose New York station was once called WABC, as is explained in these pages).

Beginning in New York radio when I did, I had the opportunity to work with people who were there in the early days and even at the creation. In 1945 I was fortunate to get a job picking records for Martin Block's "Make Believe Ballroom" on WNEW. Martin perfected that warm, persuasive manner that made you feel he was talking to a single individual while reaching a mass audience (or, as he put it, speaking "to you and you, but especially to *you*").

The broadcasting business is also a wonderful fraternity. The late Ted Cott was program director of WNEW when I worked there, and a very dear friend. When his wife was pregnant Ted held a "name the baby" contest, which I won with the entry "Boy Cott." (I doubt that the lad has carried the name through life.) I was program director at WPAT when I was just nineteen years old—probably the youngest p.d. in the country—and took the bus into Paterson every day. There I worked alongside such fine broadcasters as Chris Cunningham, Emily Deutsch, and Bill Bohack and had my own three-hour air shift. I learned a lot from them, and I hope they got a few things from me.

Here in the New York area more than 150 radio stations have had a place on the AM dial since the opening days in the early 1920s. They were entertainer, informant, and constant companion to millions of people. Some broadcasters were hopelessly stodgy and some thoroughly wacky. They all had a hand in making radio great. Sorry to say, you will never find full days of dusty radio shows tied up with string in someone's attic, and if you can restore an old Crosley "Pup," Atwater Kent, or Freed-Eisemann, it will display a regrettable tendency to pick up only present-day radio shows.

But the history is here, from the crystal set to the Walkman (both of which, I notice, require headphones). So please touch that dial, and let's go for a spin.

Joe Franklin

ACKNOWLEDGMENTS

The best source for the history of New York radio is the people who were and are part of the industry, and the authors who have been fortunate in sharing their recollections. We've known many fine people over the years but especially want to thank the following, who provided specific information and advice in the preparation of this book: Ray Adell, Herman Amis, George Ansbro, Dean Anthony, Frank Anthony, Ed Baer, Barbara Ballard, Barney Beck, Henry Behre, John Bennett, Rocky Bridges, Pete Brooks, Bob Brown, Tracy Carman, Allen Chambers, Rich Conaty, Rae Crawford, John Croft, Bob Daniels, Ed Davis, Tony Dee, Dick De Freitas, Pat Del Bene, George and Pat Dennos, Mike Derrough, Ken R. Deutsch, Del Dixon, Johnny Donovan, Jim Douglass, Ernie Duchal, Paul Ducroiset, Gene Edwards, George Edwards, Jack Ellsworth, Harry Fleetwood, Dave Frankel, Tom Franken, Bill Franklin, Alan Fredericks, Ben Freedman, Ron Furmanek, Bill Gaghan, Ed Geis, Barry Gray, Bruce Grossburg and family, Tom Hally, Arnold Hartley, Harvey Hauptman, Chuck Herlihy, Mr. and Mrs. Hillis Holt, Dean Hunter, Ed Ingles, Bob Jewell, Irving Kahn, Bob and Joen Kanze, Dan Kelleher, Mike Kennedy, Gene Ladd, David Lampel, Henry Lewis, Ed Locke, Dan Lohse, Dick London, Empress Hazel Manley, Jerry Marshall, Ron Marzlock, Dick Miller, Mark Mitchell, and Pat Montgomery.

We must also thank two men named Bob Morris. One is a former announcer at WERA; the other is a senior engineer whose career began at WEAF during the AT&T days. Also, we thank Cousin Brucie Morrow, Lee Munsick, Don Neumuller, Bob Neuwirth, Joe O'Brien, Michael Ochs, Tom O'Hanlon, Hal Ohnsman, Dennis O'Mara, Bill O'Sullivan, Bill Owen, Phil Painter, Dominick Parascandolo, Wally Parker, John Pepe, Brad Phillips, Rich Phoenix, Mrs. Garo Ray, Gene Rayburn, Jack Raymond, Joe Roberts, Ken Roberts, Richard Ross, Ed Rothschild, Dave Rozek,

Thurmon Ruth, Ed Salamon, Bob Salter, Henry Sapoznik, Ernie Schaufler, Tim Scheld, Bob Schwarz, Dave Schwarz, John Scott, Paul Sidney, Dave Siegel, Suzanne Siegel, Barry Siegfried, Dick Sifrie, Rick Sklar, Pete Socolow, Herb Squire, Irv Steele, Gary Stevens, Danny Stiles, Martin Stone, George Travis, Steve Uckerman, Jeffrey Williams, Ken Williamson, Don Wilson, David Winter, Bill Winters, and Don Worsham.

In addition, we would like to thank Fr. Lawrence MacDonnell and Fr. Donal P. Forrester of the Paulist Fathers for their accounts of WLWL and Emma Smith of Calvary Baptist Church for information about WQAO. Thanks also go to Bruce and Charlotte at WAVES and Frank Bequart at Rainy Day Books.

Recognition is due the Antique Wireless Association and curator of Bruce Kelley of the AWA Museum in Bloomfield, N.Y., especially for information on the early days of radio; the David Sarnoff Library at the Sarnoff Research Center in Princeton, N.J., for facts about RCA and NBC; and the Library of American Broadcasting. The Library and Museum of the Performing Arts at Lincoln Center contains many valuable sources, including the personal papers of Major Bowes, Dailey Paskman, and Ray Walker.

There is also a very special group of broadcast historians whose research and dogged determination continue to uncover facts about one of the great developments of the twentieth century. Some of these special people are Donna Halper, Bob Harrison, John Kitross, Barry Mishkind, and Thomas H. White.

The authors want to express their appreciation to Ed Lawlor for getting the three of us together and to Ed Brouder for receiving the text and offering helpful comments.

Finally, a very special word of thanks goes to Bob Cobaugh. For fifty years Bob was an engineer at WQXR—

he began there when it was still W2XR — and was a keen observer of the New York radio scene, which he helped to develop. His advice on historical and technical matters was invaluable to us. Bob died while this book was in preparation. We hope the final product will serve as a tribute to Bob Cobaugh's professionalism and generosity.

INTRODUCTION

The Airwaves of New York

> Well, here goes something into nothing.
> —*First words reportedly spoken into*
> *Dr. Lee De Forest's radiophone by*
> *singer Geraldine Farrar, ca. 1908*

Ever since that Wednesday, 4 October 1899, when Guglielmo Marconi flashed wireless telegraph reports of the America's Cup yacht race to the *New York Herald*, there's usually been something good to listen to on the radio in New York.

Visionary Croatian-born physicist Nikola Tesla was already experimenting with Hertzian waves at his laboratory in downtown Manhattan in the early 1890s. He conceived of a system of wireless electrical transmission and radio broadcasting and in 1901 erected a 187-foot "World Wireless Radio Telephone" tower alongside Long Island Sound at Shoreham in a fruitless attempt to send signals around the globe. (It remained a curious landmark till it was blown up in 1917 to prevent any possible use in wartime espionage.)

The new science advanced quickly. An ambitious wireless enthusiast of the early 1900s might go down to Hugo Gernsback's Electro Importing Company at 233 Fulton Street in Manhattan to buy the homely components — coils, wire, galena crystal — that somehow snatched signals out of "the ether." Soon, aerials of radio experimenters and ham operators were strung across rooftops and backyards in every neighborhood.

In 1908, the Telefunken Company of Germany conducted a series of radiotelephone experiments using the "singing arc" method of transmitting voices and music. The transmitter was located at Sandy Hook, N.J., and a receiving station was set up at Fort Wood, at the foot of the Statue of Liberty. The tests were a technical failure as well as a strain on the voices repeatedly shouting "One, two, three, four, five. Fort Wood, Fort Wood....."

On completing his electrical engineering degree at Yale, Dr. Lee De Forest moved to New York to be near the center of research and development in wireless communication. It was here he perfected the audion tube and with it the science of electronics. By 1907, Dr. De Forest was achieving some success in radiotelephone experiments from his lab at the Parker Building on Fourth Avenue and Nineteenth Street. Among the first people to speak over the air was De Forest's mother-in-law, Harriot Stanton Blatch, whose address in favor of women's suffrage may have been the first political broadcast. He even found something of an audience, though wireless operators at the Brooklyn Navy Yard who picked up music on their headphones thought it might be the voices of angels.

On Thursday, 13 January 1910, De Forest installed his transmitter on the roof of the Metropolitan Opera House and sent out a performance of the double bill of *Cavalleria rusticana* and *I Pagliacci*, the latter featuring the great tenor Enrico Caruso. Although it advanced De Forest's notion of using the wireless to spread high culture, poor audio quality and interference from a maritime transmitter at Manhattan Beach showed that the new technology was not ready to become a bearer of the fine arts. The inventor of the audion was still using the carbon arc to transmit and had merely tapped a telephone connection from the stage to pick up the singing.

De Forest moved his work to a laboratory at 1391 Sedgewick Avenue, in the High Bridge section of the Bronx. From this station, licensed with the call sign 2XG, he broadcast radio's first election returns on the night of 6 November 1916 — four years ahead of the milestone broadcasts by

KDKA/Pittsburgh and WWJ/Detroit. Returns were fed from the newsroom of Hearst's *New York American.* That night De Forest even delivered radio's first voter projection: not waiting for California to report in, he announced that Republican Charles Evans Hughes had defeated President Woodrow Wilson and signed off.

The development of the regenerative circuit and the superheterodyne receiver by Edwin Howard Armstrong of Yonkers turned the device that strained dots, dashes, and voices from the air into a means of communication that would soon be available to anyone.

This abundance of early wireless activity in metropolitan New York — including the first steps toward what would become the broadcasting industry — was not solely due to the city's role as a center of commerce, education, and the arts. It was also a natural outgrowth of the coastal location. The harbor of New York was the site of numerous military and maritime transmitters, with major communications stations at Sayville, Long Island, and Tuckerton, N.J.

There was also an important enterprise in what we might call the unwireless. In 1911–12, inspired by a "talking newspaper" that had been operating in Budapest, Hungary since 1893, the New Jersey Telephone Herald established a kind of cable-radio in Newark. The backers had wanted to set up their system in Manhattan, but failing to gain the cooperation of the New York Telephone Company, they moved across the Hudson. From facilities in the Essex Building that bore a strong resemblance to later broadcasting studios, the Telephone Herald disseminated news, sports and weather, fashion items, stock market reports, and even bedtime stories for the kiddies. Musical programs originated from nearby theaters. The Telephone Herald served some five thousand subscribers daily from eight in the morning till eleven o'clock at night.

The audio quality was reportedly acceptable for the time, but the listener had to keep an ear pressed to an earphone installed in the wall, giving the Telephone Herald an immobile audience confined to the network of wires. The New Jersey Telephone Herald was undercapitalized, the novelty soon wore off, and the system was shut down in December 1912.

During the 1910s and 1920s, all of radio was operating within what we now know is a tiny section of the radio spectrum. The useable frequencies began at about 150 kilocycles and did not extend far above the present top of the AM broadcast band. Into this space were jammed ship-to-shore radio, commercial telegraphers, hams, technical schools, and the army and navy (immediately after World War I the navy tried to wrest from the Commerce Department the authority for licensing all stations in the United States), as well as every manner of experimental and "pirate" operation.

Even the best receivers had trouble picking out one station from all those on the air — spark gap telegraphers were more readily identifiable by their individual sound than by their relatively uncontrollable frequencies. No wonder the U.S. Commerce Department's chief radio inspector in the New York area, Arthur Batcheller, tried to turn away Lee De Forest's request for modification of his radiotelephone license with the words, "There is no room in the ether for entertainment!"

Nonetheless, entertainment could be found in the ether during the years leading to the start of officially licensed broadcasting. As early as 1908, A. Frederick Collins of 51 Clinton Street in Newark was sending out music and voices from his arc transmitter, which anyone could listen to over the receiver that he had installed at the L.S. Plaut and Co. store on Broad Street. By 1911 the Radio Club of America was serenading wireless operators. Five nights a week beginning in 1919, De Forest's assistant, Bob Gowen, aired "radio concerts" from High Bridge and from his home in Ossining.

Although the wireless, both telephone and telegraph, was used primarily to carry messages, communications stations would occasionally broadcast entertainment and other features on a prearranged schedule. One such program — an admixture of broadcasting and point-to-point communication — aired in New York on the evening of Friday, 3 December 1920.

The Army Signal Corps set up a microphone in the Hotel McAlpin apartment of famed opera singer Luisa Tetrazzini and connected it by telephone wire ("without even going through the hotel switchboard," marveled the *Times*) to a transmitter atop the Whitehall Building. The station operated at 400 meters wavelength (about 750kc), chosen because it was "well adapted to carrying her songs" and would "be least susceptible to interference from routine wireless work."

At 9:30 P.M., "telephonic radio stations [were] ordered to suspend traffic for thirty minutes." The evening's broadcast began with army Private Fred Bennett at Fort Wood singing "A Tumble-Down Shack in Athione" through the transmitter at the foot of the Statue of Liberty. Then the Whitehall transmitter was switched on and Mme. Tetrazzini sang the Polonaise from *Mignon*, the Rondo from *La Sonnambula*, "Somewhere a Voice Is Calling" (a fitting selection), and finally "I millioni d'Arlecchino." At the end of the recital the stations resumed their normal communications mode. Operators at the Whitehall Building, on board the USS *Pennsylvania*, and in the Brooklyn Navy Yard exchanged comments with Mme. Tetrazzini at the McAlpin. They had enjoyed the program (and radio had taken one of its first listener surveys). It was no longer an intimation of insanity for a wireless operator to state that he heard music in his headphones.

"What is the idea of having no windows?" asked Bob.

"So there shall be no vibration from the window panes," replied Mr. Reed. "I tell you, boys, this broadcasting hasn't been a matter of days, but is the development of months of the hardest kind of work and experiment. We have had to test, reject, and sift all possible suggestions in order to reach perfection. I don't mean by that to say that we have reached it yet, but we're on the way."

—from *"The Radio Boys at the Sending Station"* by Allen Chapman (1922)

The first license issued specifically for broadcasting in the New York area was assigned to Westinghouse, which had pioneered with its stations KDKA in Pittsburgh and WBZ in Springfield, Mass. (The company's involvement in radio had actually begun three decades earlier when George Westinghouse became a backer of Nikola Tesla's experiments.) The permit for WJZ of Newark, N.J., was issued by the Commerce Department on 1 June 1921, but the station did not sign on until October. Before then, however, another pioneer slipped in with a radio spectacular that introduced broadcasting to thousands of new listeners.

The Radio Corporation of America (RCA) was less than two years old when it entered the broadcasting field in the summer of 1921. RCA had been organized at the close of World War I to nationalize, under private auspices, the U.S. assets of the British-based Marconi Company. It served also to pool the radio patents of its constituent companies, including Westinghouse, General Electric (GE), and the American Telephone and Telegraph (AT&T) Company. Guiding the operations of this nascent giant was an erstwhile Marconi telegraph boy, general manager David Sarnoff, whose vision of a "radio music box" was about to become a radio ringside seat.

The first major event to be broadcast from the New York area was a prizefight between heavyweights Jack Dempsey and Georges Carpentier, on Saturday, 2 July 1921. The fight was staged by boxing promoter Tex Rickard, who was then managing Madison Square Garden. On that hot July day the bout would take place not at the Garden but at an open-air arena in Jersey City called Boyle's Thirty Acres. These rough surroundings provided a good setting for a radio broadcast, for RCA had to construct a complete station on the site. It utilized the Lackawanna Railroad's nearby radio towers (while he was a Marconi employee, Sarnoff had overseen construction of the Lackawanna wireless) and took over a porters' shack to house the radiotelephone transmitter, which had just been built by GE for the U.S. Navy. It was granted a temporary license and the call letters WJY.

Credit for the idea of broadcasting the fight should actually go to the Madison Square Garden concert manager, Julius Hopp. Hopp arranged for ham radio operators to set up receivers in theaters and meeting halls as a fund-raising event for the Navy Club and the American Committee

for Devastated France. David Sarnoff arranged for technical support from RCA, and J. Andrew White — at the time the editor of *Wireless Age* magazine and later one of the founders of CBS — delivered the blow-by-blow description. Sarnoff also spoke some of the commentary, but his and White's voices went only as far as the transmitter shack. The voice that listeners heard was that of J. O. Smith, the engineer who repeated everything into the microphone wired directly into the modulation circuit.

The station operated on a wavelength of 1600 meters (187kc), well below the present AM broadcast band but on a frequency that facilitated long-distance reception. RCA predicted before the broadcast that the audience might number around three hundred thousand, and that number was never checked or changed. The figure now seems exaggerated by tenfold. WJY could be heard well for about a two-hundred-mile radius. Organized groups were gathered at some thirty sites, ten of them in New York City, while individuals listened in on their homemade receivers. Perhaps thirty thousand were in the radio audience (fewer than were packed into Boyle's Thirty Acres). The experiment was a success, but just barely. As Carpentier hit the canvas in the fourth round, the borrowed navy transmitter overloaded and New York's first big broadcast came to an end.

The principal candidates in the 1921 New York City mayoral contest utilized radio for election-eve addresses. On Monday, 7 November, Democratic incumbent John M. Hylan spoke from the A.H. Grebe & Co. radio factory in Richmond Hill while Henry Curran, the Coalition candidate, delivered his address "into the transmission apparatus at the laboratories of the De Forest Radio Telephone and Telegraph Company" at High Bridge.

On New Year's Day 1922, the *New York Times* reported: "An audience of perhaps 100,000 people in and about New York listen in every evening on an elaborate concert broadcasted by wireless electricity. Throughout the greater part of the day a brief concert is sent out every hour, on the hour…. These entertainments are literally free as air. A half dozen different musical numbers may often be picked up at the same time."

Something wondrous was catching on. A young listener wrote to "The Man in the Moon" at station WJZ late in 1921, "When you are talking I can even hear the inhalation of your breath and when a record is played we can hear the needle when it is placed on the record." Even if radio was considered a toy (some stores sold wireless apparatus in the toy department), there were still glimpses of how the new medium might be used for lofty purposes. In April 1922, as part of the celebration of a new Baptist church building in Jamaica, Queens, Rev. Winfrid Heath Sobey broadcast an hour-long sermon not from an ordinary terrestrial transmitter but from a radiophone in an airplane flying above the city. Rev. Sobey was hailed for having reached the largest audience ever to hear the voice of a preacher.

ATWATER KENT ● RADIO LOG No.

CITY & STATE	CALL LETTERS	WAVE LENGTH	DIAL SETTINGS 1			2	3	REMARKS
			TAP 1	TAP 2	TAP 3			
Schenectady	WGY	380		40		45	43	
Washington	WCAE		(62)	57		66	67	
New York	WEAF		72	(65)		74	75	
New York	WJY	49	40	43	49	49		
New York	W.J.Z	63	60	52	63	63		63 W.72
Philadelphia	WDAR			15		23	27	
Brooklyn	W.BBR	273	21	15 1/4		23	20	Watchtower
Rich Hill	WAHG			25		30	30	A.H.Lincoln & Co
" "	WAHG		30			30	30	Jamaica 5803 plus
New York City	WNYC			85	80	85	85	Municipal
W. W. S	15	25	25	25	53	57	53	
Cincinatti	WLW			52		52	52	53.5
Newark N.J	WOR			47		50	50	L. Bamberger
New York	WHN			35		40	38	
	WHH			30		35	33	
Newark	WAAM			20		20	19	
"	WAAM	19	20			21	19	
Pittsburg	WCAE				55	65	65	
Davenport	WOC			68		71	72	
N.Y.C.	WFBH	22			23	26	Endicott 7220	
Rich Hill L.I.	WAHG			25	30	35	30	Small Inst.
	J.F.C.			89		90	92	
Pittsfield Mass			5	8	8	5	3	
Syracuse	WFBL	15	7		17	15	End.4220	
New York City	WEBH	HOTEL MAJESTIC	22	25		23	21	Lackawana 8245
Cincinatti	WSAI			22		30	28	U.S. Playing
El Paso	W84D							Q T R Ranch
Boston	WEEI			21		29	25	
Pittsburg	KDKA			27		33	32	
Chicago	WLS	36	32		36	36	Sears Roebuck	
						56.5	35.5	

The radio spectrum is a finite resource, and the scarcity of space in the 1920s was aggravated by the fact that virtually anyone could obtain a license to put a station on the air. Obtaining a good physical facility was another matter — keeping a station up-to-date in a rapidly developing field was a technical, financial, and legal headache — but the condition was described by one writer of the time as "the gold rush of the air." The explosive growth of radio continued through the twenties, unchecked even by economic downturns. The boom could easily be felt in the New York area.

Several major players entered the game early. Westinghouse established WJZ in Newark in October 1921 as a counterpart to its stations in Pittsburgh and Springfield, Mass. The American Telephone and Telegraph Company also entered the broadcasting field with state-of-the-art facilities and a business plan to charge a fee to anyone who wanted to address the public.

But privately owned transmitters proliferated. Since broadcasting itself was not yet a money-making enterprise, stations were mostly run by businesses with an interest in some aspect of radio sales or development. Wanamaker's department store briefly operated station WWZ in the early 1920s, and Gimbel Brothers had some success with WGBS for much of the decade, while Bamberger's WOR grew to be "one of America's great stations." Electrical manufacturer Ira R. Nelson and radio entrepreneur Alfred Grebe both started small stations that would evolve into the flagships of important media empires.

And then there were all the others: hotels, churches, political organizations, the Third Avenue Railway, Hugo Gernsback, and even the city of New York itself. Ham radio operators transmitted music and sounded like broadcasting stations. They were ordered to cease and desist and get out of the way or else obtain broadcasting licenses. So from Red Bank to Tarrytown to Freeport, tiny stations came on from attics, garages, stores, and parlors. Soon, everyone was experiencing the electronic version of "New York elbows."

Until the mid–1920s, a radio receiver was customarily an assemblage of naked components. Listeners at their "receiving stations" had to delicately complete several steps, adjusting coils and variable condensers to tune the proper wavelength and — on more advanced sets — boost the signal through several stages of amplification into headphones or speaker horn. Radio logbooks provided space to jot down dial settings as an aid to tuning in the station the next time — if the listener knew at what hours it might again be on the air and if the station didn't move to a different wavelength.

Armstrong's superheterodyne, as well as the invention of "single-dial control" by John V. L. Hogan at his laboratories in Manhattan and Long Island City, changed everything. It became as simple to tune a radio as it was to switch on a light, and stations could be located along a strip as plain as a ruler. Now every station had its "spot on the dial." So one of the tenets of real estate came to apply to radio: the three most important factors for success were location, location, and location.

Try a little experiment: set an AM radio dial at 1400 and turn the knob to 1500, making note of how far you have to twist your wrist. Then do it again from 600 to 700. The physical fact should be clear on any analog tuner. The higher you go in frequency, the shorter the wavelength, the closer together the stations. Lower frequencies also require less power to get good coverage. It was apparent to New York broadcasters in the 1920s that the most spacious locations were "downtown." This was true anywhere, of course, but the nation's biggest metropolis has always had a perverse pride in its crowding. As the federal government sought to bring order to a rapidly developing mass medium, New York looked like an intractable case.

At first all broadcasting of "news, concerts, lectures and like matter" was confined to a single wavelength of 360 meters (about 830 kHz on today's AM dial). Early newspaper listings sometimes neglected to mention the station that would be radiating programs. In December 1921, the Bureau of Navigation of the U.S. Commerce Department added a second wavelength of 485 meters. In the spring of 1922, the ten stations then active in the metropolitan area (WJZ, WOR, WBS, WHN, WRW, WWZ, WAAM, WAAT, WBAN, and WBAY) agreed on a time-sharing schedule. The agreement would not endure.

Despite technical problems, radio grew in popularity and respectability. The wireless prevailed over a 1923 experiment by electric utilities to radiate broadcasts from power lines. For two dollars a month, Wired Radio, Inc. — a subsidiary of the Cleveland Electric Light Company — offered to hook up residents of Staten Island to its "Theatrome" and provide them with an electrical receiver that it said was "like a toaster." It was no more successful than the Telephone Herald had been a decade earlier.

In the spring of 1923 the Ritz Apartments at 299 Clinton Avenue in Newark wired each of its seventy-two apartments for radio reception. Only one program could be received at a time, and it was usually selected by a building employee monitoring the rooftop receiver.

March 1923 saw a development that might well mark the start of radio broadcasting as a home-entertainment industry in the United States. Rather than assigning a handful of frequencies, the Commerce Department created a broadcast band running from 550 to 1350 kilocycles, soon expanded to 1500. At that time a dozen stations were regularly operating in the New York area. Within two years the

Opposite: Station log, ca. 1925. In the early days, listeners kept records of stations they caught and noted the dial settings so that they could indeed "tune in again, same time, same station." This card, evidently kept by a listener in the New York City area, includes reception of such pioneers as WAAM, WAHG, and WLWL.

figure would double, and by the time strong federal regulation was instituted in 1927, some fifty radio stations were clamoring for a place on New York's dials.

In April 1923, New York radio inspector Arthur Batcheller convened a meeting of local broadcasters organized as the Inter-Company Radiophone Broadcasting Committee to explain the new classification of broadcasting stations, restrict the hours of experimental transmissions, and urge that stations cooperate in arranging their schedules. The assignments served to solidify the favored positions of WEAF, WOR, WJZ, and WHN. City-owned WNYC later joined the pack at the bottom of the dial — 570 kc, close by the maritime stations and too low for many home receivers — while new stations in the city and the suburbs were relegated to the higher frequencies .

In 1924, noting that the newspaper published radio schedules and technical articles but no criticism such as that given to drama, films, and music, the *New York Herald* stated in an editorial that it would now review radio programs. Some broadcasters visited the newspaper to personally express thanks, although columns by Raymond Yates and Stewart "Pioneer" Hawkins would often prove to be devastating.

Dr. A. H. Dellinger, chief of the radio lab at the National Bureau of Standards, remarked in December 1925 that "this was the year in which radio became grown up." But a week later the *Herald*'s Hawkins reviewed the play *The Show Off* and revealed how much farther radio had to go. "Mr Dorn's quaveringly magnificent groans won the highest honors of the evening, with the telephone bell a close second…. That the transmission characteristics of WGBS and all other stations still make 'S' a confusing sound dulled the edge of the most incisive sentences, causing 'Sue 'em' to come out of the loudspeaker as 'Shoom.'"

From the start, a handful of New York area stations were in distinctly favorable positions, technically and commercially, whereas another larger group would literally struggle to be heard. Often the struggle was among the stations assigned to share time on a frequency. Once the Commerce Department chose which stations were to be dial buddies, it was up to them to work out the schedule and other details.

This was not always as burdensome as it might appear. Tuning in was tricky, and listening was not as convenient an activity as it would become when loudspeakers could easily fill rooms (and, later on, automobiles) with clear sound. The challenge of maintaining a transmitter and antenna in working condition required regular downtime and even caused engineers from rival stations to fraternally cooperate. Programming in intermittent blocks was, of course, cheaper than keeping a station on the air all day long. Between broadcast times, explained one announcer, "I answered the phone and swept the floor."

By 1925, the Commerce Department considered all

available frequencies occupied and Secretary Herbert Hoover announced that no further broadcast licenses would be issued. Anyone who wanted to get on the air would have to either buy out an existing station or purchase air time from one of the growing number of "toll broadcasters."

Within a year, this situation was turned on its head. In April 1926 a federal court found in favor of the Zenith Radio Company, which had moved its Chicago station WJAZ onto an unassigned frequency and had asserted that the Commerce Department had no authority to reassign it, to rescind its license, or even to deny any citizen a broadcasting license. The U.S. attorney general examined the Radio Act of 1912 and told the secretary of commerce that Zenith was right.

Suddenly, the broadcast band was lawless territory. The National Association of Broadcasters asked its members to voluntarily show restraint and try to maintain their existing frequency and power assignments. Congress was likely to break a four-year logjam over radio regulation, and stations could later be penalized.

The plea generally fell on deaf — or distracted — ears. Between July 1926 and the end of January 1927, some twenty stations in the New York area were awarded their obligatory licenses and squeezed onto the dial.

"I am missing all the good things broadcast over WEAF because I am unable to tune out WRNY. Sometimes when I have WEAF it just shuts off and WRNY is there. This never happened before I changed rooms."
— *letter from L.S. to New York Times,
16 January 1927*

Chaos signed on during the summer of 1926. Stations that had been relegated to the upper regions looked for an open spot on a better frequency. Little WHAP dropped in between powerhouses WJZ and WOR. Half a dozen transmitters shifted during one week in July. Typical was the attitude of Hugo Gernsback's WRNY, which denied it had "pirated" its frequency and claimed that its own tests showed no interference. Unfortunately, even a slight shift can generate an annoying whistle in receivers hundreds of miles away.

The alibis were as shameful as the infractions, leaving listeners with the impression that the moves were officially sanctioned. They were not; given the legal vacuum, they couldn't be. One manager insisted his "wave jumping" was done at the urging of a major advertiser who threatened to drop an account if the station didn't provide better exposure. In some cases, the newly claimed frequency was no improvement, and stations went back to the old spots on the dial.

Opposite: **A performance from RCA's original "Radio Broadcast Central" studio in Aeolian Hall, ca. 1923.**

Revision of the 1912 radio law had been stalled in Congress, but as the 1926 congressional session drew to a close it appeared that the White-Dill Radio Act was likely to pass. Suddenly the "gold rush" went into a final sprint. Among those who met the minimal qualifications to receive a broadcasting license was a Boy Scout troop in Washington Heights.

In an opportunistic attempt to bring some order to the airwaves a bill was introduced in the New York legislature in January 1927, seeking to place all commercial stations in the Empire State under the control of the Public Service Commission (PSC). The bill would have granted the PSC the authority to make rules on frequency assignments, advertising rates, and even programming. Such a move was clearly beyond the authority of the state, and the idea became moot on February 23, when President Calvin Coolidge signed the Radio Act of 1927. The new Federal Radio Commission (FRC) issued every station in the country a temporary license good for thirty or sixty days. The FRC would use the time to devise more permanent arrangements, many of which would have the effect of rewarding or penalizing stations.

The commission was trying to balance technical necessity with political reality and to preserve as many licensees as possible despite the obvious overpopulation. In April 1927, *Radio Broadcast* magazine published its recommendations for realigning New York area radio. In an article entitled "Deliver Us from Excess Broadcasting Stations," the magazine stated: "The principle must be recognized that the fewer broadcasting stations there are on the air, the more stations the listener can enjoy. Freedom of the air does not require that everyone who wishes to impress himself on the radio audience need have his private microphone to do so."

Radio Broadcast felt that the best way to weed out the excess was for stations to consolidate through private negotiation, and it presented its own plan whereby nineteen channels then in use in the metropolitan area could be reduced to six. The proposal gives a reminder of what a New York listener could pick up during that chaotic time, and it reveals much about New York radio in the 1920s.

In the opinion of *Radio Broadcast*, only seven stations were worthy of survival: WEAF and WJZ, key stations of the new NBC Red and Blue Networks; WOR in Newark, which the writer said should absorb all other northern New Jersey stations; Loew's WHN, Gimbel's WGBS sharing time with the Atlantic Broadcasting Company's WABC, and two smaller stations, WPCH and WEBJ.

The article further proposed merging the four time-sharing stations into one, giving metropolitan New York five radio stations, which *Radio Broadcast* felt ought to be plenty. Its rationale was that silencing smaller stations would clear the air for New Yorkers to regularly receive broadcasts from Baltimore or Nashville or Omaha or anywhere. It was a scheme that failed to envision how either network or local radio would develop.

There were fifty-seven radio stations on the air in the New York area at the start of 1927. Nine of them didn't reapply as required by the Radio Act — nearly all "coffeepots" but including RCA's pioneering but superannuated WJY. The two Grebe mobile transmitters, WGMU and WRMU, were moved out of the broadcast band. Of the remaining forty-six, only eighteen were given exclusive frequencies. The FRC was careful to establish clean separation between stations and to remove offending stations from reserved Canadian channels.

But an uncomfortable problem remained for those usurpers ejected from the Canadian frequencies. "In a crowded centre like New York City," stated an FRC report, "there were not sufficient wave lengths to accommodate 'homeless' stations, for whom channels then had to be found. Such channels as had been cleared by the failure of other stations to renew their license were permitted to be shared by the homeless stations." If no room could be found, they would be invited to move up to what was then referred to as "shortwave," on 1390 and 1480 kilocycles.

With the changeover planned for Monday, 9 May 1927, Commissioner Orestes Caldwell — a Bronxville resident whose territory included his home state — returned to the city and personally reviewed permanent assignments with the station owners. The initial aim was to establish twenty frequencies at least 50 kilocycles apart for the New York area, which meant eliminating eleven channels as well as clearing the air of marginal operations. Thus began political, legal, and business struggles that would not be fully settled for more than a decade.

As station engineers trotted up to the FRC office to calibrate their measurement equipment, owners and managers examined the new orders, and in the great American tradition, some of them organized. Charles Burke of the Flatbush Radio Laboratories' WFRL issued the invitation, stating that the new assignment "has seriously embarrassed our operation and amounts to a practical confiscation of property."

Burke's invitation had been sent to twenty-nine of forty-six broadcasters, specifically those dividing the upper end of the radio dial. (Some stations were perfectly satisfied; WOR and WRNY sent messages of congratulation to the FRC for its fine work.) The Broadcast Owners Association of New York met at the Hotel Pennsylvania on 26 May 1927. An attorney was retained, and his first task was to seek a delay of new assignments and then to test the legality of the FRC orders. The greatest burdens were time-sharing requirements and the orders to move to "graveyard" frequencies.

The Broadcast Owners Association might have had more success if its members had simply been commercial rivals, but they were also in territorial conflict and battled each other, as much as the FRC, with every change that took place. The commission didn't help matters by suggesting that new stations could take over the frequency of older ones if they could prove they were better able to serve "the public interest, convenience and necessity." To help buttress any decision it might make, the Federal Radio Commission itself conducted one of the first surveys of listening habits and tried to determine which stations were the most popular in the New York area. WJZ won.

New allocations went into effect on Wednesday, 15 June 1927. Only WNYC (assigned to 560kc), WEAF (610), WJZ (660) and WOR (710, where it has been ever since) had exclusive full-time allocations. All the others were sharing time and shifting to new frequencies; they were then told to move again in an incredibly complicated situation that left both listeners and broadcasters confused. Perhaps most frustrating was that the new licenses were good for only sixty days.

As of 1 July 1927 there were fifty-one radio stations within the fifty-mile radius of Columbus Circle that defined the New York metropolitan area. Nine and a half million residents of the region owned approximately a million and a half radios.

The growing audience made New York radio a rapidly developing advertising medium. Some stations were devoted to indirect advertising in support of the station owner (Bamberger's WOR was a good example), whereas others were still trying to advance the sale of radio sets (the RCA-NBC operations). But increasingly listeners were hearing — and often complaining about — direct advertising. A 1927 column in the *Herald-Tribune* by Stewart Hawkins noted, "WMCA is a ripe example of direct advertising at its most consistent offensiveness, with talks and prize contests and repetitious address-giving standing out above its attempts at entertainment." The columnist predicted that the audience would turn to radio "not as a source of entertainment but as a bargain guide." He also envisioned direct advertising on the wane, "more desperate and intrusive as it wanes."

Despite commercial, technical, and regulatory problems, radio was clearly turning into a popular mass medium. A survey didn't even have to be conducted to find out: one could just walk down the street on a summer evening and listen to programs wafting from open windows. Beginning around 1922, the area near Cortlandt and Greenwich Streets in lower Manhattan turned into "Radio Row," with dozens of stores selling every manner of radio gear.

Radio manufacturers and broadcasters could even meet their public in Madison Square Garden at the exhibits that began in 1924. The first Radio World's Fair at the Garden — with a spillover into the 69th Regiment Armory — drew 175,000 visitors. In September 1928 the fair, at a newly built Garden, drew the unseen audience to check out the latest sets, attend broadcasts by half a dozen stations from the "Crystal Studio," and (the most exciting attraction) get a peek at the still-crude miracle of television. Several stations, including WRNY and WMCA, were scheduling experimental mechanically scanned pictures as well as sound.

As the FRC pursued its task of weeding out "excess" stations, the president of the Long Island Chamber of Commerce, William H. Ross, telegraphed Commissioner Caldwell with an appeal to spare small, local stations. In August 1928 Caldwell responded, "I feel that there is plenty of room for a comparatively large number of ... transmitters of 10 to 50 watts power, so that every community of 10,000 population and above can have its voice on the air ... if, in addition to receiving the great general programs which will always be the backbone of radio service to all listeners, there is also made available at one end of the dial, out of the way of present popular programs, a 'local' band where the listener can tune in his town or county transmitter."

The conflict for time and space on the dial was fittingly resolved on Armistice Day, 11 November 1928, when stations throughout the United States settled down on what were to be permanent assigned frequencies. The Federal Radio Commission begged everyone not to complain too quickly, but WNYC immediately made an issue of losing its exclusivity on 570kc in a time-sharing arrangement with WMCA. To reduce interference at the cost of coverage, many stations were ordered to reduce their power. Only WABC received a power increase. Listeners adjusted radios and habits to these changes and generally reported improved reception. Six stations were still found off frequency, some because they hadn't yet installed crystal-controlled transmitters.

As the twenties drew to a close, the "radiophone" was turning into a familiar companion, one of life's necessities. Many early technical objections were conquered, often by listeners who simply replaced crude receivers with more modern sets. The National Broadcasting Company's Red and Blue Networks and the Columbia Broadcasting System began national service. Schedules were filled with sopranos and "barytones," jazz, and potted-palm music. News reporting was still undeveloped, but radio showed its strength in coverage of special events and sports. The networks and major independents were bringing vaudeville, opera, and drama right into the home. The WOR morning man John Gambling was receiving five thousand letters a week.

At the same time, small stations still strained to find talent willing to appear for little or nothing: banjo ensembles, saxophone octets, virtuosi on the musical saw. Though officially neutral when it came to programming, the federal government — especially the business-oriented administrations of the 1920s — actively favored the development of a broadcasting industry with broad public appeal.

As early as 1922 the government had been willing to grant preferred status to those stations that promised not to air phonograph records. This made sense at a time when acoustical recordings were played through a morning-glory horn into a carbon microphone. But by the end of the decade, both recording and broadcasting had advanced enough (partly through application of the same technologies) that the policy against recorded music was a cultural and technical anachronism.

Nonetheless, in September 1928 the Federal Radio Commission declared a bias against "stations which give the sort of service which is readily available in another form." The rule was clearly aimed at broadcasters in the large cities, for

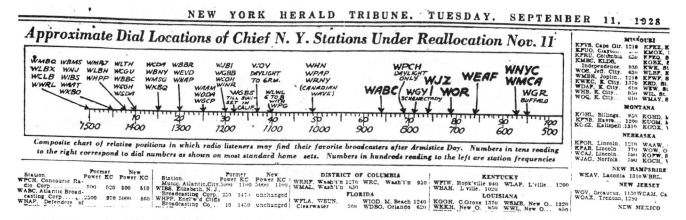

Dial locations, admittedly approximate, after the latest FRC reallocation, from the New York Herald Tribune of 11 September 1928. This was not the first such chart and wouldn't be the last.

the FRC specifically stated, "The situation is not always the same in some of the smaller towns and farming communities where program material is not always available." In other words, a station's programming would be determined by how far its audience had to travel to the theater or record store.

Radio stations in Manhattan might find an eager pool of professional or semiprofessional talent, but in the outer boroughs and the suburbs nearly every hour was amateur hour. There were several ways of stretching available talent resources, including instrumentalists or singers who would perform under several names. For stations close to the city, there was also the expedient of moving to Manhattan.

WJZ had established the precedent in 1922, and others across the Hudson and the East River saw their success tied to a closer identification with New York City (even as the Jersey swamps and Long Island meadows became favored sites for their transmitters). WOR set up studios and offices near Times Square at 1440 Broadway in 1926, continuing to identify itself as being in Newark, where it eventually maintained a recording device that said "WOR, Newark." In July 1929, the Columbia Broadcasting System and its station, WABC, moved into four floors of a new office building at 485 Madison Avenue.

The 1930 U.S. Census counted more than one million radio sets in New York City; nearly 60 percent of the local population was tuned in. Department stores conspicuously cut back the size of their record departments, often to make room for the radio displays. But the economic decline could be felt following the boom years of the 1920s. There were 350 exhibitors at the 1929 Radio World's Fair in Madison Square Garden, but only 135 one year later.

Still, there was no grander sign that radio was here to stay, and that New York was the heart of this fabulous activity, than the structure that ascended, with grace and power, seventy stories high on Sixth Avenue between Forty-ninth and Fiftieth Streets. Plans for Rockefeller Center were unveiled in March 1930, and on 4 June of that year the Radio

Corporation of America agreed to develop the entertainment areas of the complex. A lease was signed on 29 October 1931, and the RCA Building—the hub of what everyone called Radio City—was occupied during the autumn of 1933. It housed the Red and Blue Networks of NBC and their local flagships, WEAF and WJZ.

The facility was designed by Wallace K. Harrison and Raymond Hood, the latter architect responsible for the earlier NBC headquarters at 711 Fifth Avenue. NBC figured that rehearsal and broadcast activity of each network required at least sixteen studios. Twenty-eight studios were built, connected with twelve hundred miles of wire and equipped with RCA's new Model 44 microphones, which became the standard, even the symbol, of the radio industry. Studio 8H was the biggest in the world—132 by 78 feet with a 30-foot ceiling, seating fifteen hundred people. Studio 3B contained a full-size pipe organ, and four studios departed from the art nouveau design to make guests feel as if they were in a tastefully decorated parlor. There was even a studio especially designed for children's programs, with a playroom across the hall.

There were problems in the move to 30 Rockefeller Plaza. Many staff members who were crammed into small offices at 711 were disappointed to receive even less room in the new location. Performers complained about a total lack of backstage space in some studios and the discomfort of making their entrance through the audience. Several control rooms were so small that there was not sufficient space for a director. Renovations were under way as the first programs went on the air.

The inaugural broadcast on Saturday, 11 November 1933—four days short of NBC's seventh anniversary—was heard on the combined Red and Blue Networks from 8:00 to 9:00 P.M. The program opened with a fanfare by a brass choir playing from the seventieth-floor observatory to the accompaniment of a circling airplane. There were speeches by the leaders of NBC and RCA as well as a message of congratulations from the founder of the BBC, Sir John Reith, who was in New York. Ironically, NBC chairman David Sarnoff was in London and spoke via shortwave, then opened the "world's capital of Radio" by tapping out the letters R-C-A in Morse code.

Entertainment included the orchestras of Rudy Vallee and Paul Whiteman, tenor John McCormack, George M. Cohan, Amos 'n' Andy, and one of the stars of NBC's opening night in 1926, Will Rogers. Special features on WEAF and WJZ during their first week in Radio City included a "radio tour" of the facilities, "The Seven Ages of NBC," and an interfaith religious service. The public was invited to tour behind the scenes; admission price was forty cents.

The networks were often referred to during their early days as "the WEAF chain," "the WJZ network," or "WABC and its allied stations." In 1934, WOR—which had earlier decided it could make more money without a network affiliation—joined its "Quality Group" partners in Chicago, Detroit, and Cincinnati as a charter member of the Mutual Broadcasting System. A large segment of the New York audience felt little need to tune beyond the 200 kilocycle range that contained the four networks. By the mid-1930s several newspapers that had previously been printing complete daily schedules for over thirty outlets in the city, the suburbs, and beyond were listing only the most popular New York stations.

Network radio began to do many things very well. Vaudevillians like Fred Allen and George Burns mastered the sound medium. Announcers stopped "shouting from the rooftops," loosened up, and simply talked to the folks at home. Poets began to write radio plays. In December 1937 Arturo Toscanini came to the podium at Studio 8H and conducted the great symphony orchestra that NBC had organized for him.

Not all network ventures, however, were so successful, as one curious attempt proved. The name Amalgamated Broadcasting System (ABS) sounds like something out of a 1930-era movie, but was a real network with a short and sorry history, the brainchild of a comic genius with a faulty business sense. The ABS was founded in 1933 by Ed Wynn, then in his third decade as one of the nation's most popular comedians.

Ed Wynn was believed to be the highest-paid actor in America during the 1920s. He was a groundbreaking performer on radio, performing his play "The Perfect Fool" on WJZ in February 1922. Wynn is credited with bringing the studio audience out from behind glass to put both jokes and laughter on the air. In 1932 he became the "Texaco Fire Chief" on NBC, presenting the most popular of all the variety shows that took to the air during a watershed time for radio entertainment.

In the depression year of 1933, Ed Wynn was doing so well that he decided to form his own radio network. "Just now the whole thing sounds silly," he confessed. "That's what I like about it. We're not in it to make millions. It's an ide-

alistic proposition." Wynn expected that he would have 5,000 performers under contract, "and 27,000 more unemployed actors when we need them." CBS and NBC reacted by forbidding their own contract artists from appearing on the ABS.

Wynn envisioned a chain of one hundred lower-power stations in the East and Midwest and eventually a coast-to-coast hookup. The network received early commitments from sixteen stations, including WOL/Washington, WCBM/Baltimore, WPEN/Philadelphia, WDEL/Wilmington, and WOAX/Trenton. In New York City, the ABS planned to establish a flagship station with the call letters WYNN. There was to be no mistaking who was the guiding star of this network.

Ed Wynn built studios at 501 Madison Avenue, renamed the Amalgamated Broadcasting Building. It would be as grand a showplace as the CBS headquarters, just across Fifty-third Street at 485 Madison. The board of directors was chaired by Curtis Dall, President Franklin Roosevelt's son-in-law. Staff was recruited from around the country (actor and announcer Dwight Weist first came to New York from Columbus, Ohio, to begin his network career with the Amalgamated). The ABS developed a unique business plan: commercial announcements would be limited to a few words at the beginning and end of each program, and a tie-in would be established with newspapers to expand the sponsor's message and further publicize the program in the next day's editions.

The new network debuted on Monday evening, 25 September 1933, with a four-hour gala. WYNN never received a license, and the local outlet was one of the city's smallest stations, WBNX. Norman Brokenshire was host for part of the program; among the guests was Vaughn De Leath. Government dignitaries speaking included Postmaster-General James Farley, FRC Chairman Eugene Sykes, and Congressman Fiorello LaGuardia. There was even a message from David Sarnoff, head of rival NBC. The "father of radio" Lee De Forest welcomed "this long overdue reform in radio" and in his letter stated: "If you, Mr. Wynn, carry on determinedly, conscientiously as you have promised, [and] bring back radio broadcasting to approximate the high standards which I sought at its inception, [you will] demonstrate to other broadcasters that radio can be respectful and yet pay its own expenses. More power, more coverage, more wavelengths to you and may the best man Wynn!"

The general public was invited to attend the inaugural broadcast, and the prospect of a big show and free supper brought thousands of people to 501 Madison Avenue. The riotous scene at "the great pastrami and salami opening" was described by *Daily News* radio columnist Ben Gross in his 1954 book *I Looked and I Listened* as "a combination of a Marx Brothers movie and a rush-hour riot at Times Square." The network's press relations personnel were so inept and insulting that nearly all New York papers dropped their ABS listings.

One person couldn't join the crowd at the Amalgamated Broadcasting Building. Ed Wynn was still on NBC, which wouldn't release its most popular star from his contract even if he owned his own network. On that fateful date of 25 September, Wynn was in Hollywood making a movie. By the time he came to New York, the "Ed Wynn Network" was already defunct. It broadcast its final program on 29 October 1933. Personnel showing up the next morning found the door open but the electricity off. There was a nearly second indoor riot at 501 Madison Avenue when it looked as if the ABS couldn't meet its last payroll.

An attempt by a business group to immediately reorganize the ABS was not successful. Ed Wynn abandoned the network; it was estimated that he had lost about $250,000.

The network's facilities were sold the next year to the WODAAM Corporation for its new station WNEW. An embittered Ed Wynn dropped out of radio from 1937 till 1944 but continued his career on the stage, screen, and eventually on television. He remained popular as a comedian and would round out his career as a dramatic actor, best remembered for his role, alongside his son Keenan, in Rod Serling's *Requiem for a Heavyweight*. Ed Wynn died in 1966, by which time his ill-fated network had faded from most memories.

In a harbinger of changes that would come to radio with the advent of television — and would ultimately affect TV in the cable era — New York's smaller independents began seeking out niches. Foreign-language broadcasting became a mainstay of a dozen stations. An experiment in high-fidelity transmission from John V. L. Hogan's laboratory won an audience of classical music lovers and evolved into WQXR. Station WEVD remained true to its socialist origins and offered programs appealing to intellectuals of the Left. WNEW tried to stay in the vanguard of the popular music of the day, growing to tremendous success by featuring the once-forbidden phonograph records during many of the twenty-four hours that it broadcast each day.

While the Great Depression devastated and transformed the nation, the big-time radio industry grew even bigger. WOR could inaugurate its 50,000-watt transmitter in 1935 with a gala broadcast from Carnegie Hall, during which entertainer Ray Bolger remarked, "Anybody that has fifty-thousand anything today certainly deserves an auspicious occasion."

Impoverished listeners were reluctant to pawn their new touchstone with the world, which entertained them so well for so little. Within the industry, conditions were often uncertain. Many of the smaller stations in the New York area survived by the sufferance of free talent and questionable advertising schemes. WLTH in Brooklyn offered "free" air time to merchants who would merely cover their "music tax." WRNY donated time for a weekly program aimed at the unemployed and WNYC presented concerts by an orchestra of chronically unemployed musicians. But most programming avoided mention of the nation's socioeconomic crisis, which was too big even for radio's problem-solving aspirations.

In addition to providing pleasant diversion, however, radio was proving to deliver valuable public service, especially in times of emergency. In September, 1938, for example, New York radio stations made extraordinary efforts to apprise the public of a developing disaster while striving just as hard to keep the audience calm and entertained.

On Wednesday, 21 September 1938, a powerful hurricane (they didn't yet have names) rolled up the coast and ripped through New York City with winds up to seventy-five miles an hour, causing massive destruction and loss of life on eastern Long Island and through New England. The first station to be knocked off the air in New York was WOR, when its transmitter power went dead at 3:30 P.M. It switched the Carteret transmitter to another power line and so missed only a minute of broadcast time. That wouldn't be the last of the problems it had to face, and the problems weren't all WOR's.

NBC's WJZ kept going with emergency pumps bailing out the basement at its Bound Brook, N.J., transmitter to protect its generators from being swamped. At Bellmore, Long Island, the WEAF transmitter lost power at 4:08 in the afternoon — right in the middle of "Mary Noble, Backstayge Wife" — returned briefly, and then was off until 9:45 P.M. CBS's WABC went silent at 5:42 P.M. and didn't return till 10:00.

WOR kept listeners informed of weather, transportation, and other emergency conditions; Dave Driscoll reported directly from Coast Guard headquarters. WMCA relayed messages to the public from ham radio operators until its Flushing transmitter was inundated by six feet of water.

At Radio City, NBC's Red and Blue Networks continued to feed programs to the nation, as did CBS from its studios at 485 Madison Avenue. WOR offered to let WEAF broadcast through its old 5,000-watt transmitter and even interrupted "Uncle Don" with an appeal for steeplejacks to help erect an emergency antenna. Despite the storm, two tower climbers reported to Carteret within half an hour. But NBC declined the favor. In frank recognition of audience appeal, for the first time in its history NBC shifted several hours of Red Network programs to the Blue's key station, WJZ. Even after WEAF was restored, the company let WJZ finish the popular Kay Kyser show.

CBS lost its New York coverage for only forty-eight minutes. Bob Trout's 6:30 P.M. newscast was heard over station WHN, and at 6:45 a signal returned at CBS's normal spot on the dial. WNYC had signed off and retuned its transmitter from 810 to 860; fans could ride out the storm with "Lum 'n' Abner," "Gang Busters," and Paul Whiteman's orchestra. (WNYC's own backup facility atop Brooklyn Technical High School was damaged by the hurricane.)

This redeployment of storm-tossed flagships was possible because WOR's Transcription Service did recording work for almost every other station, so its master control already had permanent lines to and from all the other studios in town. NBC might not have wanted WOR's spare transmitter, but CBS required its patch panel.

The hurricane hit at the same time that radio was reporting on the Munich crisis and the deteriorating political situation in Europe. People were weary and jittery, and there was little surprise when a month later many believed a radio report that Martians had invaded New Jersey.

Despite the depression, as the 1930s came to an end radio was ubiquitous. The decade's crowning attraction, the 1939 New York World's Fair, was referred to at the time as "the biggest, breath-takingest show radio has ever poured into the air!" All the networks were on hand for President Franklin D. Roosevelt's opening address on Sunday afternoon, 30 April—which also inaugurated RCA-NBC's first major public demonstration of television.

Radio coverage continued with daily national and local programs. In addition to the network flagships, WHN, WINS, WNEW, WQXR, and WWRL broadcast from Flushing Meadow. WMCA was on with the "World's Fairest Music." The British colony of Southern Rhodesia (now Zimbabwe) sponsored a series on WWRL to attract listeners to its exhibit. WNYC had studios in the New York City pavilion, from which it aired not only New York events but also a daily "Hometown News," a reading from out-of-town papers for the benefit of visitors. Multilingual WHOM boasted that it was "a fair world in itself." WOR designed a "Periphone," a microphone that resembled the fair's symbol, the Trylon and Perisphere. But the most unusual broadcasting device at Flushing Meadow was purportedly the symbolic structure itself. Though never used, the 700-foot Trylon was intended to serve as a radio tower and the giant Perisphere and adjacent reflecting pool were designed to act as a loudspeaker strong enough to send music to every corner of the fairground.

A new form of radio transmission, frequency modulation (FM), was pioneered in the New York area on 45 megacycles. This was the invention of Edwin Howard Armstrong, who had begun his experiments in a laboratory at Columbia University in 1928, and was demonstrated publicly for the first time on 5 November 1935. NBC—following some initial skepticism within RCA—began its own FM experiments in April 1939 from station W2XWG atop the Empire State Building. Experimental transmissions were also conducted by WQXR's FM partner, W2XQR, starting on 11 December 1939. The FCC authorized commercial operation on 20 May 1940. The first full-time commercial FM station in New York City was W71NY, WOR's FM outlet, which was first heard on 1 April 1941. Three months later, commercial television began in New York with NBC's WNBT and CBS's WCBW.

The call signs of commercial FM stations prior to November 1943 were meant to immediately inform listeners of both frequency and location. W47NY was on 44.7Mc in New York, W49BN was on 44.9 in Binghamton, and so on. It was a practical concept, but existing broadcasters felt

that they lost their identity, that listeners were confused, and that there weren't enough meaningful suffixes to go around. The call letter system soon changed as a result of these concerns. New York's early FM stations and their owners included the following:

W31NY	Major Edwin H. Armstrong
W35NY	Municipal Broadcasting System (WNYC)
W47NY	Muzak Corporation
W51NY	National Broadcasting Co. (WEAF/WJZ)
W55NY	William G. H. Finch
W59NY	Interstate Broadcasting Co. (WQXR)
W63NY	Marcus Loew Booking Agency (WHN)
W67NY	Columbia Broadcasting System (WABC)
W71NY	Bamberger Broadcasting Service (WOR)
W75NY	Metropolitan Television, Inc.

By the spring of 1942 there were fifty thousand FM sets in New York.

To most listeners, FM was a promising experiment that was being carried out beyond their hearing. There was change enough already on "Standard Broadcast." Four years of engineering studies and equally complex diplomatic negotiations had concluded with the North American Regional Broadcasting Agreement (NARBA). The United States, Canada, Mexico, and several Caribbean nations agreed to rearrange frequency assignments to permit each country a fair number of high-power stations and reduce interference. NARBA caused the first major realignment of the radio dial since the FRC actions in the late 1920s. Hundreds of stations changed frequency during the early morning hours of Sunday, 30 March 1941. The following was the revised lineup in the New York market:

Station	Old kc	New kc
WJZ	760	770
WNYC	810	830
WABC	860	880
WAAT	940	970
WINS	1180	1000
WHN	1010	1050
WOV	1100	1130
WGBB/WFAS	1210	1240
WNEW/WHBI	1250	1280
WCAP	1280	1310
WEVD/WBBR	1300	1330
WBNX/WAWZ	1350	1380
WBYN	1400	1430
WHOM	1450	1480
WQXR	1550	1560
WWRL/WCNW	1500	1600

There would be a few more changes—WNEW and WOV swapped frequencies, WCNW moved down to 1190 and became WLIB, WINS moved up to 1010, WFAS shifted to 1230 — but the New York radio scene was largely stabilized after NARBA.

"'The Light of the World' comes to you as usual today. However, as important bulletins come in we shall interrupt the program to bring them to you."
— *CBS preempt announcement, 7 June 1944*

World War II seemed to begin on the radio, with Americans paying horrified attention to the news from overseas, relayed several times each day by shortwave to CBS and NBC.

As the international situation deteriorated, broadcast news rapidly gained maturity and other programming tried to become more reassuring. During the tense months before Pearl Harbor, WMCA signed off each night with a prayer written by its dramatic director, Philip Barrison. The words were as ominous as they were comforting: "From the heart of the theatrical district in New York City, from whence this voice comes, the bright lights are gradually fading.... To the men aboard the many vessels plowing the seas we wish a safe journey. To our valiant air-pilots we wish Godspeed. To those who this night are separated from their homes and loved ones, to the sick and discouraged, may the dawning of the new day bring renewed hope and courage.... And now the voice of WMCA in New York City bids you all good night, good night, good night."

Soon the bright lights would fade completely. After Pearl Harbor, "flagship stations" were protected as if they were really flagships. CBS no longer admitted audiences to programs at its headquarters at 485 Madison Avenue. Police in Carteret, N.J. checked the background of everyone living near the WOR transmitter, and other transmitters were bathed in floodlights when not under blackout conditions. The outbreak of war gave radio broadcasting a purposefulness that had not been heard before. A few announcers, newscasters, engineers, and other broadcast workers received professional deferments from the draft, their work considered as crucial to the war effort as the labor of farmers and miners.

The radio business also experienced wartime restrictions, which hit New York and other cities along the coast especially hard. Local weather reports, which might be of use to enemy ships offshore, became restricted information. Record requests could still be accepted, but to guard against coded messages, stations eliminated personal dedications and were instructed not to play a specific tune at a requested time.

Even birthday greetings were suspended during the war emergency. This was especially galling to "Uncle Don,"

whose WOR children's show was filled with such personalized announcements. But Uncle Sam couldn't be sure that "nine-year old Jimmy on 58th Avenue in Flushing" wasn't ordering U-boats to fire their torpedoes toward the North Shore at 9:58. As the war went on and anxieties turned to self-confidence, some of these restrictions were eased.

The radio was vital to homefront morale and information and provided abundant instantaneous information to rally support for everything from conducting scrap metal drives to rationing to buying that extra bond today. In August 1942, representatives of every station in the metropolitan area met to plan direct sales of war bonds to their audiences.

Radio carried a constant stream of war-related programs, including a series on WNYC for local draft boards. WOR and WHN both held contests for the best new war song. WWRL produced "Frontiers of Mercy," highlighting the work of the Red Cross and appealing for volunteers. Stations expanded their overnight programming as factories went to round-the-clock operation. WOR's "Moonlight Savings Time" included transcriptions of daytime programs that its audience probably wasn't awake to hear. "Music to Work By" was an upbeat record show piped into factories to deal with the fatigue that set in around 4:00 A.M. WPAT gave away signs reading "Quiet Please, War Worker" for display by day sleepers. Broadcasters were dedicated and imaginative in providing wartime service, sometimes excessively so. WOR readied itself for blackout conditions by creating scripts whose text would glow in the dark under ultraviolet light.

Wartime was lucrative for the broadcasting industry. Companies with defense contracts could be levied an excess profits tax, so there was a financial incentive to invest in advertising. Many people were enjoying fat paychecks for the first time in a decade. Rationing and wartime shortages meant that businesses often had to spread the word quickly that their products were available. Many new advertisers came to New York radio. WQXR saw its billings increase 40 percent from 1940 to 1942, and at WJZ income was up nearly 75 percent. With so many men away in uniform the New York radio audience was 60 percent female. The audience for women's programs more than doubled in the early 1940s, and these programs took on a new depth and urgency.

If there was one segment of the New York radio industry that felt the stress of war it was the foreign-language stations, especially those broadcasting in German and Italian. Although there was little doubt that the foreign-born audience was overwhelmingly loyal to the United States, questions were raised about pro-Fascist sentiments finding their way into foreign-language programs as political developments half a world away were argued amid the freedom of the American airwaves. WHOM found its license in jeopardy in 1938 following an anti-Semitic talk in Italian. Managers of WHOM, WOV, WBIL, and WBNX were called before the House Un-American Activities Committee during that year to explain if and how they controlled propaganda on their stations. Rallies of the German-American Bund had been broadcast over WMCA during a period of U.S. neutrality. With America's entry into the war, the Foreign Language Radio Wartime Control Committee was established to develop a code of practices and receive complaints.

In the end, no serious security problems resulted from radio broadcasts during those difficult times. Most broadcasters were outspokenly patriotic. WEVD's Italian program "L'almanacco dell'aria" ended each daily news summary with an appeal to buy war bonds and stamps. That series was canceled when its Italian food sponsor had to cut back due to wartime import restrictions. Italian station WOV even liked to identify itself as "W-O-V-for-victory." Radio's first war became radio's finest hour. During 1944, CBS's WABC broadcast 20,000 programs and announcements about the war, logging 2,933 hours and 41 minutes of airtime — equal to about one-third of a year.

"I think it would have been interesting if television had been invented before radio. Kids would run and tell their friends, 'We've got this new thing that brings you all these great shows and you don't even have to look at it!'"
— *William B. Williams, WNEW disc jockey*

The end of World War II brought the television cameras out of the mothballs. During the war years there had been limited telecasting, such as instructional programming for air raid wardens who gathered around sets installed in police stations. (DuMont engineers were preoccupied with military electronics during the war but were allowed to operate W2XWV in their spare time.) With the conclusion of hostilities, it was T-V-for-Victory. On 7 May 1945 WNBT presented fourteen continuous hours of V-E Day coverage. It was an ambitious program even by today's standards and a sign that television — which for twenty years had been predicted to be only a year or two away — would finally come out of the laboratory and into everybody's living room.

In January 1945 the FCC established the present VHF television band. Soon there were more than a dozen applicants to join NBC, CBS, and DuMont on the four remaining metropolitan New York television channels. These included radio stations WHN, WLIB, WEVD, WFAS (all unsuccessful), WJZ, WOR, and WAAT (which won channels 7, 9, and 13), Philco, Raytheon, Muzak (unlucky), the *Daily News* (lucky to get channel 11), and 20th Century Fox (which would take over channel 5 forty years later). Another hapless applicant was WABF, a pioneer on the FM band owned by the optimistically named Metropolitan Television Corp.

Despite the postwar excitement about television, radio in the late 1940s and early 1950s experienced the greatest growth since the "gold rush" days of the 1920s. So many new applications were filed for AM and FM stations across the country that the FCC feared it might run out of call letters. In the New York metropolitan area suburban radio followed the population trend; two dozen new stations with state-of-the-art equipment and ambitious young staffs signed on from Morristown to Patchogue.

The most obvious change on the postwar New York dial took place on Saturday, 6 November 1946. Two sets of call letters were retired within hours of each other and in their place appeared some new but familiar names. At 6:00 P.M. WEAF became WNBC, and at 10:00 P.M. WABC — originally the identification of the Atlantic Broadcasting Company — became WCBS. For the convenience of listeners with push-button radios, WCBS and WNBC offered free paper disks to cover over markers for WABC and WEAF — either station would supply both disks. (WJZ became WABC in 1953.)

New York City and its suburbs were served by seven television stations before many parts of the United States had any and when most major markets had only two or three. The number of TV sets in the metropolitan area doubled from 500,000 to one million in 1949, but New York radio was still going strong. The biggest loss was in the prime evening hours; in 1949 over 80 percent of the potential audience was still listening to radio after dinner; by 1950 that had fallen to 55 percent. As the network flagships prepared to lead their new video fleet, New York's independent stations were still holding an audience. WNEW felt that 1950 was its best year ever. WHOM enjoyed a 15 percent increase in time sales. WMCA, WQXR, and WINS also saw improvements over 1949. Radio remained an attractive advertising medium, especially for companies manufacturing and selling television sets.

As TV developed around the country, financing for television often came from the income of radio, so it was in the interest of the major networks to keep some of their popular radio shows on the air. This made the 1950s an era of tremendous creative activity throughout the broadcasting industry. Radio had developed high professional standards through writers, actors, musicians, and other dedicated craftspeople whose talents were honed for the microphone and not just carried over from stage or film. The sound medium had earned respect, was self-assured — maybe even cocky — and certainly lucrative.

The curtain was lowered gradually through the 1950s. Jack Benny's New York Hooperating, for one example, was in the mid-20s in 1948 but deteriorated to 4.8 by 1951. He left the sound medium to concentrate on his CBS television show at the end of the 1955 season. "Fibber McGee and Molly" was canceled in 1957. By 1960 most soap operas had been hung out to dry or transferred to television. Perhaps the biggest loss was in children's programs. Jack Armstrong gave up in 1951, the Lone Ranger rode off into those thrilling days of yesteryear in 1955. Radio never really regained the juvenile audience.

The top ten tunes of the week according to the WMGM survey for 16 May 1956 reveals a tug-of-war between the old and the new:

1. "Moonglow" and the theme from *Picnic*.
                                          Morris Stoloff Orchestra
2. "Heartbreak Hotel"   Elvis Presley
3. "Hot Diggity"   Perry Como
4. "Blue Suede Shoes"   Carl Perkins
5. "Ivory Tower"   Cathy Carr
6. "Poor People of Paris"   Les Baxter Orchestra
7. "Why Do Fools Fall in Love?"   Frankie Lyman
8. "The Magic Touch"   The Platters
9. "The Wayward Wind"   Gogi Grant
10. "Rock Island Line"   Jimmy Rogers

There were two orchestrated instrumentals, a sentimental "torch song," a couple of rock-and-roll numbers that would become classics, a country crossover, and even a nonsensical ditty ("hot diggity dog ziggity boom what you do to me") with a melody taken from the España Rhapsody by Chabrier. Such variety on the pop chart did not indicate that the public couldn't make up its mind but rather revealed that the public was splitting into many audiences, and those audiences knew what they liked.

The era of big-time network radio drama ended on the last day of September 1962 when CBS canceled the mystery adventure "Yours Truly, Johnny Dollar" and ended repeat broadcasts of the great series "Suspense." A few national programs did linger on the schedules ("Don McNeil's Breakfast Club" remained on ABC till the end of 1968), but stations across America were discovering that they could make more money — and develop a stronger identity — with their own disc jockeys playing records along with local news and information.

As TV schedules expanded to fill the daytime hours, radio remained dominant during the early part of the day. The ability of radio to cover breaking news also lent it some advantages that TV did not enjoy.

New York's four network flagships discovered for the first time that they had to creatively position themselves against the independents; they had to seek a "niche" rather than develop programs. In 1957 WOR broke away from the Mutual network, which it had helped to found. It moved to a talk format, keeping many of its established voices and going heavily into personal-advice shows that often sounded like soap operas without the organ music. WABC also dropped most of its network schedule and hired a prestigious lineup of disc jockeys. Often the niches were musical.

The rock-and-roll revolution came to radio in the mid-1950s; by 1957, WINS was playing the new sound through most of the day. Just before Easter 1958, WMCA added some rock and roll to its programming; it was soon followed by

WMGM. The "Top 40" stations instituted the notion of a "format" — with a new release here, an oldie there, and a station jingle in between — that listeners could almost set their watches by. Also during 1958 — something of a watershed year for radio programming — WNEW enhanced its middle-of-the-road music with more of an up-tempo, big-band sound. A new station, WNTA (successor to Newark's WAAT), seemed to take over where WNEW had left off.

It was also during the 1950s that the phenomenon of payola began to make itself felt in a significant way in the industry. Back in the 1920s, radio stations that played phonograph records were thought to be providing an inferior service and had to operate with lower power and a lower grade of license than those that broadcast only live music. In the 1930s, record companies and artists went to court to prevent disc jockeys from allegedly violating their copyright and undermining retail sales by airing their records (the courts found for the broadcasters). But by the 1950s the situation had taken a 180-degree turn. Song pluggers (or, more formally, "contact men") were part of the marketing effort from recording's early days and would often hand out free discs and small gifts. The proliferation of small record labels in the fifties — and some five hundred new releases during a typical week — required a more aggressive approach: record companies began to pay deejays to play their latest tunes. Soon record producers and broadcasters were back in the courtroom, this time as criminal defendants.

Payola was defined at the time by commentator David Brinkley as "the practice of paying a disc jockey to play a record so often that listeners thought it was a hit and went out and bought it — whether they liked it or not." Of course there was no quid pro quo between the record company and the public, but without regular airplay a new song would never make the charts. The transaction wasn't always a cash payment to the deejay. An individual might even be listed as a cocreator, granting undeserved credit but making him eligible for royalty payments (e.g., Alan Freed and "Sincerely").

The scandal broke on 19 May 1960 when indictments were handed down against five deejays as well as some record librarians and program directors. The air personalities included Alan Freed, formerly with WINS but then on WABC, Peter Tripp of WMGM, Tommy Smalls of WWRL, WLIB's Hal Jackson, and Jack Walker of WOV, which had recently become WADO. They were charged with "commercial bribery," a misdemeanor punishable by two years in prison. Twenty-three companies had admitted the practice to prosecutors.

None of those caught up in the payola scandal ever served jail time. Alan Freed — fired by WABC when he refused to sign an antipayola pledge — pleaded guilty. Peter Tripp was fired from WMGM and eventually found a new job in San Francisco. He was back in New York a year later to stand trial, where he denied any wrongdoing and claimed he was paid for advising record companies. Found guilty on thirty-five counts of taking a total of $36,050, Tripp was fined $500 and given a six-month suspended sentence. By then he was broke.

Alan Freed was fined $300. He too moved to California, where his drinking problem worsened, and he died in 1965 at the age of forty-three. Jack Walker left WADO for WLIB, where he was shot to death in 1970 in an incident that had nothing to do with the payola matter. Hal Jackson continued his career with Inner City Broadcasting, rising to an executive position.

For a while in the early 1960s radio stations were required by the FCC to keep a log of all "demo disks" played (for some stations, that meant almost everything on the playlist) and to identify the labels each hour. A few broadcasters took pains to point out that this was "in keeping with standard industry practice," and one deejay embellished his hourly listing with quips like, "...and the Victor Talking Machine Company." Anxiety over the need to account for free records prompted many stations to carefully file away every disc they received between 1958 and 1965. These caches would later be unearthed and would enrich the record collections of rock-and-roll connoisseurs or would return to the air as "golden oldies."

WNBC turned to talk shows in 1964, opening its mighty 50,000 watts to listeners calling in — a service vaguely anticipated by AT&T when it founded the station as WEAF. Among the first phone hosts were Tom and Mary Ewell, actor Robert Alda, musical comedy star Mimi Benzell, Brad Crandall, and Lee Leonard. Bill Mazer presented a sports talk show every afternoon.

In 1965, station WINS became the first New York station to adopt an all-news format, building on the strong Westinghouse Broadcasting news organization.

Soon after the format change, WINS and all of its peers had to cope with one of New York's major news events of the decade. At 5:27 on the afternoon of Tuesday, 9 November 1965, Bill Mazer was chatting with a caller on his WNBC talk show when both noted that their lights were growing dim. Over at WNEW, Ted Brown was delivering a commercial when he saw his turntable slowing down. "Here we go," was all he could say before everything went off. It was the start of the biggest power failure in American history, blacking out much of the northeastern United States and parts of Ontario (where a faulty circuit breaker at Niagara Falls overloaded the grid). Some thirty million people were left in the dark, and nearly all of them immediately groped for their portable radios for news and guidance.

With all television stations off the air, the big blackout triggered one of radio's greatest public-service efforts — an exercise made possible partly by radio's long-standing preparedness for defense emergencies. No New York station was off for more than twenty minutes. Announcers and reporters performed admirably, calming and informing the public. But it took imaginative and often heroic work for technical staffs to keep their stations radiating. At WOR engineers

connected a dry-cell battery with a thirty-minute charge to keep its remote control energized while someone rushed to the transmitter in Carteret, N.J., switched to manual operation, and played tapes of old Martin Block record shows, cutting back for news from John Wingate, Walter Kiernan, and others in a jerry-rigged studio at 1440 Broadway. Hearing that WOR's studio generator was running low on fuel, listeners climbed twenty-four floors with gasoline cans.

WINS's all-news staff met the challenge of reporting a story in which everyone was taking part, mixing its professionals' reports with news accounts phoned in by listeners (the telephone company used its own power system). Extraordinary effort was required to get all the news all the time, since the power outage also knocked out the wire-service teletypes.

Since areas of northern New Jersey were among the pockets bypassed by the power outage, transmitters of many New York City stations could remain operable. The problem was getting program material into those transmitters. At WNEW, crews rushed to remove batteries from their mobile news vehicles to keep studios feeding information to the Kearney transmitting station. Back in Manhattan, announcers worked by flashlight and even candlelight.

WCBS — not yet all-news — had just moved into the new CBS headquarters at 51 W. Fifty-second Street. "Black Rock" was constructed with a backup generator that restored electricity within fifteen seconds, recycled the transmitter on High Island to its full 50,000 watts, and gave WCBS the shortest downtime of all the stations in the city. Veteran announcer Kenneth Banghart was in the midst of "Up to the Minute" and simply continued on the job, smoothly and calmly.

The *Journal-American* radio-TV columnist Jack O'Brian wrote a couple of days later: "Something in the common problem spread a strangely almost holiday mood.... News staffs after the first hour took on a jolly family camaraderie, sharing the news intimately with each other as well as us.... The mood might have been a pain in the ear at some other moment but the emergency made the good-fellowship welcome and diverting." The light attitude of the broadcasters was credited with keeping the public in generally good spirits throughout the inconvenience.

Power was gradually restored across the Northeast. At WNEW the lights came back on in the midst of the 5:30 A.M. station break. Listeners could hear the newsroom staff cheering.

On Wednesday, 13 July 1977, at around 9:30 P.M., the city lights went out again, in a more localized outage. Newsradio 88 was once more off for only fifteen seconds, but WINS was able to keep going even while the power failed, since engineer Jim Stephans had learned from previous incidents and noted the signs of an imminent blackout. WMCA lost a few minutes of airtime due to a balky generator and fed reports to its New Jersey transmitter by ordinary telephone lines. A couple of stations were even able to keep their weather reports up to date, since WCBS meteorologist Bob Harris and WOR weatherman Bill Corbell phoned in observations from their homes. However, WMCA had an unexpected advantage. The station was conducting an evening staff meeting and thus had nearly all its personnel available till the electricity returned nine hours later.

CBS tried to maintain a strong network service somewhat longer than the other national chains. Arthur Godfrey continued to broadcast his daily variety show until 30 April 1972. The network would attempt to keep the radio art alive with "CBS Mystery Theatre" in the 1970s and 1980s, but the program was not heard on its New York "flagship." CBS affiliates had the right of first refusal in the choice to run the nightly hour of mystery and suspense — which reunited some of radio's best performers with veteran producer-director Himan Brown — and in New York WCBS passed so as not to interrupt its twenty-four-hour news service. (The series was heard on WOR.)

The major challenge that overtook New York AM radio in the 1960s wasn't the rivalry from television but was the competition between two different bands. Despite the high expectation with which it was first welcomed, frequency modulation had developed as little more than a static-free adjunct to AM and a haven for music lovers and audio enthusiasts. There were a few independent pioneers on the FM band and instances of a station using FM to extend its limited AM broadcast hours (WNYC after 10:00 P.M., WHLI and other daytimers inviting listeners to "switch over" to FM at sunset) or to diversify its regular service (WHOM and WEVD saw FM as a way to add more languages to the schedule). Usually, however, a New York FM listener before the mid-1960s would hear programs identical to those on the AM band during the hours when the FM transmitter might be on the air. In a simple test of FM listenership, WMCA shut off its FM transmitter in the middle of a New York Giants baseball game and waited to count the complaints. All the baseball fans in the audience must have simply switched to 570 AM, for there was not one phone call, and WMCA soon returned its FM license to the FCC.

At the end of 1960 WABC changed to an all-hits format, which would last for twenty-four years and make "Seventy-Seven" a ratings leader. It was an indication of audience fractioning that WABC's biggest rival for the top spot in the New York ratings was usually the relatively changeless WOR. Meanwhile, several rival "boomchuckers" (as *Variety* dubbed them) tried to emulate WABC's tight, clean sound.

The countercultural trends of the 1960s and 1970s stimulated "alternative media," and FM took on the innovative role that was once a mainstay of the fringe hours on New York's smaller AM stations. On 30 July 1966, WOR-FM abruptly broke away from its hoary AM partner to become New York's first progressive rock station. The station was already anticipating an FCC regulation that stations in markets above 200,000 population had to split AM and FM for at least half the broadcast day. This was supposed to add diversity on the dials, but its effect was disruptive in as diverse a city as New York. Many critics pointed out that the rule made more sense in markets below 200,000.

In earlier days it was a simple matter to move or cancel a show that had lost its snap or was flagging in popularity. But with the advent of niche programming in the 1960s, when the ratings slipped, the entire schedule had to be retooled and a new audience sought, maybe a new name adopted. WMGM dropped rock music, returned to its original call letters, and continued as WHN with "the sound of music and total information news." Then, from 1973 till its demise in 1987, WHN specialized in country and western music. WJRZ in Hackensack went from middle-of-the-road (MOR) to country music in late 1965, became WWDJ in 1971, and went to paid religion in 1974.

In pursuit of a dependable niche, radio stations pumped up their programming with the kind of talk that was once confined to announcers' lounges. In 1970, WHN picked up a Los Angeles program, "Feminine Forum." This was not a session of household hints, recipes, and other matters of concern to homemakers; it was a call-in program in which women (and men) were invited to discuss their sex lives. "Feminine Forum" was not tucked away in the late-night hours but ran from 10:00 A.M. till 4:00 P.M. every weekday. FCC action against a similar program in Chicago caused WHN to move to less provocative fare.

In 1973, however, WNBC introduced New Yorkers to a new morning personality. Taking over the time slot once occupied by "Buffalo Bob" Smith — and in the tradition of one-time "bad boy" morning man Arthur Godfrey — was Don Imus, a prankster who pushed the bounds of radio propriety. Thirteen years later the once-dignified NBC booked an afternoon drive personality, Howard Stern, whose off-color and off-the-wall remarks seemed to pick up where Imus and "Feminine Forum" left off. Fans roared with glee while critics roared to the Federal Communications Commission.

There was a time when AM radio was simply "the radio"; *amplitude modulation* was a term known mostly to radio engineers and physicists. For thirty years the FM band was a minor, albeit high-fidelity static-free adjunct, broadcasting to a relative handful of audiophiles. In 1978, WKTU-FM passed WABC to become the top-rated station in the New York market. Even in the seventies, nearly three-quarters of the radio audience was listening to AM; by the 1990s that share had fallen to 23 percent. A switch had taken place, and it was the band switch.

Over the years many broadcasters in New York earned their laurels and tended to rest on them, but laurels provide poor comfort. Typical was the case of WNEW, which changed from the big-band and ballad style to pop and soft rock in the 1970s — more Carpenters and BeeGee's, less Tony Bennett and Count Basie — then went back to the earlier styles as its fiftieth anniversary approached in 1984.

However, the station never seemed to pick up where it had left off either in listener appeal or in commercial success. In 1992 WNEW was bought by business publisher Michael Bloomberg and became WBBR, a business news service that never played a note of music. Other broadcasters tried to save the classic WNEW format and even revive the call letters (WNEW-FM kept the family name if not the swing-era music). The *Times* station WQXR, whose classical music audience had long been larger on FM than AM, stepped into the niche and changed 1560 AM to WQEW.

With a segmented audience, tape decks and CD players in cars, competition from FM, and other challenges, AM radio experienced a slump. But the development of AM stereo, the prospect of digital transmission from solid-state transmitters, and the spread of broadcast automation drew interest back to the original sector of the broadcast spectrum. The FCC relaxed the "duopoly" rules, and for the first time since NBC split up the Red and Blue Networks and Arde Bulova sold WNEW and WOV, a single company could own more than one station. There were shifts in ownership and frequency to a degree that hadn't been seen since the late 1920s. In 1991 the Federal Communications Commission expanded the AM band and opened 1600–1700 kHz, and in 1995 WJDM in Elizabeth became the first broadcaster in the United States to occupy those upper regions. Many stations applied for assignment above 1600; no one echoed the 1927 protest about "graveyard frequencies."

Radio had developed faster in the New York market than elsewhere in the nation and could diversify and experiment here more readily than in most other places. Radio proved it could fill hearts and hours, thrill audiences, inform during crises, and be an invisible friend to millions. But when the boom years ended, radio broadcasters found themselves continually trying to crawl out of one rut after another. With a single rating point worth millions of dollars and an increasing number of absentee owners running automated stations, New York radio arrived at the end of the twentieth century with a cautious, copycat reputation.

Long long ago, in September 1922, WEAF received a letter from a listener who described himself as "away down in the sticks" of Southern Pines, N.C. He was a teenage invalid whose life was brightened by the programs he heard through his earphones. What he wrote must have gratified the radio workers 575 miles to the north: "Daddy says nothing but good comes out of New York ."

Few would say that "nothing but good" has come out of New York over the years, but the possibility will continue to be there every day. Keep tuned or you may miss something.

The Broadcasters of Brooklyn

Station	Owner	Years
WARD	U.S. Broadcasting Co. (Rabbi A. Kronenberg)	1933–41
WARS	Amateur Radio Specialty Co.	1926–28
WBBC	Brooklyn Broadcasting Corp. (Peter Testan)	1926–41
WBBR	Watchtower Bible & Tract Society	1924–57
WBKN	Arthur Faske	1926–28
WBRS	North American Broadcasting Corp.	1926–28
WBYN	Unified Broadcasting Co.	1941–46
WCGU	Charles G. Unger	1926–31
WCNW	Arthur Faske	1933–42
WFOX	Paramount Broadcasting Co.	1931–33
WFRL	Flatbush Radio Laboratory	1925–27
WGAC	Orpheum Radio Stores	1922
WLIB	Elias Godofsky	1942–44
WLTH	Voice of Brooklyn, Inc. (Sam Gellard)	1926–41
WMBQ	Metropolitan Broadcasting Co.	1927–38
WMIL	Arthur Faske	1932–33
WSDA	Seventh Day Adventist Church	1923–27
WSGH	St. George Hotel	1928–30
WTRC	Twentieth Dist. Republican Club	1926–27
WVFW	Paramount Broadcasting Co.	1933–41

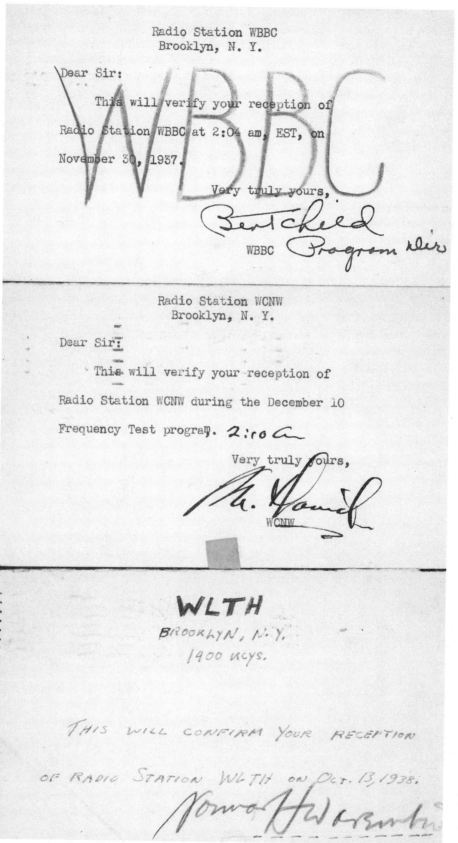

Radio Station WBBC
Brooklyn, N. Y.

Dear Sir:

This will verify your reception of

Radio Station WBBC at 2:04 am, EST, on

November 30, 1937.

Very truly yours,

Bert Child

WBBC *Program Dir*

Radio Station WCNW
Brooklyn, N. Y.

Dear Sir:

This will verify your reception of

Radio Station WCNW during the December 10

Frequency Test program. *2:10 a*

Very truly yours,

WCNW

WLTH

BROOKLYN, N.Y.
1400 KCYS.

THIS WILL CONFIRM YOUR RECEPTION

OF RADIO STATION WLTH ON OCT. 13, 1938.

These tiny Brooklyn radio stations were actually received in Cleveland, Ohio, in 1937 and 1938. Unfortunately, they could not be picked up in much of the New York City area.

Kings County embraced the proud independent city of Brooklyn until carried reluctantly into Greater New York to become the new city's most populous borough in 1897. So Brooklyn was less than twenty-five years removed from its status as the "city of homes and churches" when the first broadcasting stations began to appear.

By the 1920s Brooklyn was a thick mix of old Dutch and English families, well-established African-American communities, and hundreds of thousands of European immigrants, for many of whom a Brooklyn address represented the first step up since their entry into American society.

Given the diversity and density of Brooklyn's population, it should not be surprising that nearly a score of small radio stations were established in Kings County. And given Manhattan's business and cultural domination it may be no surprise that none of those little stations grew to be very big.

During the 1920s and 1930s, with typical Brooklyn pugnacity, the local broadcasters were often in conflict for shared air time and dial space. The "Brooklyn radio fight" began with the first attempts at regulation by the Federal Radio Commission in 1927, wasn't fully resolved until 1941, and finally played itself out when Brooklyn lost its only full-service AM station in 1946.

The story of the Brooklyn radio fight is extremely complicated. The unregulated period of the mid-1920s had overpopulated the dial, and the Federal Radio Commission assigned stations to share frequencies, generally leaving it to the broadcasters themselves to negotiate their schedules. Brooklyn stations weren't necessarily teamed up together, and those who were joined sometimes cooperated to the point of sharing facilities — WLTH used WBBR's transmitter during its first days in 1927.

Conflict broke out between WCGU and WBBC, who were sharing air time in the summer of 1928. When negotiations faltered among the stations, the chamber of commerce of Brooklyn established a radio committee to work out the problems and provide a unified voice for Brooklyn in upcoming relicensing hearings in Washington. But the committee drew a public protest from WCGU's Charles Unger, who charged that it was "acting in bad taste," favoring WBBC for a better spot on the dial and considering WBBC "above all others in Brooklyn." Committee chair Frederick Rowe denied this, though consolidation of the local stations was openly favored by some business leaders. Unger kept up his attacks on the lack of impartiality of the chamber's radio committee.

U.S. Congressman Emanuel Celler supported the mediation efforts and stated that "unless suitable protest is made Brooklyn may be wiped off the radio map." A more palpable dispute developed between WBBC and WSGH in November 1928, when both stations were heard broadcasting simultaneously on 1400kc, a frequency then also shared by WLTH and WCGU. The chamber of commerce "official radio arbitrator," Eric Palmer, phoned both stations, and WBBC signed off. "We want no radio war in Brooklyn," declared Palmer, warning of harsher action by federal authorities. He even threatened intervention by Brooklyn Borough President James Byrne against anyone with a "go it alone policy."

The disputes undermined an already weak public standing. FRC Commissioner Orestes Caldwell noted that Brooklyn radio owners preferred to listen to the popular Manhattan-based stations and placed their own local outlets "near the bottom." Nonetheless, Kings County's entire congressional delegation pressured Caldwell and his colleagues to preserve the Brooklyn broadcasters. A delegation of business and political leaders met with Caldwell and found him sympathetic but unwilling to grant Brooklyn a better frequency.

The FRC also advised that continued conflict could indeed "bring withdrawal of channel." The four stations rejected a suggestion that they alternate complete broadcast days and finally, thanks to private mediation by a New York Supreme Court justice, settled on a schedule. It allowed each to broadcast about twenty-six hours a week, which everyone complained was far less than the twelve to eighteen hours a day that most Manhattan stations were allowed.

In 1928, WBBC and WCGU merged into a single station with dual identification. Many welcomed the linkage, but the other two stations continued to stand on their own. This was the shared schedule on 1400 kilocycles in Brooklyn on Thursday, 3 October 1929:

WLTH	9:00 A.M.	Professor Hale, Dr. Hearty
	9:45	Holland program
	10:15	Pianist; Shoppers' Guide
	11:00	Rabies program; original poems
	11:30	Telephone talks

WBBC/WCGU	12:00N	Katherine Krauss, soprano
	12:15	Merchants' review
	12:30	Paul Hart, songs
	1:00	Joe Perry, jazz
	1:15	Daisy Neibling, soprano
	1:30	Bureau of Charities
	1:45	Beatrice Clyman, songs
	2:00	Joe Perry, Czar of Jazz
	2:15	Sally Ascher, soprano, pianist
	2:45	Lillian Lindeman, soprano
	3:00	Jewish Education Association
	3:15	Sirka Ketto, songs
	3:30	Philip Room, violinist
WSGH	3:45	Bob's Kiddie Hour; dance music
	4:45	Contest; Beulah Baer, soprano
	5:30	Hattie Delman, songster
WLTH	6:00	Commercial Serenaders
	6:30	Piano; Rita Hall and Kay Steel, harmony
	7:00	Dance music
	7:30	Merchant Serenaders
WBBC/WCGU	8:00	Dance orchestra, entertainers
	8:30	Sobel Jewish hour
	9:30	Parmel Brothers
	10:00	The Banjoliers
WSGH	10:30	Miriam Ray Baby Blues
	10:45	Jack Adams, songs
	11:00	Al's Tavern
	11:30	Studio program
	12:00M	Broadway Gardens Orch.; Petrie, tenor
	12:45	Harry Nelson, songs

WSGH became WFOX, which became WVFW. WCGU became WARD. WLTH and WBBC continued as independent stations, and the conflict on 1400 went on. (Meanwhile, WBBR shared 1300 with WEVD; two smaller stations, WMBQ and WCNW, dwelled with WWRL at 1500.) By 1934, the new Federal Communications Commission was still unraveling the uneasy arrangement on 1400. Then a major player entered the field. The *Brooklyn Eagle*, the most popular and respected of Brooklyn's three English-language dailies, formed a broadcasting subsidiary and applied to open a station to be called either WEGL or WBDE. The *Eagle* had been interested in broadcasting from its first days and maintained a studio to provide programs to several stations.

In November 1934, an attempt was made to unite WLTH, WVFW, and WARD into Broadcasters of Brooklyn Inc. Congressman Celler would serve as chairman of the board, with executives of the stations jointly running the station. The plan collapsed.

On 17 December 1935, the FCC canceled the licenses of WARD, WLTH, and WVFW and split the broadcast day between WBBC and the insurgent WEGL. Commissioner

Irvin Stewart dissented, declaring that the *Eagle* had never shown it could provide any service that Brooklynites weren't already receiving from the existing stations in the borough. Even worse, the *Eagle* had refused to print daily program listings for the stations whose licenses it challenged.

Stewart also stated, "In the absence of a showing that the proposed station will be used to meet needs peculiar to Brooklyn, I am unwilling to approve another station in the over-quota New York metropolitan area when there is a serious need for the facilities in other parts of the country less well served with broadcast facilities." Brooklyn's distinct identity was being further diluted.

A new series of hearings was held in Washington, and by June 1937 the FCC had turned back the *Eagle*'s application — WEGL never went on the air — and assigned the time of WARD and WLTH to WBBC, allowing the Veterans of Foreign Wars to continue to operate WVFW. But the commission did not have the last word in these disputes, for WLTH and WARD took the matter into federal court in June 1937, where the case was litigated for the next four years. Each of the stations had a small listenership, mostly among foreign-language audiences. None were very lucrative, and all seemed to delight in pointing out the others' financial problems. By the late 1930s the four stations were programming various blocks of time during the day and splitting about an hour each in the evening. In 1941, they reached a merger agreement and formed the Unified Broadcasting Corporation of Brooklyn.

The unified station was called WBYN and had the 1430 spot on the dial day and night. Rabbi Aaron Kronenberg, the owner of WARD, became president, and Peter Testan of WBBC was chief engineer. Sam Gellard of WLTH and WVFW's Sal diAngelo were also on the board of directors. A professional manager was hired, and the Brooklyn station even proudly opened a studio in Manhattan. Much of the programming was imaginative, but the partners could never put their personal animosities behind them, and the disunity finally led to the demise of WBYN in 1946. It was sold to the *Newark News* and became WNJR. Meanwhile, WCNW became WLIB in 1942, was sold to the *New York Post*, and moved to Manhattan in 1944.

Through all these disputes, the oldest station based in Brooklyn was consistent in its operation and remained under a single owner for thirty years. This was the religious broadcaster WBBR, which was content to share time with WEVD at 1330kc as it spread the message of Jehovah's Witnesses.

Hands Across the Hudson

New Jersey was the "cradle of radio" in metropolitan New York, but the cradle was robbed. Northern New Jersey was an early leader in radio manufacturing, home of Mu-Rad, Accuratune, and Newark Tool and Engineering (which built the Nerco receiver), as well as Westinghouse and Edi-son. The first major radio broadcasting stations in the area, WJZ and WOR, were in Newark. Pioneer WDY was at the RCA plant in Roselle Park. But New Jersey was, in Benjamin Franklin's words, "a keg tapped at both ends," and studios were eventually moved to Manhattan.

During the overpopulation of the air in the 1920s, New Jersey had its share of local stations in Elizabeth, North Plainfield, and other communities. Most were small and casually run, although WODA/Paterson, WAAM/Newark, and WAAT/Jersey City enjoyed loyal audiences. Regulation and the depression silenced several stations, including WNJ/Newark and WBMS/Hackensack. Even WKBO/Jersey City was shut down despite appeals from its U.S. congressman. WPAP at Palisades Amusement Park was absorbed into Manhattan's WHN in 1934. WODA and WAAM merged into WNEW, originally a Newark outlet, which became for many *the* New York station.

At the same time, new knowledge about the signal-sapping effect of skyscrapers caused New York City broadcasters to turn Jersey's swamps and meadows into antenna farms. WJZ established its first 50,000-watt transmitter at Bound Brook in 1925. Numerous Manhattan stations planted towers across the Hudson (resulting in listings like "WMCA, Hoboken" or "WRNY in Coytesville," where studio space never served for more than emergency backup).

New Jersey radio columnist Lee Page complained in 1938: "For a City of half-a-million with surrounding environs counting up into the millions, Newark, and as a matter of fact, Northern New Jersey, is decidedly lacking in efficient Radio Broadcasting facilities…. There should be at least one transmitter which will proudly and consistently announce its location as NEWARK, NEW JERSEY — and mean it. A Station that could be considered as part of community life and which would have the interests of our Communities at heart."

By 1941, only WAAT and part-time WHBI were on the air from Newark (WOR officially changed its "city of license" in 1940), and there were small stations in Red Bank and Asbury Park as well as religious broadcaster WAWZ in Somerset County. The North American Regional Broadcasting Agreement of 1941 opened the 930kc frequency, which was filled by WPAT/Paterson, and the upward trend resumed, set back by the 1942 fire that destroyed WBRB/Red Bank and WHOM's transfer from Jersey City to New York in 1946 (a move that left Jersey City the largest city in the United States without a radio station of its own).

Then, in what many Jerseyites saw as a just act of revenge, Brooklyn lost its sole full-time frequency of 1430 to Newark in 1946 with the founding of WNJR. WVNJ was fitted onto the dial at 620kc in December 1948, and that gave Newark three and one-seventh stations. Local AM and FM stations would also spring up in Morristown, New Brunswick, Elizabeth, and elsewhere. Finally — partly due to the earlier protests and pressure — northern New Jersey was assigned one of the metropolitan area's TV channels, and in 1948 WAAT established WATV on channel 13.

The Metropolitan AM Radio Stations

WAAM

(10 April 1922–29 December 1925)
(18 April 1926–12 February 1934)

1922	349m	500w.
1926	1140kc	500w.
1927	860kc	500w.
1928	1140kc s/t WODA	500w.
1928	1250kc s/t WODA, WGCP	500w.

WAAM was one of the most important stations in the early days of metropolitan New York radio, an innovator in programming, technical progress, and commercial development. It was established by the Ira R. Nelson Manufacturing Company of Newark, which made small motors such as those used in electric fans. WAAM was among the earliest stations to accept advertising and to use a sales representative, Bruce Reynolds, who came to WAAM after being turned down by WEAF. Ira Nelson was so unsure that selling time was legal that he had Reynolds pay him WAAM's share in cash. The "chief operator" during WAAM's first six months was O. B. Hanson, who left to join WEAF and rose to vice-president for engineering of NBC.

WAAM briefly disappeared from the air. Ira Nelson sold the station to Warner Brothers Pictures at the end of 1925. The call letters were changed to WBPI, then became WAAM again when Nelson reassumed control in April 1926. Studios were moved from an outbuilding at the Nelson factory to the RKO Theatre Building at 1060 Broad Street — a clear sign that showmanship was stepping ahead of technology. WAAM also operated shortwave station 2XBA on 65.18 meters.

In February 1927, a time when adventurous listeners still liked to stay up late twiddling dials and angling for distant stations, WAAM turned the fishing trip into a visit to the fish market with "Paul Godley's DX Party." Under the direction of the acclaimed radio engineer Paul F. Godley, WAAM set up a battery of receivers at a quiet location in the Jersey countryside and for several late-night hours rebroadcast stations snatched from as far away as California. (In 1921, Paul Godley was the first person to receive ham radio signals shortwaved from North America to Europe. His involvement with WAAM could be likened to Charles Lindbergh piloting for a commuter airline.)

To fill gaps between programs — a common problem during radio's infancy — WAAM installed a permanent line to the Hollywood Theatre in Orange to pick up the organist accompanying the silent films. A red light on the console was the only indication that the music was also being heard on the air. There were many programs with local New Jersey appeal; WAAM solicited home-grown talent for "Newark Night," "Elizabeth Night," and so on. It was one of the first stations to present a breakfast-time entertainment program. "The Sunshine Station" even provided a public service during a personal emergency. On 30 December 1928, when the orchestra that had been hired to play at a wedding in Belleville, N.J. failed to show up for the ceremony, WAAM's studio orchestra filled a request for the "Wedding March."

During an era when everything on the air was expected to be live, WAAM became one of the first stations to produce electrical transcriptions, which it aired in an admitted test of audience acceptance. Working with Edison engineers in 1928, Ira Nelson developed a long-playing record that could hold ninety minutes of program material.

Friday, 14 October 1927

7:00 A.M.	Sunrise Music Hour
8:00	Longines Time
10:00	Cooking School
10:30	Happy Hour
12:00 Noon	Longines Time
12:30	Newark News Late News
12:35	Luncheon Music
	Off for WODA
4:00	Clarence Hardy, baritone
4:30	Studio artists
5:00	Longines time; George Rogner, organ
5:30	Aunt Anne — Tales and Tunes
7:00 P.M.	Longines Time; Bill Fellmeth, sports
7:15	Weather; Caldwell Orchestra
8:00	Time; Maxim Entertainers
8:30	Stage — Anita Grannis
8:45	Myron Tymkevich, violin
8:30	Valley Forge Four
10:00	Great Notch Orchestra
10:45	Towers Orchestra
11:15	Organ program

Nelson even tended to enjoy good relations with stations sharing time with WAAM, and in 1928 when the FRC assigned WAAM to split its broadcast hours on 1250kc with WODA in Paterson and WGCP in Newark, WODA and WAAM joined together to request that the third broadcaster be moved elsewhere (request denied). In 1933, ownership was shifted to the newly founded WODAAM Corporation, which also bought WODA. In 1934, WAAM and WODA were merged into WNEW.

See also WODA, WGCP, WBPI, WNEW.

WAAQ

(13 APRIL 1922–15 MAY 1923)

1922	360m (833kc)	500w.

Motorcar dealers around the United States displayed an early interest in radio broadcasting. The two largest stations in Los Angeles were owned by rival auto dealers, and even the Ford Motor Company owned a radio station in Detroit in the early 1920s. The connection was not direct — the radio would not be an accessory in motor vehicles until the end of the decade — but in those days the highways were growing along with the airwaves. Some newspapers printed supplements covering both autos and radios, expecting that modern enthusiasts for one would also take an interest in the other.

There was only one radio station in the New York metropolitan area owned by a retail auto dealer, and it was also the first station in Fairfield County, Conn. WAAQ was licensed to New England Motor Sales Inc., a Franklin dealer at 22 West Putnam Street in Greenwich, just across the state line. Like other automobile dealers in the radio field, New England Motor Sales had sufficient space atop its building for an antenna and had room inside for the 1,500-volt generator that powered the transmitter. The manager and chief operator was George De Lage, who owned a small radio shop on West Putnam Street.

WAAT

(9 SEPTEMBER 1926—5 MAY 1958)

1926	1270kc	10w.
1926	1270kc	500w.
1927	1220kc s/t WGBB, WSOM	500w.
1928	1070kc (daytime)	500w.
1930	940kc (daytime)	500w.
1941	970kc	1,000w.
1949	970kc	5,000w.

Frank V. Bremer was tinkering with wireless as early as 1910 and remained active in metropolitan New York and New Jersey broadcasting until 1960. Even after he sold WAAT, the Bremer Broadcasting Corporation continued under his name on AM radio, later on FM, and eventually on television. His stature and his longevity are truly impressive when you realize that Bremer's entry into broadcasting happened without a commercial license.

In 1920 Bremer's ham radio station 2IA was leased by the *Jersey Review* of Jersey City, which paid thirty-five dollars for the semiweekly use of his facilities. At New Year's 1922 the *Jersey Journal* broadcast a one-hour show from midnight till 1:00 A.M. over 2IA. This program cost the *Journal* fifty dollars and is sometimes cited as the first commercial program, nine months before WEAF's debut as a "toll station."

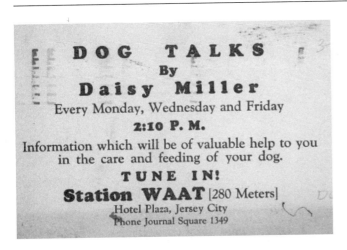

DOG TALKS
By
Daisy Miller
Every Monday, Wednesday and Friday
2:10 P. M.

Information which will be of valuable help to you
in the care and feeding of your dog.
TUNE IN!
Station WAAT [280 Meters]
Hotel Plaza, Jersey City
Phone Journal Square 1349

WAAT presented "Dog Talks" in 1929 and "Requestfully Yours"
in the 1940s with equal aplomb.

Wednesday, 25 May 1927

10:30 A.M.	Housewives Trio
11:15	Radio Shopper
11:30	Randolph Conroy, piano
11:40	Refrigeration talk
5:50	Market reports
6:00	Plaza Dinner Hour
7:00	Bill Reitz, songs
7:15	Sports resume
7:30	Cookie, songs
7:45	Marion and Bob Emmett
7:55	Today in history
8:00	Venice Orchestra
9:00	Mississippi Memories
10:00	Piano, Dorothea Padnick
10:30	Louisville Orchestra

The *Jersey Review* must have been impressed by Bremer's station, whose operation wasn't consistent with his license class. In April 1922 the newspaper received its own temporary commercial license from the Commerce Department and, with Frank Bremer at the controls, broadcast briefly with the assigned call letters WAAT. Frank Bremer continued to tend his radio shop at 210 Jackson Avenue, and in newspaper ads from the period he refers to himself as "Pioneer Broadcaster of New Jersey 1920-1926."

In August 1926—during the period when the federal government was obligated to issue a broadcast license to any citizen—Bremer got back on the air with the call letters WKBD but immediately requested a change, and on 9 September an all-new WAAT made its appearance. To publicize the new station, there was a contest to pick a slogan for WAAT;

the winner was "The Voice at the Gate of the Garden State."

Studios were in the Hotel Plaza at 91 Sip Avenue in Jersey City. Among the first programs was a nightly concert of dinner music direct from the hotel's dining room.

In February 1927 WAAT opened a Manhattan studio at 34 W. Twenty-eighth Street. WAAT was one of the first stations in the metropolitan area to serve the black community, with the "Negro Achievement Hour" starting in 1929. In 1931, WAAT moved out of the Plaza to 50 Journal Square. Frank Bremer was still the station manager, chief engineer, and occasional announcer, but in 1936 he sold controlling interest to members of his management team and continued as an engineering executive. WAAT operated

Requestfully Yours — "Mike-Shot"

Here's your latest picture in the **WAAT** Candid-Camera "Mike-Shot" series—**VIC DAMONE**. For more pictures of your musical favorites see other side . . . and keep listening to "Requestfully Yours"— 10:05 to 11:00 A. M. and 5:05 to 7:30 P. M. over **WAAT** (970 on your dial).

Requestfully Yours,

Paul Brenner

only daytime hours through the 1930s, but in 1940 and 1941 the station received permission to move from Jersey City to Newark, open a new transmitter in Kearney, double its power to 1,000 watts, shift frequency from 940 to 970kc, and stay on the air twenty-four hours a day.

WAAT was often chasing WNEW for the same audience. Against WNEW's Zeke Manners WAAT offered Dave Miller's "Hometown Frolics." Other WAAT announcers included Maurice Hart, Wat Watkins, Steve Hollis, Fred Sayles, and Bob Cook (a singer and deejay who was one of the first African-American announcers in the New York area), as well as a couple of disc jockeys who ended up at rival WNEW: Jerry Marshall and Bill (not yet calling himself William B.) Williams.

The station's biggest attraction was Paul Brenner and "Requestfully Yours," a repackaging of WAAT's "5:30 Request Club" from the 1930s. In the mid–1940s Brenner was rated the third-most-popular deejay in the nation, behind only Martin Block at WNEW and Al Jarvis in Los Angeles. Brenner was one of the most peripatetic personalities in New York area radio, hosting swing stage shows during World War II and showing up with a WAAT remote unit at store openings and community events. He was always urging listeners to visit the sponsor and "tell 'em Brenner sent me" (often there was a discount if you did).

In September 1944, WAAT prepared to enter the television era when it purchased the Mosque Theatre at 1020 Broad Street in Newark. WATV went on the air on channel 13 on 2 January 1948, and a year later WAAT and companion FM station WAAW joined it at the "Television Center." But it was still the radio era, and WAAT carried few simulcasts (one exception was the Sunday-evening "Shorty Warren Show" in the late 1940s) or cross-promotion for channel 13 (though much of its advertising revenue during this period came from television dealers urging listeners "you can enjoy television in your own living room this very evening by calling Bigelow 5").

WAAT continued to nurture an audience for country-and-western records in the nation's biggest urban market, and host Don Larkin gained a cult following. Hal Tunis played the newest big band releases. Bob Brown hosted the morning show during the 1950s, later moving to afternoon drive time. In November 1951 the Bremer Broadcasting Corporation was purchased by WAAT President Irving Rosenhaus.

On 6 May 1958 WAAT left the air for the second time. The AM, FM, and TV stations were sold for $2.5 million to National Telefilm Associates and became WNTA. The old call letters WAAT reappeared to identify a Trenton station from 1959 to 1971.

See also WNTA, WJRZ, WWDJ.

WABC[1]

(17 DECEMBER 1926–2 NOVEMBER 1946)

1926	950kc	5,000w.
1927	920kc	2,500w.
1928	970kc	5,000w.
8 Nov. 1928	860kc	5,000w.
2 Oct. 1929	860kc	50,000w.
1941	880kc	50,000w.

A. H. Grebe's Atlantic Broadcasting Company changed call letters from WAHG to WABC following an agreement with the Asheville Battery Company station in North Carolina. The new WABC set up studios in the seventeenth-floor penthouse of Steinway Hall at 113 W. Fifty-seventh Street (a thoroughfare that would act as New York's first "Broadcast Row") and began operation as a "toll broadcaster." It also was heard on shortwave through station W2XE at 58.5Mc. The secondary transmitter, WBOQ, was relicensed. In all, it was a very impressive operation that was well-publicized with one of New York radio's first printed logos.

It was Grebe's hope to expand the Atlantic Broadcasting Company into a network operation now that NBC had shown the way. But in September 1928, an opportunity arose that would make this station one of the major players of radio history. The Columbia chain did not own an outlet in New York. Its local affiliate was Bamberger's WOR, which was sure it could produce local programs of equal quality. When WOR refused to clear additional time for the CBS network, WABC stepped in to become the second affiliate, a move it hoped would justify a power increase. For a few weeks in 1928, WABC was the CBS station on Sunday, Tuesday, and Thursday, with WOR carrying the network on the other four days, but soon WOR dropped CBS completely.

In November 1928, Columbia offered to buy either of its New York area affiliates, and President William S. Paley negotiated with both Grebe and Bamberger. WOR's facilities were superior, but Paley chose the less-expensive WABC, and in December the Atlantic Broadcasting Company became a subsidiary of CBS. The sale price was $390,000, though the appraised value of the studios and transmitter was just $130,000. Grebe had apparently let the WABC studios go to seed, for Paley reported a mess on the seventeenth floor of Steinway Hall. Among the assets were goods accepted as payment from sponsors: jewelry, kitchenware, and reportedly even some live chickens.

Until that transaction the Columbia Broadcasting

Opposite: WABC/CBS tower on a man-made island in Long Island Sound, 1941.

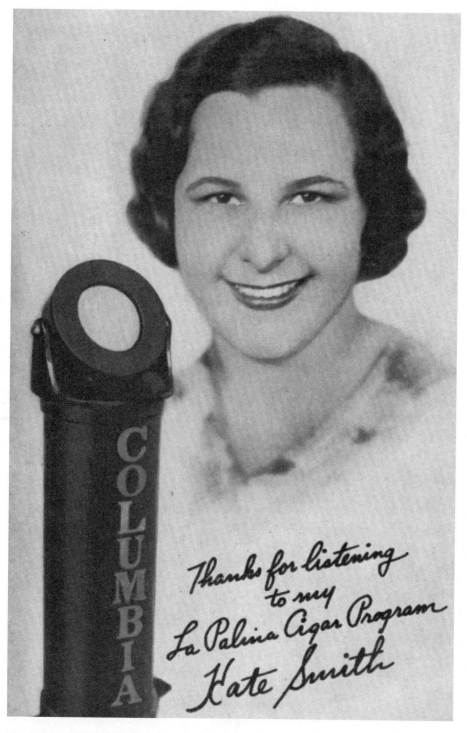

"America's sweetheart," Kate Smith first achieved stardom on the La Palina Cigar program, sponsored by the Paley family's cigar company.

In July 1929, CBS and WABC moved into six floors of a new building at 485 Madison Avenue. The network would eventually occupy the entire building as well as one across the street and various other locations around town. The local station was a very small part of this expanding empire. Shortwave station 2XE relayed all of WABC's programs to a worldwide audience. The CBS contract provided affiliates with unsponsored programs free of charge all day long with the understanding that they would clear the time for all sponsored shows. It made sense for WABC to carry a good portion of the network feed. Soon programs of purely local interest — including a few ethnic broadcasts aimed at Jewish and African-American listeners — were displaced by enjoyable but often undistinguished hours of music and talk for the national audience. Some of these, such as Rudy Vallee's program, had been on the local WABC schedule earlier, but the Columbia Network soon added new national performers to its fold: Bing Crosby, George Burns and Gracie Allen, Kate Smith, "Street Singer" Arthur Tracy, plus such irresistables as "Buck Rogers in the XXV Century." It was no surprise that WABC became one of the city's most popular stations and 485 Madison one of the nation's most important production centers.

As radio's news-reporting capabilities developed, CBS made a major effort to become "The News Network." There were as many newscasts as radio-newspaper agreements would allow and news analysis by the first generation of CBS commentators, including H.V. Kaltenborn, Elmer Davis, and Edwin C. Hill. "The World Today" brought in reports via shortwave from overseas news centers — a radical innovation for the time. All this news enhanced the value and prestige of CBS, but it added little in the way of local news in the New York area.

At 10:00 P.M. on Saturday, 2 November 1946, WABC changed its call letters to WCBS.

See also WCBS.

System was merely a program service providing entertainment features to a string of stations connected by an AT&T line. With the purchase of WABC, CBS itself was on the air. (It would confuse later generations to learn that the CBS key station was called WABC, but its parentage should now be clear; the American Broadcasting Company would not exist under that name until the mid–1940s.)

(1 MAY 1953–)

1953   770kc   50,000w.

New York's oldest call letters vanished overnight at the end of April 1953 when WJZ signed off and returned the next morning as WABC. This also marked the reappearance of letters that had identified the city's CBS station for nearly twenty years, which didn't seem to bother anyone. ABC now stood for the American Broadcasting Company, one of America's four major radio networks though still something of an upstart. In 1943, the National Broadcasting Company had been forced to divest itself of one of its two chains, partly because some programs on the Blue Network were shunted over to the Red as they began to gain popularity. When the Blue was cut loose from NBC it took few of the nation's hit shows with it, as well as losing much of NBC's news capability.

ABC did have some winners: Walter Winchell, Don Mac-Neil's "Breakfast Club," the indomitable kid shows from Detroit including "The Lone Ranger" and "The Green Hornet." It kept the prestigious Saturday matinee broadcasts of the Metropolitan Opera. The network had pulled off a coup and made broadcasting history in 1946 when Bing Crosby came to ABC, which agreed to break a long-standing network policy and allow the star to prerecord his programs. And in 1948 it had created a radio milestone (and made social history) with "Stop the Music," whose giant jackpot drew listeners away from their habitual Sunday-night favorites. ABC proved that the old Blue Network could be successful and innovative.

But the glory days of network radio were already on the wane when WJZ became WABC. Much of the ABC network schedule was fill material with scant audience appeal, and ABC affiliates were more likely than those of NBC or CBS to develop extensive local programming. That was also true for the New York flagship, which needed to loosen its network ties even as it took the network identification.

Thursday, 1 October 1959

6:00 A.M.	News; Al Lohman, Jr. Show
9:00	The Breakfast Club
10:00	Peter Lind Hayes & Mary Healy
10:10	Martin Block
12:00 Noon	News; Dick Shepard
1:55	News Reports
2:05	Fred Robbins
3:55	News Reports
4:05	Martin Block
6:15	Howard Cosell, sports
6:25	News Reports
6:30	John Daly, commentary
6:40	News Reports
6:45	Music Requests
7:00	Edward P. Morgan, commentary
7:15	Let's Travel — Paul Andrews
7:30	Alan Freed
10:00	John W. Vandercook, news
10:05	Alan Freed
11:00	Clair Hutchins, evangelist
11:30	Religious Talk
12:00 Midnight	Big Joe's Happiness Exchange
4:00	Music in the Night

The change from the "short form" parade of music, talk, drama, and game shows to the "long form" music-and-news format started when Martin Block quit WNEW and reestablished the "Make Believe Ballroom" at WABC on 4 January 1954. The pioneer deejay filled more than four hours starting at 2:35 on weekdays and in morning and evening slots on Saturdays. Part of the program was fed to the ABC Network, and although Block had lost none of his charm, in New York WNEW still claimed most of his old listeners.

In 1955, comedian Ernie Kovacs starred on WABC's wake-up show. It was a brief and strained return to radio before continuing one of television's unique careers.

"The station with the professional sound" added announcers Tony Marvin and Del Sharbutt in 1958, hosting afternoon record shows in their distinctively deep voices. In June of that year, Alan Freed brought his records over from WINS to rock and roll through the evening hours. But as WABC entered the 1960s, it was still having trouble shaking off the past and establishing a clear identity. The Metropolitan Opera matinee continued on Saturdays. The Sunday schedule was almost wholly filled by paid religious broadcasts, a common indicator at the time of economic marginality in the radio business. The music was a fuzzy mix of swing, pop, and rock and roll, and the news service still included several extended programs of analysis and commentary. The mighty WJZ had once been New York's most popular station. WABC's ratings hovered in the single digits.

A rescuer arrived in 1958 in the person of Hal Neal, formerly manager of ABC's Detroit station, WXYZ, which had surged in the ratings by specializing in rock and roll. The pop singles were out (and with them Martin Block, who retired from radio). Taking advantage of the 77 spot on the AM dial, where it had been encamped since 1941, WABC began to get lucky. The playlist of seventy records included "7 soaring singles," seven new albums, and so on, all presented by "The Swingin' 7": Herb Oscar Anderson, Chuck Dunaway, Bill Owen, Scott Muni, Charlie Greer, Farrell Smith, and Jack Carney, who was soon replaced by Dan Ingram. Neal also hired former WINS program director Rick Sklar to stimulate promotion and community involvement.

In his book *Rocking America*, Sklar explained the music formula that brought WABC to the front of the pack in New York radio. It was "a *coalition* of audiences. My targeting

An early WABC rock-and-roll deejay lineup at Palisades Park in 1962. Left to right: Bruce Morrow, Scott Muni, Charlie Greer, singer Bobby Vinton, Sam Holman, Dan Ingram, and Fred Hall. *Bruce Morrow Collection.*

OFFICIAL WABC BEATLES FAN CLUB

"WELCOME TO AMERICA"
from the
All Americans of WABC 77

WABC was not the first New York radio station to play the Beatles' records, but it organized an "Official WABC Beatles Fan Club" and sent these cards to listeners who requested them, 1964.

plan was to go after everyone…. Each record would have to do triple demographic duty or I could not afford to play it. Every air personality would have to appeal to three or more types of listeners," both urban and suburban, rich and poor, young and old. This was not Top 40. The programming policy resulted in possibly the shortest playlist in radio but one so carefully selected that exposure on WABC was nearly a guarantee that the tune would be a hit.

WABC became a power in the music business, and as it rose to the top of the ratings in the nation's first market (sixteen million potential listeners) it could make valid claim to being the most-listened-to radio station in the United States. When WABC celebrated its fortieth anniversary in 1961 with a party at the Freedomland amusement park in the Bronx, twenty-four thousand fans attended.

In 1965 WABC moved its studios around the corner to

The final moment of WABC "Musicradio" came on 10 May 1982 as Dan Ingram (left) and Ron Lundy signed the format off at 12:00 noon.

1926 Broadway and later to 1330 Avenue of the Americas. The morning slot finally stabilized, with Herb Oscar Anderson waking New Yorkers from 1960 to 1966 and with Harry Harrison for the next fifteen years.

On Monday, 10 May 1982, "Musicradio" faded out after twenty-two years — the last record was John Lennon's "Imagine" — and WABC turned into "Talkradio." In that year it also began to carry New York Yankees baseball. The original talkers included Art Athens, Ira Fistell, Ray Briem, and their English-accented colleague Michael Jackson from KABC in Los Angeles and Owen Spann from ABC's San Francisco station, KGO. Art Rust, Jr., talked sports in the early evening. There were also two straightforward psychologists counseling over the air: Dr. Toni Grant during afternoon drive time and Dr. Judith Kuriansky from 9:00 P.M. to midnight.

Then in the mid–1980s, Talkradio turned right. Reaching out for another "niche" in the mass audience, WABC booked several conservative talkers. Bob Grant's afternoon program turned up number one among listeners in the broad 18+ category in 1987, and in 1988 WABC brought Rush Limbaugh to New York from Sacramento. Initially, stations were wary of the idea of a national call-in program. "The Rush Limbaugh Show" was heard locally from 10 A.M. till noon, then a fresh two hours were fed via satellite from the same studio on what Limbaugh dubbed the EIB (Excellence in Broadcasting) Network. WABC later rescheduled Rush from noon to 3:00 P.M., picking up his national feed. To get some balance, the station brought over Lynn Samuels from WBAI-FM in June 1988. Former New York Mayor Ed Koch became a regular commentator and then host of his own morning call-in program. Bob Grant continued in the mid-morning and afternoon hours amid complaints about racist remarks.

WABC continued as "Talkradio 77" with hosts such as Guardian Angels founder Curtis Sliwa and his wife, Lisa, 1990.

In April 1996 a flip comment about the recent death of U.S. Commerce Secretary Ron Brown led to his firing.

WABC remained near the top of the ratings into the mid–1990s. Among the region's AM outlets, it was still New York's "First Station."

See also WJZ, WEAF.

WADO

(2 NOVEMBER 1959–)

1959   1280kc   5,000w

When Bartell Broadcasters bought WOV in August 1959, the station was programmed slightly more than half of the time for African-American audiences, with the remaining hours in Italian. WADO signed on in November, and black-oriented programs were absorbed into the new rock music format. Italian was heard from 7:00 to 10:00 P.M.; producers Renzo Sacerdoti and Giorgio Padovani stayed with WADO until 1964. Otherwise, WADO tried mightily to win a general audience with one of the most colorful approaches to rock in New York radio and with some frenetic news services. In April 1960 studios, moved to the Newsweek Building at 444 Madison Avenue, Bartell's corporate headquarters.

The "Musicmakers"—that's what WADO called its disc jockeys—included Happy Hare (Harry Martin) beginning the day "Hello there, this is Happy Hare," Kenny Garland, and Johnny Holiday (Mort Crowley, not the "Johnny Holliday" from WINS, who was Johnny Bobbitt). On the graveyard shift, Jack Walker, "the pear-shaped talker," played rhythm and blues with special appeal to black audiences, another carryover from WOV. The new rocker in town used the old Harry James swing tune "Music Makers" as a station jingle to identify "Radio W-A-D-O Twelve-eighty-oh."

The most striking sound on WADO was the news—not the content but the production values. News director Jack Powers personally delivered most newscasts from 6 A.M. to 6:30 P.M. Opening with the words "This is the voice of the news!" he would cup his hands and hawk, "Downtown dailies, please stand by to copy!" Along with a Walter Winchell–like delivery, Powers piled on the sound effects: teletypes clicking, bells ringing, sirens wailing, and datelines shouted through an echo chamber. The echo chamber was also cut in when WADO reported the hourly radiation measurement from it's own Geiger counter, followed by a free offer of information on how to build a fallout shelter, followed by an offer of a twenty-five-dollar savings bond for the best news tip of the week, followed by "News—no sooner done than said! Another reason for New York to choose WADO's Voice of the News!"

It was an energetic approach, but most of WADO's air personalities lacked experience in the New York market and never really connected with the local audience. Early in 1960 WADO brought back Herman Amis, a mainstay from the WOV days. The great jazz deejay "Symphony Sid" Torin came to the new station, and Jocko Henderson landed in his "Rocketship," playing rhythm and blues and speaking in an early version of rap prose. In December 1959, Alan Fredericks' "Night Train" became a doo-wop Saturday-night feature. Faced with strong competition from WMCA, WINS, and WMGM, the former WOV brought back Italian and black-oriented programming—gospel deejays Joe Crane and Charles Gibbs, Jr. joined the lineup—and some Spanish programming was phased in. "Night Train" rolled on for six years.

With the purchase of Sunday time-sharing station WHBI in 1962, WADO expanded Spanish programming and confined its English-language programs to religious broadcasts on the weekend. In the final weeks as a rock station, WADO figured it needed more news to hold on to the existing audience. There were suddenly not two but four explosive newscasts each hour —five minutes at :05, :20, :35, and :50 past the hour, or the next news in just ten minutes. WADO finally pulled the plug on rock and roll during the last week of June 1963. Among the new air personnel were Angel Richardson, who would remain as news director through the 1980s. (Jack Powers became a press officer at the Pentagon.) Also joining WADO were program director Luis Romanoche, Ismael Diaz Tirado, and Raul Torres.

WADO appealed to upwardly-mobile Hispanic listeners, including many Cubans recently exiled from their homeland following the Castro revolution. The new Radio Wado soon adapted a popular program from pre–Castro Cuba. "Radio Reloj" ("Radio Clock") awakens, entertains and informs listeners while a clock constantly ticks and tocks. The morning show became an institution in Latino households and one of the longest-running programs on New York radio.

In 1964, studios were moved to 205 E. Forty-second Street. On the first of June, 1964 WADO began to air Spanish programming from 5 A.M. till 8 P.M. WADO became a twenty-four-hour Spanish station in 1973, and with its 1979 sale to Command Broadcasting Associates, the ownership and management became primarily Hispanic. Studios moved

WADO's rhythm-and-blues disc jockey Douglas "Jocko" Henderson spoke in rhymed patter. Some consider him to be one of the originators of "rap" music.

to the transmitter in Carlstadt, N.J. and the station joined Cadena Radio Centro, a Texas-based network.

WADO later bought WGLI in Babylon, Long Island and took it off the air, removing the 1290 kHz station to open the island to 1280. By the 1990s, WADO was the metropolitan area's dominant Spanish language station. Its programming appealed to a mature audience. One day a week was devoted to Spanish popular standards. The schedule was more varied than that of many format-dominated stations and included strong news coverage on the morning and afternoon drive-time "WADO Reloj." There were also many advice programs — a formula that worked well in English for WOR — including nightly series on health, beauty, and nutrition and a daily horoscope. WADO is acquiring its first FM facility, WNWK, 105.9 MHZ, Newark, pending FCC approval.

WAHG

(24 OCTOBER 1924–16 DECEMBER 1926)

1924	920kc	500w.
1925	950kc	500w.
1926	950kc s/t WGBS	5,000w.

Alfred H. Grebe was the quintessential "radio boy." Born in 1895, he built his first wireless set at the age of nine, was a maritime operator at age fifteen, and was manufacturing his own equipment before he was twenty years old. His first "radio shack" was actually an old henhouse; the neighbors called his antenna "Grebe's pole." In 1922, Grebe (rhymes with "Seabee") razed his family home (and henhouse) on Van Wyck Blvd. and Jamaica Avenue in Richmond Hill, Queens, to construct a large radio factory on the site. At its peak the plant turned out one hundred thousand radios a year. Grebe Synchrophase receivers were among the best of their time and are prized today by collectors of antique radios.

Grebe originated one of America's first political campaign broadcasts, a 1921 speech by New York mayoral candidate John Hylan from the experimental transmitter in Richmond Hill. To guarantee an audience, receivers were loaned to Democratic clubhouses around the city. A. H. Grebe and Company developed a respected research laboratory, built the wireless equipment for Admiral Richard Byrd's Arctic expedition, and went into the broadcasting field.

WAHG ("Wait and Hear Grebe") was the principal Grebe station. It's share-time partner was Gimbel's WGBS, which occupied 950kc for most of the broadcast day. WBOQ — the call letters stood for "Borough of Queens" —

The A.H. Grebe radio factory in Richmond Hill, Queens, with the towers of WAHG and WBOQ. *Weber Collection, Queens Library.*

was a secondary transmitter in Richmond Hill, which for a while was programmed separately from WAHG. There was also a 100-watt mobile unit installed in a Lincoln sedan operating on 63 meters shortwave with the call WGMU, as well as the maritime transmitter WRMU aboard the yacht MU-1. Among the pioneering remote broadcasts on WAHG were yachting events and horse races (the latter service was said to have ruined business for some bookies).

In 1925, WAHG carried the commentary of *Brooklyn Eagle* editor H.V. Kaltenborn direct from the newspaper's own studio. Among the early announcers were George D. Hay (who later went to WSM in Nashville and created the "Grand Ole Opry") and a sixteen-year-old named Nancy Clancy.

Sunday, 17 January 1926

11:55 A.M.	Time signals; weather
12:03 P.M.	Grebe Matinee Trio
	Off for WGBS
7:30	Maude Mason, piano; vocal duets; Synchrophase Trio; H. J. Taylor, recitations
9:30	"The Land of the Pharaohs," Maj. D. Atkinson
9:45	Jean McGregor, soprano
9:55	Time signals; weather
10:03	Jean McGregor, soprano
10:20	Zimmerman's Orchestra
12:00	Utopia Orchestra
12:30	Ukelele Bob MacDonald

Not surprisingly, WAHG had one of the clearest signals among early stations in the New York area; its first 5,000-watt transmitter was referred to as "super-power" (it operated with only 2,500 watts at night). WAHG was a leader in the industry at a time when broadcasting seemed imperiled

by rapid technical change and lax regulation. A. H. Grebe took a bold step late in 1926 and reorganized his broadcast operations as the Atlantic Broadcasting Company, moved the studios from Richmond Hill to Manhattan, had the call letters changed to WABC, and developed what would become one of America's most important radio stations.

See also WABC (I), WBOQ.

WALK

(20 MAY 1952–)

1952	1370kc	500w.

In July 1950, the FCC decided to grant the Suffolk Broadcasting Company permission to operate on 1370kc with 500 watts. The company had been holding a construction permit for an FM station in Coram to be called WFSS (for "First Suffolk Station"—at least the first in twenty years), which it never put on the air. At the same time 1370 appeared to be a little close to WBNX and WAWZ at 1380, but the FCC decided that the Patchogue station would bring a new service to some fifty-eight thousand Long Islanders and so granted Suffolk Broadcasting its second construction permit. WALK-AM went on the air two years later and added an FM partner at 97.5 six months after that. The principal owner was W. Kingsland Macy, a former U.S. congressman and a major figure in the Republican Party; Nils Segerdahl was the first station manager. Program director Jack Ellsworth came over from WGSM and began a thirty-year tenure, serving for much of that time as general manager.

A teenager from Oceanside named Dan Ingram showed up one day asking for a job and was turned down. After a month at WNRC in New Rochelle, Ingram went back to WALK and this time started in earnest on a career. He broadcast from the lobby of the Bay Shore Theatre as "The Baron of Bay Shore" and later went on to WABC and CBS-FM. Announcer Ed Joyce also launched his network career from WALK.

In October 1963 WALK and its sister station WRIV in Riverhead were sold by Macy's estate to the Island Broadcasting Company. The new owners carried some clout: NBC News anchorman Chet Huntley, Cowles Publications executive Jerome Feniger, and William Mulvey, senior vice-president of the McCann-Erickson advertising agency. Edward Wood Jr., another partner, came to WALK as president and general manager. Wood had been with CBS for many years and created the "Housewives Protective League" program.

Bob Klein began his wakeup show in 1967, which soon

became an institution for Suffolk County listeners, and remained the morning man for over two decades. Part of WALK's service was the Sky-WALK traffic helicopter, which hovered over roads referred to as "the world's biggest parking lot." In 1976, WALK weathered a hurricane that struck Long Island, remaining on the air through the day and night and providing emergency information to listeners huddled by portable radios in blacked-out homes.

In 1986, American Media Inc. bought WALK. The station led the ratings in the lucrative Nassau-Suffolk market in the 1990s with its stable information service and equally stable adult contemporary-music format. It even regularly showed up in the New York City ratings book.

	Day Time	Evening Time
Monday	11:00 A.M. to 1:30 P.M.	6 to 7:30 P.M.
Tuesday	3:45 P.M. to 6:00 P.M.	9 to 10:30 P.M.
Wednesday	11:00 A.M. to 1:30 P.M.	7:30 to 9 P.M.
Thursday	3:45 P.M. to 6:00 P.M.	9 to 10:30 P.M.
Friday	11:00 A.M. to 1:30 P.M.	6 to 7:30 P.M.
Saturday	3:45 P.M. to 6:00 P.M.	10:30 P.M. to 2 A.M.
Sunday	1:30 P.M. to 3:00 P.M.	7 to 9 P.M.

In a letter to a friend circa 1938, program director Bob Becker described his situation at WARD, "It seems that I called the manager on the phone Tuesday afternoon … he asked me to come right over … then postponed decision until Wednesday ayem … when I walked in Wednesday morning I was introduced as the new PD and there I was and here I am" (ellipses in original). Becker described WARD as a "peanut whistle … with mostly foreign language programs. We have Greek, Yiddish, Hungarian, Spanish, Ukrainian, Irish, Scotch and even a Chinese program. I try to dress up what little American stuff we have. " Becker ended, "It's too damn hot for much more … this joint is not air conditioned and it gets hot as hell."

When the four feuding Brooklyn stations finally agreed to merge into the Unified Broadcasting Corporation in 1941, WARD was the lead partner and Rabbi Kronenberg the president. Call letters of the full-time station were originally to be WARD, but the former rivals settled instead on WBYN.

See also WCGU, WBBC, WBYN.

W A R D

(APRIL 1933–MARCH 1941)

1933	1400kc s/t WLTH, WVFW, WBBC	500w.
1941	1430kc	500w.

New York's large Jewish population has been served by many stations in both Yiddish and English, but no other had the special standing that WARD enjoyed among the four Brooklyn stations sharing time at the 1400 spot on the dial. WARD was run by an Orthodox rabbi. Aaron Kronenberg was a native of Warsaw who came to America in 1905 and began broadcasting in 1928. Along with attorney Morris Meyers, he bought Charles G. Unger's WCGU, which had moved from Coney Island to Fulton Street in downtown Brooklyn. Studios remained at 427 Fulton (phone Triangle 5-3300).

The "Jewish Radio Hour" was a daily Yiddish-language feature on which the radio rabbi delivered sermons, told stories, dispensed advice, appealed for support for many Jewish organizations, and even presented the commercials.

Despite this unique advantage, WARD barely held on to its license, which the FCC nearly rescinded in 1935 as a step toward establishing a single Brooklyn station. Kronenberg and the other three broadcasters with whom WARD shared 1400kc were able to keep the commission's threatened action tied up in the courts until 1941. The rabbi insisted that WARD had "no apology to make" for the quality of its programming. Among its public-service programs, the station often provided time for Catholic charitable appeals.

The one-quarter time share with WBBC, WLTH, and WVFW gave WARD an irregular schedule, which it printed on the back of its business cards:

W A R S

(3 NOVEMBER 1926–FEBRUARY, 1928)

1926	295m = 1016kc	500w.
1927	1320kc s/t WSDA, WBBC	500w.
1928 (WSGH)	1400kc	500w.

Construction of the World Trade Center demolished a section of Lower Manhattan that included the legendary "Radio Row"—a business district centered on Cortlandt Street that was to tubes, wires, and soldering irons what Wall Street is to securities or Forty-seventh Street to diamonds. The Amateur Radio Specialty Company at 77 Cortlandt sold wireless components and built complete radios for those without the knowledge or motivation to "roll their own." In small towns far from good daytime radio coverage, such businesses would often start a broadcasting station to demonstrate the wonder of radio to a skeptical customer — the broadcast period often lasted only as long as the demonstration. In New York City, when a radio store went into the broadcasting end of the business it was with the intent of joining the excitement on the air.

Wednesday, 27 July 1927

7:00 P.M.	Milton Katz, piano
7:10	Health Talk
7:20	Eddie Moss, songs
7:35	Morris Bialkin, cello
7:50	Tommy King, tenor
8:05	Announcement
8:15	Clyde Monroe, poet
8:30	Sirens Orchestra
9:00	Lillian Kellman, violin
9:15	Lillian Schurr, contralto
9:30	Scranton Sirens
10:00	Off for WBBC
12:00	Midnight program
12:10	Steeplechase Orchestra
12:30	Ken Casey's Gang

The station was not built at the Cortland Street store but in the Brighton Beach section of Brooklyn atop the Hotel Shelburne on Ocean Parkway and Sea Breeze Avenue, overlooking the beach. WARS called itself "The Voice of the Atlantic."

With the Shelburne slated for demolition, in December 1927 WARS applied to the FRC for a "remote control studio" in the St. George Hotel in downtown Brooklyn. In February 1028 the call letters were changed from the unintentionally bellicose WARS to the more respectable WSGH.

See also WSGH.

(15 MARCH 1931–1 SEPTEMBER 1984)

1931	1350kc s/t WBNX	250w.
1941	1380kc s/t WBNX	1,000w.

American religion is noted for visionaries who guided faithful adherents into independent churches. The example of Joseph Smith's Mormons and Mary Baker Eddy's Christian Scientists was emulated by Alma Bridwell White. Denied ordination by the Methodists because she was a woman, Mrs. White founded the Pillar of Fire Church in Denver in 1901. Five years later, self-proclaimed as "Bishop," she established Alma White College and a religious community called Zarephath in Somerset County, N.J. The Pil-

lar of Fire never grew into a large sect, but under the guidance of Bishop Alma White, the austere and energetic "pillar people" became important in the development of religious broadcasting.

In 1930, the Pillar of Fire applied to take over the allocated hours of WBNY, which had been operating one-quarter time on 1350kc. Owner Sydney Baruch reportedly blanched at giving up his station to WKBQ owner Allen Cahill, who was attempting to create a full-time operation, and sold WBNY to Alma White for $5,000. The Corriere d'America station, WCDA, and Madison Square Garden's WMSG were absorbed into WBNX, but WAWZ remained on the frequency (1380kc after March 1941) for over fifty years.

Monday, 3 October 1966

6:30 A.M.	Morning Hymns and Sermon
7:00	News of School, Home, and Garden
7:15	Chapel Time
7:45	News for You
8:00	Gospel in Sermon and Song
8:30	Community Gospel
9:00	Off for WBNX
6:00 P.M.	Pillar of Fire Soloists
6:15	Readings
6:30	Community Devotions
6:45	Pillar of Fire Testimony
7:00	Public Service Program
7:15	News
7:30	Off for WBNX

In its inaugural broadcast, Alma White told listeners, "The station belongs to all regardless of your affiliation." WAWZ would eventually carry every manner of religious broadcast.

WAWZ broadcast about four hours a day on most weekdays, but they were the popular breakfast and dinner hours. Sunday schedules were an intermittent eight hours and included pickups of revival meetings from the Zarephath religious community. Alma White was president of WAWZ, her husband was vice-president, and their son Ray served as program director. The sect also established stations in Denver and Cincinnati, making radio a major part of the Pillar of Fire ministry.

In 1939 WAWZ applied unsuccessfully for a license to broadcast on shortwave.

Bishop Alma White died in 1946. The Pillar of Fire began to decline in membership and, as a believer might put it, "grew cold." Alma White College closed and communal living at Zarephath waned. (Zarephath has never been an incorporated community; station breaks referred to "WAWZ in Zarephath, near Bound Brook.") But WAWZ remained on the air, and broadcasting continued to be a major occupation of the Pillar of Fire. The schedule included readings from the works of Alma White and music by Ray White's "Home Orchestra."

The Pillar's AM signal was heard weakly in New York City, but in 1954 "the old gray lady of religious radio" added an FM station at 99.1MHz, which would eventually blanket both the New York and the Philadelphia markets with paid religious programming twenty-four hours a day. The FM outlet was purchased from the *New Brunswick Home News* for $2,000, so WAWZ's place on AM and FM airwaves was obtained for less than the cost today of a family car. In 1973, Rev. S. Rea Crawford, who was born in Zarephath, became station manager.

There were newscasts and public affairs programs — some of them with religious content, but including the New Jersey governor's press conferences — which were expanded after a 1981 challenge to WAWZ-FM's license by WRNJ. The case established a public-service precedent often cited by other religious broadcasters.

In 1984, WBNX became WKDM, and WAWZ sold its part-time AM operation. For its final day on 1380kc — Saturday, 1 September 1984 — the Pillar of Fire produced a special program recalling WAWZ's fifty-three years of preaching, teaching, and zealotry and, one more time (by electrical transcription), the singularly inspiring voice of Bishop Alma White.

See also WBNY, WBNX, WKDM.

WBAB

(1 JANUARY 1958–1976)

| 1958 | 1440kc (daytime) | 500w. |
| 1961 | 1440kc (daytime) | 1,000w. |

The first of two AM stations in Babylon, Long Island, signed on at New Year's 1958 from studios and transmitter on Route 109. It was licensed to Babylon-Bayshore Broadcasting Corporation, headed by Sol Horenstein. Ray Adell was the first program director and the first voice heard on the new station. Other air personalities included John Bohannon, Tony Rousseau, Clem Cooper, Rhett Evers, and Tony James. Late that August, WBAB added an FM partner at 102.3Mc and was able to extend its programming into the evening. Less than a week after that expansion, WGLI went on the air to give WBAB some local competition.

Beginning with a middle-of-the-road music policy, WBAB switched in the 1970s to Top 40, then to an album rock format called The Happening Sound. This grasping after niches was partly due to the growing competition from what many saw as an overpopulation of radio stations on the island. Program director Bill Andres summed up WBAB's goal: "All we want is to be somebody's car button."

In 1975, Babylon-Bayshore Broadcasting sold their FM outlet, and a year later 1440 changed to paid religion and inspirational music. In 1976 it became WNYG.

WBAN

(24 APRIL 1922–10 APRIL 1925)

| 1922 | 360m (833kc) | 100w. |
| 1923 | 1230kc s/t WBBR, WABS | 100w. |

The Wireless Phone Corporation of Paterson put that city's first station on the air two months after WOR debuted in Newark.

The station shut down after three years, but its experience and some of its facilities were taken by the O'Dea family in Paterson and formed the basis of WODA.

Tuesday, 9 May 1922
MUSICAL PROGRAM — 10:30 A.M. to 6:30 P.M., every hour on the half hour
BASEBALL — Final scores every evening at 6:30 P.M., courtesy of News
PROGRAM — Will be announced daily at 7:30 P.M. by radiophone
7:45 P.M. Address by State Senator Albin Smith
8:00 P.M. Recital by G. Chrystal Brown, "Sweet Miss Mary," Neidlinger; "The Joy of a Rose," Tarbox; "For You Alone," Geehl.

Chrystal Brown will also conduct a popular sing over the radio. This has never been done from a sending station before. But it is believed all listening in will take part in the singing. The songs will include "Peggy O'Neil," "April Showers," "Why Dear," "Old Folks at Home," "Smiles," "Sweet Adeline," and others.

By special request, Mr. Brown will broadcast the popular sacred song, "I Know Not Why"; Carl Weinrich, accompanist.

W B A Y

(25 JULY–16 AUGUST 1922)

| 1922 | 360m | 500w. |

WBAY's role in the history of radio is important beyond its longevity, for it was on the air less than three weeks. It was installed by the American Telephone and Telegraph Company's Long Lines Division to be the nucleus of a national network "intended for commercial broadcasting." Even in 1922 there was a sense of "prime time": the station was available for public use at a cost of forty dollars for fifteen minutes in the daytime and fifty dollars per quarter-hour at night. An AT&T press release of 11 February 1922 stated:

> This important radio distributing station is to be equipped with the latest developments of the Bell System, including the use of electrical filters and new methods, whereby, as the business grows, several wave-lengths can be sent out simultaneously from the same point, so that the receiving stations [that is, the audience] may listen at will to any one of the several services…. It will be unique … because it will be the first radio station for telephone broadcasting which will provide a means of distribution and will handle the distribution of news, music or other program on a commercial basis for such people as contract for this service…. There have been many requests for such a service, not only from newspapers and entertainment agencies, but also from department stores and a great variety of business houses who wish to utilize this means of distribution.

Radio Broadcast magazine wrote, "Probably more thought and talent has been expended [on station WBAY] than on any other in existence." Its studio was equipped with the first audio mixers, electrical phonograph pickups, VU meters, and high-quality condenser microphones. It had ambitious program plans, including a daily "Radio Digest," which was to be an hour-long review of the day's news each afternoon at 4:30, including a regular feature to answer listeners' questions about radio. The program was to premiere on the first of September, but WBAY did not survive to present "Radio Digest."

Ironically, technical problems that only a telephone company could suffer caused WBAY to leave the air. The AT&T building at 24 Walker Street occupied a full block between Walker and Lispenard near Broadway in Lower Manhattan. It was twenty-four stories (350 feet) high, the towers on its roof were 100 feet high, and it stood "conspicuously above any other building in the immediate neighborhood." Unfortunately, WBAY's antenna was insufficiently insulated from the steel superstructure, and the entire build-ing acted like an enormous lightning rod. Even in clear weather the transmitter was plagued by "man-made static" caused by the heavy flow of electrical currents carrying phone calls within the building. The WBAY signal was weak and noisy, and when tests of AT&T's second station, WEAF, showed the newer station to have a better signal, WBAY was phased out. It had never sold a minute of airtime.

The WBAY log entry for Wednesday, 16 August 1922, states: "WBAY transmitter closed. WBAY studio broadcasting through WEAF." The staff was transferred to WEAF.

See also WEAF.

W B B C

(24 AUGUST 1926–30 APRIL 1941)

Aug. 1926	1200kc / various	500w.
June 1927	1320kc	500w.
Nov. 1928	1400kc s/t WLTH, WCGU, WSDA	500w.
Mar. 1941	1430kc	500w.

During the chaotic summer of 1926, twenty-one year old Peter J. Testan's Brooklyn Broadcasting Corporation began operation of WBBC at 1200kc and, after a few self-appointed shifts in frequency, settled down at its assigned 1400kc in 1928, sharing time with three other wavelength wanderers in Brooklyn. Their rivalry precipitated the extended "Brooklyn radio fight."

In November 1928 WBBC and WSGH at the St. George Hotel were in conflict and defying federal regulators as well as arbitration attempts by the Brooklyn Chamber of Commerce. On Friday, 23 November 1928, both stations deliberately broadcast at the same time on 1400 for about half an hour. When the Federal Radio Commission finally assigned new interim wavelengths and insisted that the protesting stations try them out, Peter Testan refused to move "until it appears that a modification of the order cannot be secured in which WBBC will receive a better wave." The FRC allowed political leaders in Brooklyn to deal with the local dispute, and following intervention by a state supreme court justice, each of the four stations in Brooklyn was scheduled for twenty-six hours a week. There were complaints from WCGU that the chamber of commerce had acted with bias in favor of WBBC.

Wednesday, 5 February 1930

1:30 P.M.	Safety topics
1:45	Kings County Observer
2:15	Madame Mitzi Welker, contralto

2:30	Miriam Ray	
2:45	Louise Holter, soprano	
3:00	Lessons in Esperanto	
3:15	Howard Joyner, piano and songs	
3:30	Hudson Bay Fur	
3:45	Frank's Electricaleers	
4:00	"How to Burn Air," H.G. Fleer	
	Off for WLTH, WSGH	
7:30	Balm Brothers & Friedberg Hour	
8:30	Merchant Serenaders	
8:55	"How to Burn Air"	
9:00	Entin's Hour	
10:00	Off for WLTH	

As the fight continued into the 1930s, WBBC was sharing one-quarter time with WLTH, WVFW, and WARD and suffering financial difficulties; it had issued some bad checks and lost over $2,000 in 1936. But in 1937, the FCC voted to allow WBBC to take over the time of WARD and WLTH — a move that would be tied up in court for four more years. "Brooklyn's Own Station" specialized in foreign-language broadcasting (one FCC examiner issued a report saying there was too much) in Italian, German, Yiddish, Polish, and several Scandinavian tongues, as well as programs aimed at Irish listeners. The influential musician Dave Tarras, a popularizer of Jewish *klezmer* music, was WBBC's music director. Another of the station's popular artists was cantor Moishe Oysher, whose performances combined Hebrew liturgical music with his own brand of Yiddish scat singing.

Finally, in 1941, the four Brooklyn stations came together to form the Unified Broadcasting Corporation of Brooklyn. Peter Testan became one-quarter owner of the new full-time station and its chief engineer. The WBBC Building at 554 Atlantic Avenue became the first offices and studios of the new WBYN.

See also WARD, WBYN, WCGU, WSGH.

WBBR[I]

(24 FEBRUARY 1924–31 MARCH 1957)

1924	1230kc (Feb.-May), 1100kc	500w.
1925	720kc (unauthorized)	500w.
1927	1170kc s/t WJBI, WLTH, WEBJ	1,000w.
1928	1300kc s/t WEVD, WHAP, WHAZ	500w.
1941	1330kc s/t WEVD, WHAZ	1,000w.
1948	1330kc s/t WEVD, WHAZ	5,000w.

Jehovah's Witnesses was one of the first religious organizations to enter the broadcasting field. The sect has always proselytized, spreading its message through a large publishing enterprise, streetcorner magazine sales, door-to-door canvassing, portable phonographs, sound trucks, and quite naturally, radio.

In 1923, the International Bible Students' Association (as it was then called — the name "Jehovah's Witnesses" was adopted in 1931) bought the equipment of WDT at Stapleton, Staten Island, which the Ship Owners Radio Service was shutting down. At 8:30 P.M. on a Sunday a year later, Judge Franklin Rutherford, successor to the sect's founder, Charles Taze Russell, dedicated the new WBBR at Rossville in southwestern Staten Island. Facilities and accommodations for the staff were in the 2½-story "Big House" at 1111 Woodrow Road. There was also a large vegetable garden at Rossville, as well as a culvert that served to drain the swampy field and the tidal flow from the Arthur Kill. The culvert also carried wiring for the station's ground radiation system and occasionally served as a baptismal font for the Rutherfordites. These baptisms were often heard live on WBBR, and perhaps charges flowing from the wires enhanced the sense of fervor.

Friday, 2 September 1927

2:00 P.M.	Studio orchestra
2:25	Radio harp study
2:50	Studio orchestra
3:10	Suggestions for dinner salad
3:15	Ronald Barclay, pianist
3:30	Lecture, Albert Clifford
4:00	Off for WJBI
7:00	F. S. Barnes, organist
7:20	Sunday school lesson
7:40	Joseph Bonaccorso, violinist
7:55	Helpful recipes
8:05	Organ selections
8:20	Health and hygiene
8:30	Lecture, H. R. Goux
9:00	Off for WEBJ

The schedule included programs in several languages, including Yiddish and Arabic.

Judge Rutherford expanded the radio operations into ownership of at least seven stations in the United States and Canada, including outlets in the Chicago, Toronto, and Oakland areas. On 5 August 1928, Rutherford broadcast on a chain of ninety-six stations, the largest radio network organized till that time (the record stood for six days). Later broadcasts were beamed via shortwave to over four hundred stations worldwide, sometimes originating from tiny WBBR. In the New York area the Witnesses also bought time on WBNX, WOV, WGBB, WFAS, and WNEW. But Rutherford's attacks on other religions led many stations to drop his programs, sometimes cutting him off before he was finished.

Like most of the other smaller broadcasters in the metropolitan area, WBBR lobbied for a better frequency assignment. In 1927, the FRC turned down its application to share time with the mighty WJZ, and WBBR was given 1170kc. It not only split the frequency with WLTH and WEBJ but leased use of the Rossville transmitter to both of them. In 1931, the main studios were moved from Rossville to the sect's headquarters at 124 Columbia Heights in Brooklyn Heights, which also served as a residence for church workers. "We produced and broadcast stirring radio dramas," longtime WBBR engineer Robert Hatzfeld recalled. "Each drama was a spectacular undertaking. And people listened. In those days of few distractions, many people sat and paid attention." There were three studios at Columbia Heights. Jehovah's Witnesses consider all adherents to be ministers, thus many people with little broadcasting experience came before the microphones of WBBR.

"The Voice from the Watchtower—Station of Origin, WBBR" shared airtime daily with WEVD and on Monday nights with WHAZ at Renssallaer Polytechnic Institute, upstate in Troy. The Witnesses' station was on the air 6–8 A.M. weekdays, 6–8 P.M. Tuesday through Friday, and Sundays 6–11 A.M. and 3–8 P.M. In 1941 the license was transferred to the Watchtower Bible and Tract Society, the religion's publishing arm, and in March of that year WBBR and its partners moved to 1330kc.

Judge Rutherford died in 1942 and was buried at Rossville in a Methodist cemetery within sight of the towers of WBBR. A fire at the Rossville transmitter in February 1945 put the station off the air briefly. In 1946, WBBR erected a 411 foot, three-tower array at Rossville, and two years later the power was increased to 5,000 watts. A new structure housed the transmission equipment. For all of its days on the air, WBBR was powered by its own electrical generator.

In 1957, choosing to emphasize its publishing activity and stating that WBBR "no longer served the interests of the Kingdom," the Watchtower Bible and Tract Society sold its station to H. Scott Killgore's Tele-Broadcasters of New York Inc. (The "Big House" was sold to the Staten Island Girls' School; the house and towers were razed in 1989.) WBBR had been the last AM radio station to identify itself as being in Brooklyn. It went silent having accomplished its mission: in New York in 1924 there was only one congregation of two hundred Rutherfordites; by 1957, sixty-two congregations in the New York area included over seven thousand members of Jehovah's Witnesses.

See also WDT, WEVD, WPOW.

Don't confuse with WBBR, 1130kc (Bloomberg Business Radio).

WBBR II

(4 JANUARY 1993–)

1993   1130khz.   50,000w.

There were already two all-news stations in New York City, and the attempt at a business news format on WMCA had proven to be a failure, when Bloomberg Communications Inc. put the city's first twenty-four-hour business news station on the air. The station was called WBBR, call letters coincidentally assigned from 1924 to 1957 to a religious station on Staten Island operated by the Jehovah's Witnesses. In this case the letters stood for Bloomberg Business Radio, owned by Michael R. Bloomberg, a publisher of businesses forms and investment publications.

In August 1992 Bloomberg bought WNEW, a longtime favorite whose swing-era programming had fallen victim to changing tastes and commercial pressures. The sale price was $13.5 million. Studios were built at Bloomberg headquarters at 499 Park Avenue.

Signing on at 5:00 A.M. on the first business day of 1993, WBBR's first program was a ten-minute talk by Mike Bloomberg. Then it began the tightly formatted ten-minute cycles of news, sports, weather, traffic reports, and of course, the latest from Wall Street and the world's financial markets. Local news wasn't covered in depth, and sensationalism was minimized. Most reports were recorded and controlled by an automation system that proved difficult to override, especially with six ten-minute feeds each hour. This was later adjusted to four fifteen-minute news blocks each hour.

WBBR has failed to draw many listeners from all-news stations WINS and WCBS. It was as different as possible from WNEW and so held few listeners from the earlier days on 1130. Bloomberg Business Radio also came along at a time when all financial news media were expanding rapidly; still, it is a small but dependable voice in the Bloomberg empire.

WBIC

(1 JUNE 1960–31 AUGUST 1967)

1960   540kc (daytime)   250w.

Five years after the FCC authorized 540kc as a broadcast frequency, WBIC in Bay Shore, Long Island, became the first station in the New York metropolitan area to set up shop at the new bottom of the dial. The call letters stood for the neighboring Suffolk County towns of Bay Shore, Islip, and Center Moriches, but WBIC's low frequency and nondirectional antenna extended the signal throughout the island and across the water into central New Jersey.

The original owner was the South Shore Broadcasting Corporation headed by Maurice Weiss, and the studios were at 1 East Main Street in Bay Shore. At first there was a middle-of-the-road music policy, and the new station attracted several experienced air personalities: Lee Murphy, Al Turk, former WNEW deejay Lonny Starr, and Mitch Lebe, who had begun as a teenage jock on WINS and went on to NBC and WCBS Newsradio 88.

WBIC added a few talk shows and changed to a rock music format in the mid–1960s. In 1963 it was sold to John Arthur's Meridian Media for $25,000; in 1967 it was again sold, with the call letters changed to WLIX.

See also WLIX.

WBIL

(17 JUNE 1937–3 JANUARY 1940)

1937	1100kc	5,000w.

One of the most curious of New York station histories belongs to WBIL, which broadcast mostly in the Italian language for about two and a half years as a sister station to WOV before, in a sense, becoming WOV and vanishing. The station was the successor to the Paulist Fathers' WLWL, which went silent after succumbing to financial difficulties and failing to gain status as a full-time broadcaster. WOV owner John Iraci had just sold part-interest in the International Broadcasting Company to Arde Bulova, owner of the Bulova Watch Company. They put WBIL on the air to operate during the evening hours on 1100kc after the 6:00 P.M. sign-off of WOV at 1130kc. The station had both prime time and 5,000 watts to WOV's 1,000.

Monday, 2 August 1937

6:00 P.M.	Dinner Musicale
6:45	People's Medical League
7:00	Pino Bontempi, tenor
7:15	Dansant
7:30	Symphonic Moods

WBIL studios were located with WOV at 132 W. Forty-third Street, and staff was shared. WBIL also shared time

with Atlantic City's municipal station WPG, which made for a cluttered condition in its corner of the radio dial. In 1938, Bulova purchased WPG (over strenuous objections among some residents of Atlantic City) for the sole purpose of shutting it down and giving WBIL exclusive rights to 1100kc.

The upgrading of the Bulova stations was supposed to create a new WBIL on WOV's frequency. Instead, Bulova moved WBIL but simultaneously changed its call letters to WOV (the FCC allowed the use of the established three-letter call for "goodwill" purposes).

See also WLWL, WOV, WPG.

WBKN

(2 NOVEMBER 1926–11 APRIL 1928)

1926	1030kc	100w.
1927	1210kc s/t	100w.
1927	1210kc s/t WWRL, WIBI, WBMS, WJBI	100w.
1928	1500kc s/t WWRL, WIBI, WBMS	100w.

Engineer Arthur Faske and his brother Dr. Leo Faske were among the most persistent—and hapless—of all the early broadcast owners in the New York area. WBKN bowed in during the "radio chaos" period of 1926 from its studios at 1525 Pitkin Avenue. The Faske brothers soon found themselves under orders from the newly authorized Federal Radio Commission to move WBKN from its frequency, one of those reserved for Canada. "The Voice of Community Service" was assigned to 1210kc, sharing time with four other stations.

Monday, 25 July 1927

12:00	Noon Organ recital
12:30	Talking-machine program
12:45	Hawaiian music
1–3	Off the air
3:00	Dance music
3:45	Window shopping
4:00	All-Star String Trio
8:00	American Trio
8:30	Dance orchestra
9:15	Rae Weisman, ballads
9:30	Pauline Blotkofsky, piano
9:45	Aeronautical achievement
10:00	Off for WWRL

Finally, the FRC told WBKN—along with WWRL, WIBI and WBMS—to move up to 1500kc, effective 1 December

1927. All protested, and Arthur Faske stated, "We are considered a good station and have quite a following in Brooklyn on the 268-meter wave [1210kc]." Leo called 1500 — too high for many older radios to tune — a "graveyard." They eventually followed the orders, and they survived. The published schedules of WBKN reveal a varied and lively program service. WBKN even aired a regular "Midnight Jamboree."

In 1928, Arthur Faske moved WBKN out to Long Beach, Long Island, and operated station WCLB. He later moved back to Brooklyn, running his station as WMIL and later WCNW, but always on 1500kc.

See also WCLB, WCNW, WLIB.

WBMS

(20 OCTOBER 1926–1933)

1926	1340kc s/t WARS	10w.
1927	1500kc s/t WWRL, WBKN, WIBI	100w.
1928	1450kc s/t WNJ, WIBS, WKBO, WSDA	100w.

WBMS was a community station that seemed content to operate part-time at low power but took that operation seriously. It was founded in North Bergen by George Showerer and R.C. Schmidt; it later moved to Union City and then Fort Lee. Unfortunately, sharing airtime was more onerous than moving facilities. WARS in Brooklyn could be heard on the air at the same time on 1340kc, covering up WBMS.

After WBMS was assigned in June 1927 to share 1120kc with WWRL, WBKN, and WIBI, the whole group was next told to move to 1500kc, at the dead end of the dial. All protested, and Showerer pointed out that WBMS "does very little commercial broadcasting, as a large part of the time is taken up with municipal notices, announcements and the like." It was later sent down to 1450kc in an all–New Jersey arrangement, sharing the frequency with WNJ/Newark, WKBO/Jersey City, WIBS/Elizabeth, and WSDA. This was no more comfortable.

Friday, 15 June 1928

9:00 A.M.	Police alarms
9:05	Sunshine Hour
10:00	The Shopper
11:00	Chimes
	Off for WWRL
5:00 P.M.	Dinner music

5:55	News; music
6:45	Russell Gilmour, tenor
7:00	Victor Album
9:00	Schroeder's chimes
	Off for WWRL

In 1929, the WBMS Broadcasting Company moved its transmitter from Hackensack to Fort Lee. But there was a new kid on the block, WHOM, which soon absorbed the airtime of WNJ and WKBO. WBMS continued operating one-quarter time until 1933, when it too was taken over by WHOM.

WBNX

(1 JANUARY 1931–1 SEPTEMBER 1984)

1931	1350kc s/t WAWZ	250w.
1939	1350kc s/t WAWZ	5,000w. day, 1,000w. night
1941	1380kc s/t WAWZ	5,000w. full-time

As the call letters indicated, WBNX was in the Bronx, but its New Jersey transmitter covered the metropolitan area, and WBNX targeted the audience beyond its home borough. WBNX began life as WKBQ at the Starlight Amusement Park, also in the Bronx, which shared time on 1350kc with WMSG, WBNY, and WCDA. In December 1930 owner Allen Cahill changed the call letters to WBNX. Some of the WKBQ program features were carried over to WBNX, including its numerology report.

In the spring of 1932, WBNX began to share its transmitter with WMSG, and that summer Amory Haskell bought WBNX from Allen Cahill. On 1 November 1933 the *Corriere d'America* station WCDA took over WMSG and WBNX and continued to operate with the call letters WBNX. It retained many of the program services of the three stations it replaced. Just before Christmas 1933, studios and offices moved from 101 Park Avenue in Manhattan to the Melrose Central Building, above the New York Central tracks at 260 E. 161st Street. Religious broadcaster WAWZ in Zarephath, N.J. took the place of WBNY and shared time with WBNX for over fifty years. In 1937 Amory Haskell changed the corporate name to the WBNX Broadcasting Corporation.

WBNX was the New York affiliate of comedian Ed Wynn's ill-fated Amalgamated Broadcasting System network (the fact that Wynn had to settle for what was then a 250-watt part-time outlet in the nation's first market was a sign that his dreams outran his plans). The network debuted on 25 September 1933 with a gala four-hour broadcast and

A *NEW* APPROACH TO THE **NEW YORK MARKET**

WBNX

With programs based on population characteristics, WBNX affords a specialized and *intimate* approach to the 6,982,635 foreign residents of metropolitan New York whose annual spendable income reaches as high as $5,000 per family.

FULL STAFF OF FOREIGN LANGUAGE PRODUCTION MEN AVAILABLE!

VARIETY'S FIRST CHOICE FOR FOREIGN LANGUAGE STATION
Speaks the Language of Your Prospect

WBNX emphasized its multiculturalism in 1937.

folded a month later. For most of its day, WBNX broadcast "from New York City to the heart of the Bronx, where it's listened to," and specialized in foreign-language programming. It boasted a "full staff of foreign language production men." The station won a Peabody Award in 1942 for outstanding service to foreign-language groups.

In 1941 WBNX moved to "1380 on everybody's dial," and its power was increased to 5,000 watts full-time. WBNX had distinctly hollow acoustics with serious leaks from outside. The studios in the Melrose Central Building were constructed with heavy wooden shutters over windows that looked out on the New York Central tracks. Announcements or performances by WBNX's "salon orchestra" (a bit of live potted-palm music that lingered on the schedule into the 1960s) might be accompanied by the noise of trains coupling, thunderstorms raging, and sirens wailing on the roof. Civil defense exercises would drown out announcers.

Programming was unique and, for many listeners, was a peculiar carryover from the earlier days of radio. In the mid–1940s, WBNX presented a late-night series of recorded arias entitled "Opera in Bed." In the 1950s, the station's broadcast day began at 9:00 A.M. with "Pinebrook Praises," whose preaching was accompanied by canaries chirping in the background. The station maintained its own orchestra long after the network stations had given up live music. Herb Mendolsohn conducted light classics at 5:30 and 7:30 each evening. "Music for the Slumber Hour" from 11 P.M. to midnight was more soothing, especially since there were fewer whistles and air brakes from the tracks below.

Among its foreign-language broadcasts was one of New York's few programs in French. "The French Hour" at 10:00 P.M. attracted both native francophones and students and lovers of French culture.

In addition to the "Tea Time Concert," WBNX proudly presented a daily 4:00 P.M. program of bar-and-grill entertainment by "The Tavern Boys": Irving, Jimmy, and Sid (their last names were never used). Thirty minutes of ricky-ticky music opened with a rousing rendition of "There's a Tavern in the Town" on the piano, rib saw, and washboard.

Aside from this esoterica, WBNX's "Record Shelf"— hosted by staff announcers Roy Baxter, Steve Hollis, Carleton Miller and others — brought back the big bands as well as the latest hits. There were several "Record Shelves" in the afternoon and evening until they were consolidated into a 4:00-to-5:30 slot on Monday through Saturday, which wrapped up with Benny Goodman's record of "Wrappin' It Up." An "Old Time Record Shelf" played the sweet bands at 10:30 P.M.

One distinctive service provided by WBNX was the daily summary from the racetracks sponsored by the Armstrong Racing Form. Each weekday afternoon at 5:45 (with a summary and late scratches at 7:55), the hornlike monotone of Charlie Vackner announced win, place, and show at Belmont, Aqueduct, Jamaica, even Pimlico and Hialeah. The program was certainly of value to bookies, but WBNX never suffered for it. In fact, Vackner sometimes led the New York ratings in his time period.

In 1960, WBNX was sold to the United Broadcasting Company (UBC), and a year later the Bronx lost its only AM station when the new owners moved studios to 560 Fifth Avenue in Manhattan. Overnight hours of rhythm-and-blues and gospel music were directed at the African-American audience, but more time was devoted to Spanish-language broadcasting till finally it was fully Latino. In 1964, a telethon on WBNX raised funds to support the Puerto Rican Day parade. "Radio X" provided good news coverage and became the center of a story on Saturday night, 13 July 1968, when six Cuban men invaded the studios — then at 801 Second Avenue — and held employees at gunpoint while they delivered a five-minute tirade against Cuban dictator Fidel Castro. The intruders left without hurting anyone. Station owner Richard Eaton was shocked by the incident, especially since the station had always maintained an anti–Castro editorial position. WBNX managed to get the tirade on tape, and newscaster Antonio Capiro had his lead story for the eleven o'clock news.

Although WBNX continued to appeal mainly to the Spanish-speaking audience, in the mid–1970s the station mixed in some Italian and Jewish programming. And although it continued to identify itself as "WBNX, New York," the former Bronx station moved its studios and offices to the Carlstadt, N.J. transmitter site in 1975.

In 1984, UBC changed the call letters from WBNX to WKDM.

See also WKBQ, WAWZ, WKDM.

WBNY

(25 SEPTEMBER 1925–MARCH, 1931)

1925	1430kc	500w.
1926	930kc	500w.
1927	1010kc	500w.
June 1927	1370kc s/t WKBO, WKBQ, WFRL	500w.
Nov. 1927	1370kc	500w.

Sydney Norton Baruch was a versatile scientist and engineer who held some two hundred patents on devices from vacuum tubes to pneumatic mail-delivery tubes. His depth bombs were used against submarines in both world wars. But Dr. Baruch—he held a Ph.D. in electrical engineering—was proudest of his system of recording sound for motion pictures, the Moviephone, which he developed to intercept illegal wireless messages sent by German diplomats in the United States. in the early days of World War I. These were some of the first "air checks" ever recorded.

Baruch's broadcasting station was also a versatile effort. WBNY's first studios were in the Warner Theatre, where Warner Bros. Pictures itself had previously operated its station WBPI. Programming consisted mostly of evening dance music with a daily news hour from 7 to 8 A.M.—an unusually early sign-on for a radio station at that time. During the summer of 1926, WBNY sent a crew with a portable short-wave transmitter to summer camps to relay back a series of programs about the outdoor life, including "campfire stories" each evening at 8:00.

In 1926 the studios were moved to 145 W. Forty-fifth Street, and WBNY tried unsuccessfully to change its corporate name from Baruchrome Corporation to the Grand Central Terminal Broadcasting Corporation. Shirley Katz assumed direction of "The Voice of the Heart of New York."

Wednesday, 27 October 1926

7:30 P.M.	Talk
8:00	Harry Zembler's Orchestra
8:10	Sid Lesser, songs
8:20	Broadway Beaus
8:30	Betty Marvin, ukelele
8:45	Studio Orchestra
9:00	Lenny Leeds, baritone
9:45	Clifford Odets, recitations
10:00	Blue Bell Dance Orchestra
10:15	Marta Lee, songs
10:30	Bert Samuels, songs
10:45	Bert Werner's Orchestra

In December 1927, WBNY created a "Jewish Department" with the expressed purpose of advancing the Americanization of Jewish immigrants.

Despite WBNY's respectable technical quality, it was constantly being shifted around on the dial and sharing time with other less-well-equipped stations. During the unregulated summer of 1926, WBNY actually "jumped" from 1430 to 1500kc but was able to get the tacit approval of the Commerce Department. Sydney Baruch stated: "This eliminates us from being classified as a 'pirate' station. We will increase our power from 500 to 1,000 watts immediately."

WBNY was then told to move to 1010kc and share time with WHAP. Dr. Baruch was especially upset about cooperating with WHAP, which was notorious for its attacks on Catholics. At a hearing before the Federal Radio Commission, Baruch challenged WHAP manager Franklin Ford to allow Baruch to reply, over WHAP, should Ford attack Jews. (Ford reluctantly granted the request.) There was more than resistance to religious intolerance in Baruch's testimony to the FRC; he wanted a change in frequency to 1070, then occupied by WNJ and WGCP.

While WBNY remained preoccupied with finding a better spot on the New York dial, Dr. Baruch was busy helping other stations around the country to develop their facilities, and in 1928 he organized twenty-six of them into the United Broadcast Chain. The UBC did not use network lines but utilized the "running magnetic wire" that Baruch had developed for his company, Sound Pictures Inc. Programs included full-length Broadway plays.

In November 1928, WBNY was assigned to 1350kc along with WCDA, WKBQ, and WMSG. These three would become WBNX in 1931, but WBNY stayed apart from the merger, and instead Baruch sold his station to the Pillar of Fire, a religious institution in Zarephath, N.J. The call letters were changed to WAWZ.

Sydney Baruch returned to his laboratory and continued research and invention till the day he died in September 1959.

See also WAWZ, WHAP.

WBOQ

(26 March 1925–28 May 1940)

1925	950kc s/t WAHG	500w.
1927	920kc s/t WABC	500w.
1928	970kc s/t WABC	500w.
1928	860kc s/t WABC	500w.

The Alfred H. Grebe Radio Company of Richmond Hill put a secondary transmitter, WBOQ, on the air five months after its primary broadcasting station, WAHG, began operation. During those days when radio was still under development, it was not unusual for an active experimenter like Grebe to hold licenses for more than one station, carrying out technical experiments on one while building an audience on the other. WBOQ's studios and offices shared WAHG's location, and the antennas were hung from the same tower in an arrangement similar to that at RCA's Radio Broadcast Central. The factory at 70 Van Wyck Boulevard in Richmond Hill was actually home to at least four stations (though, to be precise, stations WGMU and WRMU were usually far from home: WGMU were the call letters assigned to one of radio's first mobile units and WRMU was a maritime transmitter aboard the yacht belonging to Grebe general manager Douglas Rigney).

However, WBOQ was more than an instrument in the busy Grebe laboratory. The call letters stood for "Borough of Queens" and the station could serve as a local adjunct to the higher power WAHG. Programming was intermittent but Grebe didn't necessarily skimp. Among the first people to appear on WBOQ were Hollywood superstars Mary Pickford and Douglas Fairbanks.

At the end of 1926 Grebe transferred his two stations to ownership of his new subsidiary, the Atlantic Broadcasting Company. WAHG became WABC, but WBOQ remained in intermittent operation under its original call letters. Some of the company's better programs were heard there. The "Atlantic Air Theatre" presented a Nick Carter mystery series over WBOQ in 1927.

In the fall of 1928, the Atlantic Broadcasting Company was sold to the fledgling Columbia Broadcasting System. WBOQ was in the package with CBS affiliate WABC; the call letters were officially hyphenated as WABC-WBOQ. Even while the better-known station grew into a 50,000-watt network flagship operating from splendid studios at 485 Madison Avenue, WBOQ remained the "silent partner."

When CBS put up a new transmitter at Wayne, N.J. testing took place under the call letters WBOQ. The "phantom call" was used on a few occasions through the 1930s, but in 1940 the Federal Communications Commission eliminated all dual call letter assignments. Naturally, CBS elected to continue under the well-established WABC. WBOQ, a radio station that hardly ever broadcast, ended its fifteen-year history.

See also WAHG, WABC(I).

WBPI

(30 December 1925–17 April 1926)

1926	1140kc	500w.

One of the oddest short-lived phenomena of New York radio was WBPI. At the end of 1925, Ira Nelson sold his Newark station WAAM to Warner Bros. Pictures Inc. Nelson's transmitter was carried over to the Warner Theatre at Broadway and Fifty-third Street, Sam Warner himself came in from Hollywood to attend the inaugural ceremonies, and the new station took to the air just before New Year's Eve.

Mayor-elect Jimmy Walker — he would be sworn in the next day — participated in the opening night's broadcast, along with Herman Heller's Orchestra and the 113th Infantry Band. Given its backing, WBPI should have developed into one of the major broadcasters in the city.

Wednesday, 30 December 1925

11:00 A.M.	Happy Hour Program, John A. Scott
6:00 P.M.	Al Makon and his orchestra
6:30	What Shall We Do Tonight?
6:35	Al Makon and his orchestra
7:00	Theatre program
7:30	Ben Friedman and Dick Finch
7:45	Olivette Wilhelm, soprano
8:00	Elsie Miller, pianist
8:15	Olivette Wilhelm, pianist
8:30	Yale–Seton Hall basketball game
10:00	Bill McWalters, nine songs — old and new

WBPI's programming wasn't much different from that of most other stations at the time: a lot of potted palm music, some sports coverage, talks, and a daily calendar called "What Shall We Do Tonight?" which would send listeners out to see the latest Warner Bros. epic.

Warner Bros. was never as committed to WBPI as it was to its station KFWB in Los Angeles, whose long history began at about the same time. After just three and a half months on the air, WBPI was shut down and returned to Ira Nelson, who resumed broadcasting as WAAM.

See also WAAM.

WBRB

(1932–1942)

1932   1210kc s/t WGBB, WFAS, WGNY   250w.

In 1930, Robert Johnson requested that his station, WJBI, which he had operated since 1925, have its license transferred to a new entity, the Monmouth Broadcasting Company, and it became WBRB. Red Bank's "Home Town Station" established studios and a transmitter downtown at 63 Broad Street. Bob Johnson continued as chief engineer. Even with an intermittent schedule that denied it most breakfast and evening hours, WBRB was an effective and popular station. Programs like Linda Lowe's "Over the Tea Cups" highlighted local activities.

Monday, 13 January 1941

9:00 A.M.	Merrie Melodies
9:15	Dance Hits
9:30	Little Shop, Prown, County, Piano, Federal
10:00	Louise Powers Program
10:30	Radio Shopper
10:45	Fashions in Rhythm
11:00	Resume
	Off the Air
7:00 P.M.	Melodies for You
7:14	Reed's "Special"
7:15	County Sports News
7:30	Carter
7:31	Rhythm Revue (recorded)
7:35	Reed's "Special"
7:36	Rhythm Revue, cont'd
8:00	Your Favorites
8:30	Off the Record
8:45	Ruth Ellis, songs
9:00	Resume

Among the other local public affairs program were the "Home Town Forum" and its junior version, "High School Forum." And beyond the issues of the day were the remarks of WBRB's "Home Philosopher."

WBRB might have advanced to full-time status in its market — as did the three stations that shared its frequency — but in January 1942 a fire destroyed its transmitter. Wartime restrictions made it impossible to replace the equipment. The FCC granted the station permission to remain silent for the duration, a construction permit was renewed in 1944, and WBRB's license was still in effect as late as 1946. However, station manager Vera N. Sholes also managed WCAP in Asbury Park and simply transferred WBRB's personnel, as

well as some of its advertising contracts and programming. So WBRB was absorbed into the station that became WJLK. *See also* WCAP, WJLK.

WBRS

(AUGUST 1926—DECEMBER 1927)

1926	760kc	100w.
1926	1210kc	100w.
1927	1420kc s/t WCDA, WRST	100w.

Morris Halper's Universal Radio Manufacturing Company was parent of the North American Broadcasting Corporation. Despite those grandiose names, WBRS was a small station at 1062 Broadway, near Reid Avenue in Brooklyn (telephone: Bushwick 5900). WBRS took to the air during the period when the U.S. government had no authority to deny anyone a broadcast license, and so the station started up at 760kc, moved to 1210 three months later and was officially authorized to share 1420 with WCDA/New York and WRST/Bay Shore in June 1927. The assignment at least kept WBRS clear of the "Brooklyn radio fight."

WBRS offered one of the liveliest program schedules in early New York radio, thanks largely to program director Ray Walker, a vaudevillian and piano player. A listener whose radio batteries had died during one of Walker's old-time melody shows called to request that he play everything again, as she had run to the neighbors to borrow a new set of batteries. Among the performers lured out to the Bushwick studio were Blossom Seeley and young Ethel Merman. The Society of Old Brooklynites presented weekly historical talks. Evenings of Italian-language entertainment originated from the Criterion Theatre.

Friday, 14 October 1927

8:00 P.M.	Radio Shop program
8:30	Kiddy Entertainers
9:00	Hon. John H. Hylan, talk
9:30	Dance Music
10:00	Lou Hayes, songs
10:15	Duncan, Chesterfield duets
10:45	Arthur Murray
11:00	Studio party

One of broadcasting's first fund-raising marathons was held for victims of the 1927 Mississippi River floods. On 5–11 May, WBRS took song requests from its unusually responsive audience, asking one dollar for each tune and mentioning contributors' names and addresses. The music was all live, and the performers included WBRS's "juvenile orchestra. A radio reviewer tuning around the dial during the marathon reported, "Back on the station after midnight to find Ray Walker, Eddie Woods and Frank Corbett producing a splendid entertainment — still at $1 per and doing good business."

By the summer of 1927, Morris Halper was trying to get WBRS back to 760kc and applied to the FRC to allow it to share time with WHN, which had been assigned to that frequency. The request was denied, and in December WBRS consolidated its operations with Italian-oriented WCDA. In March 1928, the station was sold to the Westchester Broadcasting Corporation and moved to Yonkers, where it became WCOH, which later became WFAS.

See also WCDA, WCOH, WFAS.

(21 DECEMBER 1971–)

1971   1170kHz (daytime)   500w.

When WBRW went on the air from Somerville, N.J., just before Christmas in 1971, it was the first commercial station in Somerset County since North Plainfield's municipal outlet, WEAM, went silent in the late 1920s. Principal owners of the Somerset Valley Broadcasting Corporation were newspaper publisher William Anderson, former state senator Raymond Bateman, and New Jersey Republican chairman Webster Todd (whose daughter, Christine Todd Whitman, would become New Jersey governor in the 1990s). The studios and four-tower antenna were located off Nimitz Street in Somerville.

The Somerville station began quietly, with fifteen-minute blocks of easy and middle-of-the-road music. At the same time, its news service was one of the most ambitious for a suburban New York AM station. News director Jim Jarvis and sports director Tom Kechke were on in the morning with Bruce Kamen and Ralph Saro handling afternoon editions. WCTC's William Price was the first general manager.

By the mid–1970s Harry Haslett, formerly with WBNX and WNJR, was station manager, and the music had become adult contemporary. Deejays Mark Lewis, Dick Andrews, and Charlie Bengle added some personality to the WBRW sound, and news remained strong behind the efforts of Tom Dwyer, who left for WCBS, and Patrice Sikora, who joined the Wall Street Journal Network. The "Sunday Serenade" with Tom Hally and Don Wilson became a popular Sunday-afternoon show with its nostalgic music and comedy.

But Somerset Valley Broadcasting began to lose money in the 1980s and shut down WBRW in 1990. The Bridgewater Broadcasting Company of Dan Lohse — chief engineer of WXLX, WSKQ, and WPAT-FM — attempted to revive the station but after six years Lohse still had not completed the facilities or received final permission from the Federal Communications Commission.

Don't confuse with WBRW, Brewster, N.Y.

W B S

(11 MARCH 1922–MAY 1925)

| 1922 | 360m. | 20w. |
| 1925 | 1190kc | 500w. |

Donald W. May was one of the earliest radio suppliers in the metropolitan area, and among his clients was the Mullins Furniture Store at 325 Central Avenue in Newark. To enhance the sale of "the piece of furniture that talked," Mullins applied for a broadcasting permit and received the sixty-ninth license issued by the Commerce Department, seventh in the New York metropolitan area, two weeks after rival Bamberger's opened WOR. WBS was said to stand for the "World's Best Store." H. C. Luttgens was both chief engineer and announcer.

Thursday, 12 February 1925

5:30-7 P.M.	Bobby Brown's Orchestra
7:00	Off the air
8:30	Erv Rudin's Mannikins
9:30	Songs by Harry Knox, Joe Montgomery, Mike Plunkett, and Eddie Ginnane
10:00	Eddie Ginnane's Imitators
11:00	Walt Riggin's Orchestra

In May 1925 WBS became WGCP, moved its studios to the Grand Central Palace in Manhattan, and was sold to musician Jimmy Shearer. Donald May continued as a broadcasting entrepreneur for another decade at stations WDWM and WCAP.

See also WGCP, WHBI, WDWM, WCAP.

W B Y N

(1 MAY 1941–1 MAY 1947)

1941   1430kc.   1,000w. day / 500w. night

The complex and bitter "Brooklyn radio fight" that began in 1927 was finally resolved in 1941 when four small Brooklyn stations merged to form the aptly named Unified Broadcasting Corporation. Samuel Gellard of WLTH, Salvatore diAngelo of WVFW, Peter Testan of WBBC, and Rabbi Aaron Kronenberg of WARD joined as one-quarter owners and directors on the board, with Rabbi Kronenberg as president.

Initially, the UBC planned to continue using the WARD call letters and operate from the WBBC studios through the WARD transmitter. But new call letters were adopted, new studios were built in the Fox Theatre Building at 1 Nevins Street in downtown Brooklyn, and Westinghouse Broadcasting executive Griff Thompson was hired as manager. It seemed an auspicious start for the borough's first full-time radio station. "Brooklyn's Own Station" (a slogan previously used by WBBC) even had a studio in Manhattan, at 132 W. Forty-third Street.

Saturday, 1 September 1945

8:45 A.M.	Russian Program
9:30	Italian Program
10:00	Jewish Program
3:00	Revue
4:00	Norweigan Program
5:00	Music
7:30	Concert
8:00	Songs
10:00	Revival Hour

Much of the programming from the four unified stations continued on WBYN, including Rabbi Kronenberg's daily inspirational talks. But so did the personal conflict which had been nurtured during years of rivalry and dispute. Finally the Unified partners (who had changed the name of the company to WBYN-Brooklyn Inc.) decided it was best to divest themselves of the station. At that point WBYN was developing some of the most innovative and enjoyable programs on the New York airwaves.

In 1944, WBYN created a prototype of all-news radio by programming continuous 60-second parcels of news, sports, and other features from noon to 6:00 P.M. "The Minute Station" also presented hours of entertainment not to be found elsewhere. Art Ford broadcast an interview show from Toffenetti's restaurant on Times Square. "Sam's Bowery Follies," Mondays at 11:30 P.M., originated from the fabled McGurk's Suicide Hall and was loud, often off-key, and filled with music-

WBYN certainly reached more people than the Brooklyn stations did individually. This ad, with its spectacular view of Manhattan, appeared in 1946 — the year before WBYN disappeared.

hall ditties like "Mother Machree." The host was Johnny Kane of the tabloid *New York Enquirer,* and not only old vaudevillians but also gutsy politicians took a turn at the mike.

WBYN brought back the legendary Dolly Sisters and lured the great announcer Norman Brokenshire, then in professional eclipse as he struggled with alcoholism. Brokenshire states in his autobiography: "Although this was getting back in radio by the back door for fair, I needed the money so badly that I agreed to work for a couple of hours nightly.… It turned out to be the most distasteful bit of broadcasting I had ever done. I soon learned that the whole build-up was done in an attempt to sell the station. After the first show I began to fortify myself for the broadcasts in adjacent bars. The first broadcast of my second week was my last."

By 1945, Brooklyn's own station had found a buyer, and the FCC had found a way to reverse what was widely seen as a shortage of stations in northern New Jersey. The *Newark Evening News* purchased WBYN for slightly over $200,000 and took control at the end of 1946. It became WNJR in May 1947. The dispute that had endured for over a decade resulted in a station that had survived exactly six years. When WBYN went silent, the borough of Brooklyn — which then would by itself be the third-largest city in the United States — was left without a full-time, full-service radio voice of its own.

See also WARD, WBBC, WLTH, WVFW, WNJR.

WCAP

(JUNE 1928–1 MAY 1950)

1927	1250kc	500w.
1928	1280kc s/t WCAM, WOAX	500w.
1941	1310kc s/t WCAM, WTNJ	1,000w.

One of the soundest moves made during the uproarious period of radio reregulation in the late 1920s involved Donald W. May's WDWM. The Asbury Park Chamber of Commerce contracted to bring the Newark station to its city, and on 24 June 1927 WDWM signed on from temporary studios in Asbury Park's Isolation Hospital. Call letters were changed to WCAP during the summer of 1928, and local radio came to the "Wonder City of Asbury Park." D.W. May continued to own the Radio Industries Broadcast Company and remained as president of WCAP. The popular resort area was also the center of a region noted for its early wireless activity, and WCAP enjoyed good community support and steady growth.

Thursday, 16 August 1928

6:45 P.M.	Monterey Music
7:15	Berkeley-Carteret Orchestra
8:00	Elvira Kain, soprano
8:15	Dominick De Diego, tenor
8:30	Pryor's Band
9:15	Margaret Yarnall, contralto
9:30	Pryor's Band
10:00	Sea Girt Orchestra
11:00	Time signals

In December 1927, studios were established in the chamber of commerce building at 525 Bangs Avenue, and early in 1928 WCAP's power was increased to 1,000 watts. For a while it even received a rare exclusive frequency assignment. But in November 1928, as part of a national realignment of stations, WCAP was ordered to 1280kc, sharing time with WCAM/Camden and WOAX/Trenton (which became WTNJ). In March 1929, studios were moved to the Electric Building in downtown Asbury Park, and the transmitter was set up on the ground of Isolation Hospital.

WCAP was purchased by the chamber of commerce in January 1931. The station manager was now the Chamber's executive secretary, Thomas F. Burley Jr., and in the autumn of 1931 WCAP moved its studios to Asbury Park's new convention hall. The main arena was permanently wired for radio, giving WCAP a potential studio audience of forty-five hundred. With the move to the city's most notable address, the chamber of commerce transferred ownership of WCAP to manager Burley. The quality of programming also received a boost in 1932 when WCAP affiliated with the CBS network, a partnership that lasted only two years.

On the evening of Saturday, 8 September 1934, WCAP scooped all news media with an exclusive report on the biggest news story of the day—and it wasn't even necessary to go out to cover the story. The luxury liner *Morro Castle* caught fire off the New Jersey coast, one day after its captain had been found murdered. The burning vessel drifted helplessly as passengers and crew jumped overboard. At 7:30 P.M. Tom Burley reported: "She's here! The *Morro Castle* is coming right toward our studio!" The "safest ship afloat" came to rest in the sands a hundred yards from WCAP's convention hall location.

In January 1942, WBRB in Red Bank was put off the air by a fire that destroyed the station's transmitter, and its staff was transferred to WCAP. A year later, on 28 April, WCAP's transmitter was damaged in a brush fire. Unlike WBRB, which never returned to the air, WCAP was back by November despite wartime equipment shortages.

One of New York's pioneer African-American broadcasters, George Hudson, originated the "Downbeat Club" as an evening presentation on WCAP before moving to WNJR.

In November 1944, the Charms Candy Company and Walter Reade Theatres bought controlling interest in Radio Industries Broadcast Company and moved the studios back to the Electric Building. In 1948 WCAP moved to Charms Candy's own building on Bangs Avenue. (In 1947, WCAP-FM became one of the first stations on the new FM band at 107.1Mc.) The time-sharing arrangement with WCAM and WTNJ continued until January, 1949 when the Trenton station was moved to a new frequency and the Camden and Asbury Park stations accepted reduced power to 250 watts in return for full time on their frequency.

In April 1950 Radio Industries sold WCAP to the *Asbury Park Press* for $75,000, and on Monday, 1 May 1950, the AM station took the call letters of the newspaper's FM station, WJLK. (WCAP-FM went off the air.)

See also WDWM, WBRB, WJLK.

WCBS

(3 NOVEMBER 1946–)

| 1946 | 880kc | 50,000w. |

At the end of World War II the Columbia Broadcasting System's New York "flagship" was still called WABC, a remnant of its origin as A. H. Grebe's Atlantic Broadcasting Company. The media giant felt uncomfortable bearing the

WCBS distributed these poster-sized greeting cards for fans to sign "welcome back" greetings to Arthur Godfrey in 1959. Arthur Hull Hayes, president of CBS Radio, is holding up the poster.

letters of a new rival network. After much negotiation it reached an agreement with a station in Springfield, Ill. (an ABC affiliate), to give up call letters it had used since 1927, and WABC became WCBS.

Most CBS production in New York at that time was destined for the network. WCBS didn't even have a local news department. Metropolitan reports were prepared by network news writers; WCBS staffers sourly commented that if someone were shot on the sidewalk in front of 485 Madison Avenue, news personnel looking out the window would run to the teletypes to learn what had happened.

Network brass recognized this deficiency. At the end of 1945 CBS hired a recently discharged U.S. Navy radioman named Bill Leonard to lead in to Arthur Godfrey's Washington-based wakeup show with an offbeat local public-affairs and feature program. At first, the 6:00 A.M. "This Is New York" reported to the waking city on events that had transpired overnight—often a melange of interviews from bars and police stations—and there was an afternoon edition that attracted few listeners and further exhausted Leonard and company. "This Is New York" was both softened and sharpened and was rescheduled for once a day at 9:00 A.M. But it never lost its way, finding "the feel and smell of the city." Interview guests ranged from Harry Truman to Tennessee Williams (who mumbled through an interview after Leonard had just panned his newest play).

"This Is New York" would remain on the WCBS lineup for seventeen years, capping its run as part of the evening schedule. It was one of the first programs to take wire and tape recorders into the field. Among the memorable features was "The Other Fellow's Shoes," in which Bill Leonard (who would go on to become president of CBS News) brought listeners the day-to-day life of an elevator operator or window washer. There were also solid documentary reports on subjects like drug addiction. In the best CBS tradition, it was an authoritative and craftsmanlike hour and an affectionate reflection of both extraordinary and everyday life "here, in New York."

In March 1949 the CBS network passed NBC to lead the national ratings.

When Godfrey left the early-morning show in 1948 to concentrate on his network programs, he was replaced by Jack Sterling, then program director of CBS's Chicago station. WCBS also developed a lineup of literate afternoon talk shows, including author Emily Kimbrough and Texas storyteller John Henry Faulk (whose defense against blacklisting during the "red scare" of the 1950s made legal history and brought that sorry episode to an end). Singer Lanny Ross had a chat-and-variety show in the 1950s. Galen Drake's "Housewives' Protective League" program was one of many local broadcasts of that title heard with other hosts on other CBS-owned stations. (The program was itself a separate division of CBS.) American Airlines' all-night program "Music Till Dawn" premiered on 13 April 1953. WCBS announcer Bob Hall was the model for hosts on that program around the nation.

Network entertainment shows, including some of radio's most beloved soap operas, were canceled by the block in the early 1960s. WCBS continued to maintain a staff orchestra and programs hosted by vocalist Martha Wright and folksinger Oscar Brand.

WCBS tried to build its local news coverage in 1955 by hiring WOR news director Dave Driscoll, who brought in newscaster Lou Adler and Westbrook Van Voorhis, the muscular voice of "The March of Time." In the mid–1960s, WCBS began an afternoon drive-time news-and-information program called "Up to the Minute," anchored by Adler and Kenneth Banghart. CBS chairman William Paley was impressed by the program (and admired the all-news format that WINS instituted in April 1965) but was concerned about his flagship's otherwise low ratings. Despite management warnings to Paley that an all-news operation would lose $5 million a year, "Up to the Minute" was the prototype for what would become "Newsradio 88." Joseph Dembo was hired away from NBC to develop a format that would build on CBS's respected world news operation and provide a service to the metropolitan area.

At 4:21 P.M. on Sunday, 27 August 1967, the day before it was to start its continuous news service, WCBS found itself in the headlines when a light plane crashed into the High Island tower that it shared with WNBC. The news format was temporarily switched to WCBS-FM (which had to delay the premiere of its "Young Sound"), and the AM signal returned weakly via WLIB's old transmitter and antenna in Astoria. (Stations can put aside rivalry in an emergency. WOR offered WCBS the use of its old Conelrad transmitter in Carteret, N.J.) Two weeks later the High Island site was back in operation at 10,000 watts into a temporary 200-foot tower; Newsradio 88 didn't reach 50kw. till the end of the year.

The original anchors at Newsradio 88 included Lou Adler, Robert Vaughn, and Steve Porter from Philadelphia, former WMCA "Good Guy" Jim Harriot, and ABC newsman Charles Osgood. Sportscaster Pat Summerall—who had replaced Jack Sterling on the wakeup show in 1966—reported sports in the morning; Harvey Hauptman reported in the evening.

But it was still "all news, part of the time" until WCBS canceled Arthur Godfrey's weekday variety show. "Music Till Dawn" played its last record at dawn on Sunday, 4 January 1970. Fittingly, the record was the series theme song, "That's All," composed by WNEW deejay Bob Haymes, in a haunting arrangement by the Sy Mann Orchestra. Although WINS had been all-news for nearly five years and frequently led WCBS in the ratings, Paley's gamble with Newsradio 88 seemed to pay off. The only discrete program to remain was "Let's Find Out," a Sunday discussion slot that had premiered in 1956.

While Newsradio 88 might provide a constant flow of news and information the service is actually formatted as tightly as events permit. According to Harvey Hauptman,

WCBS morning stalwart Jack Sterling with NBC's Dave Garroway in 1964.

anchoring Newsradio 88 was not unlike disc-jockeying, demanding that an announcer always be alert to breaking news and a few steps ahead of live feeds, newsroom cues, and commercial breaks, all the while operating the control console.

WCBS has usually been ranked number two in the all-news ratings, only occasionally coming in ahead of its Westinghouse rival WINS. In 1995, Westinghouse and CBS merged, and New York's two all-news stations continued to compete under the same corporate leadership.

See also WABC(I).

WCBX *see* WNJ

WCDA

(APRIL 1927–1 NOVEMBER 1933)

1927	1250kc s/t WBRS	250w.
June 1927	1420kc	250w.
Mar. 1928	1410kc	250w.
Nov. 1928	1350kc s/t WKBQ,WMSG,WBNY	250w.

The Italian Educational Broadcasting Company operated a radio station with a clear mission: to aid in the instruction and acculturation of Italian immigrants and prepare them to become American citizens. Its station, WCDA, was named for the *Corriere d'America*, an Italian-language daily newspaper, and had backing from the Italian Historical Society of America and other Italian businesses and community groups. In 1925 the *Corriere* and publisher Luigi

Barzini had produced one of the first grand operas edited and staged for radio, *Cavalleria Rusticana*, on WGBS.

WCDA's application for a broadcast license slipped in under the regulatory wire, on 21 February 1927, two days before President Calvin Coolidge signed the bill creating the Federal Radio Commission. The new station operated briefly from the *Corriere d'America* offices at 434 Lafayette Street in Brooklyn, with its transmitter atop the Criterion Theatre at 970 Fulton Street, Brooklyn. In May the transmitter moved to Gorge Road in Cliffside Park, N.J. Studios were established on the twelfth floor of the Italian Savings Bank Building at Spring and Lafayette Streets in the Little Italy section of Manhattan. That fall the station was officially dedicated by Guglielmo Marconi himself (then in the United States to attend the 1927 Washington Radio Conference). New York Governor Al Smith also spoke on the dedicatory broadcast of 9 November 1927.

Thursday, 16 August 1928

6:00 P.M.	Educational topics; parents
6:30	Dinner Music
7:00	English lesson
7:30	Studio music; Health Talk
8:15	Angelo Palange on "Sports"
8:30	Gino Giovanetti, tenor
8:45	Stefano Caprisi, violinist
9:00	Angela Sena, soprano
9:15	Antony Di Lascia, flutist
9:30	M. K. Hoile, baritone
9:45	Margaret O'Hearn, contralto
10:00	Irene Benante, pianist
10:15	Weser Brothers
10:30	Italian Instrumental Quartet
11:00	Peppino and Paul, accordions
11:30	Studio music

Assigned to 1420kc, WCDA soon found its signal suffering interference, which it traced to harmonic radiation from WOR at 710. When requests to correct the situation were unavailing, in March 1928 WCDA sued WOR for $100,000. The FRC authorized WCDA to move to 1410kc, though it would continue to share time at 1420 with WKBQ, WMSG and WBNY (who were either unbothered or chose to suffer). All four were moved to 1350kc on 11 November 1928.

In October 1929 "The Italian Station" inaugurated new studios at 27 Cleveland Place as well as a new transmitter with a full-length performance of Verdi's *Rigoletto* by the San Carlo Opera Company. Shortly thereafter WCDA applied for a boost from 250 to 500 watts, telling the FRC that it was already reaching some 900,000 Italians in Manhattan, the Bronx, and New Jersey. It could draw in another 100,000 in Brooklyn with increased power, which would help it overcome a financial deficit. WCDA even coupled the request with an offer to allow the time-sharing stations at

1350kc to operate through its own transmitter. The commission said no.

In the early 1930s, Amory Lawrence Haskell was buying up the stations then sharing time on 1350. He took over the Starlight Amusement Park's WKBQ, changed its call letters to WBNX, and bought WMSG from Madison Square Garden. Italian Educational Broadcasting Company sold WCDA to Haskell, and that station too was absorbed into WBNX. In one way WCDA was the leading station in this new enterprise, for since 1 July 1932, WMSG and the new WBNX had been operating through its Cliffside Park transmitter.

See also WKBQ, WBNX.

WCGU

(21 NOVEMBER 1926–APRIL 1933)

1926	865kc, 855 kc (unauthorized)	500w.
1927	1300kc	500w.
1927	1370kc s/t WKBQ	500w.
1928	1400kc s/t WBBC, WSGH, WFRL	500w.

Radio engineer Charles G. Unger opened WCGU at Lakewood, N.J. in 1926 and moved it to New York on 21 May 1927, making it a strong and spunky part of the city's radio scene. The studio was located at 1587 Broadway in Manhattan's Theatre District, and the transmitter was 75 feet from the ocean at Sea Gate, Brooklyn. During its first days on the air from Sea Gate, the movement of the tides interacting with the ground transmission system caused the station's frequency to vary by as much as 4 kilocycles. In addition to its local coverage, WCGU operated on 54 meters shortwave, which Unger hoped would make his United States Broadcasting Corporation an international voice.

Friday, 14 October 1927

1:00 P.M.	Health Hour
1:30	Great Composers
2:00	Rainbow Orchestra
2:30	New Books
3:00	Off for WKBQ
6:00	Eddie Walters, ukelele
6:15	Muriel Ellis, reader
6:30	Fred Ebinger, baritone
6:45	Clyde Monroe, poet
7:00	Stanhope Hour
7:30	Donnelly Sisters, harmony
7:45	Frank Goodwin, baritone

8:00	Elaine Dale, soprano
8:30	Play
8:45	Josephine LeMaitre, contralto

WCGU was directed to share time with three stations based in Brooklyn and in 1928 seemed to be at a disadvantage in deliberations to settle scheduling problems. Charles Unger felt that the Brooklyn Chamber of Commerce was favoring WBBC and did not consider WCGU a Brooklyn station. The chamber's president stated, "WCGU is entitled to consideration as a Brooklyn station because of its direct service to Coney Island and the special value of its broadcasts and the general excellence of its programs." The praise did little to mollify Unger's suspicions.

Perhaps to solidify its position, in August 1928 WCGU moved its transmitter away from the tides at Sea Gate to the Half-Moon Hotel at Coney Island and established a studio there.

Apparently, those excellent programs weren't always well planned. One day just before sign-on, a WCGU employee had to dash out to the Brighton Beach boardwalk and shout, "Does anyone here know how to do anything?" Two young men were strolling by, and one indicated that his friend, Andy, was a pretty good piano player, so they were hustled into the WCGU studio. The young pianist was asked to introduce each number, and after the impromptu broadcast he was invited back—he spoke as nicely as he played. So Andre Baruch began one of radio's longest and most distinguished announcing careers.

WCGU's part-time status continued to offend Charles Unger and inhibit his hopes. For a while in 1929, WCGU operated jointly with WBBC, identifying with the slogan "Brooklyn's Own Stations," but that arrangement did not survive. In the spring of 1932, WCGU moved its studios and offices to the Fulton-Flatbush Building in downtown Brooklyn. In April 1933 the station was sold to Rabbi Aaron Kronenberg and became WARD.

See also WARD, WBBC, WBYN.

same time that WBKN was moved, the Long Beach Chamber of Commerce and other civic groups were planning a station to be called WLBC. It never went on the air. The Faske brothers built studios in the Ocean Crest Hotel on the Boardwalk at Laurelton Boulevard; the transmitter was one and one-half miles away at Reynolds Cove. They solicited the cooperation of the Long Island and Long Beach Chambers of Commerce as well as the U.S. Coast Guard. Away from the crowds of Brooklyn, WCLB was alone in its community and seemed to enjoy the support of local business, calling itself "the Municipal Broadcasting Station of Long Beach." Programming was informal; schedules would sometimes list merely a "two-hour varied program."

Friday, 24 August 1928

12:00 P.M.	Noon Merchants' program
2:00	Studio program
3:00	Dance period
4:00	Talk; studio offerings
5:00	Off for WBMS
8:00	Municipal reports
8:15	Fight result forecast
8:30	Bob Fridkin's Orchestra
9:00	Junior Police Band
10:00	Off for WWRL

WCLB's license expired on 31 July 1929, and the Faske brothers didn't apply for an immediate renewal, but early in 1930 they went before the Federal Radio Commission to protest that their reapplication had been dismissed without cause. The license was renewed in April 1930, but the following winter the Faskes and manager L.W. Berne moved the station back to Brooklyn and resumed broadcasting under the new call letters WMIL.

See also WBKN, WCNW.

WCLB

(15 MAY 1928–18 FEBRUARY 1931)

| 1928 | 1500kc s/t WWRL, WGOP, WBMS | 100w. |
| 1929 | 1500kc s/t WWRL, WLBX, WMBQ | 100w. |

WCLB started in 1926 as Arthur and Leo Faske's station WBKN in Brooklyn and two years later was moved to the seaside resort of Long Beach, Long Island. At around the

WCNW

(24 SEPTEMBER 1933–30 JUNE 1942)

1933	1500kc s/t WMBQ, WWRL	250w./100w. night
1941	1600kc s/t WWRL	250/100w.
1941	1190kc	1,000w.

Engineer and stamp dealer Arthur Faske spent a lot of time trying to "position" his stations. He established WBKN in Brooklyn in 1926, moving it to Long Beach, Long Island with the call letters WCLB and then back to Brooklyn, first as WMIL and then as WCNW. Faske repeatedly applied for improved dial positions, attempted to buy out other stations, and finally made lemonade out of his lemon when he was assigned what was then the highest frequency on the AM broadcast band. The station was established at 1525 Pitkin Avenue and moved to 846 Flatbush (the WCNW Building) in 1935.

Arthur Faske called WCNW, way up at 1500kc, the "First Station on the Dial," which was likely to be true on older dials calibrated in meters. Audio equipment was homemade by the Faske Engineering Company. The transmitter he built was so unreliable that Faske sometimes called other stations asking them to check his frequency. His business was so shaky that he once "lost" a stamp collection he received on consignment, actually selling it secretly to cover a purchase for WCNW. Sharing time with WWRL ("at the *right* side of the dial"), WCNW also specialized in ethnic programming. It broadcast programs in eight languages, including the city's first Chinese programs.

On WCNW you could hear New York's only female sportscast, with erstwhile Ziegfeld chorus girl Babs Brodsley covering women's sports in the early 1940s. The station also broadcast a program entitled—and the station enjoyed an identity as—"The Voice of the Negro Community." Each weekday at 5:00 P.M. and Sunday mornings at 9:00, WCNW aired a mixture of entertainment, religion, and public-service features reflecting African-American life, from the mundane to the spiritual. Musicians, poets, preachers, and news commentators all were part of the "honest-to-grits jubilee, studded through with commercials at $10 a plug," as a 1940 newspaper review put it. One of the nation's great black broadcasters, Joe Bostic Sr., began his long career at WCNW.

The North American Regional Broadcasting Agreement (NARBA) of 1941 extended the AM band to 1600kc, and WCNW was again sent to the top of the dial, sharing time with WWRL (though only after the FCC assigned it to operate for one day, 30 March 1941, at 1490kc). At the same time, the FCC determined that Faske had "operated and permitted his station to be operated, in violation of the terms of the license," and it moved to shut down WCNW. However, the changes brought about by NARBA also opened up new frequencies, and so, in Faske's final metamorphosis, WCNW was allowed to move down to 1190kc on 23 December 1941. The following spring the station was sold to Elias Godofsky, the general manager of WCNW since 1940, and on 1 July 1942 he replaced it with a new station, WLIB. Arthur Faske stayed on for a while as chief engineer.

See also WBKN, WWRL, WLIB.

WCOH

(MAY 1928–JULY 1932)

Mar. 1928	1420kc.	100w.
Nov. 1928	1210kc s/t WINR, WGBB, WRST	100w.

The city of Yonkers should have played a role in the saga of New York broadcasting. It has population and business activity sufficient to support a local radio station, and its location just north of the New York City line was a good spot from which an ambitious broadcaster could blanket the metropolitan area. However, during the era when radio receivers suffered from poor selectivity (despite rapid development due in part to the inventions of Yonkers resident Edwin Howard Armstrong), Yonkers actively tried to keep radio at a distance. In August 1926, residents and members of the Yonkers Board of Aldermen requested that the federal government not license a station "because the owners of small sets will have difficulty tuning in on out-of-town stations."

In December 1927 Brooklyn radio station WBRS consolidated its operations with Manhattan station WCDA, but on 27 March 1928 WBRS owner Morris Halper sold his broadcast property to the Westchester Broadcasting Corporation. Initially, offices for the new station were in the East Chester Savings Bank Building and studios were in the Stevens Arcade Building in Mount Vernon. The transmitter was located at 110 Highland Avenue in Greenville.

Monday, 18 May 1931

5:00 P.M.	Devotional, Rev. C. E. Karsten
5:15	Tuberculosis Association
5:30	Organ Reveries
6:01	Marcia Kulick, pianist
6:15	Brunswick Quartet
6:45	Ben Visca, fashions
6:46	Song favorites

Late in 1928, WCOH moved its operations to the Riverview Manor Apartments in Yonkers, and the "City of Homes" truly had its own radio station. The following year it moved to permanent quarters in the Strand Theatre Building at 35 S. Broadway. If there were any complaints about a local station in Yonkers, they weren't heard; receivers were improving, and the WCOH transmitter remained in Greenville.

But Yonkers was to have a hometown station for only three more years. In 1930 Selma Seitz of Yonkers purchased WCOH and two years later renamed it in honor of her late husband, real estate investor Frank A. Seitz. Frank Jr. became station manager. The new WFAS soon sought a more central location and moved to the Westchester county seat of White Plains. So the fifth-largest city in New York State was again without a radio voice of its own.

See also WBRS, WFAS.

(12 December 1946–)

| 1946 | 1450kc. | 250w. |

The postwar broadcast boom brought New Brunswick, N.J., its first radio station when the Chanticleer Broadcasting Company opened WCTC. On a "local channel" with low power but full-time service, the station quickly became a community favorite in Middlesex and Somerset Counties. Temporary studios were in the U.S.O. Building on New Street, and a few weeks later WCTC moved to the top floors of the People's National Bank building. The original owner was James L. Howe with backing from Rutgers Chevrolet, a New Brunswick auto dealer. Programming during its first days depended heavily on shows syndicated via "electrical transcription," and there was already a strong emphasis on news and community service.

WCTC's coverage of Rutgers University football and basketball began during its second year on the air. One of its noteworthy air personalities was talk show host Bruce Williams, who finally won a slot on WCTC from 11:00 P.M. to 2:00 A.M. by keeping after manager Tony Marano for over a year. It was Williams's first radio job and launched him quickly onto the NBC network. (He would later come back to WCTC via NBC's Talknet.)

Thursday, 12 December 1946

6:00 A.M.	Music without Words
7:00	News; Brunswick Bulletin
7:45	News
8:00	Let's Go Visiting
8:15	Record Reveille
8:30	Listen Ladies
8:45	Harry Horlick
9:00	Church; Organ Interlude
9:30	Public Schools
9:45	World of Song
10:00	News; State Employment
10:15	Three Quarter Time
10:30	Voice of the Morning
10:45	South of the Border
11:00	Bing Crosby
11:15	Bands on Parade
11:30	Women's World
11:45	Little Show
12:00	Noon News
12:15	Mid Day Music
12:45	Farm Bulletin
1:00	Ballads of America
1:15	Hawaiian Harmonies
1:30	Musical Bulletin Board
1:45	Accent on Song
2:00	News; Moment Musicale
2:15	Trio Time
2:30	Off the Cob
2:45	Musical Memoirs
3:00	Sunny Side of the Street
5:00	Songs before Supper
5:15	All Americans Club
5:30	Twilight Tempos
6:00	News
6:15	Lean Back and Listen
6:30	Dinner Music
7:00	Sports
7:15	Do You Remember?
7:30	Rhythm Reveries
8:00	Jerome Kern
8:30	Concert Hall
9:00	News; Let's Dance

Other WCTC alumni included newsmen Herb Kaplow, Dave Marash, and Harvey Hauptman. Joseph Dembo, who went on to become manager of WCBS, gained his early experience there. WMGM announcer Dean Hunter brought his New York experience to WCTC, becoming program director in 1976. In 1957, Greater Media Inc. bought WCTC and in 1978 moved the studios from the bank building to the transmitter site. The station was one of the first and most consistent to broadcast editorial comments. Bill Emerson became the morning man. Announcer Mike Jarmus joined the staff in the late 1960s and remained a familiar voice for over twenty years.

(14 June 1924–1925)

| 1924 | 1290kc | 5w. |

WDBX was called, with some pride, "New York's Smallest Radio Station." It was located in the back room of the Dyckman Radio Shop at 138 Dyckman Street in Inwood, near the northern tip of Manhattan. With a 5-watt transmitter feeding a 40-foot inverted-L antenna on the roof, it was certainly a small operation, though there were several rivals for the title of smallest. An article in the *Tribune* in December 1924 described WDBX as a well-equipped station for the time.

> The studio of this station is similar to that of a bigger station. Off in a corner are the piano and various other musical instruments to be used in broadcasting. The walls of the studio are covered with lath built in an arbor-like shape to prevent echoes which would make it difficult to transmit good quality. In the middle of the room is the control board, which contains the necessary switches and pilot lights. These enable the announcer to know just when the station is on the air…. The station is equipped with two double-button microphones similar to those used by larger broadcasters. One is used for announcing, while the other is mounted on a stand and is supported by rubber strips, which prevent vibration. The latter is used to broadcast speeches, vocal selections and other forms of musical entertainment.

WDBX was the project of Edward C. Wilbur and Max Jacobson, both former shipboard operators and ham radio enthusiasts. Their friend Eugene Delmar was the announcer. The station was on the air on Monday, Tuesday, and Saturday nights and despite its flea-sized power was picked up as far away as Chicago.

Thursday, 12 February 1925

8:30 P.M.	Fred Ruzika, violinist
8:45	Harry Harris, tenor
9:00	Victor Lamkay, pianist
9:15	Ivan Crisclow, tenor
9:30	Lee Kahn's Orchestra

WDBX used a portable transmitter with the call letters WOKO, and in 1925 Wilbur and Jacobson sold WOKO to radio-shop owner Otto Baur and closed down "New York's smallest station." Wilbur and Jacobson joined the WJZ engineering staff, and Jacobson eventually became supervisor of field operations for NBC.

See also WOKO.

WDT

(22 DECEMBER 1921–22 DECEMBER 1923)

1921	360m (833.3kc)	500w.
1923	405m (740kc)	500w.

The Ship Owners' Radio Service Inc. was a dealer and distributor that called itself "The Largest Radio Chain Store System in the World" in the early 1920s. It had sales locations from London to Honolulu and established wireless stations to provide shipping information in the harbors of New York and Norfolk. From "SORSINC" headquarters at 80 Washington Street in Lower Manhattan, the company operated on maritime frequencies, and since the target audience was mostly professional radio operators, it could have confined itself to transmitting Morse code. But late in 1921 it received the twenty-fifth broadcast license issued in the United States, the fourth in the New York City area.

WDT relayed tides and harbor weather to incoming marine traffic on the sole broadcasting frequency of 833.3kc. Operating intermittently while sharing time with other broadcasters wasn't an effective way to provide this vital service. But shipowners, and other radio owners, also got to hear some of the best shows on the air during radio's first years.

The studio and transmitter were located at Stapleton, Staten Island, and the station was on the air for an hour or two a day with entertainment programs. Programming was arranged by the Premier Grand Piano Company, and for a while WDT was managed by one of the most popular singers of the day, the "Original Radio Girl," Vaughn DeLeath.

Saturday, 4 August 1923

12:00–12:30 P.M.	Fletcher Henderson, piano; Edna Hicks and Emma Grove, vocalists

Monday, 6 August 1923

12:00–12:30 P.M.	Songs by Billy Frisch, Frank Goodman, Joe Trent, Vaughn DeLeath, and Lew Pollack
11:00–11:55 P.M.	Sherwood Orchestra and vocal selections

On 8 June 1923, when a second broadcast wavelength of 405m (740kc) was opened, WDT moved to this favored "class B" assignment and shared time with WOR and WJY. Programs then originated from a studio at the Premier Grand Piano building at 510 W. Twenty-third Street.

WDT's broadcasting was declared "permanently discontinued" on 22 December 1923, and the transmitter was put up for sale. A religious organization now known as Jehovah's Witnesses bought the station's equipment from the Ship Owners' Radio Service and used it for its new outlet, WBBR.

See also WBBR.

WDWM

(DECEMBER 1926–30 NOVEMBER 1927)

| 1926 | 1070kc | 500w. |
| 1927 | 1270kc s/t WAAT | 500w. |

Donald W. May sold station WGCP and the May Radio Broadcasting Company in 1925. Having thus given up his own corporate name, he founded Radio Industries Broadcast Company in 1926 and with station WDWM at least got his initials back on the air. The studios were at 20 Central Avenue in Newark. This took place during the anarchic period before the establishment of the Federal Radio Commission, and after the commission was established it ordered WDWM to double up on 1270kc with WAAT. May complained to the FRC: "We operated our station daily, putting on the very finest of programs, and were perfectly satisfied with this channel." If forced to operate on 1270, the station would lose "all commercial contracts and the total investment." May pleaded, "We feel that a grave injustice has been done."

Tuesday, 14 June 1927

6:10 P.M.	Time
6:11	Weather
6:12	Missing Persons
6:15	Ben Encherman, piano
6:30	Churchill Orchestra
7:00	Sport talk
7:15	Bernays Johnson—Radio
7:30	George Wright Jr., tenor
7:45	Dorothy Cohen, soprano
8:00	Woodfern Orchestra
9:00	Off for WNJ

In June 1927, May found a way to avoid sharing time. The FRC had given him the option of moving his station out of Newark and away from 236 meters. He reestablished WDWM at Asbury Park with the intention of transferring ownership to the Asbury Park Chamber of Commerce and onto 361.2 meters. On 13 July 1927 the station began to broadcast from the seaside community. Later that year it became WCAP.

D.W. May left the broadcasting business to become a sales executive for General Electric. In 1944 he went into business as the metropolitan New York distributor for nine electronics manufacturers, including Farnsworth Television, Wilcox-Gay, and Ken-Rad Tubes.

See also WBS, WGCP, WCAP.

WDY

(14 DECEMBER 1921–24 FEBRUARY 1922)

| 1921 | 360m (833kc) | 500w. |

Five months after the Radio Corporation of America broadcast the Dempsey-Carpentier fight through temporary station WJY, and ten weeks after Westinghouse began regular broadcasting in the New York area over WJZ, RCA signed on station WDY. Working in cooperation with General Electric, the station was housed at GE's Aldene works in Roselle Park, N.J., just west of Elizabeth. The station manager was J. Andrew White, one of the few people with anything like an extensive background in the new medium: he was editor of RCA's *Wireless Age* magazine and had described the Dempsey-Carpentier fight (five years later he would be one of the founders of CBS). The transmitter was the one that had been used for the prizefight broadcast, repaired and modified.

Despite the relatively inaccessible industrial setting, WDY's facilities were meant to be attractive and dignified. RCA historian George Clark described its "chic and cozy atmosphere":

> The studio, which was located in the station [transmitter] building, was a hexagonal-shaped little room, artistically finished with draperies of blue and gold. A large hanging lamp in the center of the room was reflected in the bright colors of the oriental rugs, the wicker furniture, the red glow of the electric heaters. On one side of the room was a Knabe-Ampico piano, and opposite it stood an Edison Re-creation phonograph. No pick-up mikes were visible, until one looked closer and noticed a tiny disc suspended by a thin wire. The general appearance of the studio was gay and friendly.

In fact, WDY's first microphone was a crude telephone pickup with a large megaphone horn attached, suspended from the ceiling by several heavy wires. Trains passing under the antenna tended to cause a slight shift in the WDY wavelength.

WDY produced one of radio's first remote broadcasts, from the New York Electrical Show at the 71st Regiment Armory in Manhattan. Opera star Anna Case was a featured guest.

Thanks to Major White's contacts on the New York entertainment scene, WDY was able to woo a few of the most talented and hopeful performers of the day out to Roselle Park. Every Friday evening the RCA station broadcast a "Radio Party" featuring both amateur and professional talent. Among the artists was a twelve-year-old xylophone player. No one was paid, but many accepted the offer of a free meal from "that cute castle of cordiality."

Andy White and J. O. Smith's hosting was witty and considerably less formal than would later be the rule when radio sought to gain status with its growing audience. White once brought on singer Dick Hanson with the words, "He's been to Honolulu and he wants to moan a song about 'Mona Lu.'"

On 22 December 1921 the station presented a piano recital by Austrian composer Richard Strauss (or at least by his piano rolls). The best-known performer to make the trip to Roselle Park was comedian Eddie Cantor, on 10 February 1922. His doubts about the new medium—and his discomfort at telling jokes in an empty room—led him to appeal to every member of the unseen audience to send him a dime, which he would donate to the Salvation Army. The response proved that there were indeed people out there and that radio could move them.

This pioneering broadcast station kept careful track of reception reports, and a map in the hallway indicated that cards had been received from as far away as Cuba and Nebraska.

WDY left the air on 24 February 1922. The last program was a "radio dance" presented for the Robert Gordon Dancing School. Westinghouse's WJZ entered into a joint operating arrangement with RCA, which then transferred its entire broadcasting effort to the more popular station. RCA's board hadn't been overly impressed and saw WDY as an unnecessary expense. Clark called it "almost the equivalent of a tryout of a Broadway play in the provinces" and was amazed that it lasted for two months.

See also WJY, WJZ, WEAF.

WEAF

(16 August 1922–2 November 1946)

1922	360m (833kc)	500w.
1923	610, 740, & 750kc	500>>1,500w.
1925	610kc	5,000w.
1927	610kc	50,000w.
1928	660kc	50,000w.

The American Telephone and Telegraph Company was involved in radiotelephone experimentation from the earliest days of the science, but its concentration was in point-to-point communication. AT&T held (and jealously protected) many of the principal patents that made broadcasting possible. It contributed to military communication during World War I and was one of the constituent companies of the Radio Corporation of America.

In 1919, AT&T inaugurated an experimental radiophone station, 2XB, at its headquarters at 463 West Street in Manhattan and a year later added 2XF in Cliffside, N.J. Reports from ham operators and others were encouraged. One radio buff in Asbury Park mounted a receiver on a wheelchair and wheeled it along the boardwalk, charging strollers a few pennies to listen to the clear voices and music from AT&T's 2XJ in Deal Beach.

AT&T's first real venture into broadcasting, WBAY, went on the air on Tuesday, 25 July 1922. The installation suffered from technical problems, and on 16 August 1922, WBAY was shut down. Its staff was transferred and its programs were fed to a new transmitter operated by Western Electric's development and research department at 463 West Street.

The Commerce Department had granted a license to AT&T's Western Electric subsidiary on 18 May 1922 to upgrade 2XB. The original call letters—issued simply from an alphabetical list—were WDAM. Concerned about the propriety of such a call, AT&T asked for something less profane, and on 29 May it received the next available designation, WEAF. The letters didn't really stand for anything, but station staff were fond of pointing out the four classic elements of matter depicted in a mural above the studio doors: Water, Earth, Air, Fire.

From the very start, under the ownership of AT&T and later as the key station of the National Broadcasting Company, WEAF would be a standard-bearer in both technology and programming. When it was launched, however, there was not yet a clear idea of what broadcasting meant. AT&T executive Walter Gifford later stated that he thought people who had something to say to the public could call the radio station, which would connect the phone to the transmitter and allow them to be heard by everyone—a vague but prescient concept.

On its first evening on the air, announcer George Peck—a manager in the Long Lines Division—told WEAF listeners: "This is the world's first toll broadcasting station. Heretofore, broadcasting was gratis to all. Now, due to the great demand by those who wish to use the air waves for good-will purposes, and with only one wave length available—360 meters—we are offering toll broadcasting services." It was intended that the station would produce no programs of its own, but that's all WEAF did for three weeks. The pioneer station collected its first toll on the afternoon of Monday, 28 August 1922. Engineer R. S. Fenimore noted in the station's operating log, "5.00/5.10 Queensborough Corpn. 'Our first customer.'" Commercial radio on WEAF began with a ten-minute talk by M. H. Blackwell, sales manager of the Queensboro Corporation, a real estate developer then in the throes of the Queens building boom. Blackwell united in flowery words the honest, earthy qualities of author Nathaniel Hawthorne and the advantages of a new coop development located on what is now Eightieth and Eighty-first Streets at Thirty-fourth Avenue in Jackson Heights. The "elevator garden apartment" was called

Hawthorne Court, "right at the boundaries of God's great outdoors and within a few minutes by Subway from the business section of Manhattan. This sort of residential environment strongly influenced Hawthorne, America's greatest writer of fiction.... There should be more Hawthorne sermons preached about the utter inadequacy and the general hopelessness of the congested city home."

According to Queensboro vice-president Robert Lassiter: "We picked a time when housewives would be listening. And, I'm sorry to say, we didn't get an awful lot of direct results." But there were already great expectations for radio. As Lassiter noted many years later, "A few people had sets but everyone was talking about it." The script seemed targeted at a public crowded into substandard housing, but the Hawthorne was definitely upscale—references were required by the Queensboro Corporation—as was most of the listening public in 1922. The apartment buildings advertised on WEAF's first commercial still stand, in excellent condition, and have helped give the Jackson Heights neighborhood historic district status.

After three months of commercial operation, WEAF had earned only $550 for selling a total of three hours of airtime. On Thursday, 21 September 1922, the log listed all its first sponsors:

7.55–8.06	Queensborough
8.16–8.26	Tidewater Oil
8.46–9.00	American Express

Business improved when the toll broadcaster hired its first salesman, H.C. Smith, and agreed to pay ad agencies a commission. But WEAF saw an income of just $5,000 in its first year of operation.

With hours to fill, AT&T recruited office personnel who could sing or play. This wasn't always a good idea. Receptionist Winifred T. Barr once got up from her piano in the midst of a performance when she heard a phone ring in the lobby and rushed off to take care of her regular job. On the other hand, featured piano player and receptionist Kathleen Stewart was popular enough to receive fan mail. A 1924 letter claimed that one "could recognize her playing very well," calling her performance "absolutely perfect."

Some listeners found commercialization an objectionable intrusion and even dismissed commercial development of the new medium. At first, advertising was low-key and indirect—what might today be considered infomercials. The Greeting Card Association presented "The Story of the Christmas Card." A talk on "Insulation Facts Every Amateur [Radio Operator] Should Know" was sponsored by the American Hard Rubber Company. Other WEAF customers during its first year included Metropolitan Life, the California Prune and Apricot Growers, and filmmaker D.W. Griffith. Two sponsors, Gimbel's Department Store and the Grebe Radio Company, disregarded AT&T's intentions and opened stations of their own.

The original toll broadcaster had trouble meeting its expenses and the expectations of its audience and in 1924 briefly launched a public fund-raising campaign in support of its concert programs. Response from listeners was weak, and contributions were returned.

On 10 April 1923 WEAF began operation from studios at 195 Broadway. The staff had learned from the inconveniences in the original setup, and so two studios were built, with an announcer's booth looking into both. On the last day of 1923, WEAF turned on its first 5,000-watt transmitter. The station was not authorized to boost its power to the full 5kw. until September 1925, but the increasingly strong and steady signal quickly dominated the local airwaves. In September 1924, WEAF vice-president W. E. Harkness stated that one million people were tuned in on any given day within the 100-mile radius considered the station's primary listening area. Nonetheless, WEAF felt the hardships of a pioneer: at the end of 1925, logbooks revealed that during that year the station had been forced to leave the air for a total of seventeen hours so as not to interfere with ships calling SOS.

AT&T's principal interest, of course, was to send voices across America. Its first experiment in interconnection was an unsuccessful link with WNAC/Boston in January 1923. On Thursday, 7 June 1923, WEAF originated the first true network broadcast, an hour of speeches and music from the Carnegie Hall convention of the National Electric Light Association. The program was fed to Westinghouse stations KDKA/Pittsburgh and KYW/Chicago and to GE's WGY/Schenectady.

A regular hookup came about because a wealthy radio hobbyist, Colonel Edward Green of South Dartmouth, Mass., received complaints from his neighbors that his station, WMAF, was interfering with WEAF. In July 1923 Green contracted to let the New York station feed programs to him via phone lines, establishing a permanent network connection. Network radio was on its way to becoming commonplace. In July, 1924, WEAF covered the Democratic National Convention at Madison Square Garden, with announcers Graham McNamee and Phillips Carlin on the scene for fifteen days following all 103 ballots. The coverage was fed to seventy-seven stations.

On New Year's Day 1925, opera stars John McCormack and Lucrezia Bori sang on WEAF and six other stations. Such high-caliber performers had seldom been heard on the air; the audience was estimated at six million, and WEAF received twenty thousand letters. It clearly did not harm an artist's reputation to appear on the radio, especially on WEAF, "the world's greatest concert hall."

RCA took over WEAF as the flagship for the Broadcasting Company of America, a name soon changed to the National Broadcasting Company. The price was $1 million. The sale by AT&T and the "merger" with WJZ were reported at the top of the front page of the *New York Times* on Thursday, 22 July 1926. The story noted, "This announcement

The WEAF transmitter at Bellmore, Long Island, around the time of World War II. Note the fountain in front of the building.

WJZ network" into permanent features, more than one hundred stations asked to be part of the arrangement.

The first broadcast of the National Broadcasting Company originated from the Waldorf-Astoria on Monday, 15 November 1926, from 8:00 P.M. to midnight. WEAF was the key station of the Red Network; WJZ was the flagship of the Blue, which went into operation six weeks later. AT&T carried the programming on its broadcast-grade lines, and NBC, in its first year, became the phone company's biggest customer. The venture was not without risk, since radio was then in a chaotic period with no solid regulatory framework. Five million U.S. households had radios in 1926, which meant that twenty-one million had yet to buy into the new technology.

On 10 October 1927, "the Voice to the Millions" shut down the old transmitter on West Street and moved to a new installation in Bellmore, Long Island, increasing power to 50,000 watts. At about the same time, WEAF and WJZ moved to 711 Fifth Avenue, between Fifty-fifth and Fifty-sixth Streets. Graham McNamee expressed delight at the advance from four rooms to five floors. Architect Raymond Hood designed eight studios to provide the proper mood for classical, jazz, and other programs. For addresses by prominent speakers, there was a studio with a Roman Forum motif, and another resembled a Gothic church. On 11 November 1928, WEAF switched from 610 to 660kc.

The move that solidified WEAF's position as the most prestigious of all broadcasters took place in the autumn of 1933, when NBC moved seven blocks to 30 Rockefeller Plaza and became the radio that gave Radio City its name. It was hailed as one of the wonders of the modern world. There were fifteen hundred switches on the master control console to tend to the functions of twenty-eight studios, which originated twenty thousand broadcasts a year.

Since the WEAF schedule became the Red Network schedule when NBC was founded, the New York flagship was lax in developing a strong local personality, in the manner of WOR or WHN. Its 50,000 watts could blanket the eastern United States and Canada, but the waves from the Bellmore transmitter had trouble penetrating sections of Manhattan and Brooklyn. On 8 November 1940 WEAF switched off the signal from the sand dunes and inaugurated a new transmitter in the marshes of Port Washington, Long Island, which opened "the salt water way" into the city.

In April 1946 journalist Tex McCrary and his wife Jinx Falkenberg began their morning "Tex and Jinx" chat show

practically foreshadows the consolidation of two of the best known broadcasting stations in the East." According to the article, AT&T had considered WEAF an "experiment," which sought to perfect "new means of electrical communication" as well as to research the commercial possibilities and public response to radio broadcasting. The paper also surmised that AT&T feared that if it remained in broadcasting, the broadcasters would feel free to enter the telephone business, providing wireless phone service.

The marriage with WJZ was not entirely happy for the WEAF staff. As part of AT&T, WEAF had prided itself on constantly upgrading its audio quality, and their engineers soon discovered that RCA gave such work lower priority.

Beginning in 1924, WEAF's day began at 6:45 A.M. with setting-up exercises led by Arthur Bagley, accompanied by William Mahoney at the piano.

By this time, WEAF staff was regularly consulting on programming with other broadcasters around the country, and when the new ownership revealed its plans to organize the temporary arrangements of "the WEAF network" and "the

WEAF's portable broadcasting van, photographed in 1942.

on WEAF. On 5 August, Bob Smith, a Buffalonian recently discharged from the navy, began a wake-up program. At first Smith was heard from 7:05 to 7:30 and from 7:45 to 8:30 each morning, which constituted the largest block of time ever given to a single personality on the grand old station. ("Buffalo Bob" left the morning show in 1951 to concentrate on TV's "Howdy Doody.") A "Metropolitan News Roundup" brought WEAF listeners local news direct from the offices of the *Bronx Home News*, the *Brooklyn Eagle*, the *Long Island Press*, and the *Newark Star-Ledger*. Most of the broadcast day was filled with music, drama, comedy, news, and sports coverage, which was some of the nation's finest, destined for the entire American audience.

In 1946, NBC came to an agreement with a small station in New Britain, Conn., to relinquish that city's initials from its call letters. On 2 November 1946 at 5:30 P.M., WEAF presented its last broadcast, entitled "Hail and Farewell," and at 6:00 turned into WNBC.

See also WAAT, WBAY, WDT, WJY, WJZ, WHN, WNBC, WRCA.

WEAM

(8 June 1922–21 December 1928)

1922	360m. (833kc)	250w.
1923	1150kc	250w.

WNYC was not the only municipally owned radio station in the New York area. It wasn't even the first. That distinction belongs to the borough of North Plainfield, N.J. Plainfield had an early experience with radio in January 1922 when ham operator Harold Blackford transmitted a message about the virtues of his hometown from his station 2QB and the chamber of commerce offered a ten-dollar prize to the first person who mailed in a correct copy.

Perhaps not to be outdone by its neighbor, a few months later North Plainfield Mayor William L. Smalley put WEAM on the air. The station was licensed to the municipal government of the borough of North Plainfield but was located at engineer William J. Buttfield's spacious home, which still stands at the corner of Rock View and West End Avenues. Harold Blackford was the announcer and official operator.

In addition to local news and entertainment, WEAM served as North Plainfield's official police radio. Mayor Smalley contacted other New Jersey municipalities with offers of airtime, hoping that their cooperation would make North Plainfield a communications center. At first WEAM was on the air from 10:15 till 11:00 P.M. but soon rescheduled itself to broadcast from 7:30 to 8:00 P.M. following complaints that it was interfering with WJZ at the later hour.

The Plainfield Chamber of Commerce and the *Courier-News* were actively involved with WEAM, and many local residents performed on the municipal station. WEAM provided the first radio experience for a young singer named Jessica Dragonette, who went on to become one of the superstars of radio in the 1930s as the "Princess of the American Air."

In 1928 the chamber of commerce took over WEAM but discontinued operation. North Plainfield considered WEAM "the Pioneer Municipal Broadcasting Station," although Dallas and Chicago actually preceded it by about two months.

WEBJ

(9 SEPTEMBER 1924–JUNE 1928)

| 1924 | 1100kc | 500w. |
| 1927 | 1170kc s/t WLTH, WBBR | 500w. |

The Third Avenue Railway Company ran the trolley cars that plied the east side of Manhattan into the Bronx and Westchester County, an operation that required a large staff of skilled electricians. In March 1923, the company instituted a "carrier current" communications system, built by General Electric, which radiated messages through the trolley wire to motormen and conductors. It was simple to turn this into an information service for the captive audiences riding the streetcars, and this was a natural step into the new field of broadcasting. WEBJ's offices and studios were located at the trolley barn at 2396 Third Avenue at 130th Street. The antenna was suspended between two 60-foot towers on the roof. On 2 August 1924, the *New York Telegram and Evening Mail* noted:

The operating room is also on the roof and is made of steel and hollow tile. A winding metal staircase leads below to the fourth floor and the studio which is approximately fifty feet from the operating room. The studio is 15×25 feet and the walls, ceiling and floor are soundproof in accord with the most modern practice. The hangings on the walls and ceiling are made of lined druid cloth and the floor is

heavily carpeted on felt. It is furnished simply but tastefully. Deeply upholstered mahogany furniture and a special system of electrical lighting together with a Duo-Art grand piano help to make this studio one of the most comfortable and efficient in the city.

WEBJ presented some lively programming, including appearances by cabaret artists who were "rushed by car to 130th Street and Third avenue and returned in time to make their next appearance on the stage." (They didn't take the trolley.) Some entertainment apparently came from within the company, with performances by the Conductors' Band and the Motormen's Quartet. Program director Henry Bruno, who was an aviator, presented his "Radio Airplane Travelogue" two evenings a week. The Red Trolley Station reviewed plays and movies, broadcast both jazz and classics, and offered much off-beat entertainment:

• The Aywon Comedy Four will present a number of farmyard ballads at WEBJ at 25 minutes after eight o' clock. These boys are all farm raised and believe that the radio audiences like to hear songs that carry them back to the farm.

• Ruth B. Gilbert, taropatch artist, and Ruth Wimp, ukelele expert, will play a program especially for people who feel blue and need cheering up. They will go on the air at Red Trolley station WEBJ at fifteen minutes to eight o'clock.

Friday, 6 August 1926

7:00 P.M.	Ormond Aces Dance Orchestra
7:30	Luna's Knickerbocker Orchestra
8:00	Brennan and Adams, songs with the uke
8:15	Tindaro Cicero, tenor
8:30	Luna's Marine Band

WEBJ gained a substantial audience, even though Bruno had to advise listeners looking for the station to "tune carefully so as not to pass through our carrier wave without detecting it." There were also educational talks, including regular appearances by Third Avenue Railway executives who spoke about transportation and safety topics. WEBJ's target audience specifically included the three thousand employees of the railway and their families.

Ranging afield from its trolley lines, WEBJ broadcast from Luna Park at Coney Island and invited community groups from the suburbs to come to 130th Street to perform. By 1927, WEBJ was utilizing one-quarter time on 256m (1170 kc), sharing with WLTH and WBBR.

WEBJ was one of six local stations that *Radio Broadcast* magazine considered qualified to remain on the air when the Federal Radio Commission reallocated frequencies in 1927. It was one of only nine New York area outlets included in a reference chart of some eighty broadcasting stations in the *Webster's Dictionary* of the period. But although it was one of the few small stations the FRC didn't try to shut down, in June 1928 the owners decided to "voluntarily discontinue operation." President S.W. Huff, according to the

New York Times, "wrote that the station was established for broadcasting safety campaigns, the relations between the public and the transportation company, relations between the employee and the employer, and kindred subjects, along with sufficient entertainment to carry the more serious subjects, that it never entered the advertising field and that it was not operated more than six hours a week." The federal regulators congratulated Third Avenue Railway for its "unselfish example."

The electrical engineering staff would continue to do experimental work in reducing radio interference from street railway lines, but the management of the Third Avenue Railway felt little kinship with the comedy teams and ukelele players it once presented so well. WEBJ had been seen as a pioneer among transit systems entering the broadcasting field, yet after its demise little was heard again of the partnership between urban rail and radio.

WERA

(16 SEPTEMBER 1961–1996)

1961	1590kc	500w.

Tri-County Broadcasting Corporation of Plainfield, N.J., said it was a new era in radio when they launched WERA. Of course, the neighboring municipality of North Plainfield had operated WEAM back in the 1920s, but this was the first station from Plainfield itself. Studios were in the Park Hotel Annex at 200 W. Seventh Street. Henry Behre came from Morristown's WMTR to serve as president and general manager, Jack McGuire was the first program director and the deejays played easy-listening and middle-of-the-road music. The day began with "Top of the Morning," hosted by Joe Reilly; he was assisted by news director Pat Parson, who went on to an anchor position at Newsradio 88.

Both WERA's news coverage and its community relations were tested by an outbreak of racial unrest in 1967. Reporters were dispatched to the scene of breaking events and squelched rumors with factual reports, but there was considerable damage to Plainfield's property and to its image.

The news-gathering efforts regularly reached beyond Plainfield to communities throughout Union, Somerset, and Middlesex Counties (the tri-counties of the corporate name). WERA sports director Barry Landers covered local high school sports; his place was taken in 1962 by John Pepe, a familiar voice for over three decades.

In 1970 WERA moved its studios to the Atlas Building at 120 W. Seventh Street. It began to add programs on the weekend for ethnic audiences in Plainfield's black, Polish, Italian, and Spanish-speaking neighborhoods. Music programming was updated, with the Carpenters replacing artists like Percy Faith on the playlist. By the mid–1970s Glen Edwards was program director and star of the morning show. Oldies aficionado Rich Phoenix presided at midday and presented a freewheeling Saturday afternoon "Solid Gold Flight of the Phoenix."

There was also an unusual hour-long news and public-affairs program called "Newsline" at 10:00 each morning except Wednesday, when Barbara Ballard presented "Sideline." WERA air personnel included Dennis O'Mara, Bob Salter, Charles Green, Jere Sullivan, Bill Franklin, and Fred Mack.

On 30 September 1985 the daytimer was allowed to expand to full-time broadcasting. Power was not increased, but a new directional antenna aimed the signal to the Jersey Shore. In January 1994 Tri-County sold the station for $555,000 to Cloud 9 Broadcasting, headed by the station's former sales manager, Jesse Carroll. The music policy was revised to include more standards and nostalgic ballads. Finally, with the start of twenty-four-hour service, WERA added an overnight country music show. But in 1996 WERA was purchased for a million dollars by WWRL, its neighbor at 1600kHz, for the sole purpose of shutting down a transmitter that blocked its own signal. Most of the purchase price would be used to pay off shareholders and cover station debts, including Cloud 9's remaining obligation to Henry Behre.

WEVD

(20 OCTOBER 1927–)

1927	1220kc s/t WAAT, WGBB	500w.
1928	1300kc s/t WBBR, WHAP, WHAZ	500w.
1934	1300kc s/t WBBR, WFAB, WHAZ	1,000w.
1941	1330kc s/t WBBR, WHAZ	5,000w. (1942)
1981	97.9MHz FM	
1988	1050khz	50,000w.

Many Americans consider socialism an alien philosophy that, in the first decades of the twentieth century, seemed to draw much of its support from immigrants. So Eugene Victor Debs was more than an inspiring leader of the Socialist Party; he was also a plain-spoken Hoosier remembered as a distinctly American type who lent socialism some native appeal. Debs ran for president four times, the last time in 1920 while jailed for sedition for resisting U.S. involvement in World War I. Campaign posters depicting Debs in prison stripes helped draw more than 900,000 votes.

Debs died in 1926, and shortly afterward a committee of Socialists—including writer Upton Sinclair and social worker Jane Addams—met in Chicago to plan a radio station in his honor. Socialists had been repeatedly frustrated when they requested airtime. In the spring of 1926 Norman Thomas, Debs' heir apparent, was turned away by WEAF and WMCA when he sought to speak against compulsory military training. Manager Donald Flamm was honest about WMCA's motivation, stating that Thomas "slammed the daylights out of the companies on which we depend for supplies." Thomas was later invited to speak on WRNY on the topic "Radio and Democracy."

The Socialists' own voice would be located in either New York or Chicago and was to be called WDEBS. In August 1927 the Debs Memorial Radio Fund, with Thomas as president, purchased WSOM from the Hotel Somerset in Manhattan. They also learned that only aircraft radio could then have five call letters.

WEVD built studios at 3 West Sixteenth Street in space contributed by the International Ladies Garment Workers Union. Its offices were around the corner at 31 Union Square. The transmitter was the one used by WSOM and earlier by WJBV in Woodhaven.

Even before the Debs station officially signed on, it produced programs over WSOM dealing with such controversial issues as the trial of Sacco and Vanzetti. WEVD premiered on 20 October 1927, the first anniversary of the death of Eugene Debs. The inaugural program opened with James Phillips performing a musical setting of one of Debs' favorite poems, W.E. Henley's "Invictus" ("I am the master of my fate / I am the captain of my soul"). One of the speakers, civil rights lawyer Arthur Garfield Hays, cautioned the station against becoming "rigid and doctrinaire." Norman Thomas called WEVD "a genuine educational force" and asked for "a multitude of small monthly gifts" to support it. Its board of directors included Roger Baldwin ACLU founder; Abraham Cahan, publisher of the *Jewish Daily Forward*; and Harriot Stanton Blatch, a feminist leader and ex-mother-in-law of Dr. Lee De Forest.

The station "dedicated to social justice and peace" was feisty in its defense of working people. Although its leftist voice didn't alone make it a target of the Republican administration during the initial days of the Federal Radio Commission, the appearance of "The Worker's Station" on a list of 162 small stations ordered to shut down brought a clearly political response. Congressman Emanuel Celler of Brooklyn defended WEVD, calling it "the only broadcasting station that can be truly termed, in the truest sense, a liberal station." Socialists and free-speech advocates around the country organized on its behalf. In July 1928, the FRC held hearings in Washington to consider challenges to the order. WEVD was the first station to testify, and it made its case in unequivocal terms:

We are not convinced that the public necessity dictates the broadcasting of descriptions of ladies' fancy dresses at receptions in Fifth Avenue ball rooms. Unless the Commission discriminates against labor we intend to carry on for the purposes for which we were organized—a service to labor…. If WEVD is taken off the air and in fact if it is not treated on a parity with others who are richer and more influential with the government, the people of the nation can truly recognize that radio which might be such a splendid force for the honest clash of ideas,—creating a free market for thought,—is nothing but a tool to be used by the powerful against any form of disagreement, or any species of protest.

The license was renewed but repeatedly challenged by rivals. The depression would limit even small gifts. Supposedly a noncommercial station, WEVD did carry some sponsored programs, but that income plus the moral support of labor and religious groups could not prevent technical deterioration. In 1928 the transmitter was moved from Woodhaven to a residential plot at 100-17 Pilgrim Street in Forest Hills. A federal radio inspector visited the site in June 1931 and found the transmitter in a corner of a basement, a transmission line snaking through a cracked window and the antenna supported by two 50-foot wooden poles. Eighteen of WEVD's fifty hours of airtime each week were programmed by a time broker who maintained his own studio on Jamaica Avenue in Jamaica, Queens. This was not what WEVD's founders had dreamed of.

Wednesday, 5 February 1930

1:20 P.M.	Clarence Johnson, basso
1:40	Elizabeth Barber, soprano
2:00	Youth Section Fellowship of Reconciliation
2:20	Mrs. W. E. Bellman, Chopin-Liszt program
2:40	Alan F. Pater, original poems
3:00	Bonnie Windsor, blues
3:20	Marcy Wahren, original monologues
3:40	Martha Grosso, lyric soprano
4:00	Cousin Betty, "World's Best Stories"
4:20	Music
4:30	Jamaica Studio
5:00	Tea Time Tunes

In October 1931, a rescuer stepped forward. The *Jewish Daily Forward*, the respected mass-circulation Yiddish language paper, contributed $250,000 to underwrite the station. In the spring of 1932 a new transmitter was put into service along Newtown Creek in Brooklyn. Morris Novik became program director, and in 1935 Henry Greenfield began his three-decade tenure as station manager. In 1937, *Der Farverts* tossed in another $100,000. The Debs Memorial Radio Fund was later merged with the Forward Association and ran WEVD as a commercial operation.

On 26 January 1933 WEVD established its "University of the Air" with a lecture by historian Henrik Van Loon.

The WEVD studios at the Hotel Claridge, Forty-fourth Street and Broadway, in 1932. Announcer Ted Weller watches the turntables as operator Kenny Arnott mans the controls inside the booth. Photo courtesy David Winter.

Philosopher John Dewey was a frequent speaker, and guests included Albert Einstein. Among the organizations that supplied program material were the AFL and the CIO (not yet merged), the New School for Social Research, and the NAACP. Station breaks were signaled by four NBC-like chimes. On the announcing staff in the early 1930s was House Jamieson, who attained national fame playing "Renfrew of the Mounted" and Henry's father on "The Aldrich Family." Ev Suffens later joined the NBC staff under the name Ray Nelson, and Gene King went on to WOR-Mutual. Hosting in Yiddish were Nuchem Stutzkoff, Ben Basenko, and Zvee Scooler, who also had a distinguished acting career. Scooler started on WEVD in 1932, commenting on the news in rhyme and was still reading his doggerel forty years later on "The Forward Hour," which WEVD proudly called "New York's oldest continuous live program."

In 1932, the station moved from Union Square to studios atop the Hotel Claridge in Times Square. On 11 November 1938 it occupied spacious and well-equipped facilities at 117 W. Forty-sixth Street. There were four studios in the WEVD Building, one of which could seat an audience of one hundred. The dedicatory program featured a dramatization of WEVD's history. Also in 1938, WEVD bought station WFAB, one of the four stations with which it shared 1300kc, boosting its airtime to eighty-six hours a week. The Debs Memorial station even attracted a wide audience with such unpolitical programs as the "Midnight Jamboree," on which Gene King filled requests for "any song, any language" from WEVD's multiethnic record library, such as the Spanish-language version of the "Beer Barrel Polka."

WEVD continued through the 1940s and 1950s to share time with Jehovah's Witnesses' WBBR—which took early mornings, 6–8 P.M. weekdays, and most of Sundays—and WHAZ at Rensselaer Polytechnic in Troy, which broadcast on Monday nights. It received one of the city's first FM licenses (107.5Mc, later 97.9) and even applied, unsuccessfully, for a TV permit.

Noted primarily for its Yiddish broadcasts (on Jewish holidays WEVD would preempt that programming and play classical music), "the station that speaks your language" was heard in literally dozens of tongues, from Japanese to Macedonian. Chinese listeners could receive special programs on an FM subcarrier. The International Ladies Garment Workers Union was still heard over WEVD on "The Voice of Local 89," the voices being mainly in Italian. Actor Robert Alda brought his Italian-American talk-and-variety hour to WEVD. "Hello Germany," featuring Jeanette van Delden and Erwin Holl, was heard for two hours each afternoon. Art Raymond's mid-morning show "Raisins and Almonds" was a longtime favorite in Jewish households. In addition to the University of the Air, WEVD had a number of general-audience programs, including jazz by Symphony Sid Torin and Latino music from Dick "Ricardo" Sugar.

In 1957, WBBR was sold, and a new station, WPOW, shared the 1330 AM spot with WEVD. In the 1980s WEVD began a series of ownership and frequency changes that are nearly unparalleled in New York radio. First the AM side of the predominantly Jewish station was sold in 1981 for $1.1 million to Salem Media, a Christian religious broadcaster, and 1330 became WNYM. WEVD continued as before on FM with a lively schedule of ethnic and cultural programming.

The demise of WNBC in 1988 gave WEVD an opportunity to return to the AM band. The Spanish Broadcasting System, which owned WSKQ-AM, wanted an FM frequency. SBS also owned WFAN, then at 1050khz, which was moving to WNBC's 660 frequency. The Forward Association, hurting financially as the *Forward* readership aged and declined, gladly agreed to sell WEVD-FM for $30 million. WEVD's 97.9 became WSKQ, and WEVD moved back to the AM band.

Programming was updated but in some ways little changed. By the mid-1990s WEVD was still speaking many languages, and some Jewish programming remained: Ruth Jacobs' daily "Jewish Home Show" in English and a Yiddish newscast prepared by the *Forward*. "The Forward Hour" and Art Raymond continued on Sundays, along with Rabbi Jacob Hecht in Yiddish. There were also shows in modern Hebrew featuring Israeli music. Danny Stiles was on overnight, playing music that stretched back to the 1920s. New York Islanders hockey was carried by "The Great 1050." In 1996 WEVD added some of the nation's top syndicated talk shows. The leftist orientation was gone, but the station that had once struggled to be a "free market of thought" on behalf of workers could now be heard with a 50,000-watt clear-channel signal. Eugene V. Debs might not be totally disappointed.

See also WSOM, WBBR, WPOW, WNYM, WNBC, WFAN.

WFAB

(29 April 1932–7 November 1938)

| 1932 | 1300kc s/t WEVD, WBBR | 100w. |
| 1934 | 1300kc s/t WEVD, WBBR | 1,000w. |

It must have been a relief to many New Yorkers, especially Roman Catholics, when the outspokenly anti–Catholic station WHAP went out of existence and was sold to Paul F. Harron to become WFAB. The Fifth Avenue Broadcasting Corporation set up studios at 29 W. Fifty-seventh Street (half a block from Fifth Avenue—this is a city where Madison Square Garden is three-fourths of a mile from Madison Square and Manhattan College is in the Bronx). WFAB had only one studio, equipped with two 78-rpm turntables whose heavy Pacent pickups used steel needles.

WFAB operated on WHAP's old schedule, sharing time with WEVD, WBBR, and WHAZ. It was on the air only thirty-six hours a week, initially with just 100 watts of power from the old WHAP transmitter in Carlstadt, N.J. It called itself "The Voice of the Foreign Language."

In 1934, Harron bought the larger WHOM and began to produce programs for the Jersey City station from WFAB's Fifty-seventh Street studio. Four years later, WFAB was sold to WEVD for $85,000.

WFAN

(1 July 1987–)

| 1987 | 1050khz | 50,000w. |
| 1988 | 660khz | 50,000w. |

Sports has always been a big part of New York radio. The first wireless demonstration here was Marconi's report on the 1899 America's Cup yacht race. The first broadcast from the metropolitan area to have important audience impact was the Dempsey-Carpentier prizefight over temporary station WJY on 2 July 1921. Three months later the area's first permanent broadcaster, Westinghouse's WJZ, premiered with coverage of the World Series between the Yankees and the Giants from the Polo Grounds. Madison Square Garden was initially reluctant to allow its major events to be heard on the air; manager Tex Rickard relented in 1926 and installed the Garden's own WMSG. New York's three professional baseball teams lagged behind those in other major-league cities in allowing play-by-play coverage, until the Brooklyn Dodgers broke the ban in 1939 and baseball became as ubiquitous on the air as it was in the city's sandlots.

But there was no radio station anywhere that specialized in sports until WFAN entered the scene. Emmis Broadcasting bought WHN in August 1986 and moved the studios across the East River to 34-12 Thirty-sixth Street in the movie district of Astoria. The change from WHN's country format to WFAN's all-sports radio took place at 3:00 P.M. on the first day of July 1987. The target audience was men age eighteen to fifty, but the first voice heard was female: Suzyn Waldman gave the quarter-hourly sports update before handing it over to Pete Franklin to begin the call-ins.

True fanatics (for whom the station was named, after all) could easily be overwhelmed by the welcome to phone in and talk about sports with the experts and the stars. During morning drive time there was Greg Gumbel, then Jim Lampley, formerly of ABC's Wide World of Sports, Dan Lovett from Mutual, and Howie Rose, transplanted from Newsradio 88. John Minko chatted overnight.

WFAN didn't have all the sports on the local airwaves, but it did carry Mets baseball and Knicks basketball beginning in 1986, the Nets from 1992 to 1994, Jets football from 1993, and Rangers hockey games since the 1992 season. It also carried the World Series, the Superbowl, the Monday-night NFL game, and Notre Dame football.

On Friday, 7 October 1988, WFAN cleaned out locker #1050 and moved over to 660khz. WNBC radio had been sold as owner General Electric withdrew from the radio broadcasting industry. For the second time in fifteen months, WFAN aired an afternoon switchover. WFAN carried over the Knicks and Rangers games from WNBC and one nonsports program: morning-drive personality Don Imus stayed at 660 to rouse and arouse the metropolitan area and then the nation via satellite radio and cable TV.

See also WMGM, WNBC.

The IMUS in the Morning Crew

SPORTS RADIO 66AM WFAN

WFAN card, 1994.

WFAS

(11 AUGUST 1932–)

1932	1210kc	100w.
1940	1210kc s/t WGBB, WBRB	250w.
1941	1240kc s/t WGBB	250w.
1943	1230kc	250w.
1963	1230kc.	1,000w.

In 1932, Selma Seitz and her son Frank Jr. moved station WCOH from Yonkers to the Westchester County seat of White Plains. WCOH was renamed in honor of the late Frank A. Seitz Sr., a real estate executive who had never been involved with broadcasting. Studios were established in the seven-story Roger Smith Hotel, and a 190-foot steel antenna was installed on the rooftop.

On 25 February 1933, with the demise of WMRJ/Jamaica, WFAS began to share 1210kc with WGNY/Newburg. WGBB/Freeport was later added to the frequency.

From its first days during the depths of the depression, WFAS brought a refined sound and ambitious programming to one of the most affluent counties in the nation. The WFAS Air Theatre was an ongoing "little theatre of the air," presenting professional and amateur productions. The station also presented Bill Bender, the Happy Cowboy, music by Wilson Ames at the console, and for those tooling about on Westchester's leafy byways, "Music for Motoring." WFAS's warm and solid sound was apparent in its slogan, "New York's Hearthside."

Saturday, 27 March 1943

7:30 A.M.	Breakfast Club
7:55	Newscast
8:00	Music for Morning
8:30	Breakfasteers
8:55	Newscast
9:00	Pleasant Valley Folk
9:15	Library Association
9:30	Varieties
9:45	Jungle Jim
10:00	Fun To Be Healthy
10:15	Mid-Morning Melodies
10:45	News Roundup
11:00	Morning Serenade
11:30	Dance Orchestra
11:55	Newscast
12:00	Noon Red & Gold Concert
12:55	Newscast
1:00	On the Homefront
1:30	Dance Music
2:00	Promenade Concert

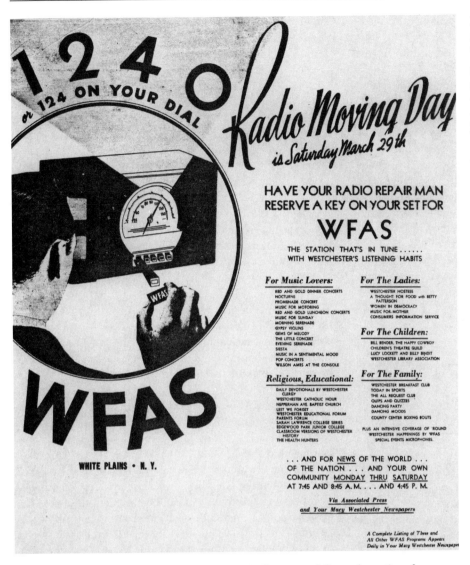

"Radio Moving Day" was no stranger to WFAS. They moved from share-time frequency 1210 to 1240 kilocycles in 1941 and finally to 1230.

2:55	Newscast
3:00	America Marches On
3:30	Invitation to Waltz
4:00	What Do You Know?
4:30	Tea Dancing
4:55	Newscast
5:00	The Air Force
5:15	This is My Story
5:30	Front Page Drama
5:45	Interlude
5:55	Newscast
6:00	Music
6:15	Behind the News
6:30	Red & Gold Concert

On 28 June 1939, Selma and Frank Seitz sold WFAS to publisher J. Noel Macy, and the station began its long and fruitful association with the Macy Westchester newspapers.

Frank Seitz continued as managing director. During December 1941, the WFAS Air Theatre presented "Santa and the White Rose," which was also serialized in the Macy papers. This was ambitious and sophisticated programming, especially for a part-time suburban broadcaster. The schedule also included some of the better syndicated series of the 1940s, including "The Adventures of Jungle Jim" and Hearst's "Front Page Drama."

On Saturday, 27 March 1943, WFAS moved from 1240kc to "1230 or 123" and an extended schedule, although power remained at 250 watts. Sign-off time changed to 7:30 P.M. on weekdays and Saturday and to 9:30 P.M. on Sundays. A press release mentioned WFAS's war preparedness: "Westchester's station will go back on the air in case of blackouts to broadcast the all-clear the moment the signal is received in the Westchester control rooms."

In December 1945, WFAS was one of the first applicants for one of the four TV channels then available (it wasn't granted). The next year the studios were moved from the Roger Smith to the Reporter Dispatch Building at 8 Church Street in White Plains. In 1947 a new transmitter went into operation from Secor Road in the neighboring town of Greenburgh, and on 1 September 1947 WFAS-FM went on the air. In 1954 "The Quality Music Station" moved all its broadcast operations to the Secor Road "transmitting plant" (WFAS continued to use that somewhat antiquated term on the air for many years).

By 1959, "the premier radio service for Westchester and Rockland Counties" was leading the Pulse ratings in its home territory during forty-eight quarter-hours, and was second in eighteen from 7:00 A.M. to midnight. Announcer Dan Vallie was a familiar voice from the 1940s through the 1970s. Sportscaster Bob Wolff and NBC newsman Tom O'Hanlon both started at WFAS; Aime Gauvin went from the White Plains station to WMGM and WHN. Bobby Lloyd did the wake-up show for years. When his program was dropped in the early 1990s, WFAS saw its billings suddenly decline by 40 percent. Lloyd was soon back on the air.

Most radio stations seem to have a young person who likes to hang around the studio, run errands, and learn about the business with the hope of getting on the air. In the 1950s a girl named Sally used to visit regularly, and by the age of thirteen she was hosting "The Junior High News." Sally Jessy Raphaël built on that experience to gain stardom on her national radio and TV talk shows.

In 1964, the Macys sold WFAS to American Greetings Corp. of Cleveland for $850,000, and in September 1965 Frank A. Seitz left the station he had founded to continue his career as manager of Fordham University's WFUV-FM. In 1986 the station was sold to Commodore Media.

WFAS maintained an affiliation with the ABC Entertainment Network from 1970 to 1988. In September 1991, WFAS backed away from the all-news/talk format and added middle-of-the-road big-band music via satellite from American Radio Network. The station also beefed up its sports coverage. By 1996 WFAS was a news-and-conversation station and an affiliate of CNN Radio. Sixty percent of the audience was age 45–64, and some had been listening to Westchester's dominant local station for their entire lives.

See also WCOH.

WFBH

(15 JULY 1924–6 NOVEMBER 1926)
1924   1100kc s/t WRW, WEBJ   500w.

WFBH should have been one of the class acts in New York radio, with studios on the ground floor of the swanky Hotel Majestic at Central Park West and Seventy-second Street and a transmitter on the roof of the hotel. Instead, "The Voice of Central Park" was one of the most hapless of the city's stations. A typical day's schedule consisted mostly of "potted palm music," including occasional recitals by the Majestic String Ensemble. There were programs on automobiling, movie reviews and reports for members of the Masonic order. A "Health Talk" at 5:30 P.M. was part of a series sponsored by an organization called the House of Health operated by Dr. Leonard Lincoln Landis; the organization was not sanctioned by the New York Medical Society or by the Hotel Majestic. One May afternoon in 1925 during "Health Talk," the Hotel Majestic literally pulled the switch on its tenant, shutting down the power and throwing WFBH off the air.

Thursday, 21 May 1925
2:00 P.M.   Kraus' Orchestra
3:00   Current Events. Mrs. Owen Kildare, Mildred Holland, Mrs. Robert Blackman
3:30   Ken Burdick, piano
4:00   Marie Cavagnero, soprano; Myrtle Hamil, piano

4:30   Byron Holiday, baritone; Ethel Whalen, piano
4:45   Frances Kirch, soprano
5:00   Four Trees Orchestra
5:30   Health Talk
5:35   Four Trees Orchestra
6:00   Scottish Choral Society
6:30   Music
7:00   Pelham Heath Inn Orchestra
7:30   Woodmere Inn Orchestra
8:00   Off for WRW
11:30   Club Kentuck Orchestra

When WFBH staff complained to the management of the Majestic, the hotel reminded them of a clause in their lease that stated, "The programs to be broadcast shall be such as may suitably be broadcast from the roof of a hotel of the standing and reputation of the Hotel Majestic and the [Concourse] Radio Corporation will not permit to be broadcast any program which may in any way interfere with the business of the hotel company, or which is objectionable to the management or guests of the hotel." Paragraph six of the lease pointed out that the Majestic "caters to guests of refinement and social standing." The station had also agreed not to employ anyone objectionable to the hotel. Hotel manager Copeland Townsend explained that criticism of WFBH "has been brought to our attention and it is apparent that there is a strong false impression that the station belongs to us."

The power was turned on a few days later but was again shut off when the offending broadcast was next scheduled. A station engineer ran down to the basement to restore the power but was physically restrained by hotel employees. During a meeting on Thursday, 21 May 1925, the hotel agreed to allow WFBH back on the air until 5:30 P.M., when the health talk was scheduled, and to resume again in the evening. But while this meeting was in progress the power was again shut off, and the scene at the basement switchbox was repeated.

WFBH was able to return. "One reason for permission to broadcast last night," explained the *Times*, citing hotel manager Townsend, "was to allow the speech of Arthur Woods, former Police Commissioner, to go on the air."

The Concourse Radio Corporation sought a restraining order in New York State court against the Majestic, pointing out that their power line was separate from the hotel's electrical system and that the hotel had no right to install a switch on it. While the landlord specifically objected to the health talks as "positively indecent" (Dr. Landis was, in fact, later found guilty of unprofessional practices), Hotel Majestic officials testified that there were other programs they did not want the name of the hotel associated with, including "broadcasting jazz music from the Cotton Club up in the Harlem section, thereby creating the erroneous impression that the music was being played at the Majestic."

The state supreme court denied WFBH an injunction against the hotel. However, the station did obtain a ruling in federal court that its license superseded its lease in the realm of broadcast operation. The Hotel Majestic could not be a censor, but WFBH was obligated to return 5 percent of gross receipts and hadn't paid up and also owed a $300 electric bill.

In the autumn of 1926, George F. George (professional name of clothier George Sultzbach) bought WFBH as well as WRW and organized the Peoples Broadcasting Company. Program director was Eunice Brokenshire, wife of announcer Norman Brokenshire. But the bad luck persisted. On 6 November 1926, the *Herald* radio reviewer Stewart Hawkins wrote in his column:

> Not quite six months ago Station WFBH, at that time one of New York's most graceless radio urchins, passed into new and avowedly reformatory hands. Mr. Georges Jr. the eager, if untutored (?), managing director of the station, promised to eliminate the noxious uncouthness and to set WFBH up among the elite parlor entertainers. Because summer is a lean season for program-picking, and because Mr. Georges so prettily admitted that broadcasting was a bigger business than he had anticipated, this department has not scowled too fiercely at WFBH's still uneradicated blemishes.

Like so many New York radio stations, WFBH took on an entirely new identity. Columnist Hawkins welcomed it in these words: "Tonight WFBH will cease to be WFBH and will henceforth identify itself by the more lisping mouthful WPCH. Freed completely from its inherited bad name, and with the Lewis Reed–Walter Neff–Norman Brokenshire Trio [of announcers] quite at home in their mutual harness, WPCH is presumably ready to knock at the portals of polite society."

WFBH's chief engineer William Reuman went on to found WWRL. In January 1927, the old WFBH facilities in the Hotel Majestic became home to station WGL.

See also WRW, WGL, WPCH.

(1929–1933)

1929	1400kc s/t WCGU, WLTH, WBBC	500w.

On 29 November 1929 the St. George Hotel asked the Federal Radio Commission to reassign the license for its station WSGH to the Paramount Broadcasting Corporation. Studios were established at 1 Nevins Street, the location of the Brooklyn Paramount Theatre.

In September 1931, the FRC was trying to put WEVD off the air and replace it with WFOX (moving it down to 1300 but still sharing with three other stations). Examiner Elmer Pratt lauded WFOX: "WFOX is operated on a commercially successful basis, has well-trained and efficient personnel, has excellent studio and reasonably good transmitter facilities, has rendered and is now rendering a good program and community service, has available sufficient talent for the increased hours and operates substantially in accordance with the commission regulations." But no change was made. In October 1933 WFOX manager Salvatore D'Angelo applied to have the call letters changed to WFWV and then to WVFW.

Sunday, 17 May 1931

12:15 P.M.	Wagner's Juveniles
12:30	East New York Hospital
1:30	Off for WLTH
4:30	Brooklyn Mission
5:00	Erin's Orchestra
5:30	Edmond Day, tenor
6:00	WFOX Trio
6:30	Judge Nathan Sweedler
6:45	Nip and Tuck
7:00	Off for WBBC

See also WVFW.

WFRL

(21 SEPTEMBER 1925–31 JULY 1927)

1925	1460kc	100w.
1926	910kc (unauthorized)	100w.
Apr. 1927	1460kc	250w.
June 1927	1370kc s/t WKBO, WKBQ, WBNY	250w.

Flatbush Radio Laboratories at 1421 E. Tenth Street was operated by Robert Lacey and James A. Bergner. In the fall of 1925 they put up station WFRL and brought in Charles Burke to manage the station. It was a small but aggressive enterprise. When radio entered a period of suspended regulation in 1926, WFRL reassigned itself to 910kc and occupied that frequency for five months until the new Federal Radio Commission sent it back to 1460. Unhappy with the commission's actions, WFRL was a leader in organizing the smaller stations in the New York area to formally protest to Washington.

Sunday, 24 July 1927

8:00 P.M.	Elliot Sisters
8:30	Peggy Jordan, songs
8:40	Billy Sticks, songs
8:50	Josephine Clancy, songs
9:00	Russell Howard, piano
9:15	Pauline Wilkinson
9:30	Fique concert

In May 1927 WFRL moved to the Strand Danceland building at 635 Fulton Street. Direct pickups from the popular dance hall were a regular part of the station's schedule. In July of that year, however, the station was sold to the Leverich Towers Hotel and became WLTH.

See also WLTH.

WFYI

(1959–1965)

1959	1520kc. (daytime)	10,000w.

For your information, the *New York Herald-Tribune*'s radio network reached into Long Island. The four-station chain, based at WVIP in Mount Kisco, was organized by *Tribune* owner and Manhasset resident John Hay Whitney. Station WKIT hadn't yet officially changed hands when the network service began on 3 March 1959, but after the purchase, the power of the new WFYI was increased from 250 to 10,000 watts through a new directional antenna erected on "Jock" Whitney's property. The studios remained at the Roosevelt Field Shopping Center.

For most of the broadcast day WFYI carried music and *Herald-Tribune* news and features piped down from Mount Kisco with only local breakaways for Long Island news.

When the *Tribune* folded, WFYI was again a local station. A new information program, "Long Island A.M.," started the day, and "Musicana" continued till sunset. Whitney attempted to turn WFYI into a classical-music station, but facing the growing popularity of FM and the loss of the news resources of his newspaper, in 1965 he sold his Long Island station and it became WTHE.

See also WKIT, WVIP, WTHE.

WGBB

(15 DECEMBER 1924–JANUARY 1988)
(1 APRIL 1991–)

1924	1230kc	150w.
1927	1220kc s/t WAAT, WSOM	400w.
1928	1210kc s/t WINR, WCOJ, WJBI	100w.
1941	1240kc s/t WFAS	100w.
1956	1240kc.	250w.
1962	1240kc.	1,000w.

"Long Island's First Station" was founded by one of Long Island's oldest families. The Carmans came from Hemel Hempstead, England, to settle Hempstead, Long Island in the mid–1600s. In the early twentieth century some of their descendants owned a grocery store on Merrick Road in Rockville Center. Wireless became an avocation in the Carman family before World War I. Beartreas Carman, a Western Union telegrapher, operated amateur station 2AUQ; her brother Harry was 2EL. The Carman kids shared war dispatches and election returns with their neighbors in Freeport and invited friends over to hear the Dempsey-Carpentier fight in 1921. Soon the grocery store was displaying a line of Grebe radio gear, and Harry was ready to give up butchering for broadcasting.

The 100-watt station was assigned call letters WGBB— they would later say it was "Where Good Broadcasting Begins," but the initials were merely the next entry on the Commerce Department's alphabetical list—and signed on from the garage behind the Carman residence at 215 Bedell Street in Freeport. The antenna was hung from two wooden poles in the backyard. During the summer of 1927 WGBB's power was raised to 400 watts, and it was moved to 1220kc to share time with WAAT/Newark and WSOM/New York. In November 1928, WGBB was ordered to shift to 1210kc and divide the new frequency with several small suburban stations. Transmitter power was also trimmed back to 100 watts. "The Voice of the Sunrise Trail" was losing its potential to become a station with metropolitan reach. Carman protested to the FRC, citing WGBB's cooperation with the Girl Scouts as an indication of its public service. The commission offered praise but no relief.

Wednesday, 13 June 1928

7:00 P.M.	Lynbrook Merchants' Program
8:00	Marie Becker, piano
8:15	Girl Scout Program
8:30	F.W. Richard, baritone
8:45	Neger-Mead recital
9:00	Correct time
9:01	Hoffman and Curley, songs
9:30	Harry Gillen, baritone

9:45	Studio program
10:00	Dance program
11:00	off for WEVD

Despite the imposed limitations, in 1931 WGBB demonstrated that it was more than a family's avocation when studios were moved from the residence to the Freeport Post Office building at 64 South Grove Street (now Guy Lombardo Avenue). The transmitter remained in the Carman backyard. In 1937 WGBB relocated to a spacious loft at 44 S. Grove. During most of the 1930s, WGBB shared time with WFAS/White Plains and WGNY/Newburgh. Long Island, Westchester, and the lower Hudson Valley each had only one radio station, and they had to take turns on the air.

Harry Carman was a devoted but parsimonious owner. He was known to work an air shift himself, using more than once voice in an attempt to give the impression of a larger announcing staff. WGBB's main control booth contained an audio board, a microphone, and turntables placed so far apart that air personnel were forced to introduce a recording, walk to the board, shut off the microphone, walk to the turntable, start the record, return to the control panel and bring up the volume, later turn down the volume, step back to the microphone … and so on for hours. This procedure surely gave WGBB a sluggish sound and wore out a lot of shoe leather. One hot summer day Carman took pity on announcer Mike Sands, who was pacing the sweltering studio (which wasn't air conditioned); Carman went on a mission of mercy and returned to hand the suffering man a dripping ice cream cone.

Low power and languid pace hardly mattered as long as WGBB enjoyed a monopoly in its market. News director John Frogge presented his authoritative "News of Nassau" for a quarter-century. Bandleader Guy Lombardo, a Freeport resident, was an occasional guest. In 1941, WGBB and WFAS

Freeport resident and bandleader Guy Lombardo was a frequent guest on WGBB.

were reassigned from 1210 to 1240kc, and on Monday, 22 March 1943, WFAS moved down to 1230. After more than eighteen years on the air, WGBB was finally a full-time broadcaster.

In 1946, Carman erected a 290-foot vertical antenna at his Bedell Street property. New studio equipment was also installed in a professionally efficient arrangement; the station's old carbon mike was made into a lamp and mounted beside the modern Gates console. Upgrading was necessary, since after 1947 WGBB was no longer the only radio voice on the island.

Carman was gravely injured in an auto accident shortly before Christmas 1953 and died in July 1954. Murray Evans, WGBB's long-time sales manager, took over direction of the station until it was purchased for $95,000 by a group of Long Island businessmen led by the new station manager, John Whitmore. At the time the Carman era ended, Long Island's "First Station" was still filling much of its broadcast day with electrical transcriptions ("Now fifteen minutes of music by Tony Lane and his Airlane Trio…") and with aging 78-rpm discs. The new owners quickly updated programming, most notably adding the "Night Train" doo-wop session with Lee Donahue and then Alan Fredericks to the evening hours on "Nassau County's only day and night station."

In February 1956, the FCC granted WGBB permission to increase power to 250 watts. It had been the last station in the New York area, and one of the last in the country, to operate with only 100 watts. Carman had earlier discouraged the FCC from authorizing a power increase, which would have required an expensive transmitter upgrade. A station legend claimed that Carman had even turned down an offer to boost WGBB's power to 50 kilowatts to fill the need for another major coastal station. The story reflected a staff attitude that Carman and program director Ada Cheesman had all they could do to keep their centiwatt going.

In August 1956 WGBB was again sold, this time to Edward Fitzgerald Sr., the owner of WGSM in Huntington, and it became part of the Long Island Network (WALK/Patchogue and WRIV/Riverhead were affiliated but carried few programs). The stations were individually programmed, although news director Bill Goddard set up the network's news headquarters in Freeport. During the late 1950s, WGBB participated in a groundbreaking technical experiment. Operating with the experimental call sign KE2XSS, WGBB chopped its signal in half and broadcast in compatible single-sideband (AM stations normally send out twin signal patterns carrying audio information on each side of the carrier wave). Listeners reported that they couldn't tell the difference; WGBB had demonstrated that adjacent "local channel" stations could run higher power, and in 1962 it went to 1,000 watts.

Fitzgerald would regularly offer his stations for sale just to see how much they were worth, and in 1965 he accepted a bid from Susquehanna Broadcasting and sold WGBB for

Bill Jaker on the air at WGBB, 1960. Photo by Bette Barr.

$452,000. The new absentee owner moved the studios from Grove Street to "1240 Broadcast Plaza" on Brooklyn Avenue in the neighboring village of Merrick. WGBB continued to identify itself as being in Freeport.

WGBB's programming evolved from a middle-of-the-road music policy in the 1960s and 1970s to "adult contemporary" and then hard rock by the 1980s. In 1981 it was purchased for slightly more than one million dollars by the owners of WBAB AM/FM in Babylon, Long Island, and both stations were sold again to Noble Broadcasting five years later. In 1987 it went to a news-talk format. Then in January 1988 the owners changed the call letters to WBAB (WBAB-AM had become WNYG) to merely rebroadcast WBAB-FM. Seventeen staffers were laid off and held a farewell gathering in front of Broadcast Plaza.

The historic call WGBB disappeared from the dial for three and a half years—they had been the last sequentially assigned call letters still in use in the New York area—but were restored in April 1991 when its news/talk format again became separately programmed. Studios were still housed with WBAB in West Babylon, but the transmitter remained in Freeport, at the spot where Harry and Beartreas Carman had strung up their ham radio aerials during the second decade of the twentieth century.

WGBS

24 OCTOBER 1924–14 JANUARY 1932)

1924	950kc	500w.
1927	860kc s/t WAAM	500w.
1928	1180kc s/t WIP, WOO (Phila.)	500w.
1929	600kc s/t WACA (Conn.)	500w.
1931	1180kc.	500w.

Gimbel Brothers Department Store on Thirty-fourth Street and Eighth Avenue—right across from arch-rival Macy's—was one of radio's earliest advertisers. In March 1922 Gimbel's put station WIP on the air from its store in Philadelphia. The Gimbel program on WEAF beginning 1 March 1923 was the first time a sponsor bought time from the toll broadcaster for a musical show (Gimbel Brothers was WEAF's biggest client during its first year). The series originated from a radio exhibit at the store. Soon Gimbel's followed the example of Wanamaker, Bamberger, and numerous stores around the United States: it ran an antenna across its roof and built a showcase studio downstairs. On 17 July 1924 the *New York Times* wrote:

> The entire station, including the studio in which the artists perform, the transmitting room and power room, will be in a glass enclosure, so that the public can see how broadcasting is done and how the apparatus functions. Each instrument will be labeled and its purpose briefly explained. Visitors will be allowed in the studio when programs are being sent into the air and a special receiving room will be provided which will enable people to gather and hear important events broadcast by various stations.

Saturday, 7 August 1926

1:30 P.M.	Scripture reading
1:35	Milton Yokeman, tenor, Evelyn Hurst, soprano
2:05	Radio Gym Class
2:15	The Four Tars
3:00	Orchestra selections
	Off for WAHG
6:00	Uncle Geebee
6:30	Oscar Blank, tenor
6:45	Perla Amado & Henriette Chevillon, Spanish duet
7:00	Officers of SS Chantler on Polar expedition
7:15	Baseball and news items
7:20	Ukelele Bob MacDonald
7:30	Hyman Novick, baritone
7:45	George Hall's Arcadians
8:45	Clifford Cheasley, "Philosophy of Numbers"
9:00	Pauline Watson, violinist; classic dance
9:30	Nassau County hour
10:30	Arrowhead Dance Orchestra

WGBS's premiere broadcast on 24 October 1924 was one of radio's classiest opening nights. Eddie Cantor was the master of ceremonies, and the guests included George Gershwin, Rudolf Friml, Cliff (Ukelele Ike) Edwards, Rube Goldberg, the Dolly Sisters, and the Vincent Lopez Orchestra. Isaac Gimbel welcomed listeners. The program was fed to sister station WIP. Two days later WGBS presented a rare, early broadcast of a Broadway play, Morris Gest's production of *The Miracle*. When the Ziegfeld Theater opened, WGBS covered the event, including scenes from the play *Rio Rita*. Sylvia Golden, the assistant editor of *Theatre Magazine*, interviewed such luminaries as Eva LaGalliene and Sophie Tucker. This was radio fare as fine as could be found anywhere.

In the October 1925 edition of WGBS's program magazine *On the Air*, station manager Dailey Paskman set out the Gimbel station's philosophy: "We are distinctly a noncommercial station. We do not sell time to advertisers who put on orchestras or artists to feature the name of some canned goods or merchandise. Gimbel Brothers derive as the sole benefit from the operation of WGBS the feeling that they are helping to further the cause of radio—to help develop it to a point where it will be treated eventually with the serious consideration commensurate with its merit."

Paskman believed that radio entertainment was already becoming cut-and-dried. In the quest for serious consideration and freshness, he organized the Radio Minstrels. This retro outfit performed on WGBS and toured the country, drawing nostalgic audiences in the South.

In February 1926 the WGBS transmitter was carried from the store and installed in Astoria, directly across the East River from Carl Shurz Park. The improved facilities included the latest in metering equipment and a recording device to monitor distress signals. Back at the store, WGBS added a second studio "so that one orchestra may be tuning up and be in readiness to broadcast immediately after its predecessor has gone off the air, thus doing away with one of the worst nuisances of radio," the long pauses between programs. WGBS believed it was the first broadcaster to originate a program from an airplane; it was involved in early transatlantic shortwave tests and presented shows direct from the ocean liner *Leviathan*.

Also in 1926, WGBS instituted a regular network connection with WIP as well as a link to a studio in Atlantic City. As the radio industry burgeoned, WGBS seemed in the perfect position to become one of the nation's major broadcasters. On 28 November 1928, Gimbels reorganized its radio operation as the General Broadcasting System (GBS) and, with WGBS and WIP as key stations, planned to spread across the country. It also presented some of the first transcribed programs—initially using a wax-recording device called a "homophone"—which the station manager recognized as an alternative to the network. On 1 December, the *Herald-Tribune* wrote:

> Mr. Paskman does not believe that recorded programs will compete with chain broadcasting. Despite his views on the advantage of transcriptions he pointed out that WGBS is still going ahead with its plans for a wire-line chain hookup. "Of course the chains will still have their place," Mr. Paskman continued, "for as elaborate and interesting as electrically transcribed programs may be, there is a certain thrill for the listeners in knowing that the persons to whom they are listening are actually in the studio."

But GBS's plans for a national network—Paskman's dream that "later on, of course, we will bring in television"—were thwarted by the Federal Radio Commission, which assigned the Gimbel stations in New York and Philadelphia to share time on 860 kilocycles, undermining them in both markets. On 10 October 1931, Dailey Paskman, J.W. Loeb, and Fred Gimbel sold WGBS to William Randolph Hearst, who in 1932 changed the call letters to WINS.

See also WINS, WICC.

WGCP

(MAY 1925–1933)

1925	1070kc	500w.
1926	1190kc	500w.
1927	1250kc s/t WAAM, WODA, WNJ	500w.

In 1925 Donald W. May moved his station WBS from the Mullins Furniture Store in Newark to the palmier environs of the Grand Central Palace and Clover Garden, a giant exhibit hall that ran from Lexington to Park Avenue between Forty-sixth and Forty-seventh Streets in Manhattan. Designed along the same lines as the neighboring Grand Central Terminal and referred to as "New York's perpetual circus tent," Grand Central Palace hosted a constant parade of industrial exhibitions, as well as the motorboat show, auto show, flower show, sportsmen's show, and many more. The first New York Radio Exposition was held there during the last week of 1922. Attractions at the Palace drew over two million visitors a year.

The WBS call letters were changed to WGCP, and Grand Central Palace management assured potential clients that the station's facilities "can be harnessed to the interests" of the current exhibitors.

But "The Four Leaf Clover Station" remained licensed to Newark, with headquarters at the Mullins store at 325 Central

Avenue. May had transferred control of the station to manager James Shearer, a veteran vaudeville performer, who programmed it in a livelier manner than the Grand Central Palace.

Wednesday, 6 June 1928

9:00 A.M.	Theatre Program
10:00	Off for WNJ, WAAM
3:30 P.M.	Irving Porter, songs
4:00	Joy Hour
5:00	Dance Music
5:30	Alice from Wonderland
6:00	Telecrone Time
6:00	Off for WAAM
8:00	Rutherford Orchestra
8:55	Holly Park
9:00	Musical Bankers
9:30	Jimmy Shearer, songs; time
10:00	Off for WNJ

Congressman Frederick Lehlbach (R-N.J.), ranking member of the House Committee on Merchant Marine and Fisheries—which drafted the Radio Act of 1927—went before the FRC on 18 July 1928 on behalf of WGCP. He was asked if all New Jersey stations should remain on the crowded air but begged off an answer. He said that WGCP served 750,000 people and thought three stations in Newark should be enough. The city of Newark had an advertising contract with WGCP, but WODA and WAAM wanted WGCP off their frequency. The political dispute resulted in victory for WGCP.

When the Grand Central Palace withdrew from operation of WGCP in 1933, owner Jimmy Shearer continued to broadcast for another thirty years with call letters WHBI.

See also WBS, WHBI.

WGL

(30 JANUARY 1927–15 SEPTEMBER 1928)

Jan. 1927	422.7m (710kc)	1,000w.
June 1927	1020kc s/t WODA	1,000w.

Less than two months after WFBH was shut down, terminating its uneasy relationship with the Hotel Majestic, a new station went on the air from the swanky hotel on Central Park West at Seventy-second Street. Hotel manager Copeland Townsend had objected to WFBH's programming, stating that it often gave listeners the impression that the station was owned by the Majestic. WGL was owned by the International Broadcasting Corporation, and Townsend was named to the station's advisory board.

The Radio Act of 1927 was moving toward passage when WGL went on the air, and frequency assignments still did not have the force of law. The announcement of WGL's inaugural program invited listeners to "tune in at about 422 meters. Definite wavelength will be announced later."

WGL president Colonel Lewis Landes stated on the station's inaugural broadcast, "The International Broadcasting Corporation's aim is to adhere to truth, to be free of partisanship, religious or political." But by opening its microphones to a broad range of speakers, WGL was often embroiled in controversy and confusion during its twenty months on the air. WGL quickly found itself in the midst of a dispute between two of Ireland's major political figures, Liam Cosgrave and Eamon de Valera. After de Valera delivered a St. Patrick's Day speech over WGL, Cosgrave cabled a response, which WGL read after omitting personal attacks on the future president of Ireland.

Thursday, 10 November 1927

10:00 A.M.	News flashes
10:15	Sports talk
10:30	Vegetable market
10:45	Food talk
11:00	Radio instruments
11:30	Uplift Hour
12:00 Noon	Off for WODA
2:00	Sports features
2:15	Cele Green, songs
2:30	Travel talk
2:45	Wilson and Addie, duets
3:00	Bamboo Revue
3:30	General hints
4:00	Off for WODA
6:00	Time; news; racing
6:05	Variety music
6:25	American Legion series
6:35	Grizzle, Rudolph, duets
6:50	C. Levy
7:00	Medical Centre series
7:10	Burke's Varieties
7:35	Belais white gold
7:40	Flying school
7:50	Georgette Nyriele, songs
7:55	Today in History; lost children
8:00	Talk—Prof. B. F. Gilman
8:15	Wright's Orchestra

WGL appears to have been unaware of the potential for controversy. On Monday, 2 May 1927, an impromptu pacifist speech by Mary H. Ford at a banquet of the All Nations Association was censored by the station. Ford wasn't cut off but was instead drowned out by a studio orchestra. "We let her continue to actuate the microphone," explained WGL studio manager Charles Isaacson, but "the music was much louder than the voice, and therefore sounded like two programs overlapping [a common phenomenon on unselective older receivers] with the orchestra blanketing the voice, so that no one could understand the pacifist plea." He told the *Times*, "No protests have been received ... except from Mrs. Ford."

Later that same week, WGL canceled the broadcast of the play "*Spread Eagle*," another pacifist statement that had found its way onto the station's lineup. "This action was decided upon after due consideration of criticism made by veterans organizations," explained Col. Landes, "and as this company consists mainly of veterans of the World War, it will under no circumstances broadcast anything that has not the full endorsement of veterans and patriotic organizations." (After being turned down by several stations, *Spread Eagle* was finally heard over WPCH on 6 June 1927 at 11:15 P.M.)

WGL's programming could be very offbeat. Among the features on the schedule were "Jack Clark, radio tapper" (tap dancing was popular on the radio for many years), lectures on phrenology (a pseudo-science purporting to reveal personal character by feeling bumps on the skull), and "Columbia University Yells and Cheers" (no game, just Columbia students in the studio yelling and cheering). There's no record that the Hotel Majestic ever complained.

In search of good reviews, Landes invited New York's radio editors to suggest a program. Stewart Hawkins of the *Herald-Tribune* declined and wrote, "WGL, at present, is busily disseminating inaccurate facsimiles of sound, without tonal fullness or beauty."

WGL shared time uneasily with WBBR, and on 26 April 1927 both stations were heard operating on the same wavelength at the same time. WGL had earlier refused to share with WHAP. In May, 1927 WGL was the first station to protest reallocations by the new Federal Radio Commission, calling into question the assignment of ten New York area stations on five different frequencies. It had been sent to 1170kc instead of the 720 it wanted. WOR was awarded 710, and both stations journeyed to Washington to defend their positions, complete with witnesses (U.S. Senator Royal Copeland testified for WGL but also praised WOR). WOR was favored, since it had been operating since 1922 and had "a record of unique popularity in New York and vicinity," according to Commissioner Orestes Caldwell when questioned by Lewis Landes, who was a lawyer. In the midst of the dispute with WOR, Charles Isaacson disclosed that both stations had been approached by Paramount Pictures as a New York outlet of a radio network proposed by the movie studio.

On 14 June 1927 WGL and WMSG filed suit in federal court in the District of Columbia seeking to have the Radio Act of 1927 declared unconstitutional. WMSG later stepped back from demanding court action, and WGL was alone before the court in arguing that its new frequency assignment had the effect of depriving it of property without compensation. It also raised some fine points about the way the FRC was constituted.

Meanwhile, WGL was interfering with WODA, signing on five or ten minutes before the time-sharer in Paterson left the air. Listeners complained to the FRC, and some members of the commission suspected that WGL was trying to set up a situation that would challenge its authority. But the suit was withdrawn in August, and no action was taken against WGL.

Perhaps to keep controversy under control, WGL turned to another dimension for its programming. On the night of 13 July 1927, Rev. Mary Freeman of the Liberty Spiritualist Church beckoned the spirits of Voltaire, Woodrow Wilson, and murder victim Albert Snyder. WGL prepared the studio to Freeman's specifications, dimming the lights and setting out drums, a bell, a cello, and other objects that would vibrate in response to messages from the beyond. WGL listeners heard various sounds, which Rev. Freeman later interpreted as ambiguous messages. On 1 August a second experiment was conducted, with noises emanating for a half-hour from an empty, darkened studio. On 21 August 1927 Charles Isaacson announced one of the city's first attempts at local news coverage. WGL was organizing listeners to volunteer as radio reporters and call the station with breaking news stories. "If it sounds worthwhile we will immediately put it on the air." By now WGL was striving to be commercially successful and hired the Theatre Sales Company as its agency. Twenty-four announcements of one hundred words cost $47.50. The company said it was to receive $30 of the $47.50 and sued for $32,812 in damages, charging that the International Broadcasting Corporation had broken its agreement. WGL stopped dealing with the company.

Despite its ambitious programming and distinctive three-letter call, WGL left the air in late 1928, to be replaced by WOV.

See also WFBH, WOV.

WGLI

(1 SEPTEMBER 1958–1989)

| 1958 | 1290kc. | 1,000w. |
| 1966 | 1290kc. | 5,000w. |

WGLI was established in Babylon, Long Island, by one of the veterans of New York radio, WWRL founder William Reuman, along with WWRL's longtime station manager Edith Dick and program director Fred Barr. It was just the second AM station on the Island, after WGBB, to broadcast day and night, and was the first suburban station to adopt a Top 40 rock-and-roll format (only WINS, WMCA, and WMGM in the city were then specializing in the new sound). Among the personalities on WGLI during its early days were

Alan Fredericks, who kept his "Night Train" stoked with doo-wop records, and former WINS overnight deejay Jerry Warren.

Reuman also started WTFM at 103.5Mc to relay programming from his station WRFM in New York. When off-air FM pickup proved too fluttery in Babylon due to interference from traffic at the nearby Republic Aviation airport, the network plan was scuttled, and WTFM continued simply rebroadcasting WGLI. (News concluded with the latest forecast from "the Wigli Witfum Weather Bureau".)

In 1966 Reuman's Long Island Broadcasting Company sold WGLI to Martin F. Beck, who moved studios from the Madison Avenue transmitter to 1290 Peconic Avenue in Babylon. But programming didn't change, and in fact, WGLI continued to play Top 40 longer than almost any other New York area station. In the mid 1970s it stepped back to a middle-of-the-road nostalgia format and also added extensive sports coverage with Islanders hockey and New York Mets baseball.

WGLI went through several changes of ownership in the 1980s, trying an oldies and chat format. In 1986 it was purchased by Noble Broadcasting, which programmed it with album rock. But the Long Island dial was already over-populated, with the AM audience declining, and the best offer Noble received for its 1290kHz property was from the owner of WADO at 1280. In 1989 the New York Spanish-language broadcaster bought WGLI with the sole purpose of clearing away interference from an adjacent frequency. A station with distinguished parentage and a powerful potential went silent.

WGMU *see* WAHG

WGOP *see* WIBI

WGRC *see* WRRC

WGSM

(1 September 1951–)

| 1951 | 740kc. (daytime) | 1,000w. |
| 1980 | 740kHz(daytime) | 25,000w. |

WGSM was the first radio station to go on the air in Suffolk County, Long Island, since the demise of WRST/Bay Shore in the early 1930s. The Huntington-Montauk Broadcasting Company was founded by advertising executives Byron Sammis and Edward Fitzgerald. The corporate name suggested a signal spreading the entire length of the county (Sammis' home was in Montauk), but the "World's Greatest Suburban Market" initially covered by WGSM was imposing: western Suffolk, the North Shore of Nassau County, and sections of Westchester and southern Connecticut.

The first day on the air was also impressive. Among the guests who dropped by or recorded greetings were musicians Duke Ellington, Vaughn Monroe, Benny Goodman, and Mindy Carson, baseball stars Leo Durocher, Roy Campanella, Gil Hodges, and Carl Furillo, and political leaders including Allen Dulles, who would later become director of the CIA.

At 740kc ("Seven-four-oh on your radio"), WGSM benefited from being right in the middle of the four big New York network flagship stations. Studios were on New York Avenue in Huntington's central business district. The station's original program director and morning man was Jack Ellsworth, who would later take charge of WALK and then own WLIM. Another early staffer was Walter Nieman, who went on to manage WQXR. Among the air personalities during WGSM's first decade were Dave Rosehill, Bruce Herbert, and Lee Carle. Joe Roberts took over the wakeup show, and Ray Adell became program director and station manager as well as presenting the "Fisherman's Forecaster," an institution for anglers on the island for more than twenty-five years.

In addition to its news service, WGSM had one of radio's most forthright editorial policies. In 1980, station manager Richard Scholem delivered over one hundred editorials, including several that bit the hands feeding it by criticizing the Huntington Chamber of Commerce and local businesspeople. Said Scholem when he accepted an award for his editorials from the New York State Broadcasters' Association, "You can't be a nervous Nelly." National talk show host Alan Colmes got his start working part-time at WGSM while a student at Hofstra University.

The 1980 increase in power planted WGSM's signal even more firmly in the world's greatest suburban market, though its required directional antenna restricted it to the north and east. With the sale to Greater Media Inc., WGSM became a sister station to WPEN in Philadephia and adopted its big-band and standards format, which remained after the station was sold to WGSM president Gary Starr in 1994.
See also WGBB.

WHAP

(26 March 1925–29 April 1932)

1925	1250kc	500w.
1926	various frequencies	500w.
1927	1270kc s/t WMSG	500w.
1928	1010kc s/t WBNY, WODA	500w.
1929	1300kc s/t WEVD, WBBR	500w.

The Defenders of Truth Society stated that WHAP stood for "We Hold America Protestant" but it could just as easily have meant "We Hate All Papists." The society and their station were overtly prejudiced and virulently anti–Catholic as well as anti–Semitic.

WHAP was constantly embroiled in religious and social controversy. It was established by followers of Augusta Emma Stetson, for many years the closest disciple of Mary Baker Eddy, the founder of Christian Science. In 1903, under "Gussie" Stetson's leadership, Christian Scientists built an impressive church at Ninety-sixth Street and Central Park West. But in 1909 Stetson was excommunicated, with "malpractice, perverted sexual teaching [and] self-deification" among the many charges of "unscientific practice." She continued her ministry at her church near the park and retained a following despite powerful objections by mainline Christian Scientists. The station stated it would be operated "in cooperation with the ideas of Mrs. Augusta E. Stetson," although Stetson insisted she had no ties to WHAP management.

Wednesday, 25 May 1927

1:00 P.M.	J.W. Erb, organ; Irene Perceval, harp; Marion Kener, soprano
2:00	Sacred program
2:25	WHAP Madrigal Singers
2:45	Sybil Huse, reading
3:15	Dorothy Hoyle, violin
3:35	Cruelty to Animals—Mary Price
4:00	Dorothy Hoyle, violin; Vida Milholland, soprano
4:35	Franklin Ford, news
5:00	Talk—Hickman Price

The original licensee of WHAP was the W.H. Taylor Finance Company (William H. Taylor was a board member at Stetson's church). The first studios were at 426 W. Thirty-first Street in Brooklyn, and when WHAP moved to 393 Seventh Avenue in Manhattan, the management asserted that it would "depart from the neutral and passive attitude generally maintained by broadcasting stations, as it has definite convictions, which will be expressed on the air." The convictions were most often those expressed by station manager Franklin A. Ford. Ford was a Princeton graduate and a newspaper and advertising writer as well as a composer. He would earn a reputation as a professional bigot.

In April 1926 WHAP moved its studios and offices to 9 W. Ninety-sixth Street, site of both Stetson's church and the headquarters of the Defenders of Truth. The *Times* described the setup: "The main floor will be used as a reception room, with the control room and batteries in a separate room in the rear. On the second floor are two large broadcasting studios, both completely equipped and thoroughly soundproof with monk's cloth. The ceilings as well as the walls are covered to destroy echoes and the floors are heavily carpeted. Silent but powerful ventilators will provide fresh air in the studios.... Microphones will be suspended from the ceiling to protect them from jars and 'carbon packing' instead of being on floor stands. The third floor is occupied by business offices of the station."

WHAP saw itself spreading education and culture, but more typical of its programs were "Lectures in Political Romanism." These talks were also published in pamphlet form ("Governor Smith kissed the cardinal's ring in City Hall!"), and each pamphlet concluded with an appeal for support. This is from the back page of the lecture on "Mussolini's Persecution of Freemasons":

> The work which station WHAP is carrying on, is for the benefit of every Protestant American. The welfare of the United States of America, and the protection of its traditional principles, is involved. Will *you* do your part in this fight for Americanism?... The loyal and wide-awake patriots, who understand these issues, are helping us to finance station WHAP. Its cost for running expenses is high; we have no commercial income; we do not and shall not "sell time" to business firms, because we must not be hampered, as to policy, by commercial dictation.... Let us all contribute what we can, be it little or much, to support this vital work, in defense of our country and its vital ideals.

For Franklin Ford, the defense of vital ideals became the defense of his personal political and religious views. Ford was banned from jury duty in December 1926 because the defense attorney was convinced that he would be prejudiced against the defendant, who was black. Enraged at this rejection, Ford took to WHAP to offer trial judge Otto Rosefsky fifteen minutes of airtime on Christmas Eve to comment. The judge didn't appear.

Meanwhile, the schism between Augusta Stetson's brand of Christian Science and the mother Church continued. William H. Taylor and his wife were expelled in 1922, and in 1927 a federal appeals court in Boston dismissed their lawsuit against the church. Also in 1927, the Christian Scientists' publishing arm issued a circular denouncing the anti–Catholic and anti–Jewish broadcasts from WHAP, a station "conducted by a group of persons using the term 'Christian Science' without authority." It wasn't the only outrage they heard from New York. Stetson was predicting that Mary Baker Eddy would soon return to life, and she even claimed immortality for herself.

Not unexpectedly, controversy surrounding the Defenders of Truth could interfere in the operations of WHAP. During a time when small stations were expected to work out time-sharing arrangements on their frequency, WHAP was rejected as a partner on the dial by several broadcasters, including WGL and the Catholic Church's station WLWL.

The ultimate in public protest may have come in a letter from U.S. Representative Sol Bloom to Mayor Jimmy Walker in April 1927. Noting the limitations of the new federal Radio Act and his personal distaste for censorship, the Manhattan congressman nonetheless recommended that the city exercise its power to control incendiary "public utterance within its jurisdiction." Bloom wanted the city of New York to declare WHAP a public nuisance. "At an earlier day Station WHAP's present speakers could have reached only a street corner crowd," wrote Congressman Bloom. "If this nuisance is not abated, we may also expect that Station WHAP will have imitators." Despite many such complaints, the city could take no legal action.

In November 1927 WHAP moved its transmitter from the Printerian Building at 406 W. Thirty-first Street to a site in Carlstadt, N.J. Studios were relocated to 154 W. Fifty-seventh Street, the Carnegie Hall building. The improved signal carried shrill attacks against Democratic presidential candidate Al Smith, a Roman Catholic. But WHAP lost a powerful voice in 1928 when Augusta Stetson, then eighty-five years old, told listeners: "I have decided to withdraw from the microphone and rise still higher into the wholly spiritual work of mental reflection. To my air audience I say, 'Listen for my mental voice in the wholly spiritual chambers of thought.'" Despite her predictions, Stetson died in October 1928.

Ford later tried to purchase WOAX in Trenton and move it to Camden, aiming to spread his message to the Philadelphia area. This transaction was supported by members of the Masonic and Loyal Orange orders but was protested by Catholic and Protestant churches as well as Camden city officials and did not take place. In 1932 station WHAP was sold and became WFAB. The church on Central Park West was transferred to the mainstream Church of Christ, Scientist.

WHBI

(1933—MARCH 1962)

1933	1250 kc s/t WAAM, WODA	
	(1934-41 s/tWNEW)	100 w.
1941	1280 kc s/t WOV	2,500 w.

WHBI was one of radio's longest-lived part-time stations. It belonged to James L. Shearer, a musician and music publisher who was reputed to possess the world's largest collection of sheet music, which he once peddled by riding around Newark playing the piano on the back of a flatbed truck. Shearer went into radio in 1922, singing over WJZ from its Waldorf-Astoria studios. He was manager of the D.W. May Company's WGCP; he later came to own the station and changed the call letters to WHBI to reflect an unusual change in operations.

WHBI was named for its landlord. The letters stood for Hoyt Brothers Inc., a chemical manufacturer that owned a warehouse at 100 Shipman Street. Hoyt Brothers had no share in the ownership—the corporate name of May Radio Broadcasting was never changed—but allowed Shearer to occupy a loft free of charge in return for the constant promotion: "WHBI, Hoyt Brothers, Incorporated, in Newark." Studios were located on the seventh floor of the warehouse,

accessible by freight elevator; the lobby resembled a beer garden, complete with plastic vines.

Sunday, 16 November 1941

7:00 A.M.	Musical program
7:30	Uncle Pete and Louise
8:00	Goodwill Mission
9:00	Rev. Cornelius Stam
9:30	Mission program
9:50	Music
10:00	Off for WNEW
12:30	Music
1:00	Jimmy Shearer, songs
1:30	Music
2:45	Hoffman Sisters, songs
3:00	Variety Hour
4:00	Goodwill Mission
4:30	Back to God
5:00	Gospel Hour
6:00	Gospel Services
6:30	Off for WNEW
9:05	Jimmy Shearer
10:00	Brookdale Baptist Church
11:00	Words and Music
11:15	Dance Music to 2

At first, WHBI broadcast on Sundays and Monday nights, sharing time with WAAM in Newark and WODA in Paterson. When these two stations merged to form WNEW in 1934, many more radio dials were parked in place

General advertising air time basic rate without talent.

CLASS A

		1 time	13 times	26 times	52 times
Sunday	12:30 P.M. to 6:30 P.M.				
Monday	8:00 P.M. to 10:00 P.M. S				
1 Hour		350.00	332.50	315.00	297.50
½ Hour		210.00	199.50	189.00	178.50
¼ Hour		140.00	133.00	126.00	119.00
5 minutes		87.50	83.12	78.75	74.37

CLASS B

		1 time	13 times	26 times	52 times
Sunday	7 A.M. to 10 A.M.				
Sunday	9 P.M. to 12 midnight				
Monday	2 P.M. to 5 P.M.				
1 Hour		200.00	190.00	180.00	170.00
½ Hour		120.00	114.00	108.00	102.00
¼ Hour		80.00	76.00	72.00	68.00
5 minutes		50.00	47.50	45.00	42.50

CLASS C

Sunday 12 midnight to 7 A.M. Monday

	1 time	13 times	26 times	52 times
1 Hour	130.00	123.50	117.00	110.50
½ Hour	78.00	74.10	70.20	66.30
¼ Hour	52.00	49.40	46.80	44.20
5 minutes	32.00	30.40	28.80	27.20

1 MINUTE ANNOUNCEMENTS

	1 time	13 times	26 times	52 times
CLASS A	25.00	23.75	22.50	21.25
CLASS B	15.00	14.25	13.50	12.75
CLASS C	10.00	9.50	9.00	8.50

This is what it "officially" cost to advertise on WHBI in 1938.

to also hear WHBI. Jimmy Shearer played the same style of music as WNEW and tried to capitalize on the shared time by referring to his spot on the dial as "the metropolitan popularity wave-length."

WHBI was not an easy station to listen to. For most of its history, the signal radiated from a wire antenna atop the Hoyt warehouse, and for many years there was an annoying hum on the station's audio. Its equipment was so undependable that for a while in March 1936 WHBI had to operate through WNEW's transmitter. A 1938 radio critic called its programming "entertainment that consists mostly of phonograph records (scratchy and with poor quality)—and wheezy athsmatic groans."

When WNEW and WOV, then jointly owned, swapped frequencies in December 1941, WHBI found itself sharing time with an ethnic broadcaster and took the opportunity to play to Newark's growing black population. Monday-night broadcast time was dropped in favor of twenty-four continuous hours on Sundays. From 6 A.M. till 4 A.M., WHBI broadcast church services, commonly originating from a different church every half hour. Four crews worked through the day, leapfrogging between churches, often simply feeding music and voices through a microphone clipped into the church's telephone. WHBI dubbed itself "the Gospel Station of the Nation."

Danny Stiles began his broadcasting career in 1947 with a Sunday midnight jazz, blues, and swing show over WHBI. He wasn't paid but rather had to buy the time at the regular commercial rate of $65 an hour. Stiles took a job as elevator operator at the Hoyt Warehouse and soon was earning enough to expand his program to two hours.

Bernice Bass was WHBI's news director, not an easy job since the station never subscribed to a wire service. Bass later conducted the "Party Line" interview program from midnight to 2 A.M. Monday, and Jack Bilby—who held the title of promotion manager and was a kind of Major Bowes to the night owls of Newark—broadcast his "Talent Showcase" from 2:00 to 4:00 A.M. Jimmy Shearer stepped away from active participation in WHBI during the 1950s, although he did appear on television singing and playing his piano on Newark's original channel 13, WATV.

By 1962, WOV had become WADO, and Shearer sold WHBI to his cohort on 1280. The price was $635,000, which must have been a record for a station that was on the air only one day a week. WHBI did leave behind a portion of goodwill, for the call letters later returned, assigned to new ownership, on the FM band.

See also WGCP, WNEW.

WHLI

(22 JULY 1947)

| 1947 | 1100kc | 250 w. |
| 1960 | 1100kc | 10,000 w. |

Paul and Elias Godofsky, owners of WLIB from 1942 through 1944, established WHLI in 1947. It opened up one of America's most lucrative markets, expanding local radio on Long Island just as the suburbs were mushrooming.

WHLI debuted on a summer morning, offering $1,000 in prizes to its first-day listeners. It was one of the first AM/FM pairs; its FM station, then called WHNY, began only weeks later at 98.3. (It became WHLI-FM on 1 January 1948.) Music director was Eddy Brown, formerly with WQXR and WLIB. The Godofskys even carried over some programs and program titles from their WLIB days, including the dinner music of the syndicated "Candlelight and Silver."

Initially, WHLI looked to its local audience for talent and encouraged both amateurs and professionals to audition, welcoming everyone from classical musicians to pop singers and comedians. Studios and offices were in a frame house at 245 Baldwin Road in Hempstead, but the Godofskys already owned a site at 384 Clinton Street. The plan was to expand when WHLI added television and even facsimile broadcast service, to deliver printed matter by radio. Neither medium was granted, and WHLI didn't move until 1957.

From its first days, "The Voice of Long Island" aimed at an upscale audience and quickly became the dominant local station in Nassau, with good reach in Queens and Suffolk Counties. Jerry Carr, the station's program director, and Alan Stewart were familiar voices of WHLI. By 1951 WHLI could boast that it had more daytime listeners in its primary coverage area than the four network flagships and major metropolitan independents combined. "Commuter's Time" was the top-rated morning show, and the day was filled with "familiar good music and local news." Programs included the "Long Island Pops Concert" and hours of "Music from the Country Club." After the AM signoff at sunset the light classics continued heavier on FM. Even the transmitter location, towering alongside the Southern State Parkway at Hempstead, provided excellent publicity. Originally 250 watts, the daytime station increased to 10,000 watts and covered more than Long Island. WHLI puts a weak signal into Bermuda!

In February 1979, the Godofskys sold WHLI to Williams Broadcasting Corp. for $1.5 million, and it was sold again in 1984 to Barnstable Broadcasting for $5 million. The market was certainly worth more, but starting in the 1980s WHLI's primary competition came not from the New York

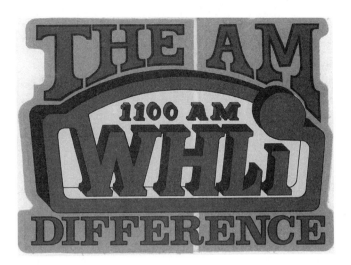

WHLI was the "AM Difference" in the early 1980s.

City stations but from its rivals on Long Island. With the "Music of Your Life" program service, the station continued to appeal to a large suburban audience, some of whom had been listening since 1947.

WHN[1]

(18 March 1922—15 September 1948)

1922	360m. (833.3 kc)	15 w.
1923	830kc s/t WQAO, WPAP	500 w.
1927	760kc s/t WQAO, WPAP	500 w.
1928	1010kc s/t WQAO, WPAP, WRNY	250 w.
1934	1010kc	5,000 w.
1941	1050kc	50,000 w.

Ridgewood, astride the Brooklyn-Queens line, still felt like a small town in 1922. Its daily newspaper, the *Ridgewood Times*, advertised "No Home Complete Without a Player Piano," and the Montauk Electric Company urged "Wire Your House Now—Increase the Value of Your Home." Telephone repairmen made their rounds by bicycle, and one of them took a moment one day to pass along some news to his friend Bill Boettcher: *Ridgewood Times* president George Schubel had just asked a local electrical contractor for an estimate on a broadcasting installation.

Boettcher went to work for the contractor and installed a 15-watt De Forest transmitter atop a three-story building on Cornelia Street and Cypress Avenue, in the heart of Ridgewood's business district. The building was occupied by the *Times*, a bank, and the Ridgewood Chamber of Com-

merce. An antenna was strung between two flagpoles, and a chamber of commerce meeting room was converted into the first studio of WHN. Music-store owner Joseph Stroelein supplied pianos and phonograph equipment and was program director and announcer. Boettcher became chief engineer. This was the third broadcasting station licensed within the Five Boroughs and the first to survive to radio maturity.

WHN went on the air with a schedule that included talks by schoolchildren on the WHN Radio Forum at 4:45 each afternoon. "Radio broadcasting is full of great possibilities as an educational activity of a high order of excellence," enthused the *Ridgewood Times* on 2 June 1922.

As WHN grew in power and popularity, George Schubel was approached by Nils Thor Granlund, since 1914 publicity chief of the Loew's Theatre Organization, with one of the first offers of its kind in the radio industry. On 28 July 1923 the *New York Times* wrote: "Reports that the radio broadcasting station WHN of the Ridgewood Times, Brooklyn, had been purchased by the Loew Theatrical Enterprises, were confirmed last night by Nicholas M Schenck, Vice President of the company. The station, Mr. Schenck said, is being transferred to the Loew State Theatre, 1,540 Broadway, Manhattan, and will be put in operation about August 14th [1923]. Mr. Schenck said that the Loew organization would broadcast shows from the State Theatre, and they hoped to make the wireless station not only a valuable advertising medium, but to use it for the benefit of persons in rural districts who are not able to get their entertainment first hand."

At first, the station wasn't sold but was leased by Schubel to Loew's for $100 a week. Even before this transaction—and only six weeks after AT&T's first network hookup—Loew's announced that it would establish a chain of stations at its theatres in New York, Boston, and other cities.

WHN moved to Loew's State Theatre in September 1923 to become "The Voice of the Great White Way." Granlund brought Al Jolson, George Jessel, and other stars to the WHN microphones. Listeners also enjoyed poems declaimed by "N.T.G." himself. A new AT&T transmitter was installed, and WHN took its first steps into the new field of "toll broadcasting," selling commercial time. This precipitated one of the watershed legal cases in the history of broadcasting.

The American Telephone and Telegraph Company contended that WHN had no right to sell commercial time, since it had never been granted a license to operate commercially—a license from AT&T, that is. In March 1924, AT&T filed suit against WHN. Throughout the industry, and among many public officials and the citizenry at large, there was a feeling that AT&T was trying to establish a monopoly. Since AT&T's patents covered some circuitry found in nearly all radio equipment, it was difficult for a radio station to operate without at least a professional debt to the communications giant, which stated that obtaining its permission was merely a formality.

WHN was selected as the object of the lawsuit partly because it was located in New York and the plaintiff wanted to spare both itself and the defendant large travel expenses. (There was also the impression that WEAF was trying to rid itself of an up-and-coming local rival.) The case was decided out of court in favor of AT&T, for even WHN had to recognize the validity of patent rights. AT&T would receive a license fee of $1,500 from WHN, but the case also earned AT&T general ill will and sent the message that the telephone company could not monopolize the American airwaves.

Tuesday, 23 November 1926

12:30–1:00 P.M.	Theatre Organ Recital
2:00	Overture and Vaudeville
3:10	Sports events
3:20	Theatre Orchestra
4:00	News; sports events
4:10	Theatre Orchestra
5:10	Al Plantadosi, songs
5:25	News; sports events
6:30	Entertainment
7:00	Dance Orchestra
7:30	Will Oakland's Chateau
8:00	Treasureland Ensemble
8:30	Ethel Hartley entertainers
9:00	Wright and Wrong, harmony
9:15	Frances Spear, contralto
9:30	Orchestra selections
10:00	Prince Plotti, entertainer
10:15	Belle Osborne, contralto
10:30	Estelle Rubin, violinist
10:45	Pease & Nelson, songs
11:00	N.T.G. and Pals
11:30	Dance Orchestra

Under the guidance of Granlund ("he is responsible for its jazzy, vaudeville type of program into which he injects a personality as whimsically humorous as there is in all of Radio"), WHN became a prime outlet for jazz and the "snappy dance music" of the 1920s. Sophie Tucker, Fletcher Henderson, and mind reader Prince Joveddah were part of the WHN schedule. Probably the most culturally significant of WHN's programs were the pickups from the Cotton Club in Harlem featuring "Duke Ellington's Jungle Music." In the fall of 1926, WHN arranged to carry all of Columbia University's home football games with sportscaster (and sometime WHN program director) Ted Husing at the microphone. In October 1928, George Schubel sold WHN to the Loew's organization; the official licensee became the Marcus Loew Booking Agency.

Despite the high quality of much of its entertainment, WHN still had to fill a lot of empty hours. "If it wasn't for its pipe organ," wrote a critic in 1930, "no telling what would happen to it."

For its first decade WHN shared time with two or three other stations, including WQAO at Calvary Baptist Church, Palisades Amusement Park's WPAP, and Hugo Gernsback's WRNY. Finally, on Tuesday, 9 January 1934, WHN absorbed its partners. "This is WHN, dial ten-ten" could be heard all day and evening. At the time this development was announced, Loew's also revealed plans to change WHN's call letters to WMGM. In February 1936, WHN's power was raised to 5,000 watts daytime and 1,000 watts at night. The station boasted that it could be heard by more daytime listeners than any other 5,000-watt station in the country.

It was on his weekly WHN Broadway gossip show in 1932 that columnist Ed Sullivan provided comedian Jack Benny with his first exposure to a microphone. Young Judy Garland gave her first radio performance on WHN. Through the early 1930s, WHN was managed by one of America's leading showmen, Edward Bowes. Major Bowes had been a vaudeville impresario and was involved with the Loew's circuit for many years; he brought an old stage format to radio:

The original WHN lost no chance to cross-promote the MGM and the Loew's Theatres connections. This ad dates from 1937.

amateur night. Of course, throughout its first decade, amateur performers were the only kind heard on most stations. "The Original Amateur Hour" premiered on WHN in April 1934 (a time when many among the 30 percent unemployed would try anything) and was such a hit that the CBS network picked up both the program and the major. For the next couple of years New Yorkers could hear two "Amateur Hours" a week; the "WHN Amateur Hour" continued locally, hosted by Jay C. Flippen.

Major Bowes' national success with the "Amateur Hour" took him away from his duties at WHN, and in March 1935 he was fired from his "day job." He showed up for work on a Monday morning to find his desk on the sidewalk in front of Loew's State Theatre.

WHN's network hopes hadn't been realized in the 1920s, but from 1937 to 1939 it had network affiliation as the New York City outlet for the Yankee Network, a New England regional chain that was ranging slightly afield. For a short while in 1938 WHN also carried some programs from Cincinnati's WLW. In 1939, WHN learned that it would receive authorization to increase power to a full 50,000 watts and took the opportunity to give NBC an idea: it would like to become the flagship of a new NBC White Network, to join the Red and the Blue. NBC wasn't interested.

The North American Regional Broadcasting Agreement moved WHN to 1050kc and on 1 December 1941 power was increased with a gala show from the Barbizon Plaza. On 28 October WHN had begun testing its 50kw transmitter and discovered that the signals were causing interference to WINS, whose transmitter was 3,000 feet away in Carlstadt, N.J. WHN loaned WINS its old 5,000-watt transmitter in Astoria and took on the responsibility of demolishing the WINS towers. WINS was already building a new transmitter at Lyndhurst, N.J.

WHN was an innovator among New York stations. "Radio Newsreel" at 6:00 A.M. and 11:00 P.M. was renamed "Newsreel Theater" in 1945. This program established the kind of cycle that would later be adopted by all-news stations: a ten-minute newscast was repeated five times, and the final minutes of the hour were left for other announcements.

WHN news analysts included Fulton Lewis Jr. and George Hamilton Combs as well as a "Commentators Round Table." Combs also hosted "Now You Decide," which dramatized court cases with the home audience in the imaginary jury box. Brooklyn Dodgers baseball moved to WHN from WOR in 1942, with Red Barber at Ebbets Field. Giants football and Rangers hockey were heard over WHN, which is also where Marty Glickman perfected the art of describing a basketball game. Another popular sportscaster was Bert Lee, the air name of WHN executive Bertram Lebhar Jr. "The Avenger," a weaker version of "The Shadow," debuted on WHN in July 1941 before moving on to national syndication in 1945.

Much of the broadcast day was popular music, live and recorded. The late-night "Music to Read By", an undistract-

ing hour of songs without words, was later referred to as the most imitated program in radio. WHN also pioneered on the FM band in 1942 with WHNF at 46.3 Mc.

In September 1948, Loew's fulfilled a fourteen-year-old intention and changed its station's name to WMGM. Fourteen years later the old call letters would return. The new owner, Storer Broadcasting, publicized the change with the slogan "Remember WHN." Many New Yorkers did.

See also WQAO, WPAP, WMGM, WHN[II], WEVD.

(28 February 1962–1 July 1987)

1962   1050kc   50,000w.

The transfer of WMGM from Loew's to Storer Broadcasting was a transaction between two of the nation's media giants and marked the entry of the Miami-based Storer stations into the New York market. Storer could have called the station anything that was available, but it opted for history and the opportunity to have a station with just three call letters and chose to restore the original name.

On the day of the big changeover, newspaper ads showed two radios side by side. One radio was vibrating and captioned "5:59 P.M. WMGM Beat"; the other radio sat still, and the caption read "6 P.M. WHN Sweet." Actually, WMGM said goodbye to New York before 5:30, when deejay Bob Callen played the "Peppermint Twist" as the last of the great hits, followed by a special thirty-minute WHN preview. Short biographical pieces introduced the program hosts—most of them familiar voices from WMGM—and there was even a sample of the revived station's new jingle package. The music on WHN would range through the easy-listening middle, from Mantovani to Les Elgart. Fans of the "Peppermint Twist" started twisting their dials. The new format had originated on Storer stations in Miami and Cleveland and was prepared by Storer Central Music Programming.

News was provided by a new audio service called Radio Press International (RPI), founded by George Hamilton Combs, a commentator who had been on WHN in the early 1940s. RPI was soon sold to R. Peter Strauss, who owned WMCA, and WHN affiliated with the Mutual network in October 1962.

Also in late 1962 the comedy team Bob and Ray came to WHN from 4:00 to 7:00 P.M. on weekdays and 4:00 to 8:00 on Saturdays. Soon WMGM morning fixture Ted Brown left WHN, and after a short stint by Dick Shepard, Bob and Ray were again entertaining New York at breakfastime. Lonny Starr and Jack Lazare came over from WINS. Veteran broad-

After WMGM switched back to being WHN in 1962, the station tried to sound "very New York City." Even personality Dick Shepard was posed in a Hansom Cab on Park Avenue.

caster Jim Ameche (Don's brother, he had once played "Jack Armstrong, the All-American Boy") took over the midday slot. Hans Anderson was heard during the afternoon drive time, and WMGM alumnus Dean Hunter worked overnight. With such talent in the New York market, Storer soon allowed WHN more autonomy in music programming.

The station began coverage of the New York Mets games in 1964. Bob and Ray left the wake-up show in 1964 to be replaced by Lonny Starr, then by Jim Ameche, and then, in 1967, by longtime WCBS morning man Jack Sterling.

WHN targeted the thirty-to-fifty year-old group with an adult music policy that was detailed in a November 1969 staff memo from program director John Moler. "WHN programs for *sound* and sound alone. The sound must be right at any moment of the day. Record sales charts are to be completely ignored…. WHN never programs music which is *even suspect* for being (1) teen-age oriented (2) country (3) folk/rock (4) concert (5) hard jazz or (6) old fashioned or date-sounded." Moler further explained the playlist, "WHN's music *must always* possess two or more of these qualities: (a) melodic (b) pretty (c) familiar (d) beautiful and (e) interesting."

In 1970 WHN began a middle-of-the-road music policy and brought in another established wakeup man, Herb Oscar Anderson. Its appeal was still to an older audience. In 1972 WHN dropped its Mutual affiliation (Mutual would be back) and signed with ABC's American Entertainment Network.

On 26 February 1973, WHN made a change that brought in a whole new audience and signaled a major development in American popular culture. There had always been a devoted public for country-and-western music in the New York area; devotees of Don Larkin on WAAT and other country-and-western deejays formed a cult following. Country music fans may have been the only group of listeners in New York since the 1920s to strain at their speakers into the wee hours trying to pick up Nashville or Wheeling. But now there was a 50,000-watt station airing country music twenty-four hours a day right in li'l ol' Manhattan. The first country tune played on "1050 Country" was "The Race Is On" by George Jones, introduced by "the kosher cowboy from Coney Island," Jack Spector.

Making the transition from middle-of-the-road to the

During the country years, WHN publicized the current fads in country music. This "CB Talk Guide" was distributed during the citizen's band radio craze in 1975. The autographs are from the deejay lineup at the time.

Bob Elliott and Ray Goulding began in New York on WNBC, then went to WINS and WHN. Later they were on WOR.

country roads were Lee Arnold, Stan Martin, and Del DeMontreux, and they were joined by Big Wilson, Sheila York, and Dean Anthony. Gene Ladd and Dirk Van did the news, and Jim Gordon was the voice of the New York Rangers hockey.

By 1976, WHN's adult audience was just behind WABC's. Key to its success was the fact that it never called itself a country radio station, just a station that played country music. But it was a time when country was becoming cool, helped along by the CB radio craze.

On 29 February 1980 WHN was sold by Storer to the Mutual Broadcasting System. Mutual had begun in 1934 as a cooperative and remained so throughout radio's "golden age." The sale of Mutual to the Amway Corporation allowed the famous network to finally own its own stations, and the 50,000-watt New York station was a prize worth $14 million. WHN dropped its ABC Entertainment affiliation and picked up Mutual News; "modern country" programming continued unchanged.

In January 1985 Mutual sold WHN to Doubleday Broadcasting, a subsidiary of the publisher whose holdings at the time also included the New York Mets. The deal also involved the purchase of WTFM, the Queens-based station that became WAPP. In July 1986—reversing a practice that had taken hold sixty years earlier—Doubleday moved WHN's facilities out of Manhattan to 34-12 Thirty-sixth Street in the moviemaking district of Astoria, Queens. The executive offices remained in Manhattan. A month later WHN was sold to Emmis Broadcasting.

The historic station WHN went silent for the second time at 3:00 P.M. on Wednesday, 1 July 1987, when Emmis adopted an all-sports format and changed the call letters to WFAN.

See also WHN^I, WMGM, WFAN.

WHOM

(13 APRIL 1930—29 MARCH 1976)

1930	1450kc s/t WNJ, WBMS	
1941	1480kc	1,000w.
1948	1480kc	5,000w.

"This is WHOM, New York. We invite you to stay tuned for the program that follows." For much of its history, only the greatest linguists could have stayed tuned through all the programs that followed on WHOM. A 1955 ad referred to WHOM as "America's Foremost Foreign Language Radio Station" and boasted of its service in Spanish (sixty-two hours a week), Italian and Polish (eighteen hours each), German (twelve hours), and lesser time in Russian and Ukranian. And that was only on AM. Over on FM, WHOM could be heard in thirteen languages, including Carpatho-Ruthenian, Ukranian, Greek, Swiss German, and most notably, Cantonese.

WHOM was founded in 1930 by the New Jersey Broadcasting Corporation, owned by Outdoor Advertising executive Harry O'Mealia, whose company owned thousands of billboards around the metropolitan area. He was also president of the Jersey City Board of Education. WHOM was originally a Jersey City station, having taken 1450kc from the merged WIBS/WKBO.

Studios were on the third floor of the Stanley Theatre at 2870 Hudson Blvd. WHOM debuted with a fifteen-minute inaugural broadcast on 13 April 1930 at 5:45 P.M. The host was chief announcer Howard Lepper, previously the manager of WIBS. O'Mealia made a brief speech, and there were

prayers from several clergy. Then the station left the air to make time for WNJ and WBMS, returning at 9:00 P.M. for a gala show that lasted until 2:00 A.M. In 1931 WHOM absorbed the airtime of WNJ, and the following year it became a full-time station with the demise of WBMS.

Initially, WHOM's schedule was filled with local North Jersey talent, Hawaiian combos, coverage of marathon dance contests, and other general-audience programs in English. In 1934, O'Mealia sold WHOM to Paul Harron, owner of WFAB, a small part-timer in New York. Before long WHOM adopted WFAB's polyglot programming, as well as sharing its studios at 29 W. Fifty-seventh Street.

In 1939, WHOM became the broadcast outlet of one of America's major media companies when it was bought by Gardner Cowles, whose publications included *Look* magazine. The new owner was the Atlantic Broadcasting Company (no relation to Grebe's ABC of the late 1920s). WHOM offered some respectable programming in English, bringing on jazz disc jockey Symphony Sid Torin in 1946 and news director Ron Cochran, later a prominent CBS correspondent. Joe Franklin was on WHOM in 1944 with "Vaudeville Echoes," a pioneering nostalgia program that he conducted without pay. Cowles tried, without much success, to convert WHOM into a full-time English language station. Instead it continued to pursue its "natural and maximum audience," adding Norwegian, Yiddish and Lithuanian to the schedule.

Broadcasting foreign languages during the turbulent days before and during World War II—especially German and Italian—was risky for WHOM, even with a station policy requiring that English translations be submitted in advance. Many of its broadcasts were produced by "time brokers" and were beyond the direct control of the station. There were several troublesome incidents, including an allegedly anti–Semitic Italian program in 1938 that jeopardized renewal of the station's license. During the war years WHOM presented many special war-emergency programs produced by Charles Baltin. Baltin also hosted a Jewish-oriented program in English and was later WHOM's program director and vice-president.

Wednesday, 31 July 1946
In Italian

8:00 A.M.	Request Program—Ralph Costantino
8:30	News—Pasquale Cajano
8:45	Invitation to Opera
9:00	Popular Music and Songs
9:30	News; Popular Music

In English

2:00	News—Alois Havrilla
2:05	Old World Gems
2:30	Music to Remember
3:00	News; Caravan Crooners
3:30	Highlight Special
3:45	Name Band of the Day
4:00	News—Alois Havrilla

WHOM served up a variety of ethnic and special programming. Wrestler Antonino Rocca even had his own show.

4:05	Top Tunes
4:30	Highways to Safety
4:45	Highlight Special
5:00	News; Request Time
5:50	Latest Sports Picture

In Italian

6:00	Musical Interlude
6:05	My Rights—M. Sarullo
6:15	News—Giulio Scotti
6:30	Recorded Music
6:45	Enrico Ruiz, tenor
7:00	Question and Answer
7:15	Musical Album
7:30	Paolo Dones, songs
7:35	Nino Rolli, songs
7:45	Musical Program
8:00	Presenting Clara Stella
8:15	The Incredible Truth
8:30	Gems of Opera—Pietro Novasio
8:45	The Cavalier of Justice
9:00	News—Mario Capelloni
9:15	Recorded Music
9:30	Popular Melodies
10:00	Serenade
10:45	The "Il Progresso" Program—Gino Pagliari (international, national, and local happenings with the latest news from Italy from *Il Progresso's* exclusive sources)

Lingering questions of loyalty also emerged when Cowles moved to sell the Atlantic Broadcasting Company in 1946 to Fortune and Generoso Pope, owners of the city's major Italian daily, *Il progresso*. The sale was approved after doubts about the Popes' patriotism were put to rest, and on 24 November 1946 the Pope family took over WHOM, with a distinctly Italian program featuring opera star Lucia Albanese and the Italian consul in New York. Also in 1946, WHOM officially relocated from Jersey City to New York.

In 1948, WHOM moved its studios to 136 W. Fifty-second Street and boosted power to 5,000 watts. Affiliated with a popular daily paper, "The Il Progresso Station" might have been expected to concentrate on the half-million Italian-born people in its coverage area, but Spanish-language broadcasting was begun in 1947, and by the early 1950s, shows aimed at the black community featured Ray Carroll, Willie Bryant, and Carlton Coleman. "Fiesta Mambo" was a mid–1950s Latin rhythm program presented by Don Mambo in both English and Spanish. Alan Fredericks' "Night Train" program came to WHOM briefly in the late 1950s, and Ralph Cooper presented the "Rocket Party" from midnight to 5:00 A.M.

In December 1949, Generoso Pope prepared to buy WINS from Crosley with the intention of moving WHOM to 1010kc with 50,000 watts, but the sale was never approved

by the FCC. WHOM then looked forward to the television era and contemplated a merger with WOV when it applied for UHF channel 31 in 1952, seeking to start a foreign-language TV station to be called WHOV-TV. Citing economic problems in opening up the UHF band, the plan was abandoned in April 1954.

The biggest change came on Monday, 6 June 1960. Although the Italian family ownership and top management remained the same, weekday programs were now all in Spanish (some Italian and German continued on Sundays). From "Buenos Dias, Nueva York" in the morning to "El Correo del Amor" and other soap operas, WHOM developed a full-service operation at a time when English-language broadcasters were moving into thinner niches. It was "la emisora del corazón latino"—the station with the Latin heart. Among its air personalities were Raul Alarcon, Freddy Baez, and Polito Vega. Sports director Buck Canel reported mainland and Caribbean scores, and WHOM carried both Mets and Yankees games in Spanish, occasionally feeding the coverage to stations in Latin America. As the first full-time Spanish voice in the city, WHOM easily led the ratings along "the Spanish Main," the cluster of Latino stations at the upper end of the dial. In 1975, the Popes sold WHOM to the San Juan Racing Association, and a year later the call letters were changed to WJIT. So an Italian-owned Spanish-speaking station with an Irish name finally became fully Hispanic.

See also WIBS, WKBO, WZRC.

WHPP

(11 FEBRUARY 1927–30 APRIL 1929)

| 1927 | 1450kc. | 10w. |
| 1928 | 1420kc s/t WMRJ, WLBH | 10w. |

The development of radio was due partly, in the effusive words of Commerce Secretary Herbert Hoover, to "the genius of the American boy." Youthful enthusiasm was certainly the driving force behind the Bronx Broadcasting Company's station WHPP. WHPP was built and managed by William Elster, a twenty-two-year old insurance agent and radio buff, and his friend Herman Rubin, who was only sixteen when the station went on the air. The pair modified a ten-watt navy transmitter designed originally for Morse code transmission and built a small studio in Rubin's house at 953 Southern Boulevard in the Bronx. The station received its license during the unregulated period of the mid–1920s and signed on less than two weeks before the Radio Act of 1927 became law.

Thursday, 14 July 1927

7:00	Battery program; sports; correct time
7:15	Jules Rosenberg, songs
7:30	Natalie Gural, songs
7:40	Clock novelty
7:45	Crane entertainers
8:00	Harmonica band
8:15	Eisenbach Novelty
8:30	Ukelele Buddy Raskin
8:45	Billy Kuback Jr., piano
9:00	Prudy program
9:30	Miriam Burdow, soprano
9:45	Andy and Johnson, songs
10:00	Sylvia Hirsch, contralto
10:15	Camp Harlee-Mitchell program
10:30	Insurance tips—W. Elster
10:35	Amateur Announcers Contest
10:40	Hartford music

Although Rubin and Elster stated that their purpose was "to present patriotic programs on a small scale," WHPP enjoyed a remarkable period of growth. In September 1927 the Bronx Broadcasting Company moved its studios to 150 Delancey Street in Manhattan; in January 1928, the city of license was changed to Englewood Cliffs, N.J. and in the fall of that year, WHPP moved its transmitter to Englewood Cliffs, directly across the Hudson from the Bronx.

On 11 November 1928, WHPP moved to 1420kc to share time with WMRJ/Jamaica and WLBH/Farmingdale. But Rubin and Elster couldn't keep up with technical and programming demands and they allowed WHPP's license to expire in April 1929. On 6 November 1929 the FRC denied a request to transfer WHPP's license to James A. Lodice, and a happy little station disappeared.

WHTG

(1 NOVEMBER 1957–)

1957	1410kc.	500w.

When WHTG began broadcasting in 1957, it was only the fifth commercial radio station to ever operate from Monmouth County, N.J.—a center of telecommunications activity since the days of Marconi—and three of those had already disappeared from the air. The other station was the well-established WJLK in Asbury Park, which at the time had only half the power of WHTG. A new outlet could surely find an audience and room to grow, especially since the station's studio and transmitter on Hope Road was "centrally located

in New Shrewsbury to serve the entire North Jersey shore." The official city of license was Eatontown.

WHTG was a mom-and-pop station: the call letters stood for Harold and Theo Gade. Harold was a retired engineer and civilian employee of the U.S. Army Signal Corps at its Fort Monmouth headquarters. In one sense, the station was a throwback to the early days of radio: the first facilities were in the Gade home. In other ways, WHTG sounded like it should have been on FM, with continuous easy-listening instrumentals and community announcements.

Each afternoon at 4:55 there was a newscast for personnel and dependents at Fort Monmouth. Music would then continue in WHTG's relaxed style, introduced with an announcement such as, "You're listening to Dusk on 1410 Radio."

In October 1961, WHTG added an FM service at 105.5Mc. This would seem to be the natural habitat of such a station, but WDHA in Dover was on the same frequency and blanked out much of the coverage area. In 1965 WHTG-FM moved to 106.3, taking the frequency of Red Bank station WFHA, which had forfeited its license. Things remained as Harold and Theo had begun them until 1984 when the music policy was revised, with the AM station playing "adult contemporary" and the FM station carrying album-oriented rock.

Theo died in the late 1970s, and Harold was in ill health in 1985 when WHTG Incorporated was transferred to their daughter Faye. In 1989 another change was made to return the station closer to its less frantic sound, with a big-band and nostalgia format.

WIBI

(15 SEPTEMBER 1925–19 NOVEMBER 1927)

1925	1370kc.	5w.
1926	1370kc s/t WJBI	50w.
June 1927	1120kc s/t WBMS, WBKN, WWRL	100w.
Dec. 1927 (WGOP)	1500kc s/t WBMS, WBKN, WWRL	100w.

Frederick B. Zittell Jr. opened an electrical contracting and appliance business at 49 Boerum Avenue (150th Street) in the Flushing section of Queens shortly after World War I. The Murray Hill Electric Company added a line of radio equipment when the first broadcasting stations went on the air. Soon Zittell installed a five-watt army-surplus Western Electric transmitter in the back room, added some heavy curtains and carpets for acoustical treatment, and hung an antenna between a pair of steel poles in the yard. His station was given the alphabetically issued identification WIBI and assigned to share time on 1370 with WJBI in Red Bank, whose similar call letters were a coincidence.

The station staff consisted of Zittell and his assistant, Norwood Bradshaw. Local entertainers came to perform, and WIBI's publicity material asked for audience reaction and added, "If you hear a good educational and instructive talk tell us so—and we will give you more."

Early in 1927—after WIBI's power had been increased to 50 watts—Zittell moved the studios to the Roosevelt Theatre at 55 N. Fifteenth Street in Flushing and the transmitter to Twentieth Street and Northern Boulevard. The theatre publicized the radio station at the bottom of each day's newspaper ad. WIBI became an outlet for local talent with its "Shadowland on the Bay" revue; news from the *Daily Star* of Long Island City and services from the First Baptist Church were broadcast. It boosted Flushing merchants with hours of entertainment and "Dollar Days" commercials, produced by a business committee.

Thursday, 5 May 1927

2:30 P.M.	Vaudeville program
7:00	Daily Star Hour
8:00	Roosevelt Theatre Hour
9:00	Shadowland Orchestra
10:00	Frank Kelly, tenor
11:00	Midwood Orchestra

In June 1927, the new Federal Radio Commission assigned WIBI to switch to 1120kc and share time with WBKN/Brooklyn, WWRL/Woodside and WBMS/Union City, N.J. In November 1927, the four stations at 1120 were ordered to move up the dial to 1500kc. All but WIBI immediately protested, for Zittell was then busy dismantling his station with the aim of moving it to Port Washington, Long Island. Despite the services of salesman Robert Lake, Zittell was losing money on WIBI. His financial problems even caused him to try to bypass the Con Edison electric meter serving his store.

In December 1927, WIBI changed its call letters to WGOP. Its transmitter was now at Orchard Beach in the Bronx, and Zittell hoped the station would have special appeal for Republicans. But his broadcasting activity caused Zittell to neglect the once-lucrative Murray Hill Electric Company, and declining financial fortunes finally led to the breakup of his marriage. WGOP's license expired in August 1928, before it could be of service in that year's election. Frederick Zittell eventually moved to Bucksport, Maine, where he was working at a gas station when he died, by suicide, in the early 1940s.

WIBS

(1925–1930)

1925	1480kc		10w.
1926?	1470kc		100w.
1928	1450kc s/t WNJ, WBMS, WKBO, WSDA	100w.

WIBS began as a portable transmitter belonging to the 57th Infantry Brigade of the New Jersey National Guard and licensed to Lt. Thomas F. Hunter at 921 Edgewood Road in Elizabeth. The station outgrew its demonstration status and by 1928 the owner was the New Jersey Broadcasting Company headed by Capt. Howard J. Lepper.

The new Federal Radio Commission ordered WIBS to share time with New Jersey stations WBMS, WNJ, WAAT, and WKBO. "We have no objection to a three-way split on 1,450 kilocycles," stated Captain Lepper in October 1928, "but we do object to a four or five way split." The studios and transmitter were on the roof of the Levy Building in Elizabeth, but construction began on a two-room single-story building on Black Brook Parkway on the Kenilworth-Union Township line. From that location it overlooked Irvington, Springfield, Cranfield, Westfield, and Union.

Friday, 15 June 1928

5:00 P.M.	Melody Hour
6:00	Shore Highway program
6:30	Carteret Ensemble
7:00	News flashes
7:05	Baseball results
7:15	Majestic program
7:45	Kitty Smith, soprano
8:00	Off the Air
10:30	Dance program
11:00	Crane and Kisley, songs
11:30	Dance program

On 8 June 1929, WIBS applied to the FRC to temporarily operate through the transmitter of WKBO. It may not have been wise to return to its own equipment, for on 11 April 1930 the FRC refused to renew WIBS's license because it was deviating from its frequency. Shortly thereafter, WIBS began to operate with the dual call letters WKBO-WIBS and then was sold for $16,000 to Harry O'Mealia and became WHOM in Jersey City. Howard Lepper remained as chief announcer of WHOM.

See also WHOM, WKBO.

WICC

(8 NOVEMBER 1926–)

1926	1400kc. s/t WCWS, Danbury	250w.
1928	1130kc s/t WCWS	500w.
1928	1430kc s/t WBRL, Tilton, NH	500w.
1929	1190kc	1,000w.
1931	600kc s/t WCAC (till 1935)	1,000w.

Bridgeport, Conn., lies beyond the New York City metropolitan area, but WICC should be considered among New York area stations because it easily reaches listeners on Long Island and in the northern suburbs and because at one point it had a role in the evolution of New York radio.

Touting the "Industrial Capital of Connecticut" in the call letters, station WICC was founded during the deregulated days of 1926 by a group calling itself the Bridgeport Broadcasting Station, headed by textile chemist Harold Foyer. A year later, the new station was sold and tried to move its operations from Bridgeport five miles to Sport Hill in Easton. It encountered objections from local residents fearful that its signal would block out superior New York stations. The Easton residents filed a protest with the new Federal Radio Commission—the first appeal of its kind, but to no avail.

In 1931, WICC emerged as the victor to obtain the 600kc frequency from Manhattan station WGBS. The Federal Radio Commission had cited the "superabundance" of stations in the city and forced WGBS to vacate the favored 600 spot. WICC then shared time with WCAC at Connecticut Agricultural College in Storrs until that station went silent in 1935. With a choice frequency to itself, WICC erected a new transmitter on the shores of Long Island Sound at Pleasure Beach, beaming toward New York. Both masts and wires alongside the Pleasure Beach Amusement Park were brightly lit; the antenna array had the shape of a bird in flight and could be seen for miles.

WICC seldom drew many listeners from New York, partly because it was heavily committed to serving the New Englanders in its audience. In 1932, the station was sold to Boston department store magnate John A. Shepard III and became part of Shepard's Yankee Network (YN). In addition to the YN's ambitious entertainment programming and high-quality news service—Shepard was a founder of Trans-Radio News and by the mid–1930s his network had one of the industry's best news organizations—WICC gained a CBS affiliation that lasted until the YN stations moved to NBC (Red and Blue) in 1936. A year later Shepard founded a second regional chain, the Colonial Network, to carry Mutual programs in New England. WICC's schedule at one time or another included broadcasts from all the networks.

From 1936 to 1939 WICC maintained a studio at the Hotel Stratfield in New Haven. It was easily the dominant voice in southern Connecticut. In 1940 WICC moved from 184 Church Street to 1241 Main Street in Bridgeport. With the sale of the NBC Blue Network in 1943, the Colonial Network was absorbed into the Yankee, and WICC continued with a Mutual affiliation. Also in 1943, John Shepherd sold the Yankee Network stations to the General Tire and Rubber Company, keeping the YN affiliation. In 1950, when General Tire bought WOR, WICC was sold to the Bridgeport Broadcasting Company, which had been operating that city's smaller WLIZ. A sale was necessary because WICC penetrated part of WOR's New York market area—a vestige of the 1931 FRC decision to assign 600kc to Bridgeport.

The new management team at WICC included station manager Dickens Wright and sales manager Charles Parker, both of whom left in 1955 to become owner and vice-president, respectively, of WPAT in Paterson, N.J. In the late 1950s WICC's studios moved to 2190 Post Road in Fairfield.

WICC continued to offer some of the best local news coverage in the country, and under news director Walt Dibble in the 1950s it was the proving ground for several top broadcast journalists. Dibble's assistant Tony Bruton went on to become executive editor of CBS News. Newscasters Bill Whalen and Christopher Lindsay moved to ABC, while Steve Young and Christopher Glenn became familiar voices on the CBS network. Deejay Ed Baer went to WMCA, WHN and WCBS-FM. Morning man Bill Codare later broadcast on WCBS and WHN, while Reed Upton went to WINS and WABC. Announcer Phil Cutting became owner of WNLK in Norwalk. Some of the WICC personalities, such as Wally Dunlap and Frank Delfino ("Franklin D"), stayed in Bridgeport and became community institutions. Bob Crane was program director through the 1950s before going to Hollywood and getting a starring TV role in *Hogan's Heroes*.

In 1953, WICC-TV began operation as one of the nation's first UHF television stations, on channel 43 (Bridgeport had been the site of an early RCA field test of UHF; WICC owner Phil Merryman was a former RCA executive). It was a tragicomic effort. In the days before most sets could receive UHF, WICC-TV became known as "the television station without any viewers." It even seemed as if the Bridgeport Broadcasting Company kept channel 43 on the air just for fun, and for giving its radio personalities TV experience and exposure. In 1959, WICC AM/TV was sold to Connecticut–New York Broadcasters Inc. for $1.4 million, and the TV venture was shut down. WICC could afford such experimentation. It liked to refer to itself as "the most listened-to station in the richest retail market in the United States."

WICC had better luck with an FM station established at 99.9Mc in 1960. With the catchy call letters of WJZZ, it was one of the first stations to specialize in jazz.

In 1967 WICC was again sold, this time to Tribune

Broadcasting, which, through interlocking ownership, also controlled the *New York Daily News* and station WPIX TV/FM. In 1974 a new antenna beamed WICC's signal away from the New York area. Studios were also relocated back to Bridgeport, at 177 State Street. In 1989 M. L. Limited Partnership, which owned WEBE-FM, bought WICC from Tribune and moved the studios up the block to WEBE's location at 166 State. Both stations soon moved to 2 Lafayette Street.

Through many changes in location and ownership, WICC retained a stable position with its listening audience. Its music stayed middle-of-the-road; its air personalities were not only personable but well informed, linking the entertainment and community-service aspects of the station. Local news coverage remained strong, a tradition nurtured during the days when the Yankee Network delivered "news while it is news."

See also WGBS.

W I N R *see* W R S T

W I N S

(15 JANUARY 1932–)

1932	1180kc	1,000w. (daytime)
1941	1000kc	10,000w.
1943	1010kc	50,000w. (June 1947)

Newspapers were among the earliest broadcast operators, but no major metropolitan daily entered the field in New York until William Randolph Hearst, owner of the *New York American* and the tabloid *Daily Mirror*, purchased the Gimbel's Department Store station WGBS. (The *American's* interest in broadcasting can be dated from 1916, when it supplied returns to Dr. Lee De Forest for his experimental election-night reports.) The new call letters, WINS, stood for Hearst's International News Service, then one of the nation's three major wire services. In July 1932, WINS moved out of the WGBS studios in the Hotel Lincoln to a Park Avenue locale at 110 E. Fifty-eighth Street, the Ritz Tower.

Such well-heeled patrimony should have won WINS the role of New York's premier information source. The Hearst station was even experimenting with television, oper-

ating the Jenkins mechanical scanner through experimental transmitter W2XCR. However, in the early 1930s, radio was still struggling for status against restrictions imposed by newspaper interests, who tended to accept the new medium as a promotional tool rather than a full-service news source. Also, WINS was initially just a low-power daytime operation, hardly in keeping with the Hearst image.

On 29 March 1941, WINS became a beneficiary of the reallocations caused by the North American Regional Broadcasting Agreement (NARBA), and it switched to full-time operation at 1000kc ("Easy to remember, easy to dial") with its power authorized at 10,000 watts. This was the widest of some eighteen NARBA shifts on the New York dial, the result of good planning and early application by Hearst engineers. It opened up 1190 for later occupancy by WLIB. WINS also moved to new studios at 28 W. Forty-fourth Street and began to live up to its name. Popular music and low-budget quiz shows highlighted the broadcast day. There was also news reporting by "Mr. and Mrs. Reader," a couple who read the papers to each other every morning.

At about the time of its frequency and power change, WINS had to shut down its transmitter at Carlstadt, N.J., due to interference with WHN, 50 kilocycles up the dial but just half a mile away in East Rutherford. WHN let WINS move to its old transmitter site in Astoria till it could occupy a permanent plant in Lyndhurst, N.J. But signal problems caused WINS to temporarily return to daytime operation till it became full-time at 1010kc on Saturday, 30 October 1943. The FCC also authorized an increase to 50,000 watts, but wartime equipment shortages delayed this until 1947.

In 1946, Hearst sold "New York's Home Station" for $2 million to another media powerhouse, the Crosley Broadcasting Corporation, owner of the giant WLW in Cincinnati. In October 1946 Crosley began feeding New York programs from "The Nation's Station." From "Top o' the Morning" at 5:45 A.M. to the dulcet late-night "Moon River," New Yorkers could now listen in to some of the Midwest's best programs. The schedule even included concerts by the Cincinnati Symphony. Yet New Yorkers responded weakly to being plugged in to WLW, and the Crosley network was phased out.

WINS needed little help from Cincinnati. Since 1946 it had been the outlet for New York Yankee baseball, with Mel Allen as play-by-play announcer. This was the first time any station had carried all of a team's games live, home and away.

In 1953, Crosley sold WINS to the Gotham Broadcasting Corp.—despite its name, a West Coast organization controlled by Seattle businessman J. Elroy McCaw. "Ten-Ten Wins" entered one of the most exciting and tempestous periods in any station's history.

Stan Shaw conducted "The Original Milkman's Matinee" at night. Veteran NBC sports director Bill Stern presented a breakfast-time talk show. Disc jockey Alan Freed and his record collection came to WINS on 8 September 1954. Often cited as the man who coined the expression

When not playing music, WINS was very active in sports broadcasting. Here sportscaster Joe D'Urso reads the ball scores in 1950.

Jack Lacy and his wife, Agnes, were both leading WINS personalities. Agnes often covered for Jack on events such as "wives day," when the wives and girlfriends of WINS deejays took over the shows.

"rock 'n' roll," Freed was certainly a pioneer; he had already garnered an audience in the New York area through his Cleveland program syndicated through WNJR. He stayed with WINS through 1958, at a time when the station had one of the strongest program lineups in the city. Bob Elliott and Ray Goulding moved over from WNBC in 1954 to fill the morning slot, bringing newscaster Peter Roberts with them. Deejay Jack Lacy played records on "Lacy on the Loose" and "Listen to Lacy" ("spinnin' the discs with finesse / just set your dial to 1010 awhile / to WINS"), and Bob Garrity presented live late-night jazz from Birdland. In 1956 Herbert G. "Jock" Fearnhead became general manager, and under his leadership and the efforts of programmer Rick Sklar, the rock-and-roll revolution seized complete control of WINS.

Monday, 30 September 1957

6:00 A.M.	Wake Up to Music—Irv Smith
9:00	Listen to Lacy
12:00	Orbit Universe with Stan Z. Burns ("The High Noon to 3 Orbit to Be for Stan Z")
3:00	Listen to Lacy
7:00	Alan Freed's Rock and Roll Party
11:00	All Night Show—Stan Shaw

In August 1957 WINS moved its studios to 7 Central Park West, overlooking the park and Columbus Circle (dubbed Radio Circle by WINS). It was a roach-infested building topped by a Coca-Cola sign and had been constructed, coincidentally, for William Randolph Hearst.

News director Tom O'Brien, Lew Fisher, Brad Phillips, and Paul Sherman reported the news at twenty-five and fifty-five past the hour. Each newscast opened with the words "Sounds make the news!" and some significant noises. Les Keiter covered pro, college, and even high school sports.

Deejay patter was heard through a "Soundarama" echo chamber, which WINS introduced after surreptitiously operating on reduced power for a couple of hours to make the new sound even more impressive. A Western Union wire brought in record requests and dedications and WINS won listeners through a constant stream of audience-participation

ROCK 'N ROLL with ALAN FREED

KING of the Rock-N-Roll—Listen to the absolute monarch in the Kingdom of Rock-N-Roll. WINS is where the beat first began. Every night Alan plays your favorite knights of the round turntable—Elvis Presley, Pat Boone, and other such court favorites.

Mon.	6:30-9:00 PM
Tues.	6:30-9:00 PM
Wed.	6:30-9:00 PM
Thurs.	6:30-9:00 PM
Fri.	6:30-9:00 PM—11:00 PM-1:00 AM
Sat. ....10-12 AM—6:30-9:00 PM—11:00 PM-1:00 AM

So dial 1010, you Maidens and Squires, for the best—the most—and the latest in Rock-N-Roll.

For your favorite Rock-N-Roll requests, write to Alan direct at WINS, New York 36, N. Y.

WINS really hit its stride with the rock-and-roll era of the 1950s. Alan Freed, who was the first of the big-time rock deejays, broadcast from WINS from 1954 to 1958.

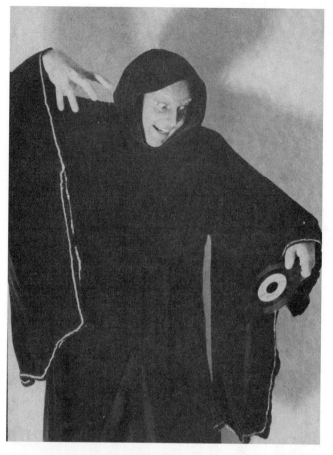

Old-time straight-ahead WNEW deejay Pete Myers' alter ego was the effervescent "Mad Daddy" on WINS in 1964.

gimmicks and contests, like a trumped-up treasure hunt for a silver subway token that supposedly kept Murray Kaufman living underground for a week. On April Fool's Day 1958—the same day that WMCA moved to a rock-music format—"Murray the K" took over the all-night shift.

Burned by the payola scandal that threatened renewal of the station's license and a four-month announcers' strike in 1958, and losing its rock-and-roll audience to WABC and WMCA, WINS briefly stepped back to a more middle-of-the-road format. Al "Jazzbeaux" Collins inherited the 6:00–10:00 A.M. program in the autumn of 1959, and Cousin Brucie Morrow was on from 7:00 to 11:00 P.M. Late in 1960, WINS briefly replaced WOR as Mutual's New York outlet.

Westinghouse purchased WINS for $10 million on 28 July 1962. The original owner of WJZ had returned to the New York market after an absence of nearly forty years. As one of the Group W stations, WINS beefed up its news and public-affairs programming. In addition to five-minute summaries every half hour there was Charles Scott King's thirty-minute "Radio Newsday" each evening at 6:00. John Henry Faulk—behind the mike again after his successful blacklisting lawsuit—hosted a weeknight call-in, "Contact." Sunday evenings were four hours of public-affairs and cultural programming, including the "WINS Press Conference," and special reports on transportation, race relations, and science. There were even comedy and quiz shows from the BBC. WINS took full advantage of the 1964 Beatle "British Invasion" when Murray the K befriended the group and milked as much publicity as possible from the arrangement.

On Monday, 19 April 1965, the station shut off the

WINS changed to an all-news format in 1965. The photo of the main newsroom was taken a few days before the change.

music—its last record was the Shangri-La's "Out in the Streets"—and became "All News, All the Time." Westinghouse had commissioned a study to ascertain the best-possible format for their New York outlet. The survey indicated that a "talking newspaper" would have a good chance. Hearst's foray onto the New York dial had evolved into the nation's third all-news station and the metropolitan area's first twenty-four-hour radio news source. It was a service that would keep WINS consistently at or near the top of the New York ratings.

WJBV

(JULY 1926–FEBRUARY 1927)

1926	640kc	100w.

George Cook, an engineer at WFBH, founded Union Course Laboratories, a radio shop and school at 924 Seventy-eighth Street in the Woodhaven section of Queens (an area known as Union Course, near the site of Aqueduct Racetrack). Union Course was granted a license during a period when the federal government was obligated to allow any citizen who had the proper equipment to put a broadcasting station on the air, and WJBV was the first such station in the New York area to take advantage of that situation. Cook's colleague at WFBH, William Reuman, started WWRL a few weeks later.

WJBV lasted for only six months. The entire installation was sold to the Hotel Somerset in Manhattan to become WSOM and, less than a year later, the long-lived WEVD. George Cook went on to work as an electronic engineer for the U.S. Navy and also was president of the American Society of Professional Magicians.

WJDM

(11 MARCH 1970–)

1970	1530khz (daytime)	500w.
1986	1530khz (daytime)	1,000w.
1995	1660khz (additional)	10,000w. day
		500 w. night

WJDM originated as WELA, owned by Radio Elizabeth Inc., with studios at 9 Caldwell Place in Elizabeth and a transmitter on a former dairy farm in Linden. Following protest by WERA in nearby Plainfield, which argued that the similar call letters might confuse listeners and sponsors, the station adopted WJDM, for the first names of its three owners: John Quinn, Dominick Mirabelli and Michael Quinn. Its local service featured middle-of-the-road, adult contemporary, and rock oldies and a solid news service. Among its staffers were former WMGM/WHN deejay Dean Hunter, announcer Jerry Carroll, and Rich Phoenix, a Beatles historian. Newscaster Fred Fishkin went on to Newsradio 88, and WFAN public-affairs moderator Bob Salter also began at WJDM.

John, Dom, and Mike's station added a Sunday foreign-language schedule and was soon broadcasting throughout the week in Spanish, Italian, French, and Hungarian. There were also a bilingual Polish-American show and programs for the Irish-American audience.

At 10:00 A.M. on Friday, 8 December 1995, WJDM opened up the attic of the AM band. In the first expansion of the band since 1955, when the lower end was dropped to 540kc, the FCC authorized operation on frequencies between 1600 and 1700 kHz. It was hoped that this expansion would provide space for hundreds of daytime-only stations to operate around the clock. Through the application of WJDM owner John Quinn, with some help from Congressman Matthew Rinaldo, Radio Elizabeth became a pioneer and test case. WJDM was authorized to add a second transmitter and to duplicate its daytime programs on 1660kHz, remaining on the air on a noncommercial basis into the evening. The 1530kHz transmitter would be shut down in 2001.

WJDM had little company in the region above 1600: a religious broadcaster in Anguilla called the Caribbean Beacon has long operated at 1610kHz, and Vatican Radio has a high-power transmitter on 1611. Several small European, Asian, and Australian stations were established above 1600, but this had remained largely a frequency frontier beyond the tuning capacity of most radios.

The commercial viability of a station so far up the dial would need to be proven. Broadcasters complaining about "graveyard" frequencies in the 1920s and John Hogan's bold experiment with W2XR in the 1930s suggested that listeners might be willing to change their listening habits if and when the proper equipment became available. The great hope was that scanners on new car radios, which already reached to 1700, would stop on WJDM. But the technical effectiveness was easy to measure. Within weeks of operating all alone on 1660, WJDM had received reception reports from radio buffs as far away as California, Finland, and India.

On 1 February 1996, WJDM-1660 took another bold step, affiliating with the Minneapolis-based Children's Broadcasting Corporation to bring back radio for listeners age twelve and younger. "Radio Aahs" came to the New York market with a four-hour special from the FAO Schwartz toy store in Manhattan. Programming for and by kids began with "The All-American Alarm Clock" at sunrise and continued around the clock, to the delight of children who could twist their AM dials far enough.

```
┌─────────────────────────────────┐
│                                 │
│          W J L K                │
│                                 │
└─────────────────────────────────┘
```

(1 MAY 1950–)

1947	94.3Mc	xxx
1950	1310kc	250w.
1980	1310kHz.	2500w.

On 20 November 1947 the *Asbury Park Press* established a station at 94.3 on the FM band with call letters honoring its late editor and publisher J. Lyle Kinmouth. Two and a half years later the *Press* acquired 94 percent interest in WCAP, the Asbury Park AM station whose history dated from the 1920s. WCAP-FM was put off the air, WJLK-FM moved its transmitter to the old WCAP location and studios were established at "Press Plaza," 605 Mattison Avenue in downtown Asbury Park. Some personnel and a few programs were carried over from WCAP, but most of the schedule was filled with the old WJLK-FM lineup.

The schedule included hourly five-minute newscasts plus fifteen-minute summaries at 1:00, 6:00, and 11:00 P.M., prepared by the *Press*. The 1:00 P.M. newscast was one of WJLK's most listened-to programs, since it included the daily obituary column. Each day began with the "Alarm Clock Club" featuring Dick Lewis and ended with George Hudson's "Downbeat Club"—the former an established program on WJLK-FM, the latter a carryover from WCAP.

Thomas Tighe was general manager of WJLK-FM, replaced by Ernest Lass when the consolidation took place and then by program director Everett Rudloff in 1954. Among WJLK's air personalities in the mid-1950s were Bill Bransome, who went on to major stations in Philadelphia, as well as newsmen Lincoln Harner, who left for WNEW, and John Wheeling and Andy Parish, who graduated to CBS News.

"Your listening post on the Jersey Coast" quickly became the dominant local voice with its authoritative *Press* news services. At one point there were fifteen-minute reports on the top of each hour with a headline summary on the half hour—nearly all-news radio. The middle-of-the-road music policy was designed to hold a broad adult audience. In response to requests that the station play some rock and roll, one afternoon WJLK announced that it had selected "the worst rock and roll records we could find" and broadcast a half-hour show that must have repelled the entire listenership through either content or attitude. When the show was over, things returned to normal on a station fairly secure about its standing.

In 1970, longtime air personality and programmer Dick Lewis was promoted to station manager. Lewis continued to host the morning drive-time show but changed it to a three-and-a-half-hour "Newsmorning Radio." The new program included reports from news director Jack Christie, interviews on Larry Brennan's "Coffee Break," and Phyllis Kessel's "Woman Talk." For the remainder of the day, WJLK aired the Drake-Chenault "Hit Parade," which featured some of the best contemporary hits. There was also play-by-play coverage of high school football and basketball, which kept local communities at the "Listening Post."

By the 1980s WJLK switched to something it had once sworn it would never do and moved the AM side to a rock-oldies format while keeping an adult-contemporary sound on FM.

On 9 March 1988 the *Press* sold WJLK to former WOR manager Rick Devlin and adman Jon Ferrari for $12.5 million. The rock oldies were replaced by a big-band and nostalgia format, and in 1991 the station took on a country sound.

See also WCAP.

```
┌─────────────────────────────────┐
│                                 │
│          W J R Z                │
│                                 │
└─────────────────────────────────┘
```

(1 APRIL 1962–16 MAY 1971)

| 1962 | 970kc. | 5,000w. |

National Telefilm Associates' WNTA replaced the thirty-two-year-old WAAT in 1958. Four years later, WNTA was sold to Communications Industries Corporation, which changed the call letters to WJRZ but initially left WNTA's programming untouched. Then on Wednesday, 15 September 1965, at 6:00 A.M. WJRZ became the first station in the New York metropolitan area to play country-and-western music twenty-four hours a day. Country music was winning new audiences at that time, but WJRZ was actually reaching back to the days when WAAT's schedule featured shows like "Hometown Frolics." Many country fans happily turned their dials back to 970.

WJRZ's country format was initially imported from the Midwest. Music director and deejay Bob Lockwood brought his talents and even his jingle package from Chicago's WJJD. Ed Neilson—part of the old wake-up team of Fraim and Fortune—continued as the morning man, and holdovers from the WAAT era included Steve Hollis and Paul Brenner ("You tell 'em you heard Brenner say it on the station with the 97 Brand marked on it"). Lee Arnold, a nationally respected c&w deejay who later went to WHN, promoted concerts by the cream of country talent. Arnold and WJRZ were among the first to advance the career of singer Tammy Wynette. In 1965 WJRZ presented three hours nightly of classic drama and variety shows from radio's "golden age" under the title "Theater of the Imagination."

The original WJRZ studios were at 32 Green Street in Newark, but in 1968 it moved both studios and transmitter. Abandoning the old WAAT transmitter in Kearney, the improved antenna location was on the banks of the Hackensack River, and power output was boosted to 5,000 watts full-time (it had previously been 1,000 watts at night). The FCC also allowed WJRZ to change its official "city of license" when it settled down at 497 Hackensack Avenue in Hackensack.

The ABC Entertainment Network provided news on the half hour, and WJRZ's own news staff, including Dick Jennings, Bob Leeder, and John O'Shea, did local reports at the top of the hour. Also in 1968, WJRZ added some sports coverage to its schedule and positioned itself to be part of one of baseball's greatest chapters. Through their years as the dregs of the diamond, the New York Mets had been heard over WABC, but in the late 1960s enthusiasm about the national pastime was in a general slump and both the Yankees and the Mets moved to less-powerful stations. And so it happened that as "the amazin' Mets" surged into first place and a historic National League championship and World Series victory, their radio voice was a small station over in Hackensack. Ralph Kiner, Lindsay Nelson, and Bob Murphy continued as the play-by-play crew, but WJRZ staff announcer Bob Brown conducted the pre- and post-game shows. The fans found WJRZ, and it shared the glory. The Mets would remain on the WJRZ schedule for the rest of the station's history.

The WJRZ studios were damaged in a fire that broke out after sign-off at 3:43 A.M. on 17 October 1970, forcing the station to move to a temporary prefab at the transmitter site. As 1970 drew to a close, WJRZ revised its music format and switched from country and western to rock.

On 6 January 1971, the FCC approved the sale of WJRZ to Pacific and Southern Broadcasting for $6 million. That spring, the call letters were changed to WWDJ. WJRZ joined WAAT and WNTA in the memorial park of radioland. It had endured for twice as long as its immediate predecessor but less than a third of the life of the pioneer.

See also WAAT, WNTA, WWDJ.

W J X

(13 OCTOBER 1921–JUNE 1924)
1921   360m (832.8kc)   500w.

Dr. Lee De Forest, the "father of radio," was experimenting with radiotelephone transmission in New York as early as 1907 and was responsible for some of the most notable efforts of the pre-broadcasting era through transmitter 2XG. By 1916, De Forest's station at 1391 Sedgewick Avenue in the High Bridge section of the Bronx was radiating on a regular basis. One of his listeners was young Carl Dreher, later a radio engineer and author, who described the De Forest programs in his biography of David Sarnoff: "In 1916 I had a station of my own, for receiving only, in the Bronx, a few miles from Highbridge, so I got a fairly strong signal from De Forest's transmitter. The quality was quite good, and I would listen to the station for hours at a time. It broadcast phonograph records, with De Forest himself sometimes officiating as disc jockey, and he was at the microphone when the station broadcast the 1916 election returns. The station also did some remote pickups by telephone lines."

In his autobiography, *Father of Radio*, De Forest tells about the Highbridge operation and his later experience after World War I with a station in Manhattan which was shut down by radio inspector Arthur Batcheller with the comment, "There is no room in the ether for entertainment." By the time commercial radio broadcasting became a reality, De Forest had come to think that the field was getting crowded. Nonetheless, on 13 October 1921, the De Forest Radio and Telegraph Company received the nation's eighth broadcasting license, the first in New York City. De Forest makes no mention in his autobiography of WJX, since by 1921 he had begun to shift his personal attention to the development of sound in motion pictures and had also moved with his family to Germany. Indeed, when he returned to America, he remarked with some surprise on the progress that broadcasting had made during his absence.

The person most responsible for WJX was Robert F. Gowen, chief engineer of the De Forest Radio Telephone and Telegraph Company and an early radiophone experimenter from his station 2XX in Ossining. He even broadcast vaudeville acts by such stars as the Duncan Sisters and assured radio fans that "there will positively be no phonograph music." By the end of 1921, WJX was planning a series of nightly one-hour concerts, each preceded by a news program, but it appears to have kept an irregular schedule.

An article in the *Boston Post* in April 1922 lists WJX as one of the strongest stations received in its area, but this New York pioneer soon became "dead wood" on the cluttered broadcast dial. As part of a general reduction in broadcast stations, the Commerce Department deleted the WJX license in June 1924.

W J Y ᴵ

(2 JULY 1921)

1921   1600m. (187kc.)   3,500w.

The story of WJY must be divided into two chapters. The first appearance of station WJY lasted only one day, to broadcast one event: a heavyweight championship bout between Jack Dempsey and Georges Carpentier from Boyle's Thirty Acres, alongside the Lackawanna Railroad tracks in Jersey City. The announcer was J. Andrew White, with RCA general manager David Sarnoff, a boxing fan, at his elbow. Speaking into a telephone, White could be heard only as far as the makeshift transmitter shack (a railroad porters' locker room), where his commentary had to be repeated by engineer J. O. Smith.

"The transmitter to be used in this unusual voice broadcasting is the most powerful wireless telephone set of commercial type ever built," explained an RCA publication at the time. It was installed at the Lackawanna railroad yards (while he was with the American Marconi Company, Sarnoff had overseen the development of Lackawanna's radio links), and a six-wire antenna was strung between the railroad's 400-foot radio tower and the clock tower on the terminal building.

The transmitter proved no more able to stand the punishment than was Carpentier, who fell to Dempsey's blows in the fourth round. By then, WJY had overheated, and the station was forced off the air. This was doubly unfortunate for RCA, since it had borrowed the transmitter from General Electric, which was set to deliver it to the U.S. Navy. The equipment was simply not designed to remain on the air continuously for four hours. However, this pioneer broadcast was also a charitable event to raise money for the American Committee for Devastated France, and it enjoyed the support of the Navy Club and its president, Franklin D. Roosevelt.

WJY's groundbreaking sportscast would be a landmark in the "pre-history" of radio.

W J Y ᴵᴵ

(15 MAY 1923–JULY 1926)

1923   405m (740kc) s/t WOR   1,000w.

WJY (the reissued call letters of the RCA station, not the burned-out transmitter) later returned to the air as sister station of WJZ at Radio Broadcast Central. WJY was on 405m (740kc) while WJZ was at 455m (660kc). The two stations operated from twin studios on the sixth floor of Aeolian Hall at 29 W. Forty-second Street, and in an admirable engineering accomplishment, the transmitters fed a duplicate pair of antennae on the roof. The RCA house organ *World Wide Wireless* noted in June 1923 that there would be "a dual program to be broadcast; one, that of classical or serious entertainment; the other, popular airs, dance music and lectures." WJY was to be oriented toward high culture, but the schedules of programs from Radio Broadcast Central didn't always reflect that plan. The major distinction was that WJZ was usually in continuous operation, whereas WJY had to share time with WOR and so was subordinate to two stations.

Friday, 13 February 1925

7:30 P.M.	Billy Wynne's Orchestra
8:15	Travelogue, "From Burma to Java," by Dr. Sigel Roush; musical accompaniment
10:00	"Motion Pictures," Dr. A. B. Hitchens
10:15	Ace Brigode's Virginians

The twin stations at Radio Broadcast Central were occasionally on the air at the same time, but it was apparent that WJY was something of a "spillover" for WJZ. It was also a proving-ground for programming, as in the "Omni-Oral Productions" that were instituted in June 1924. For two hours WJY broadcast half-hour shows that had some connection but that could also stand on their own—a concept still applied by programmers seeking audience flow.

When WJZ moved its transmitter from Forty-second Street to Bound Brook, N.J., with plans to boost power to 50,000 watts, its partner became extraneous. WJY's operation was phased out, and in July 1926 it went off the air. RCA still held a license for the station, but when WEAF was brought into the RCA fold and the National Broadcasting Company was founded, WJZ became the key station of the Blue Network. The newly formed Federal Radio Commission ordered every broadcasting station in the country to present a new license application in 1927, but WJY was not among the applicants. For the second time in a decade, WJY disappeared.

See also WJZ, WEAF.

WJZ

(1 OCTOBER 1921–31 APRIL 1953)

1921	833kc (360 meters)	3,000w.
1923	660kc	variable
1927	660kc	30,000w.
1932	760kc	50,000w.
1941	770kc	50,000w.

GROUCHO: This is a map and diagram of the whole Cocoanut Section. This whole area is within a radius of approximately three-quarters of a mile. Radius. Is there a remote possibility that you know what radius means?

CHICO: It's WJZ.

—*from "The Cocoanuts" (1929)*

WJZ used the slogan "New York's First Station." Although it was the first in the New York area to be officially licensed for broadcasting, Bremer, De Forest, and other experimenters predate it, and RCA's WJY was on the air for a single day three months before Westinghouse's WJZ was heard for the first time. But it would not be unfair to state that the broadcasting industry in the New York area begins with WJZ. Although the Westinghouse Electric and Manufacturing Company had already established KDKA in Pittsburgh and WBZ in Massachusetts, there were those in the Westinghouse organization who believed that radio didn't really take off until WJZ was founded. This is where we find many of radio's milestones. Yet for most of its first two decades, WJZ operated in tandem with another transmitter, first the resurgent WJY at RCA's Radio Broadcast Central and then as the NBC Blue Network flagship and partner to NBC-Red's WEAF.

The beginning was humble. During its first days, WJZ was housed in a shack on the roof of the Westinghouse meter factory on Orange and Plane Streets in Newark; it was accessible only by ladder. It then expanded into the one available space downstairs. Manager Charles Popenoe described it:

Half of the ladies' rest room of the Newark works was set aside for [the WJZ studio], making a space some thirty feet long by fifteen feet wide. Microphones were installed, the necessary wiring from these instruments to the roof, a control panel placed in order to keep announcers and operators [the engineers] in direct communication, and the room draped in a dark red material not only to add to its appearance, but to subdue any noticeable echo. A few

pieces of furniture were secured and a piano rented of the Griffith Piano Company of Newark.

Just as sister station KDKA debuted with the 1920 presidential election returns, WJZ opened with a big show, the 1921 World Series between the Giants and the Yankees, starting on 5 October. There was no play-by-play direct from the Polo Grounds (home field for both teams); announcer Tommy Cowan in Newark simply repeated the description phoned from the ballpark by a newspaper reporter.

WJZ soon gained the support of the Aeolian Company, which supplied a grand piano and a Vocalion record player and helped attract such notable artists as pianist-composer Percy Grainger and singers Johanna Gadski and John Charles Thomas. One of the early guests was opera singer Margaret Namara, whose initial impression of WJZ left her "thoroughly disgusted," according to Tommy Cowan. He quickly redecorated the studio. Writer John Floherty made his first visit to WJZ and was "shocked at its resemblance to an undertaking parlor. Its atmosphere was dead and silent." Westinghouse soon set up a permanent studio at a more comfortable location, the Waldorf-Astoria Hotel, then located at Fifth Avenue and Thirty-fourth Street (now the site of the Empire State Building). Refused a hookup by AT&T, the studio was connected to Newark by a noisy Western Union line.

Radio News magazine wrote of WJZ in December 1921, "Never before has a radio telephone station sent out broadcast, on a regular schedule day after day, so complete and satisfactory a musical and bulletin service."

As the first broadcaster permanently operating in the New York area, WJZ felt a special claim on the sole broadcast wavelength of 360 meters and was reluctant to cede its time to such upstarts as WOR (it did sign off for an hour to allow WOR to broadcast an inaugural program). The Radio Broadcasting Society of America, an early listeners' group, complained that WJZ ought to be shut down if it couldn't go along with time-sharing agreements. In response, Westinghouse and RCA—which by 1922 jointly operated WJZ—offered to let the audience decide between the station's "giving to other broadcasting stations a large part of the time" or going off the air forever. It was pointed out that the station had cost $50,000 to build and cost $50,000 a year to operate and that the Commerce Department authorized "not over two hours a day." WJZ wanted the prime evening hours. It stated that only WOR and WBAY approached it in quality, and it complained, "Other stations have been sending out music from the phonograph." The station reported receiving scores of letters and phone calls asking it to maintain the 7:00 P.M.–midnight schedule. WJZ then recommended that the 400-meter wavelength be made available for broadcasting and maybe even a third additional frequency "so that three strong stations may operate simultaneously."

WJZ continued to be the leading pioneer. On 15 March 1922, WJZ broadcast a studio performance of Mozart's *The*

This broadcast was made from the original WJZ "tent studio" in Newark, N.J., in 1923. The device on the right is a Phonotron, or "dishpan microphone."

Impresario, probably radio's first full-length opera. Comedian Ed Wynn brought the cast of his hit play *The Perfect Fool* out to the Newark studio. In October 1922, WJZ aired its second World Series, this time feeding it to WGY in Schenectady.

Friday, 5 May 1922
In addition to a musical program every hour from 11:00 A.M. to 6:00 P.M., the Newark station sent out the following broadcasting programs by radio telephone.

11:00 A.M.	Official weather forecast
12:00 Noon	Official weather forecast and agricultural reports
2:05	Shipping news
5:00	Official weather forecast
6:00	Agricultural reports
7:00	"Man in the Moon" stories
7:30	"Oral Hygiene" by T. P. Hyatt
7:45	"The Trend of Business Conditions," a financial letter, read by Richard D.

	Wyckoff, editor of the Magazine of Wall Street.
8:00	"Art and Interior Decoration," by Jesse Martin Breese of "Country Life"
8:30	Concert by Colgate Band, 50 pieces, under leadership of Harry Murphy
9:30	Concert by Temple Four quartet of Yonkers
9:52	Official Arlington time
10:01	Official weather forecast

Westinghouse intended that WJZ would be a high-power "super-station" (the term was coined in the early 1920s) that would cover much of the nation and be operated on behalf of all of RCA's affiliated companies, including AT&T and General Electric. When the time came to take that step, it decided to keep the WJZ call letters, and the license was simply transferred to RCA.

"I announced, Good Night and Good Bye, on the night

of May 14, 1923," Tommy Cowan later recalled. "These words signed off forever Station WJZ of Newark, NJ. As ACN [he wasn't allowed to use his name on the air] I had pioneered radio broadcasting through this station. The old station was through. Transferred to New York and new ownership. Signing off was my greatest thrill and sorrow."

WJZ and sister station WJY operated from Radio Broadcast Central on the sixth floor of the Aeolian Building, 29 W. Forty-second Street (across from the public library). RCA president James Harbord stated, "This station will gather from every part of New York City and from all available sources all that will instruct and entertain, and hurl it over millions of square miles of territory … the world's first national theater." There were twin studios with wax-treated muslin over felt walls. Two transmitters fed dual 115-foot high antenna arrays on the roof. RCA intended this to be "the Model Broadcast Station of America," but there were still shortcomings that the technology of the day couldn't overcome: on hot summer days the studio temperature climbed to well over 100 degrees.

Program logs from 15 May to the last day of December 1923 reveal that WJZ aired 3,426 programs, including 723 talks, 67 church services, 205 bedtime stories, and 21 sports events (football, baseball, boxing, and polo). Most of the broadcasts were musical and ranged from Carnegie Hall and Aeolian Hall recitals to harmonica and banjo solos.

Toward the end of 1925, WJZ fired up a 50,000-watt transmitter on the banks of the Raritan River in Bound Brook, N.J., thirty-five miles from the Aeolian Hall studios. Four years after its genesis in a rooftop shack, WJZ occupied a two-story, 100-by-75-foot building. The station could now be picked up on the smallest crystal set, and Bound Brook residents found that the signal overwhelmed everything else on the air. WJZ switched to lower power while its engineers visited hundreds of homes in central New Jersey to deal with complaints, and federal regulators took another look at high-power transmission. It did not operate regularly at 50kw. till 1935.

In 1926, WJZ conducted a survey of listener tastes. More than four thousand questionnaires were returned; they revealed that WJZ's audience preferred jazz to classical music, wanted more news, liked baseball, football, boxing, and horse racing in that order, and preferred travel talks over all other topics, followed by politics, health, and literature. The listeners split evenly on the question of advertising, but most seemed ready to accept "indirect" announcements at the start and end of programs.

Most stations in 1926 were still broadcasting for goodwill alone, and RCA was learning that goodwill had a cost. "WJZ was operating on a budget of over $100,000 a year, without visible and tangible earnings of any kind," wrote radio pioneers Alfred Goldsmith and Austin Lescarboura in 1930. "Once amply repaid by publicity for its organization, the competition of many other broadcasting stations had reduced the publicity value to the point where it was considered hardly worth the cost."

In July 1926, AT&T agreed to transfer station WEAF to RCA ownership, setting the stage for NBC's networks and making permanent the wired "syndication" that both WEAF and WJZ had been conducting for several years. On 15 November 1926, the National Broadcasting Company came into America's homes for the first time. Both WJZ and WEAF broadcast the inaugural gala. On New Year's 1927, the NBC Blue Network debuted, with WJZ as the originating station. A March 1927 poll by *Radio Listeners' Guide* found WJZ to be the most popular station in the United States.

In October 1927 WJZ moved into NBC studios still under construction at 711 Fifth Avenue. A month later WEAF and the Red Network joined WJZ and the Blue. The National Broadcasting Company was finally under one roof. In November 1933 WJZ, WEAF, and all of NBC and RCA corporate headquarters moved to 30 Rockefeller Plaza.

Over the years WJZ and the Blue Network presented many of America's most popular programs: Lowell Thomas and the News, "Amos 'n' Andy," "Little Orphan Annie," "America's Town Meeting of the Air," and excellent western drama on "Death Valley Days." Each midday "The National Farm and Home Hour" brought news and entertainment to rural listeners. Ted Malone read poetry. Milton Cross conveyed children "Coast to Coast on a Bus," as well as bringing opera lovers the Saturday matinees from the Met. NBC found plenty of material to program two networks. WJZ was New York's connection with the world more than it may have been New Yorkers' connection with each other. The first superstation had little time to spend on its local audience.

Occasionally a show would premiere on NBC-Blue, which had a weaker lineup of stations nationwide, and be shifted to the Red Network if it grew in popularity ("Fibber McGee & Molly" is one example). NBC seemed to be competing unfairly with itself, and this was one reason for an antitrust action against RCA. In 1942, the FCC ruled that no broadcaster could own more than one station in a market. WJZ was the most valuable asset of the BLUE (as the newly independent network preferred to be listed so that its name would stand out like NBC and CBS). On 12 October 1943, the BLUE and its New York outlet were sold to Edward J. Noble, owner of station WMCA. Due to wartime shortages, the new company and its proud flagship, WJZ, continued to broadcast from Radio City on a ten-year lease. The company also continued to identify itself on the air as "The Blue Network"; "ABC, The American Broadcasting Company," would not become official until 15 June 1945, when negotiations were completed with George B. Storer, who had owned the defunct American Broadcasting System and still owned the name.

To divide the company into two, NBC and the BLUE appointed managers who would then "invite" employees to choose a network. Several staff announcers waited to see what decision the great pioneer Milton Cross would make, then followed him to ABC.

In January 1944, WJZ moved its transmission facilities from Bound Brook to Lodi, N.J., six air miles from Manhattan.

The 640-foot mast erected at Bound Brook in 1925 was dismantled and trucked to Lodi, where it dwarfed all other radio towers. The primary coverage area reached all the way to Philadelphia, and WJZ had regular daytime listeners as far south as North Carolina.

WJZ and the ABC network finally got a home of their own when studios were moved in November 1948 from Radio City to a renovated building at 7 W. Sixty-sixth Street. A block west of Central Park, the edifice had formerly been the stables of the New York Riding Club.

Supplementing the ABC schedule were local chat shows featuring Walter Kiernan, Galen Drake, and Ed and Pegeen Fitzgerald, during a 1945 escape from WOR.

On 1 May 1953—six and a half years after the other two network flagships had changed their names—WJZ became WABC. The familiar old Atlantic Broadcasting Company call letters that had been used for nearly twenty years by CBS were heard again in New York, and in 1957 Westinghouse regained the letters WJZ to identify its television station in Baltimore.

See also WEAF, WJY, WABC (II).

Wit Henry Morgan returns from army duty in 1945 to his "Here's Morgan" radio show to renew his long-standing feud with sponsor Jesse Adler—"Old Man Adler" of Adler elevator shoes.

WKBD *see* **WAAT**

WKBK *see* **WBNY**

WKBO

(1926–1931)

1926	various freq.	xxx
1927	1410kc s/t WFRL, WBNY, WKBQ	xxx
1927	1370kc s/t WIBS, WBMS, WNJ	xxx

The Camith Corporation of Jersey City put WKBO on the air before 1926 and changed frequency about four times in the first year before being set to 1410 by the FRC in April 1927. It was a station whose sense of public interest included broadcasting church services and police bulletins. Then in May 1927, WKBO was ordered to share 219 meters (1370kc) with WFRL, WBNY, and WKBQ (a Bronx station with which WKBO would sometimes be confused). The proliferation of small stations soon made it likely some would be combined, and as early as 1928 WKBO was seen as a candidate for consolidation with WIBS in Elizabeth and WBMS in Hackensack. By that autumn it was splitting hours with WIBS, WNJ, and WBMS.

Thursday, 28 April 1927
12:00 Noon   F.N.T. and Charles Coleman

12:30	Weather Reports and News
12:50	Police Reports
1:00	Musicale
	Off the Air
6:15	Complete Baseball Returns
6:25	Police Reports
6:30	Orchestra
7:30	Jack McGown, songs
7:45	Saul Kaplan, pianist
8:00	John R. Fasson, baritone
8:15	Ben Gordon, tenor
8:30	Goodwill Industries Program
9:00	Dd. O'Hanlon, Talk
9:15	Manzke and Goellner, violin & piano
9:30	Phil Duckman, pianist
10:00	Club Abby

By the summer of 1931, WKBO's service had become inconsistent and clearly inferior to that of its newest partner at 1450kc, WHOM. A Federal Radio Commission report pointed out that WKBO was "inadequately financed and renders a comparatively poor program service." Its elimination "would deprive the Jersey City area of no substantial broadcasting service not available through other existing stations." Despite protests filed by Congressmen Hartley and Lehlbach—and despite Lehlbach's appeal for intervention by the Hoover White House—the station was shut down and the license deleted in October 1931. WKBO's hours were given to WHOM, which also absorbed WNJ. The consolidation foreseen three years earlier had taken place.

WKBQ

(25 September 1926–31 December 1930)

Sept. 1926	1040kc s/t WJBV	500w.
June 1927	1370kc s/t WKBO, WCGU	500w.
Nov. 1928	1350kc s/t WMSG, WBNY, WCDA	250w.

Bronx residents who didn't want to travel all the way down to Coney Island could take the trolley out 177th Street to the Starlight Amusement Park. WKBQ signed on the air from the Starlight during a period of regulatory limbo before the creation of the Federal Radio Commission, when broadcast licenses were easy to obtain.

To draw people away from the radio, WKBQ plugged the day's leading attractions along with a daily broadcast called "Starlight Parking," an advisory on the best way into the park and one of the city's first traffic bulletins.

Thursday, 2 June 1927

2:00 P.M.	Mara Gold, piano
2:15	Pauline Kittner, soprano
2:30	Home Talk—Irene Phillips
2:45	Radio Rowdies
3:15	Financial Review
3:30	Dave Herman, harmonica
3:45	Starlight Parking
4:00	Same as WPCH
Off for WKBO, WCGU	
7:00	Daly Theatre
7:30	Boy Scout program
8:00	Harlem hour

Starting in 1927, WKBQ regularly relayed the programs of WPCH in Manhattan. However, the Bronx station also drew on it own "stable" of speakers and musicians for a nice mix of popular and classical music. The park's major attraction was a series of full-length operas staged each summer as a showcase for young American singers and broadcast over WKBQ. The station also covered local happenings on the "North Side News Hour."

With the beginning of serious radio regulation in 1927, WKBQ was told to share its frequency with WKBO in Jersey City and briefly with WCGU at Coney Island.

On 11 November 1928—a day when hundreds of stations around the country were reassigned—WKBQ moved to 1350 and a time-sharing arrangement with WMSG at Madison Square Garden and the Corriere d'America's WCDA, two stations with which its history would be linked. WBNY was also assigned to share the WKBQ frequency.

Among the structures at the Starlight Amusement Park was the New York Coliseum. Not to be confused with the Columbus Circle venue of the same name that opened a quarter-century later, this was a large wooden exhibit hall that Allen Cahill had transported intact from Philadelphia. WKBQ moved into the structure early in 1929 and erected twin towers there to support the antenna. This would be its home when the station was sold to Amory Lawrence Haskell at the end of 1930, and so "the official broadcasting station of the New York Coliseum" became WBNX at New Year's 1931.

The depression drove the Starlight Amusement Park to failure; the shacks of a squatter colony went up alongside it, and an observer in 1938 said the park "was "overrun with weeds ... which gives an effect of a deserted city."

See also WBNX.

WKBS

(1 SEPTEMBER 1948–30 NOVEMBER 1956)

1948   1520kc.   250w.

The first station on Nassau County's North Shore was established by the Key Broadcasting System in distinguished surroundings. The original studios of WKBS were in the Moore Building on the corner of Main and South Streets in Oyster Bay, which had served as the nation's administrative center whenever President Theodore Roosevelt was at the "summer White House" at Sagamore Hill. R. Lee Hollingsworth was the station president, general manager, commercial manager, and chief engineer. With his strong technical background—he once designed a single antenna that would have simultaneously sent a 50,000-watt signal to a domestic audience and 500,000 watts overseas—Hollingsworth built an effective plant. The 250-watt WKBS transmitter was alongside Oyster Bay Harbor, and the signal crossed Long Island Sound so strongly that the Key Broadcasting System contemplated studios at Port Chester, in Westchester County, and in Stamford, Conn.

The prospect of competition from a new station in Huntington worried WKBS. Disc jockey Bob Holmes was sent to originate remote broadcasts from a storefront in Huntington, beneath a large sign that suggested WKBS was the only local radio the North Shore needed. That didn't hold back the founding of WGSM, and failing also to solidify an audience on both sides of the Sound, in 1952 Hollingsworth moved WKBS to a more central location on Maple Place near Jericho Turnpike in the Nassau County seat of Mineola. Studios, offices, and transmitter were now crowded into a small cinderblock building with the tower beside the Long Island Railroad tracks.

"The Jericho Turnpike Station" developed a faithful audience through an active involvement with community groups. The day began with Perry Samuels' "Tune-Up Time" (a title chosen in a listeners' contest), followed by a phone-in auction at 9:00 A.M., an event often interrupted by calls of a general nature because the auction used WKBS's central office number.

Lee Hollingsworth was a man of strong opinion, utterly convinced that his 250-watt daytime station was the finest on the air, he was intolerant of any suggestion otherwise. He also was known to occasionally walk in on record shows to interrupt the disc jockey and deliver editorial comments; his favorite topic was the potential threat to the U.S. economy caused by Japanese imports driving down American wages—a view that turned out to be prophetic.

In 1956, the Key Broadcasting System sold WKBS, which became WKIT.

See also WKIT.

WKDM

(1 SEPTEMBER 1984–)

1984   1380kHz   5,000w.

The United Broadcasting Company of New York had taken over station WBNX in 1960 and continued to run it as a share-time station until 1984, when the Pillar of Fire religious organization in Zarephath, N.J. relinquished WAWZ-AM; 1380kHz was finally occupied by only one station in the New York area. As if to proclaim its liberation from an intermittent schedule, the station changed the call letters to WKDM—an echo of San Juan's popular WKVM—during Labor Day weekend festivities.

The "Spanish contemporary hits" format wasn't much different from what "Radio X" had been playing for the previous twenty years. Longtime WBNX afternoon host Polito Vega took over the morning show, with newscaster Coco Cabrera. Among WKDM's other air personalities were Manolo Iglesias, Nelson Rodriguez, and Pedro Juan. Building on the sudden popularity of the Puerto Rican group Menudo, WKDM played Latin contemporary music. In 1988 studios were moved to 570 Fifth Avenue.

The competition was strong among New York's Spanish-language stations, and WKDM usually trailed the better-established WADO and the more-powerful WSKQ.

In 1993 WKDM was purchased by Arthur Liu's Multi-Cultural Broadcasting, owner of WNWK-FM in Newark (the former WHBI-FM). The new owner cut back the Latino programming to the prime morning and early afternoon hours and instituted Chinese programs in the evening.

WKER

(3 OCTOBER 1964–23 AUGUST 1993)

1964   1500kc (daytime)   1000w.

Pompton Lakes is in New Jersey's scenic Ramapo foothills, at the other end of Passaic County from Paterson. In 1964, former NBC executive Robert Kerr and his wife, Joan Brooks Kerr (whose radio experience went back to the "Lavender and New Lace" show on the Blue Network), founded Kerradio Inc. and started a local radio station. The studios and transmitter were close by N.J. Route 23, the Pompton Turnpike, locale of some of the great "swing era" roadhouses.

WKER started out playing Top 40 mixed with some middle-of-the-road music. Station manager Ron Hickman did the wake-up show, news director Jack McElen had a mid-morning record show, and program director Tom Niven hosted afternoon drive time. Local news was presented in cooperation with the *Paterson News*. Joan Brooks Kerr returned to the microphone with a daily afternoon talk show.

In 1993 WKER was sold to Mariana Broadcasting, headed by John Silliman, and became WGHT.

WKIT

(1 December 1956–1959)

1956   1520kc (daytime)   250w.

When Lee Hollingsworth's Key Broadcasting System sold WKBS, it was housed in a tiny cinderblock building in Mineola. When WKIT took to the air, it had settled into more spacious and accessible facilities. The studios were located on the lower level promenade of the Roosevelt Field Shopping Center in Garden City, and broadcast operations were behind floor-to-ceiling windows. Thousands of shoppers each day looked over the announcers' shoulders or paused to read the news for themselves as it came in on the UPI teletype. It was an excellent public-relations gesture and probably also served to keep the on-air work neat.

Seymour Weintraub was the president of WKIT Inc., Walter Ware was the station manager and Frank Costa, a veteran of WKBS days, became program director. Chief engineer Stan LoPresto was also a familiar voice on the air. Among the announcers was Hempstead's Telly Savalas, who went on to fame as an Oscar-winning actor and as the irrepressible TV detective Kojak.

The music was mostly easy-listening LPs. "The Station Where Women Keep In Touch" cultivated its relationship with the audience of suburban housewives through its Community Club Awards and other activities. Always lagging WHLI in the local ratings, WKIT still attracted advertisers aware of the responsiveness of its well-targeted public. And being housed in the island's biggest shopping mall didn't hurt.

WKIT lasted only three years; it was sold to the *New York Herald-Tribune* to become WFYI, the Long Island outlet for the newspaper's suburban radio network.

See also WKBS, WTHE, WVIP.

WLAW

(September 1922–August 1924)

1922   360m. (833kc)   500w.

The New York City Police Department installed its first permanent radio station on 11 June 1920, a point-to-point communications setup with the call KUVS. Police officials viewed earlier attempts at radio as unsatisfactory due to the lack of confidentiality on the air, the very phenomenon that broadcasters were happily exploiting. But when the police radio was upgraded in the fall of 1922, it was with a broadcast license and the name WLAW, one of the first instances of call letters that meant something. (The letters were issued from the Commerce Department's alphabetical list, but someone must have been looking to do the cops a favor.) WLAW was managed by M. R. Brennan, superintendent of the NYPD's Telegraph Bureau, and shared time with WJZ, WOR, WHN, and other pioneers on the sole broadcast wavelength of 360 meters.

WLAW sent out bulletins for use by police officers, but it was also a medium for obtaining the cooperation and goodwill of the city's "radioists." Listeners could follow the progress of police activity, especially after the city put its first radio-equipped motorcycle patrols on the street in 1923 (the apparatus was in a sidecar surmounted by an enormous loop antenna).

WLAW soon grew obsolete. In 1924, despite many developments in radio and the expansion of the broadcast band, WLAW was still operating irregularly at 360 meters. In August 1924 Brennan reported it "out of commission" and turned in the license. A month earlier, however, the city of New York seriously entered radio through station WNYC, whose service included police advisories. WLAW had served in part as a model for municipal broadcasting.

Of course, the NYPD never left the air. By 1931 all police cars were equipped with radios, and there were three police transmitters operating above the broadcast band: WPEG in Manhattan, WPES in the Bronx, and WPEE in Brooklyn. Avid radioists still enjoyed monitoring the police frequencies, but millions more preferred to follow the cops and robbers on "Gang Busters" or "Dick Tracy."

See also WNYC.

WLBH

(6 DECEMBER 1926–APRIL 1928)

1926	1320kc s/t WMRJ	30w.
1927	1290kc	30w.
1928	1420kc s/t WMRJ, WHPP	30w.

WLBH was owned by Joseph J. Lombardi of Farmingdale and sometimes operated as a portable station at fairs and radio exhibits. In April 1927 the new Federal Radio Commission assigned it to share time with WMRJ at 1320. Then it was kicked up to 1490 in June to share with Grebe's WGMU and WRMU, which were actually being moved out of the broadcast band.

Lombardi organized his operation as the Nassau Broadcasting Corporation and arranged for an operating agreement with the Patchogue Elks' Club. In 1928 WLBH became WPOE, Patchogue.

See also WPOE.

WLBX

(24 DECEMBER 1926–25 JUNE 1932)

Dec. 1926	1070kc	250w.
Apr. 1927	1300kc	
	(unauthorized)	250w.
June 1927	1470kc	250w.
Nov. 1927	1500kc s/t WMBQ,	
	WCLB, WWRL	100w.
Nov. 1930	1500kc	250w. (unauthorized)

John N. Brahy's Radio Service Laboratories was one of those small shops that went into radio broadcasting during the unregulated days of 1926. WLBX operated from 283 Crescent Street in Long Island City, first on 1070kc; it then jumped in April 1927 to 1300 and, in June to 1470 and finally, in November, was ordered to 1500, sharing with WMBQ, WCLB, and neighboring WWRL.

"The Radio Voice at the Gateway to Long Island" was not a powerful voice. Brahy had strung his antenna so close to the ground that any large vehicle passing on Crescent Street could absorb some of the radiated power. Every time a truck drove by, listeners heard a dip in WLBX's signal.

By the end of 1930, WLBX was on the air only Tuesday and Thursday evenings. Three or four hours of each broadcast day were in German. WLBX seldom issued an advance schedule.

John Brahy moved his transmitter to Twenty-fourth Street in Long Island City and raised power from 100 to 250 watts, all without permission of the Federal Radio Commission. These violations, plus Brahy's use of an unlicensed transmitter operator (his father), caused the FRC to revoke the license. Brahy fought the FRC in court, but in June 1932 a cease-and-desist order was issued and WLBX was forced off the air.

WLIB

(1 JULY 1942–)

| 1942 | 1190kc (daytime) | 1,000w. |
| 1967 | 1190kc | 10,000w. |

Beginning in 1926, Brooklyn radio engineer Arthur Faske consecutively operated several stations: WBKN, WCLB, WMIL and WCNW, and in each case he shared time with other small stations near the end of the dial. Just before Christmas in 1941, Faske moved WCNW from 1600 kilocycles down to 1190, operating continually but on a dawn-to-dusk schedule. Faske had been cited by the FCC for irregularities in his operation of WCNW, so it was to be expected that it would soon be sold.

On Wednesday, 1 July 1942, station manager Elias Godofsky took control of WCNW and adopted call letters WLIB. During those early days of World War II the station's slogan "The Voice of Liberty" had an especially patriotic ring. Studios remained in the WCNW building at 846 Flatbush Avenue—the new station identified itself as "WLIB in Brooklyn"—and a Manhattan studio was added in the RKO Building. Arthur Faske stayed on as chief engineer.

WLIB's described its programming as "the popular classics with a blend of the modern … and news." Former WQXR music director Eddy Brown joined the new station and it became the first commercial competition with WQXR for the classical music audience. Murray Jordan was chief announcer and other air personalities included Charles Sidney Freed, who'd been heard on WQXR, and Alan Courtney, whose credits included WNEW and WOV. In October, 1944, the *New York Post* realized a long-standing ambition to enter radio when publisher Dorothy Schiff Thackery bought WLIB for $250,000. Godofsky went on to found WHLI in Hempstead. In November the "city of license" was officially changed to New York and studios were soon moved to 207 E. 30th Street. *Post* newscasts were heard at 45 minutes past each hour, but programming was little changed.

Wednesday, 1 November 1944

7:45 A.M.	Studio music
7:50	N.Y. Post News
8:00	Young People's Church
8:30	Morning Overture
8:45	N.Y. Post News; Household hints
9:15	Concert Music
11:45	N.Y. Post News; Luncheon Music
12:45	N.Y. Post News; Concert Music
3:45	N.Y. Post News; Tea Music
4:45	N.Y. Post News; Candlelight and Silver
5:55	N.Y. Post News
6:00	Clifford Evans, news
6:15	Little Classics
6:25	Sign Off

In September 1949, with financial difficulties facing the *Post*, WLIB was sold for only $150,000 to the New Broadcasting Company, led by former WNYC manager Morris Novik and his brother Harry, who was in the ladies' garment business. Classical music was proving unprofitable, and ethnic programming had already begun in a small way on WLIB. The Noviks expanded broadcasts for Jewish and black audiences and added Spanish, Polish, and Greek programs. The Jewish-oriented programs were mostly in English and emphasized culture and public affairs, while a Harlem studio was planned to better serve the African-American community. On 11 December 1952, WLIB moved its entire broadcast operation to the Hotel Theresa at 2090 Seventh Avenue, which the station dubbed Harlem Radio Center.

WLIB developed a respectable schedule of community-affairs programs. News director Clifford Evans went on to head RKO-General's Washington bureau. Among those heard during the "Anglo-Jewish" hours was noted commentator Estelle M. Sternberger. Drawing listeners to the black-oriented programming that filled nearly 90 percent of its schedule were personalities like Buddy and Sara Lou Bowser, Doc Wheeler, Ora Brinkley, George W. Goodman, and former NAACP president Walter White, whose discussion show was nationally syndicated by WLIB. Disc jockey Hal Jackson came to WLIB briefly in 1949 and returned in 1953 with "The House That Jack Built." One of the most respected programs was "The Gospel Train," created by veteran broadcaster Joe Bostic Sr. Bostic had begun his career at WCNW and often acted as the conscience of WLIB, effectively outspoken within the staff in opposition to paid religious broadcasts.

During those years, WLIB was New York City's weakest AM station—the only daytimer in the city—and was still using the old WCNW transmitter in Greenpoint. In July 1953 it was installing a new transmitter and completing erection of a tower on pilings in Hallett's Cove near the East River in Astoria when the 212-foot tower tore loose from its base and collapsed across Vernon Boulevard, injuring five people and just missing a playground filled with children. The new

transmitter and antenna were finally put into service on 21 February 1954.

By 1960 WLIB led the daytime ratings among African-Americans in New York City. The station held on to its reputation for community spirit and service. In 1962, it moved from the Hotel Theresa to the United Mutual Life Insurance Building at 310 Lenox Avenue at 125th Street, still in the center of Harlem. Five years later WLIB went from 1,000 to 10,000 watts, still a daytimer. On 6 June 1967, Mayor John Lindsay presided at the ceremony that shut down the Queens transmitter and switched over to Lyndhurst, N.J.

WLIB's power was not to be measured merely in kilowatts. It became a soapbox and safety valve for the black community, especially during the "hot summers" of the 1960s and 1970s. The "Community Opinion" call-in show conducted by program director Leon Lewis gave listeners an outlet for outrage, frustration, or just puzzlement. Lawyers, doctors, and even psychologists were regular guests. Following the assassination of Dr. Martin Luther King Jr. in 1968, WLIB turned over entire broadcast days to news and a wide range of public comments and won some of the credit for keeping New York City relatively calm while riots broke out in other cities. The radical Black Panther Party even had its own program on WLIB in 1969, "The People's Information Slot." All this provided an outlet for black opinion as well as a listening post for the entire community to share that opinion, and in 1970 WLIB earned the first Peabody Award given to a black-oriented station.

As early as 1945, WLIB was one of the first stations in the city to apply for an FM license and finally was awarded 107.5MHz. in the spring of 1966. The Harlem station had always enjoyed the collaboration of some of America's top musicians, including Mercer Ellington. Jazz pianist Billy Taylor joined the staff as program director of WLIB-FM, which quickly attracted the city's jazz fans. WLIB had always recognized the diversity within the black community and now added programs targeted to the growing Afro-Caribbean audience.

A disagreement that began with the dismissal of a producer who refused to act as a lunch-hour switchboard operator led to a rupture of labor relations at WLIB, forcing the station to shut down both AM and FM for two weeks in October 1970. Employees set up picket lines outside the studios and handed out pamphlets accusing the New Broadcasting Company of being "the scavenger of black radio." Staff members, both black and white, publicly complained about technical and working conditions as well as the relevancy of the programming. The dispute ended on 28 October 1970 (the producer was offered her job back), but the strained relations added to the pressure on Harry Novik to sell WLIB, and he looked for an African-American buyer.

In July 1971, WLIB-AM was purchased by Inner City Broadcasting Corporation, headed by former Manhattan Borough President Percy Sutton and by Clarence Jones, publisher of New York's major black newspaper, the

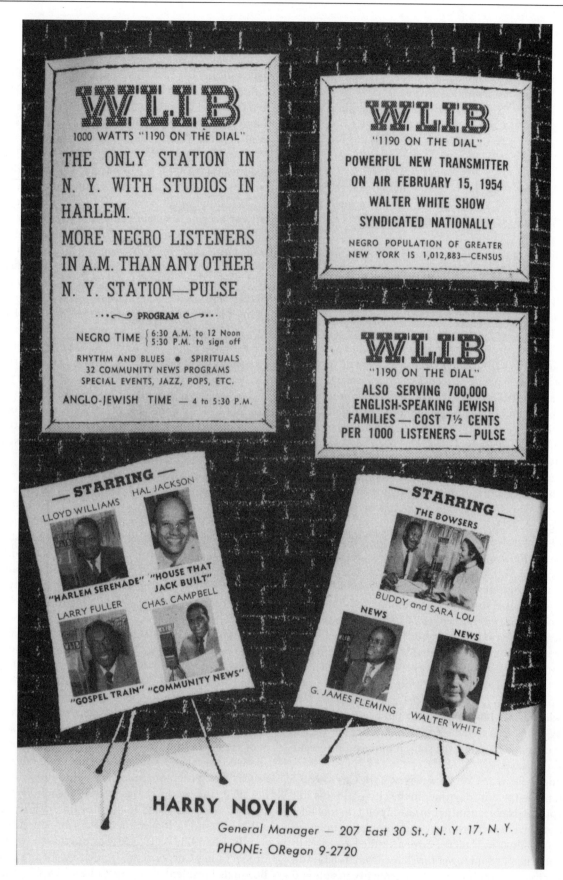

WLIB told its entire story in this 1954 ad.

Amsterdam News (which had been purchased by Jones and Sutton a year before). Other owners included Billy Taylor, Percy Sutton's son Pierre, Hal Jackson, and "three black housewives." Novik held onto WLIB-FM but gave Inner City an option to buy it two years later. In 1975 WLIB, AM and FM, moved from Harlem to 801 Second Avenue. In that same year the FM call letters were changed to WBLS. From 1979 to 1983, Arbitron found WBLS to be the top-rated station in the New York market.

WLIB's newscasts had about one-fifth the audience pull as all-news WINS, and surveys revealed that the station's listenership was 97 percent black.

As intended when Inner City Broadcasting Corporation was organized, WLIB soon became the center of an African-American media empire, which added stations in the Los Angeles, San Francisco, and Detroit markets as well as cable TV systems. In 1980, Inner City bought and restored Harlem's historic Apollo Theatre.

In November 1980 Inner City applied to move WLIB from 1190 to 1200kHz in order to escape the dawn-to-dusk restrictions imposed by its operation on the clear channel frequency of 50,000-watt WOWO in Fort Wayne, Indiana. The request to the FCC pointed out that since Inner City "came to be a broadcast station owner relatively late in the day, as have most minority broadcasters, it has found that the stations available to it for purchase have tended to be those with less adequate facilities." It contrasted the success of WBLS (FM) with the plight of its AM partner, which had "suffered substantial operating losses in every year since its acquisition." But the FCC feared that WLIB would interfere with existing stations at or near 1200 and denied the application.

Public affairs continued to be a key part of WLIB's schedule, and as racial issues grew sharper in New York and public involvement in broadcast discussion more commonplace, WLIB became a dominant and controversial voice. It brought together various African-American communities and had hopes of starting a national network for black-oriented talk shows. WLIB assumed a conspicuous role in local politics, especially with the election of David Dinkins, the city's first black mayor and a close friend of Percy Sutton's. Dinkins' transfer of Inner City Broadcasting stock to his son had become an issue in his mayoral campaign. Harsh criticism of Mayor Dinkins over WLIB caused Sutton to go on Gary Byrd's "Global Black Experience" program on 14 May 1990 and tell listeners, "WLIB cannot be used for us to destroy each other." He threatened to cancel the talk shows.

In September 1994, in a move unprecedented in the broadcasting industry, Inner City Broadcasting purchased WOWO for the sole purpose of reducing its power and redirecting its signal. The Fort Wayne station was then resold and continued operating as a local broadcaster while WLIB, after forty-three years, could finally increase its power to 50,000 watts daytime and 30,000 watts at night and be heard full-time in the entire New York market.

See also WCNW, WHLI.

WLIM

(1978–)

1978?   1580 kc   10,000 w.

Patchogue's WPAC turned out to be something of a bad-luck station for its owners, and its successors didn't seem to be doing any better. WLIM was seriously on the ropes when a veteran broadcaster came to its rescue, restored its health, and impressed his own personality on it.

In the early 1980s when Patchogue's other station, WALK AM/FM, was up for sale, Jack Ellsworth was a prime bidder for ownership. Ellsworth had come to WALK as program director in the early 1950s, was promoted to station manager, and was the guiding force for thirty years. His bid to buy that station fell short, and he left early in 1981. By July 1981 Ellsworth, his wife, Dorothy, and former WALK newscaster George Drake had formed the Long Island Music Broadcasting Corporation and owned WLIM.

The day began with morning man Bob Dorian, who would go on to host cable television's *American Movie Classics*. WLIM played big-band and swing music, which was Jack Ellsworth's passion. Deejay Bob Stern said of his WLIM colleague, "Jack is a big band missionary." "Memories in Melody" became one of the longest-running shows on Long Island radio, drawing on Ellsworth's extensive record collection and even more extensive knowledge of the swing era. The biggest memory in melody for WLIM was its 1982 daylong salute to Benny Goodman. The aging King of Swing himself was persuaded to come out to Patchogue and was a little puzzled by all the fuss. Asked on the air how he felt about a full day of his music being played over WLIM, Goodman replied, "If you can take it, so can I." The visit was covered by NBC Television and was a spectacular turning point for the popularity of WLIM.

The swing-era sounds drew to WLIM a loyal audience —not all of them senior citizens—who appreciated the music and the expertise that Jack Ellsworth had gained during a half-century in radio.

WLIR

(1984–)

1984	1300kHz.	500w. day / 83w. night

When Rockland Media Corporation took over Spring Valley's WGRC in 1984, new owner Elton Spitzer requested a reissuance of the call letters WLIR, the spunky FM station on Long Island that he had previously owned. The programming of Rockland County's new WLIR was initially the "Music of Your Life," a nostalgiac package of big bands and ballads. In 1993 Rockland Media sold the station to Talkline Broadcasting, headed by Zev Brenner. Talkline was then producing a Saturday-evening block of Jewish programs on WMCA, and Brenner built on that experience to transform WLIR into one of America's unique broadcast operations.

With studios on Route 59 in Monsey, at the center of a region with a large traditional Jewish population, WLIR became "all Jewish all the time." The broadcast day was expanded to twenty-four hours and was filled with the spectrum of Jewish entertainment and ideas, from rabbinical discussions of the Torah and Talmud to contemporary Jewish rock music. There were shows in Yiddish and Hebrew and even a few hours a week of Christian programming. The Monsey station soon extended its service nationwide with a satellite uplink.

WLIX

(1 FEBRUARY 1967—1995)

1967	540kHz (daytime)	250 w.
1976	540kHz	250 w. day / 220w. night

With call letters meant to signify "Long Island Crossroads," Malcom Smith's Long Island Broadcasting Corporation (no relation to the company that founded WWRL and WGLI) took over WBIC. Studios were moved from Bay Shore to Islip, the station's official hometown. The easy-listening format continued, and some talk shows were added.

In 1975, WLIX subscribed to the Drake Chenault Hit Parade and began specializing in rock oldies from the 1950s and 1960s. News was heard at six minutes before each hour. At about the same time, studios were moved to 2960 Sunrise Highway in South Islip. A few hours were scheduled each week for the Italian-American audience, featuring host Joe Rotolo.

On 13 October 1976 WLIX was sold to Living Communications Inc. and studios were moved back to Bay Shore. Programming was changed to paid religion, and nighttime service was added at slightly reduced power.

WLIX was sold at the end of 1995 and became WLUX. *See also* WBIC, WLUX.

WLNA

(25 NOVEMBER 1948–)

1948	1420kc (daytime)	500 w.
1951	1420kc	1,000 w.
1982	1420kHz	5,000 day / 1,000 w. night

The postwar suburban broadcast boom gave Northern Westchester its first station since WOKO moved from Peekskill to Poughkeepsie in 1928. WLNA was established by the Highland Broadcasting Corporation with studios and transmitter on Dogwood Road in Peekskill, a site that soon became known as Radio Terrace. Peter J. Housekeeper was WLNA's first president and chief engineer, and the program director was former WPAT announcer Joel Blake.

With WFAS as its primary local competition, WLNA started out specializing in easy listening "Music from Radio Terrace." News director Sam D'Onofrio and announcer George Birdas were familiar voices, and Birdas became program director in 1958.

With the addition of WLNA-FM at 100.7MHz in 1958, the Peekskill station could serve its audience from "Top of the Morning" at dawn, through musical programs with titles like "Journey into Melody" and "Midday Medley," to "Evening Medley" and "Your World of Song" after the AM sign-off. The "After Hours" program ran till 2:00 A.M. The biggest break with the format came on Saturday afternoons with Clee Everett's black-oriented rhythm-and-blues program.

By the 1970s WLNA was presenting extended news blocks under the title "Newswatch 14," and the musical hours were called "Music 14." WLNA-FM was split from the AM operation, and the call letters were changed to WHUD. In 1982, Highland sold WLNA and WHUD to Gary B. Pease's Radio Terrace Inc. for $4.2 million. The AM side finally went to full-time operation, and programming was revised to add more news and talk as well as an adult-contemporary-music format.

At the start of 1996 WLNA moved to a full-time news and talk format. "Good Morning Hudson Valley" begins the day on the "Local News Authority," and in addition to local talk shows are several nationally syndicated programs, including the "Fabulous Sports Babe" and psychologist Dr. Laura Schlesinger. WLNA also broadcasts local high school football and basketball, Hudson Valley Renegades baseball and U.S. Army football from West Point.

In October 1996 WLNA and WHUD were again sold, this time for $20 million.

WLTH

(23 July 1927–31 April 1941)

1927	1370kc s/t WARD, WBBC	250w.
June 1927	1320kc	250w.
Nov. 1928	1400kc s/t WBBC, WCGU, WSDA (WVFW)	500w.
March 1941	1430kc s/t WARD, WVFW, WBBC	500w.

The call letters of WLTH stood for the Leverich Towers Hotel, a grand structure constructed by one of Brooklyn's leading real-estate developers, A. Lyle Leverich, at 25 Clark Street in Brooklyn Heights. Construction began in 1926 at a cost of $4 million, and the hotel company bought station WFRL planning to move it to the new building. Studios on the mezzanine floor were to be equipped with the latest equipment and modern soundproofing, and there was to be a studio in Manhattan. A new transmitter on the shores of Jamaica Bay would "obtain the greatest degree of clearness for the broadcasting," but when WLTH took to the air, it was through the old WFRL facility atop the Strand Danceland at 635 Fulton Street.

By 1928 the Leveriches were facing bankruptcy and trying to scale back their hotel through such compromises as lowering the height of the ceilings. For a while station WLTH was operating through the Staten Island transmitter of WBBR. Station manager Samuel Gellard became head of a new parent company called the Voice of Brooklyn Inc., which was one of the creditors (for $434.18) when the Leverich Towers went into foreclosure in 1929. The hotel was renamed simply The Towers. WLTH apparently didn't feel stigmatized being named for a bankrupt institution.

WLTH shared time with as many as three other Brooklyn stations. In 1930, it moved into new quarters and identified itself as "WLTH, the Voice of Brooklyn in the *Brooklyn Daily Eagle* Building." The station was not owned by the *Eagle*—it occupied only two rooms on the ground floor in exchange for the airtime it provided to the paper—but the respected Brooklyn daily did have a good relationship with WLTH for a while. *Eagle* "news flashes" were

presented several times each day, delivered by *Eagle* reporter Maurice McLaughlin or radio editor Joe Ranson.

During the depression, WLTH was able to survive through a clever (and questionable) scheme. The station broadcast daily periods of recorded music interspersed with brief commercial messages. According to announcer Ken Roberts, who began his career at WLTH in 1930 at a salary of $25 a week, the "Voice of Brooklyn" would approach butchers, grocers, clothiers, and other small merchants around the borough and offer them participating sponsorship of a musical program. The plug would be free of charge, but WLTH asked that the business absorb a "music tax" that the station claimed it was obligated to pay—$50 for a thirteen-week run. Many businesses gladly shelled out, and so the audience heard something like, "The next musical selection comes to you courtesy of the Pitkin Lingerie Shop at 200 Pitkin Avenue." Then, Roberts recalled, there would be a few seconds of a record, which faded under as he said: "That was Bing Crosby, brought to you courtesy of the Pitkin Lingerie Shop. And now…" The federal government never took action against WLTH for making up the "music tax," nor did any sponsor ever renew.

Wednesday, 5 February 1930

4:00 P.M.	News flashes, *Brooklyn Eagle*
4:06	Brooklyn Federation of Churches
4:22	Tea Music
4:37	Clarine Cordler, soprano
4:50	News flashes, *Brooklyn Eagle*
5:00	Commercial Serenaders
5:15	Lillian Keating, songs
5:30	The Four Rasa Brothers
	Off for WSGH (6–8), WBBC (8–10)
10:00	The "Mixit Boys"
10:20	Henrietta Oleta, contralto
10:30	Henri's Rendezvous
10:45	Ernie Valle's Orchestra
11:00	Moulin Rouge
11:15	Milton Spielman's Orchestra
11:30	Allen's Dreamers
12:00 midnight	Village Grove Nut Club

WLTH was so hungry for business that it sold sixty seconds of air time each day for a week to a "mysterious bearded old man" who used his minute to say, "I love you, I love you, I love you…." In a more conventional marketing effort, the station organized the WLTH Radio Foodstores to serve Jewish grocers and advertisers.

On 21 October 1931, WLTH opened a studio at 105 Second Avenue in Manhattan, in the heart of the Yiddish theatre district. Station owner Sam Gellard moved his office there, and the station became known as "The Radio Theatre of the Air." The station maintained a one-hundred-seat auditorium, and among its programs were shows aimed at the Italian and Scandinavian population.

WLTH was "tops in Jewish programs" in 1938 and even had the grocers organized. Mazeltov!

The variety of WLTH's shows was impressive: "Ben Bolt and His Nuts," a very local Yiddish news and chatter show called "Brunsviller Zeide" ("Brownsville Times"), "The Brooklyn Foreign Affairs Forum," "Voices of the Street," "Legends of Palestine," and a comical series called "Happy Tho' Married." In 1933, in cooperation with the Long Island Historical Society, WLTH produced a series called "Looking Back in Brooklyn," which dramatized "vital incidents that have gone into the making of this—the world's largest residential center." Sunday nights at 10:30, listeners could learn about such events as Long Island's attempt in the nineteenth century to declare itself an independent state.

WLTH was at the center of the "Brooklyn radio fight" of 1936–38. Along with WARD, WBBC, and WVFW, it was found to be operating in a "negligent and haphazard" manner by FCC examiner George H. Hill. It was recommended that their frequency be assigned to a new company formed by the *Brooklyn Daily Eagle*. In January 1936, the FCC voted to take the stations off the air, but a dissent by Commissioner Irvin Stewart granted a stay of execution.

WLTH and WARD filed petitions to voluntarily turn over their facilities to the "Kings Broadcasting Corporation of Brooklyn" and on 2 October 1936 applied for a construction permit for a new station on 1400kc. At about the same time, the Yiddish-language *Daily Forward*, which operated WEVD, formed a corporation to give Brooklyn a full-time radio station. Sam Gellard held tight to his station, and by 1937 the time-sharing matter was before the court of appeals.

The programming continued to be ambitious, with musical programs under the direction of Sholom Secunda, president of the Society of Jewish Composers, Publishers, and Songwriters and the man who wrote "Bei Mir Bist du Shoen." WLTH reworked some of radio's most popular program concepts for its ethnic audience, including "The Jewish Amateur Hour," "Jewish Court of Arbitration," and a "Jewish Health Food Hour."

In 1941, WLTH was merged with its time-sharing partners and became WBYN.

See also WFRL, WBBC, WVFW, WARD, WBYN.

WLUX

(1995–)

| 1995 | 540kHz. | 250w. day / 218w. night |

The first station on Long Island's radio dials had been WLIX for twenty years when the religious broadcaster was purchased by Long Island Media Partnership and the call letters were changed slightly, to WLUX. Studios moved to Main Street in Bay Shore. The new name of the station could stand for "light" or "luxury" or just "luck"—the station didn't really try to make it symbolize anything in particular in the audience's mind. What was different was a new secular sound, although the sale of WLIX by Living Communications did stipulate that its successor retain about 6 percent of its airtime for established religious programs.

Music was a mix of big bands, ballads, and adult contemporary. Bruce Barlow did the wake-up show; Mary Perez hosted at midday and program director Joe Roberts at afternoon drive time. WLUX presented a heavy schedule of news, traffic reports, and a feature called "Info Minutes," sixty seconds on general topics scattered throughout the day.

The station appealed to the same demographic that it had attracted when 540 was all religion, but the ratings did begin to show an improvement.

See also WBIC, WLIX.

WLWL

(25 SEPTEMBER 1925–16 JUNE 1937)

1925	1040kc (288m)	3,500w.
1928	780kc, 1020kc	5,000w.
1934	1100kc s/t WPG	5,000w.

"We Listen, We Learn." The Paulist Fathers have always seen themselves as fulfilling a distinctive role within the Catholic Church, a role reflected in the 1920s and 1930s by station WLWL. It was launched to coincide with a Papal Jubilee Year and was originally to be called WPL. In a sermon at the Church of St. Paul the Apostle on 15 February 1925, Father John Handly, who was in charge of raising funds for a radio station, told parishioners: "When the sower went out to sow, as our Lord tells us, we used to call it 'broadcasting.'… Our Lord thought it worthwhile to broadcast the word of God, in spite of the fact that some of the seed fell by the wayside."

Paulist broadcasting tended to be eclectic, intellectually stimulating, and tolerant in tone, generally shunning polemics and controversy. Its schedule highlighted classical music, with lectures on literature and science. There were movie reviews, sometimes prepared by the watchdog Legion of Decency. WLWL broadcast the Mass only once a year, at midnight on Christmas Eve. The very fact that the Paulists ventured to be the radio voice of New York's large Roman Catholic community was considered a reflection of the progressive nature of the order.

Monday, 1 October 1928

6:00 P.M.	Dominican Hour
6:05	Edwin Breen, baritone
6:20	Viator Instrumentalists
6:45	"Christian Peace," Welsh
7:00	Dupree Ensemble
7:15	Iseo Ilari, tenor
7:30	"Question Box," J. I. Malloy
7:45	Concert Orchestra
8:00	Off for WMCA

The Missionary Society of St. Paul the Apostle organized itself as the Universal Broadcasters Corporation and installed studios and transmitter in the Church of St. Paul the Apostle at 415 W. Fifty-ninth Street near Columbus Avenue. The 226-foot towers beside the rectory were likened to modern-day steeples.

For the first three years, Father James Cronin was the guiding force behind WLWL, as station manager and principal announcer. In a 1926 survey he was "proclaimed by a number of leading radio critics as the foremost announcer

on the air." Perhaps someone else was at the microphone when a *Trib* reviewer wrote in March 1926: "To the announcer of WLWL goes the honors of the 'musicale' that opened the station's program last night. Aside from pronouncing 'musicale' as though its last syllable were a beverage, the gentleman occasioned a number of sympathetically humored smiles with his naiveté and his homeliness of diction. His trick of sending his station call-letters over inflectional roller coasters is nothing if not infectious."

Cronin was followed as head of WLWL by Father Henry Riley and Father Henry Malloy. A Paulist priest observed many years later: "Under Riley there was a snap to it. Under Father Malloy there was no snap to it." Broadcasts included "The Quiet Hour," a Sunday-afternoon program with a poetic, meditative quality, and a regular "Question Box," hosted by Father James Gillis, who patiently responded to even hostile letters. Sacred music was performed by the Seventy-voice Paulist Choristers. It was on WLWL in 1926 that Father (later Archbishop) Fulton Sheen began his broadcast appearances, speaking before an overflow "studio audience" at the church. At a time when stations begged for audience reaction, WLWL was pleased about its strong mail pull. The *New York Sun* regularly reviewed WLWL and once compared the station's programming to "a return to a favorite woodland spot.… One wanders peacefully about, content to find no change."

Thursday, 5 November 1936

6:00 P.M.	Bob Cox, songs
6:15	Concert Orchestra
6:30	Alma Creasy, violin
6:45	Sports Talks—Andy Burke, Arthur Dailey
7:00	Kyser Orchestra
7:15	Lithuanian Ensemble
7:30	Talk—Rev. J. M. Gillis
7:45	Dance Music
8:00	Off for WPG

The station was so well received (in every meaning of the word) that it was one of only five New York area broadcasters included on a short list of "standard wave stations" packed in with each Atwater Kent radio sold in the early 1930s. Despite its high-quality programming, its active support from the Archdiocese of New York, and the clarity of the signal—WLWL started with 5,000 watts licensed for full-time operation at 1040 on the dial, making it one of the most powerful stations in the country at the time—the Paulist Fathers still had to struggle. In 1926, WLWL found itself sharing its frequency with WPAP at the Palisades Amusement Park, an assignment the Paulists felt discriminated against them "in favor of a mere dispenser of jazz and cheap entertainment."

In 1927, WLWL moved its transmitter from the church in midtown Manhattan to the Belleville Turnpike in Kearney,

N.J., which improved reception but complicated its financial situation. Despite fund-raising among the faithful and an unsuccessful try at selling commercial time, a deficit grew. In 1930 WLWL attempted to lease its facilities to the Hearst Newspapers, but the deal fell through—to the relief of those who felt that commercialization would undermine WLWL's true mission.

WLWL repeatedly protested time-sharing and asked to return to a favored full-time frequency. However, when the newly formed Federal Radio Commission asked stations in 1927 to state the minimum hours they felt they could viably operate, the Paulists responded that WLWL could get by with twenty-four hours per week. The "minimum" was later misinterpreted as "sufficient," and WLWL found its shared time pared back to what it called a "starvation allowance," divided first with WMCA and later with WPG in Atlantic City. Federal regulators pointed out that when it had been full-time, WLWL was on the air for only three or four hours daily.

WLWL's battle for survival took many turns. The Roman Catholic Church asked its members to write to federal authorities. Katherine McCarthy of the Catholic Daughters of America, insisting that the station was "being crowded off the air," called for support of "clean radio programs as a serious part of the program of Catholic action." But the most significant step was a proposed amendment to the Communications Act of 1934 that would reallocate frequencies at a 3:1 ratio between commercial and nonprofit broadcasters. Commonly referred to as "Harney's Amendment" in honor of Paulist Superior-General (and titular director of WLWL) John Harney, who proposed the measure at a Senate hearing, the idea was opposed by commercial broadcasters and rejected by Congress even though it drew over sixty thousand letters of support. It is considered one of the pivotal moments in the history of American broadcasting.

In January 1935 the Paulists applied to move back to 810kc, then occupied by WNYC (which they suggested should split 1130 with WOV). Such a change would, of course, also affect broadcasters all over North America. The Paulists suggested that WWL in New Orleans, owned by Loyola University of the South, a Jesuit institution, be moved to 810 and share with WLWL. Father Harney expected a fraternal welcome from the Jesuits, and when WWL (which operated commercially as a CBS affiliate) refused to cooperate, he grumped that they would "rue the day."

The public struggle attracted much support for WLWL—it even finished 1936 slightly in the black. But negotiations to find sufficient room for Paulist broadcasting proved fruitless, and in 1937 WLWL agreed to be purchased for $275,000 by John Iraci, the owner of WOV, and by WNEW's Arde Bulova. WLWL became WBIL, which was merged with WOV.

In June 1937, Father Gillis bade a final farewell to listeners of WLWL. The station would be fondly remembered by the Paulists, who could take satisfaction in the trailblazing role they played in religious and educational broadcasting.

In 1946, the Missionary Society of St. Paul the Apostle challenged the license renewal of WNEW, then operating with 50 kilowatts on a frequency that some Paulists felt should have been theirs. A new superior-general withdrew the application before the FCC could consider it.

See also WPG, WBIL.

W M B Q

(28 JANUARY 1927–24 JUNE 1938)

Jan. 1927	1430kc	100w.
June 1927	1450kc s/t WTRC, WLBX, WIBS	100w.
1928	1500kc s/t WWRL	100w.

Despite its name, the Metropolitan Broadcasting Corporation ran a station that could barely be heard beyond the northwestern corner of Brooklyn. WMBQ was a low-power station at 95 Leonard Street in Williamsburg (phone: STagg 2-9307). It shared time with other stations in the outer boroughs, including at one point or another WTRC, WHPP, WMRJ, WCNW, WLBX, and WWRL.

Sunday, 17 May 1931

7:00 P.M.	Civic, fraternal, social
7:15	String Music
7:45	Entertainers
8:30	Kanzer Sisters, songs
8:45	Recital
9:30	Jewish program
9:45	Lillianette, songs
10:00	John Kiefer, songs
10:15	Italian program
10:45	Studio party

President Paul J. Gollhofer and his wife, Lillian E. Kiefer (who held the titles of station manager, commercial manager, publicity director, musical director, and director of the artists' bureau), even spoke proudly of how "the Home Sweet Home Station" had a primary coverage area of about a mile and a half. But within that radius of the studios and transmitter at Leonard Street and Broadway lived about 464,000 people, a third of them foreign-born.

WMBQ was among the first broadcasters in the city to specialize in foreign-language programming, presenting shows in Polish, Lithuanian, Italian, Yiddish, and other languages. Many of these programs were produced by "brokers," who would arrange for talent, prepare scripts, and sell commercial time, returning a share to WMBQ. Unfortunately for the Gollhofer-Kiefer partnership, brokering time turned out to be its downfall. An FCC examiner asserted, "Control over these programs presented in foreign languages is practically non-existent."

Even more unfortunately, the personal partnership between Paul and Lillian also dissolved. The station's assets were placed in receivership, and in 1938 WMBQ's broadcast time was given to WWRL. Equipment and furniture were sold at public auction at 95 Leonard Street. Keifer and Gollhofer continued to try individually to renew the license of WMBQ. In February 1941 the FCC rejected both applicants.

WMCA

(6 February 1925–)

1925	880kc	500w.
1927	810kc	500w.
1928	570kc s/t WNYC (till 1933)	1,000w.
1941	570kc	5,000w.

Hotels were among the earliest station owners, and the first broadcast from a New York hotel was probably the 1920 recital by singer Luisa Tetrazzini from her apartment in the McAlpin. It was arranged by the Army Signal Corps, and the success of the experiment may have motivated the Hotel McAlpin to enter radio in a serious way. In 1922, the McAlpin became one of the first hotels to tie ship-to-shore radios into their room phones.

When WMCA's circular glass-enclosed studio was installed on the twenty-fourth floor of the hotel at Broadway and Thirty-fourth Street, the management declared, "Only professional entertainers will broadcast, as it has been decided not to extend the use of the microphone to amateurs." After a period of testing under the call sign 2XH, WMCA not only went on the air but also was wired into room phones at the McAlpin and Martinique Hotels. It called itself the station "Where the Searchlight Flashes and the White Way Begins," and for the next three-quarters of a century, WMCA would continue as a lively, often provocative, station.

Monday, 8 August 1927

6:10 P.M.	H. Normanton, songs
6:25	Baseball scores
6:30	McAlpin Orchestra
7:00	Home Adornment talk
7:10	McAlpin Orchestra
7:30	Minnie Weil, piano
8:00	Christian Science lecture
11:15	F. Cohen, piano
11:45	Manhattan Serenaders

The McAlpin soon yielded control of WMCA to Donald Flamm, who had connections to Broadway as the publisher and printer of playbills. WMCA was both dividing its own airtime on 810kc with other local stations and—in the first of several attempts to become a network "flagship"—sending out its programs to a small chain, including WOKO in Peekskill, WCAM in Camden, N.J., WDRC in New Haven, and WNJ in Newark. By December 1926, WMCA was airing popular music continually from 9:00 A.M. till 5:00 P.M.—an unusually long broadcast period for that time. WMCA soon became the first station in the metropolitan area to regularly program the postmidnight hours.

In the autumn of 1928, WMCA was granted FRC approval to move from 810 and share time on the 570kc frequency then occupied by WNYC. The municipal station protested, but Flamm had better connections with Tammany Hall than did the professional politicians who ran the city and for whom WNYC was a small and controversial city agency.

According to FRC Commissioner Caldwell, WMCA was "shown by all surveys conducted by the commission to be among the first five most popular New York stations, along with WNYC." WNYC was using only a few evening hours, but when the two stations failed to work out a fair division of the day, the FRC ordered them to broadcast on alternate days. That arrangement didn't work out either. Each regularly complained about the other's intrusion into its scheduled airtime.

Even while battling for its spot on the dial, WMCA bought station WPCH—which occupied its old 810kc frequency—and on 23 December 1928 both stations moved to new studios in the Hammerstein Theatre Building at Fifty-third and Broadway, studios "decorated in futuristic style, which has as its basis the art of the American Indian." The inaugural broadcast featured Eddie Cantor, Ruth Etting, Major Bowes, Helen Kane, and other stars and was carried on the WMCA network.

Among the WMCA alumni from this era were singer and bandleader Rudy Vallee, dialect comedian Henry Burbig, Arthur Tracy (the "Street Singer"), Vaughn DeLeath, and producer-director Phillips J. Lord, who later created "Gang Busters." On one typical night in 1932, WMCA presented live pickups of the bands of Ozzie Nelson, Don Redman, Chick Webb, and Cab Calloway. The team of Billy Jones and Ernie Hare, who pioneered as The Happiness Boys, concluded their careers on WMCA. Comedian Henry Morgan started there in 1932, not as an entertainer but as a page boy.

As early as September 1929, WMCA was syndicating programs on motion-picture sound-track film. WMCA also experimented with television, in 1931 utilizing the mechanically scanned system of Scottish inventor John Logie Baird, who at that time was also working with the BBC.

By the end of 1930, Donald Flamm could point out that WMCA had been on the air 4,702 hours during the year then ending, which he said was a record for part-time and regional stations. But the time-sharing arrangement with WNYC was growing more uncomfortable. The municipal station carried its conflict with WMCA all the way to the U.S. Supreme Court, basing its constitutional appeal on the question of whether broadcasting could be considered "commerce." The courts rejected this argument. WNYC performed valuable civic services, but it could not deny the professionalism of WMCA, which now had acknowledgment of its worth from the highest tribunal.

In March 1932, WMCA recommended that WNYC take over the frequency of its daytime-only sister station, WPCH. Under protest by WNYC, the switchover was made and the WPCH license was soon relinquished. On Monday, 5 June 1933, WMCA finally stood alone, "First on Your Dial in New York."

Since 1932, WMCA's signal had blanketed the metropolitan area from a transmitter in the College Point section of Queens. In consideration of the long and irregular hours worked by engineers, the transmitter building contained three apartments.

WMCA's next foray into network broadcasting was short-lived. In October 1934 it affiliated with the American Broadcasting System (not to be confused with today's ABC; there were many former CBS people running it) but severed its relationship with the twenty-four-station chain early in 1935. Shortly afterward, WMCA organized the Inter-City Broadcasting System, serving a dozen stations in the Northeast.

In the spring of 1938, WMCA moved to 1657 Broadway at Fifty-second Street, upstairs from the famed Lindy's Restaurant. The new facilities included a three-hundred-seat auditorium and wire connections to over one hundred nightclubs and hotels. WMCA had some of the most ambitious programming of the independent stations, from the "Bar-O Ranch" to the "Broadway Newsreel" and female-oriented programs such as "The Bride's House" and "How to Hold a Husband." Its 1939 evening schedule was filled with repeats of network daytime soap operas, including "John's Other Wife," "Young Widder Brown," and "Just Plain Bill."

WMCA seldom aspired to high culture. Among its early features were the Sunday-afternoon services from the Chinatown Rescue Society, which featured "the flotsam and jetsam of life." A. L. Alexander, who started in 1925 as WMCA's chief announcer, created the "Good Will Court" and later "Alexander's Mediation Board" to spread legal counsel via the airwaves. His program soon became an NBC network feature (until bar associations and the real courts forbade lawyers and jurists from appearing). Despite Alexander's entanglements, John J. Anthony ("no names, please") came to the WMCA microphones in 1937 to dispense personal advice personally; he moved to WOR and the Mutual network within a year.

WMCA aired "Amateur Night" at Harlem's Apollo theatre, as well as "New World A-Comin'" and a black-oriented magazine show, "Tales from Harlem." Also during the 1930s,

"Five Star Extra" was a local version of "The March of Time," dramatizing the day's events. Hillbilly singer Zeke Manners came to WMCA in 1939, and a Radio Guide poll declared this the most popular of "programs not on networks." WMCA even broadcast the first commercials for condoms, which drew a reprimand from the FCC. And, of course, there were pickups from a hundred hotels and nightclubs. This was truly "Broadcasting in the New York Manner."

In December 1940, owner and president Donald Flamm sold WMCA to Edward J. Noble, the manufacturer of Life Savers candies and undersecretary of commerce in the Roosevelt administration. But Flamm then refused to transfer title to Noble, who finally took control of WMCA in mid–January 1941. Three years later Noble bought the NBC Blue Network, including station WJZ, and founded the American Broadcasting Company. In September 1943 he sold WMCA to real estate developer Nathan Straus, as required by new FCC regulations forbidding ownership of more than one station in a market. It soon appeared that this was not the first forced sale of WMCA.

In August 1943, Flamm sued Noble in Manhattan Supreme Court to block the resale of WMCA. An injunction was denied, but as legal action continued, a congressional investigation was launched that soon reached into the highest levels of the U.S. government. Flamm contended that he never wanted to sell WMCA and that Noble's offer of $750,000 was "ridiculously low." He had earlier turned down a one-million-dollar offer by President Roosevelt's son Elliott.

Flamm charged that he had been warned by Noble's attorney, former FCC chief counsel William Dempsey, that he would lose the license if he didn't sell WMCA and that the move was "greased from the White House down." Flamm stated that Dempsey had personally threatened violence and that Noble had told him, "I'll get your station whether you want to sell it or not." At the time of the transaction, Flamm's protests had come to FDR's attention and had been referred to the FCC. The White House later denied having any interest in the case. Closed-door investigations dragged on like a long-running radio serial of mystery and intrigue until November 1944, when ex–WMCA manager Donald Shaw retracted his story of threats and intimidation.

In January 1945, the congressional committee issued a report exonerating Noble and the FCC (the Republican minority called the findings a whitewash). But a year later a jury in New York awarded Flamm $350,000 in damages, and he said he would try to "recapture" WMCA. By then, however, the Straus era was irreversible. (Flamm later owned WMMM in Connecticut.)

In the mid–1940s, some of the biggest names in popular music became WMCA disc jockeys. Duke Ellington and Tommy Dorsey played their own and others' records; announcer Andre Baruch and singer Bea Wain became "Mr. and Mrs. Music." "Symphony Sid" Torin had an "all night, all frantic" jazz program starting in 1948.

WMCA was certainly a station of superlatives when it published this ad in 1930.

In 1946, the Giants baseball team—then in last place in the National League—signed WMCA as its local outlet, even though Nathan Straus neither liked nor understood baseball. With Russ Hodges leading the radio team at the Polo Grounds, this association would last through two pennants and a 1954 World Series victory and end with the Giants' 1957 departure for San Francisco.

In 1950 Barry Gray began one of the longest-running of radio's late-night talk shows. It originated first from Chandler's restaurant and was brought to an initially reluctant WMCA by Chandler's. With the show debuting during the "red scare" days, the outspoken Gray was investigated by Senator Joseph McCarthy and incurred the wrath of columnist Walter Winchell, who wrote that the station's call letters stood for "We Make Communists Adorable." The remark enraged Straus, who stood by Gray even when it became difficult to line up guests. Gray's program moved from its restaurant setting to the WMCA studios, where one night a member of the studio audience tiptoed away and expressed his displeasure by defecating in a darkened hallway. Gray outlasted his critics—and survived physical assaults—to become a New York radio institution.

WMCA gained a reputation as a crusader, taking a stand on such matters as public housing and presenting a 1951 documentary series on driving safety, ominously entitled "The Killers"; one controversial angle was the reading of license numbers of cars observed breaking traffic laws. WMCA initiated regular station editorials in 1954, and on 27 October 1960 it became the first station to editorially support a presidential candidate when Straus read an endorsement of John F. Kennedy.

Controversial talk-show host Barry Gray. His nightly program, broadcast from 11:00 P.M. to 1:00 A.M. during WMCA's rock and roll years, caused teenage tuneout to WABC and WINS.

The classic WMCA "Good Guys" lineup in 1964.

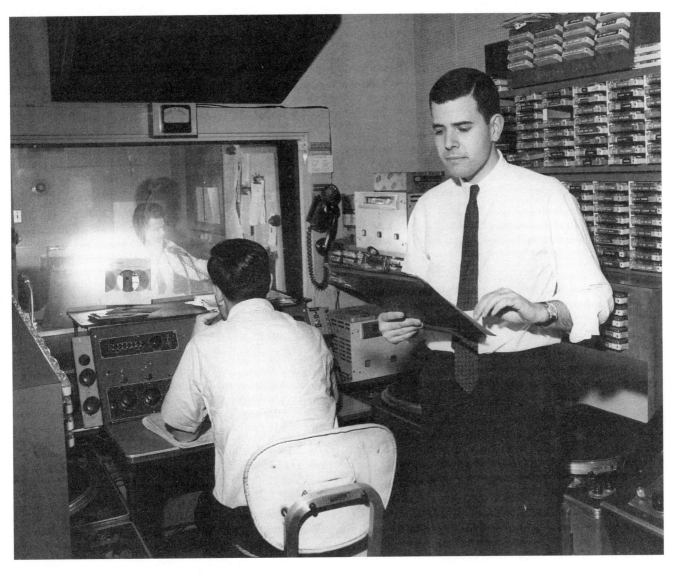

Control room shot of Gary Stevens, who replaced B. Mitchel Reed at WMCA in 1965.

Probably WMCA's most ambitious public service was "Call for Action," in which the station itself acted as soapbox and ombudsman. Starting in 1963, listeners could call PLaza 9-1717, where volunteers would answer questions about housing, consumer fraud, discrimination, and other problems. The brainchild of Helen Straus, "Call for Action" later became more activist, with callers advised to phone back and tell whether their problem was solved. If it was not, there might then be an investigative report or editorial comment. "Call for Action" was copied by stations across the country.

Always a station playing pop music, WMCA drifted into rock and roll in about 1958. Herb Oscar Anderson replaced Roger Gallagher and Joe O'Brien on the wake-up shift; Gallagher left, and O'Brien moved to afternoon drive time. Ted Steele's "Bandstand" was heard from 1:00–5:00 P.M.; Scott Muni's "Music with Muni" was heard from 8:00 P.M. to midnight. Staff veteran Alun Williams did WMCA's

first all-night rock show. Later, under the guidance of station manager Steve Lubunski and program director Ruth Meyer (from WMGM), it vied or tied with WINS or WABC for stature as the city's top rocker. Dandy Dan Daniel, Harry Harrison, Gary Stevens, Frankie Crocker, Dean Anthony, B. Mitchell Reed and the rest of the deejays were known as the "Good Guys" (a name coined at WABC and lifted by WMCA). At 570kc WMCA seemed to be push-button number 1 on most car radios. Teenagers gained status wearing an orange-and-yellow "Good Guy" sweatshirt. On 29 December 1963, WMCA signaled a cultural revolution when Jack Spector played the first Beatles record heard on New York radio, "I Want to Hold Your Hand."

If WMCA had trouble staying at the top of the New York rock ratings, one of the reasons may have been that it kept losing its best talent to its higher-rated rivals. Herb Oscar Anderson, Scott Muni, and Harry Harrison all jumped to WABC.

With rock music taking hold on the burgeoning FM band, in April 1969 WMCA took the unusual step of becoming talk radio from 10:00 A.M. till 10:00 P.M. and rock radio overnight and through the morning drive time. But in September, 1970, deejay Frankie Crocker signed off the format for good. WMCA turned to all-talk, mostly call-in programs. "Long John" Nebel and his wife, Candy Jones, dwelt on the offbeat and occult from midnight to dawn; Jones continued on her own after Nebel died. The erudite Dominic Quinn accepted calls but was a stickler for proper American English usage. Provocative talk-jockeys like Alex Bennett, Bob Grant, and Barry Farber gained an opinionated audience. To others they were the "bad guys." The station that started out allowing no amateur performers had put its program content into the hands of the listening audience. The firing of counter-culture hero Bennett brought a thousand demonstrators to the street in front of WMCA.

In 1987, J. Peter Straus sold WMCA to Federal Broadcasting for $10 million. This time there was no duress but certainly regret; WMCA had been the last family-owned radio station in New York City. In April 1988 Federal sold WMCA—which by then had the lowest Arbitron rating in the market—to Salem Communications, which had tried unsuccessfully to buy either WHN or WNEW. Salem switched WMCA to a financial news format and then on 16 September 1989 to all religion.

See also WPCH, WNYC.

WMGM

(15 SEPTEMBER 1948–28 FEBRUARY 1962)

1948   1050kc   50,000w.

In 1934, when the Marcus Loew Booking Agency consolidated its station WHN with three other time-sharers on its frequency, it announced the intention of creating an entirely new broadcast entity called WMGM. The added sparkle of Loew's Hollywood subsidiary (the movie company was always headquartered in New York) would more than compensate for the loss of three well-known but meaningless call letters. In December 1946 Loew's quietly changed its FM station's call from WHNF to WMGM and two years later brought the name to the AM dial amid great publicity and big plans. With the change of call letters came a change of address, from Loew's State Theatre to "new million-dollar studios" at 711 Fifth Avenue, the old NBC location.

"The Call Letters of the Stars" brought to New York, and the nation, some of the most entertaining shows to be found anywhere. The premiere broadcast from 8:00 to 11:00 P.M. on

15 September 1948 originated from both coasts. Live from New York were stars including Lena Horne, Vic Damone, Morton Downey, and Morey Amsterdam as well as two full orchestras. The Hollywood hour featured a salute from Frank Sinatra, Gene Kelly, Esther Williams, Red Skelton, and the 128-piece MGM orchestra. The gala broadcasts continued for four more evenings.

In 1949, WMGM syndicated the radio version of the "Dr. Kildare" movies, with Lew Ayres and Lionel Barrymore reprising their movie roles. The "Maisie" series, which had begun on CBS radio, was revived by WMGM in 1949 with its original star, Ann Sothern, and a supporting cast that included Lurene Tuttle, Frank Nelson, Hans Conreid, and Sheldon Leonard. These were among radio's finest actors, and an attentive fan would notice that they all usually worked out of California. Metro-Goldwyn-Mayer Radio Attractions was packaging some of the parent company's most popular material and trying to move its screen stars into the electronic medium in anticipation of founding an MGM-TV network. The Marcus Loew Booking Agency even applied, without success, for a UHF channel in New York. (This was a period when Washington was looking closely at possible antitrust violations by the dominant Hollywood studios and wasn't ready to increase their empires.)

Other MGM attractions included "Crime Does Not Pay," "Judge Hardy's Family" starring Mickey Rooney, and the hour-long "M-G-M Theater of the Air." There were Hollywood chat shows conducted by Paula Stone, George Murphy, and Lionel Barrymore.

The Hollywood connection helped give WMGM a "big network" sound. However, WMGM retained many of the local programs developed during the WHN era. "Newsreel Theatre" was all-news for an hour from 6:00 to 7:00 A.M., then Robert Q. Lewis carried on with his record show till 9:00. Sports remained an important part of the schedule with Brooklyn Dodgers baseball, Giants football, Knicks basketball, and the Rangers hockey games in season.

In 1950 Robert Q. Lewis left for CBS, and into the morning slot slipped Ted Brown and the Redhead (Rhoda Brown, Ted's real-life wife), whose nasal New-Yorkese belied a pleasant voice that was never heard on the air. Actress Sylvia Miles later played the Redhead. Ken Roberts, Hal Tunis, and Aime Gauvin hosted daytime record shows, and Joel Herron's orchestra continued to perform live three times a day. The most celebrated of the WMGM disc jockeys during its first years was former WHN program director and CBS sportscaster Ted Husing. He greeted listeners to his twice-a-day "Bandstand" with "Hello, kiddies," fitting words for one of radio's senior announcers. Husing remained at WMGM till 1954, when ill health forced an end to his thirty-year career.

MGM/Loew's network dreams were never realized, but on 10 December 1951 WMGM began an affiliation with the Liberty Broadcasting System (LBS), a Dallas-based chain that specialized in studio re-creations of baseball games (and

WMGM was born when WHN moved to new studios at 711 Fifth Avenue in September 1948. Here commentator George Hamilton Combs participates in the dedication ceremonies of the new "million-dollar studios." Staff announcer Phil Goulding (with script) stands by.

thus was shut out of major-league cities). The LBS was founded in 1949 and went silent in May 1952. It was heard in the nation's number-1 market for only six months.

The midmorning hours on WMGM were aimed at a female audience, with nutritionist Carlton Fredericks followed by a record-and-chat show called "It's a Woman's World," hosted by Aime Gauvin and other male announcers. Even before the advent of Top 40 programming, WMGM was pushing the day's big hits on the "Record Bandwagon," "Best Sellers," and "Your Hits of the Week," which allowed the station to make an easy transition into the rock-and-roll era. Big Joe Rosenfeld's "Happiness Exchange" dispensed overnight sunshine ("Have no fear, Big Joe is here"), coming to WMGM in 1955 after filling the late-night hours on three other stations. When Big Joe left for WABC in 1958, the late-night spot was taken by singer Johnny Johnston.

In the spring of 1957 Jerry Marshall departed WNEW's top-rated "Make Believe Ballroom" to join WMGM. Other air personalities included Dick DeFreitas, Bill Silbert, Ed Stokes, and Phil Goulding (brother of Ray Goulding of the Bob and Ray comedy team). Vaudevillians Blossom Seeley and Benny Fields had their own show, and Harold Peary, the rich-voiced actor who created and abandoned "The Great Gildersleeve," became a WMGM disc jockey.

Sunday, 6 April 1958

9:00	Record Rack with Dick DeFreitas
	(Dateline New York at :55 past the hour)
12:00 Noon	American-Jewish Caravan of Stars
1:00	Record Revue & Preview: DeFreitas
1:55	Dateline New York
2:00	Warm-up Time with Gussie Moran
2:30	Exhibition Baseball: Yankees vs. Phillies
4:30	Sports Extra with Marty Glickman
5:00	The Nation's Hits with Peter C. Tripp
	(Dateline New York at :55 past the hour)

7:45	Dateline New York
8:00	Best Sellers with Bill Reddick
	(Dateline New York at :55 past the hour)
10:45	What's With New York?
11:00	Newsreel Theater

In 1957, the corporate name was changed from the historic Marcus Loew Booking Agency to WMGM Broadcasting Company and two years later to Loew's Theatres Broadcasting Company. Early in 1958, WMGM moved from Fifth Avenue to an even more splendid address, 400 Park Avenue, across Fifty-third Street from Lever House. Hotel owners Larry and Robert Tisch had been on the Loew's board of directors since the mid–1940s, and in 1960 they gained control of the corporation. In October 1960 the Crowell-Collier publishing company announced it would buy WMGM for $11 million, but the FCC denied the application, citing Crowell-Collier's mismanagement of its Los Angeles station, KFWB.

Loew's continued to operate WMGM and deal with its own problems. In 1960 deejay Peter C. Tripp ("the curly-headed kid in the third row") and music director Joe Saccone were charged with accepting bribes from record companies. Tripp had received over $35,000 in payola since 1958. (Tripp was fined and given a six-month suspended sentence, charges against Saccone were dropped.) Tripp's suspension from WMGM checked a noteworthy career that at one point made medical history. Beginning Tuesday, 20 January 1959, Tripp, then age thirty-two, remained awake for over a week, broadcasting from the Armed Forces Recruiting Station in Times Square as a fund-raising stunt for the March of Dimes. He was under constant observation by doctors, who studied Tripp's physical and mental strain—periods of clarity alternated with moments of hallucination, and at one point he forgot the name of the charity he was supporting. Naturally, WMGM's ratings soared as listeners tuned in to hear Tripp bumble his way through his own two daily record shows and in guest spots at all hours of the day and night. After the first day, WMGM brought in other announcers to read his commercials. Crowds gathered around the booth in Times Square to catch a glimpse of the "curly-headed kid," who usually looked amazingly fit. Finally, after 201 hours and 10 minutes Tripp, the March of Dimes, and WMGM reached the end of the record-breaking wake-a-thon. Tripp played his final record, a tune by the Bell-Notes called "I've Had It!," and went off to nap for thirteen hours.

In the wake of the payola scandals, Mike Lawrence took over Tripp's programs, and Saccone was replaced by one of rock radio's patriarchs, former WINS music director Rick Sklar. With the addition of overnight service in 1960, WMGM brought in one of the city's first female deejays, Bea Kalmus, and Bill Edmonds moved into the "swing shift" from 2:30 to 5:00 A.M., carrying over the contemporary daytime sound. The station now specialized in rock and roll, though music on the Ted Brown and Jerry Marshall shows

stayed middle-of-the-road. News time was doubled to five minutes every half hour.

During the late 1950s, WMGM called its news team the Minute Men; they cruised the streets in a radio car looking for breaking news. WMGM's striving for respectability as a news organization sometimes left the station with egg on its face (see below). The Minute Men seldom came on hot news in progress. Bill Reddick once drove the vehicle with emergency lights flashing to the home of fellow announcer Dean Hunter and rushed in with fireman's gear trying to fool Hunter into thinking the house was on fire. This method of news-gathering was finally abandoned when someone crashed the car.

But that was not the news program's only embarrassment. In the late 1950s, WMGM at 1050kc, then specializing in rock and roll, was receiving heavy competition from its neighboring rocker, 1010-WINS. Since the two were usually playing the same records, their news coverage was one way to distinguish themselves. WMGM tried to step ahead in international reporting by placing calls to the major overseas news centers in the hope of getting world leaders on the air. It was a fine idea, but WMGM wasn't wise to inform its listeners about who they were trying to reach.

At 10:30 on Tuesday morning, 27 May 1958, the WMGM newsroom received a message from an overseas operator that General Charles DeGaulle was returning its call. DeGaulle was then preparing to assume power in France amid national turmoil. The call was put through to newscaster Bill Edmonds, who wanted to tape an interview with the general. DeGaulle insisted that he would speak only if the interview was live. So Edmonds broke into Jerry Marshall's record show, and amid the whistling and static that accompanied transatlantic phone traffic in the days before satellites, a French-accented voice explained that he was ready to answer his nation's appeal and seek a peaceable solution to France's problems. (DeGaulle did speak English, though haltingly and unenthusiastically.)

The voice from Paris then asked, "Who am I talking to anyway?" Edmonds explained it was WMGM. "MGM? The motion picture company?" asked the Frenchman. No, responded Edmonds, it was a radio station in New York City. Suddenly the voice lost its French accent and shouted: "Everybody knows in New York the best station is WINS. Vive la France!"

WINS denied any knowledge or complicity, though it rubbed in the incident by announcing the time in French all that day. WMGM manager Art Tolchin called Jock Fearnhead, his counterpart at WINS, and threatened bodily harm. Fearnhead professed innocence. WMGM complained to the FCC but couldn't prove who had carried out the prank. The next day WMGM received a cable from Paris: "I was cut off. What happened?—Charles DeGaulle."

It was WINS news director Tom O'Brien who, unbeknownst to others at his station, made the DeGaulle call. The background noises were taped and mixed in, not a

WMGM's Peter Tripp was second in popularity only to Alan Freed. Like Freed, he was caught up in the payola scandals. Here Peter contemplates the "extras" to his nightly Top 40 record countdown.

difficult task at a station whose newscasts sometimes included heavier sound effects than "Gang Busters." O'Brien then sent everything through an ordinary phone line, the way WINS did its normal news feeds. The telegram was written by Tom O'Brien's fiancée, a flight attendant for British Overseas Airways, who happened to be in France.

Loew's surely didn't skimp on making the station a first-class facility (station manager Art Tolchin occupied one of the swankier executive suites on Park Avenue), and WMGM always had some of the best voices and smoothest sounds in the city. But early in 1962 Loew's agreed to sell WMGM to Storer Broadcasting for $10,950,000. It was a record sum for a single station but also the same price that Crowell-Collier had offered two years earlier.

The Hollywood specials, "Newsreel Theater," Ted Husing's "Bandstand," Ted Brown and the Redhead, and Red Barber and the Dodgers all occupied a distinguished place in radio history, but the "Call Letters of the Stars" faded out. At 5:30 P.M. on the last day of February 1962, Bob Callen played the "Peppermint Twist," and WMGM said goodbye with a half-hour show that was actually a preview of the sweet music soon to be heard at 1050. Many familiar voices would remain when, at six o'clock, New Yorkers could again tune to station WHN. At the time of its final sign-off, WMGM was rated third among adults in New York. The first Arbitron book to appear after the sale to Storer listed WHN as simply "also in market."

See also WHN[I, II], WINS.

WMHA

(17 JANUARY 1927?)

1927	230m.	30w.

One of the glories of the radio age was the skill and enthusiasm of young people who built their own radios and operated ham stations. Some of these "radio boys" were members of the Young Men's Hebrew Association (YMHA) in New York. As early as 1921, the Bronx YMHA was hosting meetings of the Radio Club of the Bronx, and the Washington Heights YMHA, at 975 St. Nicholas Avenue at 159th Street, was operating a "carrier current" station in 1922, sending programs by wire around its building (and possibly around the neighborhood).

An announcement in the New York Times of 9 January 1927 said that Boy Scout Troop 707, which met at the Washington Heights YMHA, would put station WMHA on the air at 8:00 P.M. on 17 January. The permit to broadcast was issued shortly before the Radio Act of 1927 came into effect,

and WMHA was one of the last stations licensed during the anarchic period of 1926–27.

There were many Boy Scout programs on the air in the late 1920s, and a station in Kingston, N.Y., was also licensed to a Boy Scout troop. It's not known how often WMHA broadcast.

WMIL

(APRIL 1931–18 SEPTEMBER 1933)

1931	1500kc s/t WMBQ, WLBX, WWRL	100w.

As early as 1930, Arthur Faske applied to the Federal Radio Commission to change the call letters of WCLB in the city of Long Beach, Long Island, to WMIL. His license was then under scrutiny, and by the time the new name was approved, Faske was moving his station from Long Beach— where his lease had expired—back to Brooklyn. On 18 February 1931 the new call letters were assigned, and soon the studios and transmitter were reinstalled at 1525 Pitkin Avenue in Brownsville, where Faske rented five rooms above a store.

"Brooklyn's Premier Independent Station" shared time with WMBQ, WWRL, and WLBX. In August 1932, Faske applied to the FRC for WMIL to take over the airtime and facilities of station WLBX, with whom it shared time on 1500. That autumn, Faske applied to take over WFAB's operating time on 1300kc. Both applications were denied. In September 1933, Arthur Faske changed WMIL to WCNW.

See also WCLB, WCNW.

WMRJ

(9 JULY 1926–SEPTEMBER 1932)

1926	1320kc	10w.
1927	1450kc s/t WHPP, WLBH	10w.
1930	1210kc s/t WGBB, WCOH, WGNY	100w.

As the hub of Queens County, Jamaica could easily stand on its own as an independent city. The community's history dates back to 1650, and it was settled early by people of English, Dutch, and African descent. The local population in 1930 was over 26,000, and nearby neighborhoods added hundreds of thousands more.

Jamaica's radio station was a small operation that came on during the anarchic days of 1926 when anyone with the equipment could go into the broadcasting business; it faded six years later. WMRJ—"Merrick Radio, Jamaica," named for the area's principal thoroughfare—was built by owner Peter J. Prinz in his Merrick Radio store at 12 New York Boulevard. It had a ten-watt transmitter with a six-wire "inverted-L" antenna on the roof, and it split its airtime with other small stations. Garry Howard was studio manager and chief announcer.

WMRJ had a strong tie-in with Queens' ubiquitous newspaper *The Long Island Daily Press*, and it joined with the paper during the 1927 Christmas season to present a series of fund-raising marathons on behalf of holiday aid for the needy. WMRJ did attract local listeners, not least because the *Press* printed its schedule prominently at the top of each day's radio listings.

WMRJ, "In the Heart of Queensboro," occasionally stayed on the air into the wee hours, with "The Gloom Chasers" or a "Midnight Frolic" from the Merrick Theatre and a 2:00 A.M. aid to insomnia called "The Coffee Testers." There were frequent request programs, and Prinz even arranged with record stores and companies to play records before their official public release.

Tuesday, 4 February 1930

7:00 P.M.	Al Lynn and his Music Makers
7:35	Chester Glasson's children's program
8:35	Banjo Eddy
9:05	Jerry Moore, pop pianist
9:20	Agnes Lewis, soprano
9:40	Charles Coleman, Edward Fraenkel, violin
9:50	Ethel Lockwood
10:00	Henry Kean and Mitchell Sadewitz
10:30	Al Lynn and his Music Masters
11:30	Studio
12:00	Good night

When it appeared as if the Federal Radio Commission might revoke WMRJ's license in 1928, Queens Borough President Bernard Patten personally intervened on its behalf, citing frequent community service programs, and Congressman Robert Bacon called the station "indispensable" in Queens. The license was renewed, but WMRJ was still squeezed in too closely to other local stations. In May 1930 it was authorized to move to 1210kc but had to keep its power down to ten watts.

The station moved studios and transmitter to 146-10 Jamaica Avenue in July 1930, for the New York Avenue site was due to be torn down. In February 1931, Prinz moved WMRJ to 162-14 Jamaica Avenue, and in April it finally increased power to 100 watts. The station at "the Gateway

of the Sunrise Trail" then found its license under challenge from a rival one hundred miles away. Peter Goelet, scion of a wealthy banking family, was establishing a station on his Orange County estate and wanted WMRJ off the 1210 frequency they were sharing. Goelet and the FRC examiner alleged violations of radio regulations, which Prinz denied in a Washington hearing.

It was around this same time that WMRJ initiated its most memorable and influential program. In April 1932, John J. Anthony—the professional name of Lester Kroll, a prankster who once served a jail term for not keeping up his alimony payments—began a series "dedicated to helping the sufferers from an antiquated and outmoded domestic relations code." Troubled listeners in Queens could "Ask Mister Anthony," a self-styled expert on human relations. It was one of radio's first, and frankest, advice programs.

Unfortunately, Mr. Anthony couldn't solve Mr. Prinz's problems. The challenge from Peter Goelet was successful, and in September 1932 Goelet bought WMRJ and put it off the air, its time transferred to WGNY. John J. Anthony went on to national fame on the Mutual Network. Peter Prinz continued his career as an engineer for NBC.

W M S G

(5 APRIL 1926–31 OCTOBER 1933)

1926 (WWGL)	1410kc	500w.
1927	990kc	500w.
1927	1070, 1270kc s/t WHAP, WBNY	500w.
1928	1350k s/t WCDA, WKBQ, WBNY	500w.

Madison Square Garden deserves to be considered one of the pioneers of New York broadcasting, even though its own station never lived up to its potential. The Garden's chief executive, boxing promoter Tex Rickard, and his concert manager, Julius Hopp, were instrumental in the experimental 1921 broadcast of the Dempsey-Carpentier fight over WJY. In 1925 a new Madison Square Garden (the third to bear that name) was built at Eighth Avenue and Fiftieth Street. A new medium was then gaining popularity, and Rickard was rethinking radio.

Tex Rickard had banned radio from his arena in November 1924, fearing that it would reduce attendance at prizefights. But early in 1926 he changed his mind after hearing from shut-ins and disabled veterans who couldn't make it to the Garden. Rickard purchased WWGL, which the Radio Engineering Corp. of Richmond Hill had put on the air in August 1925. The equipment was moved to the new sports palace to operate as the Madison Square Garden Broadcasting Corporation. WMSG's studios were in the Garden itself with transmitter and antenna on the copper roof, initially considered an excellent siting for the ground radiation system.

The new station planned to air all events taking place at Madison Square Garden, concerts as well as sports. As it turned out, sports coverage was never the biggest part of the WMSG schedule. For one thing, the station had to share time on its frequency and therefore might not be on the air when a prizefight or basketball game was scheduled, nor could it extend its hours to cover an entire track meet. Also, major events usually attracted the interest of larger stations and networks, which could easily outbid the Garden's own station.

Friday, 2 September 1927

6:00 P.M.	Carlton Lorraine Orchestra
7:00	Kathryn Connolly, soprano
7:15	Willy White, pianist
7:30	Muriel Ellis, readings
7:45	Bill Rietz, composer
8:00	Warren Nash, talk
8:15	Jack Davis, baritone
8:30	Anton Civoru pupils' concert
9:00	Off for WBNY

As the radio industry developed in the late 1920s, Madison Square Garden was the scene of the annual "Radio World's Fair" exhibits, showing off the latest in radio (and even television!) equipment. Several New York radio stations set up remote studios and broadcast from the Radio World's Fair but WMSG never bothered to join the show taking place under its own roof. There is evidence that after the NBC network was launched in the fall of 1926 and a national audience was created, Tex Rickard's interest in his own broadcasting station began to wane. In August 1927, WMSG applied to change its call letters to WPUB and its corporate name to "Public Broadcasting Corporation." Although the FRC approved the request, the Garden management had second thoughts, and even though the letters WPUB were never spoken on the air, the commission went through the formality of changing them back to WMSG.

One aspect of the 1921 Dempsey-Carpentier broadcast continued to haunt Rickard. In May 1927, Julius Hopp sued Rickard, Frank Coultry and J. Andrew White, charging that he had been forced out of their partnership. He stated that he "was the first to perfect measures to use wireless telephones and telegraph in the dissemination of news, addresses, sporting events and other public matters" and that he had exclusive rights to such events. He wanted an accounting of all profits since 2 July 1921.

Some of WMSG's programs were worthwhile. There were French lessons and a children's series called "Tots from

Tottysville." Composer and conductor Morton Gould made some of his earliest radio appearances playing the piano on WMSG. The station even escaped the confines of the Garden to cover golf matches and other events.

Unfortunately, poor operating conditions caused WMSG to lose some of its best fans. On 4 May 1929 the *Times* reported that the Radio Association of Reliable Merchants was campaigning, along with sports fans and athletic societies, to get WMSG a better frequency. Its 500 watts had been cut to 250 in 1928, and many listeners complained that the signal couldn't break through interference from adjacent stations. "Many radio dealers are reported to have trouble in selling radio sets," the newspaper stated, "because they cannot guarantee reception of the Garden events."

The Garden reorganized its radio operation as the New York Metropolitan Broadcasting Corporation, but it was always a minor adjunct of the nation's greatest sports palace. In a series of steps between December 1931 and November 1933, the Madison Square Garden studio was shut down, the transmitter moved to the Bronx, and operations transferred to the new station WBNX. During the summer of 1932, WMSG was broadcasting from the Bronx through the New Jersey transmitter of WCDA. Finally in 1933 it was absorbed, along with WCDA, into WBNX.

See also WJY, WCDA, WBNX.

WMTR

(12 DECEMBER 1948–)

1948	1250kc (daytime)	500w.
1951	1250kc	1,000w.
1960	1250kc	5,000w.
1984	1250kc	5,000w. day / 1,000w. night

In the forested hills twenty-five miles west of the Hudson, George and Kenneth Croy founded the Morristown Broadcasting Company. The Croy family was in the ice and coal business, and with the advent of oil burners and refrigerators, brothers George and Ken branched out into radio. Studios and offices were located on the Green in Morristown, N.J., at 10 Park Avenue, and the transmitter was on Evergreen Avenue. The first program director was Jack Allen, later a WOR newscaster, and Merrill Morris was news director and farm reporter.

The programming was pleasantly attuned to the exurban/rural lifestyle, beginning with hourly news, "Morning in Morris [County]" at 7:00 A.M., country-and-western music at noontime, and the syndicated "Candlelight and

Silver" during the dinner hour. The Croys were very sensitive about keeping the musical selections quiet and slow, even destroying records that were too up-tempo. During the 1950s Susan Bond brought her women's talk show to WMTR, including "Women Are People" weekdays at 9:45 A.M.

Bob Vessel replaced Jack Allen as program director and on-air host in 1951, and later news directors Bob Stopker and Nick Di Rienzo maintained respectable information service that made WMTR the dominant local station in its corner of New Jersey. In the 1960s, WMTR subscribed to Peter Strauss's Radio Press International, giving it the added prestige of audio reports from around the world. Studios were moved to the new transmitter site in Hanover Township.

In 1971, WMTR was sold to Drexel Hill Associates, which owned WDHA(FM) in Dover. The WMTR news department began supplying newscasts to WDHA. Its music became adult contemporary, but the station still had an easygoing feel.

With the sale to Legend Broadcasting, WMTR briefly became a business news and talk station, but when Northern New Jersey Radio took over the station in 1991, it dropped the business news format to play big-band oldies, a switch that gave Morristown's station a pace and mood that listeners may have missed in its quiet early years.

WNBC

(12 NOVEMBER 1946–7 OCTOBER 1988;
WRCA: 18 OCTOBER 1954–1 JUNE 1960)

1946   660kc.   50,000w.

When WEAF turned into WNBC, it added a touch of new luster to an old, established station. During the days of the Red and Blue Networks, either of the National Broadcasting Company's two New York flagship stations could have claimed the corporate monogram, but with the demise of the Blue—and with the concurrence of a station in New Britain, Conn. that then held the call letters—the switch was a natural development. To make sure everyone remembered, WNBC levied a small fine on speakers if they called the station by its old name.

The year 1946 was still network radio's "Golden Age," and the NBC chimes were as familiar to most Americans as the sound of their own doorbell, bringing Jack Benny, Kate Smith, Burns and Allen, "Your Hit Parade," "The Great Gildersleeve," Fred Allen, and Edgar Bergen with Charlie McCarthy. Daytime bubbled with soap operas, many of which had been unfolding their episodes for a decade or

more. Toscanini was still conducting the NBC Symphony; Lowell Thomas and H.V. Kaltenborn were still commenting on the news. The spirit of WEAF, "the world's greatest concert hall," continued to dominate NBC. The network was so well established that it seldom had to develop its own programming—sponsors and their advertising agencies simply contracted for time and facilities. Beginning with the "Paley Raids" of late 1948 and early 1949, CBS carried away some of NBC's most popular programs, including Benny and "Amos 'n' Andy." After two decades, "America's #1 Network" was losing its primacy.

By the mid–1950s, network radio was flagging as a profitable enterprise, but local radio was proving its value with recorded music, news, community service, and simply companionship. WNBC still had a pool of talent that was nurtured on the network. While rival stations opened the day with long-running morning personalities—Jack Sterling on WCBS, John Gambling *père* and *fils* on WOR, George Edwards on WQXR—WNBC had a greater turnover of talent in the early hours. "Buffalo Bob" Smith was replaced by musician Skitch Henderson. Failing to attract the team of Rayburn and Finch from WNEW, in 1951 WNBC brought in Bob Elliott and Ray Goulding from Boston. Bob and Ray introduced New Yorkers (and soon the entire nation) to such characters as Wally Ballou, Mary McGoon, Wealthy Jacobus Pike, and "Mary Backstayge, Noble Wife," the ultimate soap opera parody, heard daily at 7:50 A.M.

In 1954, "Your Community Station" developed an expanded series of regular public-service features not heard before, including the daily pollen count for allergy sufferers. Reporter Gabe Pressman was hired to cover breaking events around the city from a mobile transmitter installed in a Ford Thunderbird sports car. The day then began with "Pulse," a music-and-information show hosted by Bill Cullen, already well known on NBC radio and TV as a quiz-show host. "Pulse" was bold in its promotional efforts, especially the 1956 treasure hunts that would reward a lucky listener who deciphered the clues and found an object hidden somewhere in the metropolitan area. Despite Cullen's reminder that "you don't have to move anything or disturb anything to find the hidden object," WNBC listeners could cause minor disturbances at a suspected mystery location. Most encounters were friendly, and "Pulse" fans at least got to meet each other, but the *New York Times* commented editorially that the whole thing was "childish."

Beginning in 1952, "Music through the Night" presented classical and semiclassical works from midnight to 5:30 A.M., hosted by staff announcer Fleetwood (first name: Harry, seldom used on the air). The haunting theme song, a lush Mantovani arrangement of "Greensleeves," drew many comments from its surprisingly large overnight audience. The program had its origins in the cold war. WNBC had been signing off following the nightly dance band remotes, but Civil Defense authorities felt that its signal and facilities should be available around the clock. In the public interest,

Mary Margaret McBride was the first woman radio interviewer to achieve "superstar" status. She developed many of radio's effective interviewing techniques. This 1950 photograph at WNBC is with socialite Sharman Douglas.

the night was filled with Tchaikovsky, Beethoven, Liszt … and Fleetwood.

Seeking the maximum promotional tie-in with its parent Radio Corporation of America, on Monday, 18 October 1954, WNBC changed its call letters to WRCA (the call had been in use by RCA's shortwave station; WNBC went back to New Britain, Conn., where NBC operated a UHF-TV station). WRCA instituted a trailblazing program concept in 1959 when veteran newscaster Kenneth Banghart began "Up to the Minute," a news and feature program interspersed with music in the manner of the NBC weekend-long network program "Monitor." Ironically, Banghart and "Up to the Minute" jumped to WCBS in 1962 to plant the seed for that station's all-news format. Also in 1959, WRCA worked up a blend of pop and easy listening that it called "Wall-to-Wall Music." The announcers were among radio's best, including Ed Herlihy, Wayne Howell, and two former WNEW personalities, Jim Lowe and Bob Haymes. The music lived up to its wall-to-wall promise, for it could be heard in "binaural sound," a stereo system that required two radios tuned to WRCA AM and FM.

In 1960, WRCA went back to being WNBC. There was a little inaugural program, and the first person to officially speak the reissued call letters was New York Mayor Robert F. Wagner.

With the added space requirements of television, in October 1962 radio operations at 30 Rockefeller Plaza were shrunk from five floors to two. If NBC needed more room, a program could originate from a studio across the street in Radio City Music Hall. The following year WNBC shut down the Port Washington transmitter and moved to a new facility on High Island in Long Island Sound, sharing a 527-foot tower with arch-rival WCBS.

The station broadcast NBC News on the Hour and the weekend-long "Monitor" program, but WNBC was still caught between its local and national identity. Big Wilson continued to play records at breakfast time, but at the end of March 1964, WNBC turned to talk and instituted the first major call-in format in New York. Hosts included actor Robert Alda, musical comedy star Mimi Benzell, satirist Mort Sahl and one of the provocative pioneers of talk radio, Joe Pyne.

The talk shows endured for six years, and then the music returned, mostly up-tempo current hits. Music policy was regularly redirected as "66 WNBC" went to a "contemporary" format, then to something approaching Top 40 in form if not in content, and then to "all-hits" programming, trying to rival WABC. In 1970 the lineup included former WMCA morning man Joe O'Brien during the morning drive time, Ted Brown at midday, Big Wilson on afternoon drive, and Jim Lowe and Jack Spector on weekends. The overnight host was Reggie Lavong, formerly "Dr. Jive" on WWRL. It was a skilled and savvy team, but the ratings didn't improve. The flagship station was becoming an embarrassment to NBC.

The year 1972 marked a major turning point for WNBC and American radio generally (possibly even for American life) with the arrival of Cleveland disc jockey Don Imus. He was the first "shock jock" to crack the New York market; the cracks were spontaneous, often brilliant, and occasionally off-color. Music policy was a combination of Top 40 album cuts with some "adult contemporary." Joining Imus on the WNBC lineup were Oogie Pringle, Dick Summer, and Bob Vernon. Newscasters included Charles McCord, Judy De Angelis, Mitch Lebe, and Don Rollins. Some of the top personalities in radio were later featured on WNBC, including Wolfman Jack, Soupy Sales, and Cousin Brucie Morrow. Nothing seemed to pull WNBC out of the ratings cellar. General manager Bob Pittman was brought in from NBC's Chicago station in 1977. One of his first acts was to dismiss Don Imus and give the morning slot to Ellie Dylan and then Lee Masters. When Pittman left two years later, Imus returned.

Howard Stern took over afternoon drive time in 1982 with a show that made Don Imus seem like Buffalo Bob. Stern was more than suggestive, and his blue humor offended large segments of the audience, from religious leaders to feminists. "How-weird" (as he was known around WNBC) was eventually fired, not for his off-color comments but for on-air badmouthing of the Statue of Liberty restoration committee, which was headed by friends of some high-level RCA executives.

Late in 1987, WNBC added some oldies to its music mix and began a nightly sports-talk program with Jack Spector and later Dave Simms. The next year would be its last. The demise of WNBC was a result of the breakup of the parent Radio Corporation of America. RCA's broadcast operations were sold to the General Electric Company, one of the partners when the Radio Corporation was organized in 1919. GE decided to concentrate on NBC Television and sold the radio network to Westwood One. WNBC and it's FM partner WYNY were sold to Emmis Broadcasting for $39 million.

In its final moments, WNBC's life flashed before its ears. "The First 66 Years" was a sixty-six-minute show that few other stations could attempt. It was produced and narrated by program director Dale Parsons as a labor of love. Once again, by transcription, Vincent Lopez, Rudy Vallee, the Silver Masked Tenor, Amos 'n' Andy, and Fred Allen were heard from Radio City. Mae West reprised the performance that had caused any mention of her name to be banned from NBC. Pearl Harbor, D-Day, the death of FDR, the assassination of JFK—all reminded listeners that this was once the station that millions were likely to tune to first at a time of crisis, and stay with the longest. For one more time there were Toscanini, Tallulah, Imus, and the words of Mister Blackwell of the Queensboro Corporation urging tenement dwellers to come out to Jackson Heights.

At 5:30 P.M. on 7 October 1988, WNBC signed off forever. WFAN would move down from 1050kHz to air its all-sports programming (and Don Imus) at the superior 660

Don Imus and Howard Stern were featured in WNBC's subway advertising campaign, ca. 1985.

spot. The Radio City studios had been dismantled, old equipment and memorabilia picked clean by staff and visitors. At its last sign-off, WNBC had been reduced to two model RE-20 microphones. As Alan Colmes delivered the final farewell, in the background a little xylophone rang three chimes.

See also WEAF, WJZ, WFAN.

WNEW

(13 FEBRUARY 1934–15 DEC. 1992)

1934	1250kc s/t WHBI	1,000w.
1939	1280kc s/t WHBI	5,000w. day / 1,000w. night
1941	1130kc	10,000w.
1949	1130kc	50,000w.

During radio's first two decades, federal regulators assigning stations to share a frequency hoped that the cum-bersome arrangement might motivate them to merge into a single, stronger, full-time operation. This did occur a few times (usually a dominant station took over the weaker partners), but there was only one true marriage in the New York area that turned out sweetly successful.

In June 1933, WAAM in Jersey City and WODA in Paterson—two well-regarded stations that occupied 1250kc with unusual equanimity—began the process of creating a new licensee called the WODAAM Corporation. From September 1933 through February 1934, the New Jersey stations broadcast jointly with dual identification as WODA-WAAM. Advertising executive Milton Biow joined watchmaker Arde Bulova (a Biow client) and WODA's Richard O'Dea as one-third owner and president of a thoroughly new station. The call letters WNEW were chosen not necessarily to stand for Newark, the station's original home, or even New York, but because it was going to be "the newest thing in radio." WNEW's original transmitter was a secondhand unit that had been used by CBS's station WABC in Wayne, N.J.

For its dedication on 13 February 1934, WNEW boldly spotlighted its own contract talent, without big-name guest stars. The first day's schedule was filled with WAAM holdovers like the "County Roscommon Boys," an "Old Family Almanac," the "Homespun Philosopher," several children's shows, and seven "to be announced" listings. During its first year WNEW offered a standard mix of popular and classical music, sports, and news commentaries. Its first newscaster was WMCA veteran A. L. Alexander. Then WNEW made a change that would revolutionize radio. It seems that Milton Biow didn't like the house orchestra, which he felt made every tune sound alike. He was paying twelve musicians a total of $1,200 a week, and since the union wouldn't let WNEW out of its contract, the musicians were soon being paid to sit around idle.

Tuesday, 12 November 1935

2:00 P.M.	Harmony Keyboards
2:15	Sons of Pioneers
2:45	Uncle Lum
3:00	Medical Talk
3:15	Social Problems
3:30	In Italy
4:00	Dwight Butcher, talk
4:15	Key Reed, organ
4:30	Pickard Family
4:45	Helen Forest and Alan Courtney
5:00	Michael's Little Theatre
5:30	Cocktail Trio
5:45	Marathon
6:00	Dinner Rhythms
6:30	Dal and Ann
6:45	Dinner Rhythms
7:00	Earl Carpenter Orchestra
7:15	Headlines Talks
7:30	Jack Feeny, songs
7:45	Courtney's Rhythm Roundup
8:15	Duck Call Contest
8:45	Amateur Revue
9:30–2:00 A.M.	Dance Music
2:00–7:00	Dance records

"One thing we did have that the networks could not use was records," Biow wrote in his autobiography, *Butting In.* "We could play all the music they were playing if we just put records on the air.... I discussed this with [station manager Bernice] Judis. I was sure the public didn't care a whit whether they had records or the live band, as long as they had their favorite music. If we used records, we could offer Guy Lombardo, Tommy Dorsey, Bing Crosby—anyone at all. We could give the public what they wanted."

The biggest news story of the day in February 1935 was the trial of Bruno Hauptmann for the kidnapping and murder of the infant son of aviator Charles Lindbergh. To fill time during breaks in the trial, announcer Martin Block purchased six records from a corner music store. Once the trial ended, Block's record show continued as a Monday, Wednesday, and Friday feature from 11:15 to 11:30 A.M., and soon grew to ninety minutes a day. The original format called for one performer to be featured for a quarter-hour, supposedly performing beneath a "crystal chandelier." WNEW was not the first station to broadcast phonograph records—a scorned but common practice since the earliest days—but starting with Martin Block and the "Make Believe Ballroom," programs were created merely from "wax" and the personality of the announcer.

Soon most of WNEW's schedule was recorded music, although live performances continued from the former WAAM studio in the RKO Theatre Building at 1060 Broad Street in Newark. Among the stars on this paragon of swing era radio was Zeke Manners, who called himself "America's Number One Hillbilly" and had two shows a day. Block also presented a live "Battle of the Bands" from Randall's Island on Saturday mornings, attracting thousands of fans and thousands more listeners to hear the big bands in live, competitive performance.

From its first day on the air, WNEW also occupied Manhattan studios at 501 Madison Avenue built for comedian Ed Wynn's defunct Amalgamated Broadcasting System (this could be the origin of the mistaken notion that N-E-W stood for "Network Ed Wynn"). WNEW even had hopes of reviving the ill-fated ABS but soon abandoned the network plan to become one of the most successful independent stations in America. On 20 October 1936, WNEW adopted New York as its official "city of license," and by April 1938 it had closed the Newark studio. In 1939, WNEW was the top-rated independent in the city, its 10.4 Hooperating more than double the runner-up.

Audience response to "platters" was enthusiastic, but bandleader Paul Whiteman and RCA sued WNEW for violating the "not for radio broadcast" warning written on every record label. In 1940 a federal court ruled that copyright protects against reproducing a work and that WNEW "never invaded any such right." The record show was legal for everyone.

Even then not everything was recorded. Among the vocalists to appear live on WNEW in the 1930s were Frank Sinatra, Dinah Shore, Bea Wain, and Helen Forrest. Merle Pitt and the Five Shades of Blue was the station's (improved) house band, and Roy Ross also led the WNEW studio orchestra.

Another innovation put WNEW in a class by itself: it was the first station to regularly remain on the air twenty-four hours a day. All-night operation was not unknown in radio—during the 1920s some stations would stay on through the night for the benefit of distant listeners, then sign off at dawn. But WNEW recognized that there was a significant overnight audience in the New York area, and on Tuesday, 6 August 1935, Stan Shaw ("your very good friend the milkman") began a record show that would join the "Make Believe Ballroom" as one of the anchors of WNEW's schedule. At first, the "Milkman's Matinee" began at 2:00 A.M. and ran till "Dolly Dawn [Teresa Stabile] and the Dawn Patrol" at seven o'clock, making it as much a wake-up show as an overnight program. Art Ford took over the "Milkman's Matinee" in 1942.

WNEW's early success came despite the handicap of

Martin Block, host of WNEW's "Make Believe Ballroom," demonstrates his secret remedy for all-night partying.

being on the air only six days a week. A third station, WHBI in Newark, was also sharing the WAAM-WODA frequency and remained in operation on Monday evenings and all day Sunday at 1250kc. In March 1941, WNEW and WHBI were both reassigned to 1280 but WNEW would soon escape the frequency and the time-sharing that came with it. Station WOV was also owned by Arde Bulova and broadcast mostly in Italian at the preferred dial position of 1130. The FCC authorized a swap of call letters, which was in effect a change of frequency. On Monday, 1 December 1941, WNEW's studios were patched into WOV's transmitter and vice versa, the renamed stations took over each other's programming, and WNEW commenced to swing 168 hours a week at eleven-three-oh. A month later the power was boosted to 10,000 watts.

Alan Courtney had originated WNEW's "1250 Club" in

1937. With the frequency change it became WNEW's "1280 Club," and Courtney stayed with the show at that spot on the dial, continuing on WOV until the mid–1940s.

Although WNEW took the International News Service wire in 1939, it was not really a "music and news" station until the outbreak of World War II, when arrangements were made with the *Daily News* to provide "News around the Clock" on the half hour. There was also a "War Diary" each evening at 7:35 with commentators "Richard Brooks" and "George Brooks"—both the same person, chief announcer John Jaeger. Newscaster Henry Walden also did a Sunday morning children's program reading comic strips and nursery rhymes, accompanied by Merle Evans and the Circus Band. Programming continued to feature several country-music programs, including the Sons of the Pioneers and "singing cowboy" Elton Britt.

During this era, WNEW dispensed with the position of program director, and programming decisions were made by a committee. Under the hands-on guidance of general manager Bernice Judis—she was known to call in at 3:00 A.M. to advise an announcer to tone down his delivery—the station cultivated a smooth, sophisticated personality. To its fans, WNEW would become as distinct a New York institution as the brownstones and the bridges.

During the summer of 1942, WNEW organized the Atlantic Coast Network (a plan that originated with Arde Bulova and WOV) and fed programs to ten stations from Boston to Washington, including Philadelphia's WPEN and WFBR in Baltimore.

In 1946 WNEW began to awaken New Yorkers each day with zany deejay teams. The pioneers were Gene Rayburn and Jack Lescoulie, staff announcers who were notified on a Friday that they would begin the wake-up show that Monday. They created a dawn-breaking gagfest called "Scream and Dream with Jack and Gene," soon retitled "Anything Goes." After a year Lescoulie was fired, and staff announcer Dee Finch took his place. Rayburn and Finch—who were close friends before they became a radio team—entertained New Yorkers till 1952. In that year WNBC tried to recruit the team, and Rayburn signed a contract, but at the last minute Finch insisted on remaining with WNEW. A replacement was quickly found for Rayburn: Washington deejay Gene Klavan (the abrupt change and similarity in their names made the switch almost imperceptible for some listeners). The Klavan and Finch partnership lasted till Finch retired in 1968. Klavan continued solo in the morning till 1977.

On 24 August 1946 the station moved to 565 Fifth Avenue; a small, second-floor balcony fronted by large golden letters W N E W became a genuine midtown landmark. Among the novelties in the seven color-coded studios were clocks that ran backward to show the time remaining, and scripts that were projected on the wall (the latter innovation never caught on). WNEW took over 50,000 square feet at its new location, most of it in anticipation of needing space for television studios. In 1949 "America's Razzle-Dazzle Station" was sold for over $2 million to a group headed by Rhode Island businessman William S. Cherry and including Bernice Judis and her husband, sales manager Ira Herbert. Power was increased to a full 50,000 watts. In 1954 ownership passed to Richard D. Buckley, and in that year Judis ended her two-decade leadership of WNEW.

The rock-and-roll era of the 1950s should have signaled the end of WNEW's big-band and ballad sound, but ironically the rise of the rockers and the demise of big-time network radio helped make "The Big W" the most listened to

Co-owned WOV and WNEW trade places on the dial, 1941.

and profitable station in the New York market. Martin Block remained beneath the Crystal Chandelier through the end of 1953, when he departed for WABC, whose network was already carrying another of his daily shows. On 1 January 1954 Jerry Marshall took over the "Make Believe Ballroom" for three years, eventually surpassing Arthur Godfrey in the morning ratings. Al "Jazzbeaux" Collins played jazz nightly from the Purple Grotto with "Harold, the purple-tailed Tasmanian owl," keeping silent watch. In the afternoons "Collins on a Cloud" drifted above the city on Cloud 9 with a harp plunking Debussy's "Au Claire de Lune" in the background. Well into the 1950s there were daily live variety shows featuring singer-announcers such as Bob Haymes, Bill Kemp and Bill Harrington. WNEW cultivated a friendly, often antic sound; but mostly it could be described by the title of its afternoon record show, "In a Sentimental Mood." The "newest thing in radio" had segued into nostalgia.

Over the years "The Milkman's Matinee" had some twenty different deejay hosts. Jazzbeaux Collins took over radio's original all-night entertainment from Art Ford but

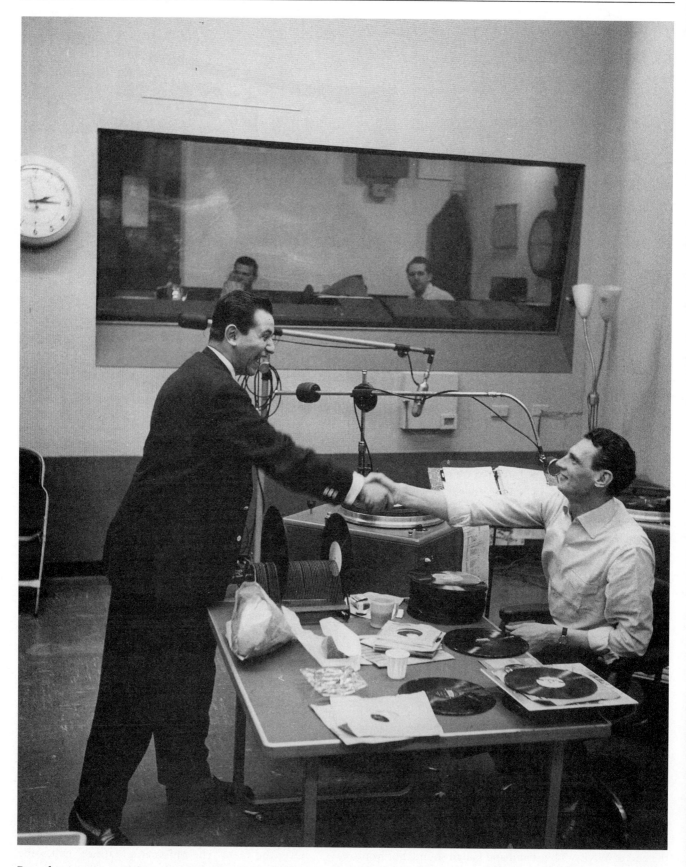

Record company promotion men were an integral part of New York's radio scene. Here's an unidentified song plugger meeting WNEW's Ed Locke at 2:15 A.M.!

WNEW was as well known for its personalities as for its music. Here's Ted Brown looking sartorially splendid...

was fired after spending the entire night repeatedly spinning one record, the Chordettes' "Mr. Sandman." The NYPD even called at about 2:30 A.M. to ask if anything was wrong; Jazzbeaux explained simply, "Nothing, man, I'm just doing my thing." He got his walking papers the next day, and Ed Locke was brought in from WIP in Philadelphia (a station that served as the WNEW "farm team" for many years).

Monday, 8 November 1954

6:00 A.M.	Klaven and Finch
9:30	Bill Harrington and Company
10:00	Make Believe Ballroom with Jerry Marshall
11:30	Bing Crosby Show (recorded)
12:00 Noon	Bill Harrington and Company
2:00	Music Hall, with Lonny Starr
4:00	Art Ford at Four
5:00	The Bill Kemp Show
5:30	Make Believe Ballroom
7:30	Art Ford Evening Show
9:00	Bill Williams
12:00 midnight	Milkman's Matinee—Al Collins

Morning stars Klaven and Finch as well as William B. Williams had special contracts with WNEW, but most of the

other disc jockeys, including Dick Partridge, Bob Landers, Jack Lazare, and Al Collins, each did two-hour daily broadcasts and were actually part-time employees.

In 1957, the station was sold for $7.5 million, the biggest price paid till that time for a single radio station. The new owner was the DuMont Broadcasting Corporation, a reorganization of the defunct DuMont Television Network. DuMont was then bought by John Kluge's Metromedia, and with this era WNEW became the radio partner of TV channel 5. (WNEW filed an application for channel 31 when the UHF band was opened in 1952; the application was later withdrawn.) Surprisingly, "your favorite station for music and news" didn't actually establish its own news department until 1958, when the station's new TV involvement forced an end to the association with the *Daily News*, which owned channel 11. WNEW gained respect as a news source through the work of such journalists as Ike Pappas, Marlene Sanders, John Laurence, Jim Gash (who few reporters ever beat to a story), sportscaster Chip Cipolla, and former CBS foreign correspondent David Schoenbrun.

There was little crossover activity between WNEW-TV and radio. By the 1960s WNEW radio was earning over $7 million a year, with stars like Pete "Mad Daddy" Myers, a unique comic talent who moved to WNEW from WINS. His delivery was a precursor to the rap artists who would come a dozen years later. But he fell into debt; fearing that WNEW would move him out of his afternoon time slot, in 1969 Myers, an avid gun collector, committed suicide.

An attempt in the early 1970s to mix in light versions of current rock-and-roll hits bombed with listeners, as did the try at an "adult contemporary" format. The station expanded its sports coverage, including New York Giants football, and the "Milkman's Matinee" even had its title temporarily changed to "The Nightmare Show." WNEW could never stray far from its listeners, but neither could the melody linger on forever.

...and William B. Williams on a subway poster in the early 1960s.

WNEW's record library was once considered the world's largest, and disc jockeys had individual collections in their own offices. In the mid–1960s a new program director, objecting to what he saw as personal fiefdoms, gave all the deejays a week to vacate the space. William B. Williams returned from vacation to find his office empty and his record collection missing. By the mid–1970s the station was even playing some rock tunes again and decided to "prune" the library. Nearly ten thousand records—LPs, 45's, even some classic station jingles—were placed in a hallway; staff members and visitors were invited to help themselves. Additional purges depleted the fabled WNEW library till it consisted of some two thousand cartridge tapes and a cabinet of scratchy albums.

In the 1980s, WNEW seemed to find itself continually on the sales block. Metromedia divested itself of the property in 1986 and sold out to some of its own executives, d/b/a Metropolitan Broadcasting. In 1988, the Westwood One network, which had already built a media empire by purchasing the remnants of both Mutual and NBC Radio, bought a 50 percent interest from struggling Metropolitan. Westwood's talk shows soon took over the nighttime hours, with Larry King displacing the Milkman. Seven months later, Westwood One sold out to Legacy Broadcasting; it would become the last owner.

"If you love us today, you'll love us tomorrow," proclaimed the new slogan, but the sophisticated sound was losing its glimmer. The death of William B. Williams in 1986 was as much an institutional as a personal loss. Like the lyric of one of the ballads that once filled WNEW's days and nights, the thrill was gone. In mid–December 1992, WNEW said goodbye forever; its passing was regretted as if it were another solid structure falling to the wrecker's ball. William O'Shaughnessy, the owner of WVOX and WRTN(FM) in New Rochelle, tried to have the WNEW call letters reassigned, to renew the name and the format. O'Shaughnessy even offered to buy the legendary record library, apparently unaware of how much had been lost.

"The station that invented music and news" was sold to Bloomberg Business Radio, which changed the call letters to WBBR and stopped the music to specialize in business news. The *New York Times* station WQXR changed its AM call letters to WQEW and hired several of the personalities from eleven-three-oh, including Jonathan Schwartz and program director Stan Martin, to continue one of radio's richest legacies.

See also WAAM, WODA, WOV, WHBI, WBBR (II).

WNJ

(15 OCTOBER 1924–31 MARCH 1933)

1923 (WRAZ)	233m (1290kc)	50w.
May 1924 (WCBX)	1290kc	100w.
July 1925	1190kc s/t WGCP	100w.
1926	1190kc	500w.
July 1926	860, 850kc (unauthorized)	500w.
April 1927	1070k s/t WGCP, WDWM	500w.
1927	1120kc	250w.
Nov. 1928	1450kc s/t WBMS, WIBS, WKBO	250w.

It was *not* the legendary David Sarnoff who heard the SOS from the luxury liner *Titanic* in 1912 and relayed the news to a shocked world. The future head of RCA was merely a Marconi operator at Wanamaker's Department Store in Manhattan hearing signals from the S.S. *Carpathia*, which came to the aid of the *Titanic*'s survivors. The distinction of copying the actual distress signals should belong to Herman Lubinsky, who served as a member of the wireless crew on board the *Carpathia*. Lubinsky was a naval radio operator and following World War I spent a few years enforcing Prohibition as a federal revenue agent.

Then he took up a quieter occupation and opened the Radio Shop of Newark at 58 Market Street and established station WRAZ in June 1923. The July 1924 edition of the trade journal *Radio Dealer* stated that Lubinsky was the only radio wholesaler in Newark "interested in broadcasting activities." In the days when broadcasters were often forbidden to use their names on the air, operator Herman Lubinsky called himself "OHL."

The WRAZ call letters were changed to WCBX in April 1924. Lubinsky then requested the letters WNJ, which he said stood for "Wireless New Jersey," and on 15 October 1924 received his third set of call letters in sixteen months.

Despite its close identification with the Radio Shop, WNJ was located in the attic of the Lubinsky home at 89 Lehigh Avenue. A generator was installed in a dormer and the transmission tower took up the entire backyard. In 1925 Lubinsky built a studio in the Paradise Ballroom in Newark and operated a shortwave transmitter for local remote pickups.

Thursday, 3 October 1929

8:31 A.M.	Radio Shop program
9:00	Sunshine period
9:30	George Zoen, pianist
10:00	Off for WIBS-WKBO

Herman Lubinsky, founder of WNJ. *Collection of Bruce Grossberg.*

6:01 P.M.	Mildred Graham, soprano
6:15	Readings, Harry Mack
6:30	Arthur Lang's Gang
7:00	Italian program
7:30	Coast Guard Ripples
7:45	Herman Halperin, uke
8:00	Violin and piano recital
8:30	Penn's Pennsylvanians

Lubinsky was appointed by Secretary of Commerce Herbert Hoover to an industry committee to advise the department on radio frequency allocations. The former government agent could understand the problems well, for during the period of legal limbo in the mid–1920s, WNJ had moved itself around the dial a couple of times.

WNJ, "The Voice of Newark," presented programs in Polish and Lithuanian and some of the earliest Italian programming in the New York metropolitan area, featuring Ben D'Avella. Sam Barnowitz, the chief announcer and program director, produced dramatic hours featuring the WNJ Players. In 1928 WNJ established a studio in the Hotel St. Francis in Newark. A year later, Lubinsky reorganized as the Radio Investment Company.

Through these years, WNJ was sharing time with several other New Jersey stations, including WBMS, WIBS, WKBO, and finally WHOM, which was absorbing the other stations on 1450kc. In November 1932, the FRC denied WNJ's request for license renewal. Lubinsky fought the action in the federal courts but lost and was ordered off the air. The equipment remained in the Lubinsky attic till the family moved in the 1950s.

A decade after the demise of WNJ, Lubinsky went into the record business. He founded Savoy Records at 54 Market Street, the old Radio Shop location. Savoy has been called "the first rhythm and blues label of consequence" and attracted some of the best jazz, blues, and gospel performers of the era. Lubinsky gained a reputation as a penny-pinching tyrant, but he also advanced the careers of Little Esther Phillips, James Cleveland, and other African-American performers. Lubinsky also haunted the Manhattan jazz clubs and signed such jazz greats as Coleman Hawkins, Ben Webster, Hot Lips Page, and Johnny Guarnieri for Savoy recordings that are today treasured by jazz fans.

Herman Lubinsky died in March 1974 at the age of seventy-seven. His radio station WNJ had been just one chapter in an exciting life.

WNJR

(20 NOVEMBER 1947–)

1947   1430kc.   5,000w.

The demise of Brooklyn's only full-time commercial station, WBYN, was the opening for Newark to bring added radio service to the northern New Jersey market, which many considered underserved. WBYN officially changed hands on 27 December 1946, and on that same day it was authorized to increase its power to 5,000 watts full-time. The original applicant for 1430 was the Newark *Sunday Call*—a paper whose experience as a radio producer and sponsor went back to the earliest days of WJZ—but the *Call* was absorbed into the *Newark Evening News*, and the station planned as WNJW went on the air in 1947 as WNJR. North Jersey Radio Inc. ran "Brooklyn's Own Station" for nearly a year until facilities were ready at 91 Halsey Street in Newark.

The gala inaugural broadcast featured drama by actors from the Paper Mill Playhouse, scenes from *Rigoletto* by the Griffith Music Foundation (whose own station, WVNJ, was still a year away), and the music of the WNJR Orchestra conducted by Leo Freudenberg. With its *Evening News* connection and the leadership of news director Tom Costigan—once the narrator of Fox Movietone Newsreels—WNJR quickly developed the Garden State's best radio news coverage. Announcers included Alois Havrilla, one of the finest voices in network radio whose credits included the Paul Whiteman and Jack Benny programs. He gave the new station a refined sound as both news commentator and in the presentation of a musical program, "Alois Havrilla Presents."

Carl Ide was heard during the morning drive time and from 1:00 to 3:00 in the afternoon playing jazz on the "S.S. Cool," as well as at 11:00 p.m. with a transcribed hour of music and poetry. WNJR's early programming also included some western swing and Latin dance music. By the early 50s, WNJR was moving toward a mixture of jazz, jive, and a musical phenomenon called rhythm and blues which especially appealed to the black audience. Alan Freed's rock-and-roll party was first heard in the New York area on WNJR in a syndicated show that originated at Cleveland's WJW. Freed called himself "the Moondog" and his listeners "Moondoggers" until a lawsuit by blind troubadour Louis "Moondog" Hardin forced him to cease and desist.

New personalities included some of the nation's outstanding African-American broadcasters, including George Hudson and Ramon Bruce ("I am **the Bruce!**... called Ramon"). Hal Wade did the overnight hours, replaced in 1953 by Danny ("the Cat Man") Stiles, whose theme song,

"Jeep's Blues," was wailed and meowed by a chorus of alley cats. Charlie Green, Pat Connell, Herman Amis, Enoch Gregory, and Hal Jackson also came to the WNJR microphones.

In the fall of 1953, the *Newark News* took over WVNJ and sold WNJR to Rollins Broadcasting. The new owner completed the switch to black-oriented rhythm-and-blues programming (the station's collection of 78 rpm pop records was trucked off late one night to a Rollins station in Delaware). The Bruce extended his show to six and a half hours a day and went into syndication; George Hudson was on for six hours a day. The station also picked up syndicated rhythm-and-blues deejays from around the country, including Dewey Phillips from Memphis, Daddy Sears of Atlanta, and L.A.'s Hunter Hancock.

The turbulence and impatience of society in the 1960s did not bypass WNJR. In August 1967 the staff of the Rollins station walked out on strike, putting WNJR off the air for six hours. The dispute was ostensibly over salaries and work rules, though George Hudson blamed "white management." Rollins denied discrimination in any form. The company had been reorganized as Continental Broadcasting, and in November 1968 the FCC refused to renew its license citing fraudulent advertising, falsified logs, and other violations. Continental continued to run WNJR during the appeals process, but early in 1971 the courts upheld the commission, and in July of that year WNJR was left without an owner. It went silent on Saturday, 17 July 1971.

The Newark city government requested permission to operate WNJR until a new licensee could be found, stating that the station was vital to the city's black community. The interim arrangement was delayed until terms were worked out with Rollins, which still owned the building and equipment (actually located outside of Newark, in Union, N.J.) and it wasn't until 29 July that WNJR returned under the banner of "Radio Newark." New Jersey's largest city had joined New York, at least temporarily, as a municipal broadcaster.

It would take thirteen years to settle WNJR's ownership. In December 1971 the interim license was transferred from the city to a consortium of station staff and applicants known as the WNJR Radio Company. The station was finally under private, de facto control of African-Americans (and by coincidence in an arrangement similar to that of the ill-fated WBYN). Despite its transitional status WNJR made some major advances in 1972, becoming the New York area affiliate of the Mutual Black Network (later the Sheridan

Bobby Jay, WNJR deejay, 1967.

Broadcasting Network) and joining the new National Black Network a year later. The temporary license of the WNJR Radio Company was canceled in May 1975, and a new group of four applicants known as 1430 Associates, took control. In 1976 one of the applicants, Sound Radio Inc., was awarded the license. An FCC review board reversed that decision in June 1978. By that time, WNJR had been caught up in another fraudulent advertising scheme.

One of the station's religious broadcasts had publicized a "Money in a Hurry Prosperity Package," which was really giving out information on illegal gambling in the guise of Bible verses. The speaker's "blessings" referred to "numbers". The FCC's chief administrative law judge found the licensees and management innocent, however, "because they did not play the numbers and were not familiar with its subculture."

The legal twists finally came to an end in 1982 when

Sound Radio received permanent authorization to run WNJR. License limbo hadn't seriously affected the audience, which remained faithful to the gospel and urban contemporary programming directed at a mature African-American public. From 1983 to 1986, mornings were filled with big band music of the swing era.

In 1986, Sound Radio Inc. put up a new transmitter and antenna in Hillside for WNJR, but improved audio didn't lead to improved returns, and the company fell into bankruptcy. In 1989, Spanish American Radio Communications Inc. (a group that included Danny Stiles) bought out Sound Radio for $4.1 million but ultimately couldn't meet its payments. In 1991 it was sold for $6.75 million to Douglas Broadcasting, a West Coast black-owned corporation.

Douglas made major changes at WNJR, in line with the ethnic programming on its stations in Los Angeles and San Francisco. Many English-language programs for the black community were replaced by broadcasts in Spanish, Portuguese and Haitian Creole.

See also WBYN, WVNJ(I).

WNO

(19 JANUARY–24 JUNE 1922)

1922   360m (833 kc)   20w.

The Wireless Telephone Company of Hudson County was the radio voice of the *Jersey Journal* in Jersey City, whose rival, *Jersey Review* had contracted to broadcast over Frank Bremer's 2IA as early as 1920. That made station WNO something of a laggard in Jersey City, even if it did hold the thirty-sixth broadcast license issued by the Commerce Department.

WNO was located in the Lerner Building on Journal Square and operated on the only frequency available to all broadcasters. Each evening at 6:30, announcer-engineer Clarence P. Bowyer would speak into the microphone, "Tune your instruments for 360-meter waves."

As was the case with most stations of that era, programming was unorganized and spontaneous. There were regular appearances by a quartet of Jersey City policemen, and occasionally Wireless Telephone owner John F. Meyers would bring in some vaudevillians from Manhattan. If no one showed up, Bowyer would sing, accompanied by a player piano, while cranking up the phonograph to play the next record. As he remarked in a 1965 newspaper interview, "It took unusual coordination." As the record spun, the announcer-engineer installed the next roll in the player piano.

In June 1922, the Wireless Telephone Company took WNO off the air with the intention of installing a new transmitter. The station never returned, and its license was canceled in March 1923.

WNRC

(1953–1958)

1953   1460kc   500w.

After five years, Julian Gins sold WGNR to James Iodice, whose company was called Radio New Rochelle Inc. The cost was $21,000 plus assumption of the station's $2,000 mortgage. Much of the programming that had begun during the WGNR era continued on the renamed station. Finances were so shaky during the first days that teenage deejay Dan Ingram quit his first radio job when his first paycheck bounced.

Ralph Cooper brought his "Rock and Roll Party" to WNRC every afternoon from 3:00 to 5:00, and Mort Fega presented "Jazz Unlimited" on Saturdays from noon to 3:00, supposedly originating from the cool cave behind the radio station, "since no self-respecting jazz fan would listen to a show coming from an ordinary studio." Sundays were filled with bilingual ethnic programs for the German, Polish, and Italian communities.

In 1958 the call letters were changed to WVOX, and 1460 became the Southern Westchester outlet of the Herald-Tribune Radio Network.

See also WVIP, WVOX.

WNTA

(6 MAY 1958–31 MARCH 1962)

1958   970kc   5,000w. day/ 1,000w. night

WNTA was a short-lived but ambitious broadcast operation, replacing the venerable WAAT at a time when radio was trying to find its way in the television age. Of course, when it purchased the Bremer Broadcasting Corporation, National Telefilm Associates was primarily seeking control of Newark's channel 13 with its metropolitan coverage.

WNTA-TV was as much an innovator as its radio counterpart, widely hailed for the syndicated "Play of the Week" and David Susskind's Sunday night "Open End"—simulcast on WNTA radio—a talk show that theoretically continued till everyone was talked out or fell asleep. A WNTA jingle stated, "Forty records fill a drawer / But this station gives you more," a promise the station tried mightily to keep.

Among WNTA Radio's programs was a breakfast-hour talking newspaper called "Nothing But News," anchored by Mike Woloson. "NBN" reported news and sports, weather every five minutes, and a time signal every minute. It was a faster-paced version of WMGM's "Radio Newsreel" and another forerunner of all-news radio.

The music policy seemed to take over where WNEW left off, playing more down-tempo ballads in a format called "The Golden Sound." Mantovani's lush strings were heard in a weekly "binaural" program simulcast with WNTA-TV. The most ambitious bit of music programming was a 1958 series of Sunday noon-to-midnight musical marathons hosted by former WNEW "Milkman" and WNTA program director Art Ford. The first of these paid tribute to Rodgers and Hammerstein with a well-intended but clumsy attempt to play most of the show tunes of the prolific team, interspersed with snippets of recorded interviews. Succeeding weeks presented half-day salutes to "Italians in American Popular Music," "Negroes in American Popular Music," "Jews in American Popular Music," and so on.

In addition to his Sunday stint, Art Ford presented two ninety-minute record shows a day. Longtime WHN/WMGM sportscaster Bert Lee came to WNTA with a nightly sports show. Among the other air personnel were Lee Arnold, Vince Lindner, and WOR veteran Herb Sheldon. But the "Golden Sound" turned out lackluster and often a bit strained. In 1962 National Telefilm Associates divested itself of channel 13, which was reassigned for educational television and became WNDT, later WNET. AM and FM radio remained commercial and continued as WJRZ.

See also WAAT, WJRZ, WWDJ.

WNYC

(2 JULY 1924–)

1924	570kc 1928: s/t WMCA	500w.
1931	810kc	1,000w.
1941	830kc	1,000w.
1987	820kHz	10,000w.

SOUND: Chimes, in and under
ANNCR: Seven o'clock, by the century-old chimes in historic City Hall. This is New York, the city of opportunity, where more than eight million people live in peace and harmony and enjoy the benefits of democracy.
SOUND: Chimes, up to conclusion

Four times a day—at 7:00 A.M., noon, 7:00 P.M., and midnight—a clear-voiced announcer at "New York City's Own Station" would intone radio's most impressive time signal, a message of pride and confidence in the greatest city in the world. At morning and midday it was a statement of vitality, whereas the midnight version (heard only on FM) created a mood of power in repose, the perfect lead-in to a program called "While the City Sleeps." But the city's fates are always shifting. First the population dropped below eight million. Then, during the social upheavals of the 1970s, the remaining millions ceased to "live in" and began to "strive for" peace and harmony. Then the single male voice was replaced by a group recitation, as if this were a pledge of allegiance. Finally, the announcement was canceled. It had become a flowery anachronism.

A "municipal wireless broadcasting station" was first proposed to the New York City government early in 1922 by Queens Borough President Maurice Connolly, a friend and admirer of radio pioneer Alfred Grebe. A committee chaired by department store owner Rodman Wanamaker (whose New York location was home to WWZ) was appointed to determine the feasibility and cost and came up with a price-tag of $50,000. "The station will be conducted as a municipal venture," wrote the *New York Times* on 5 May 1922, "with a view to making it one of the largest broadcasting stations in the world. Under favorable conditions it will be able to reach Chicago."

Although supporters spoke of the public-service value of a municipal station, its political potential was not denied. Mayor John Hylan made this clear in May 1922: "When the Citizens Union sends out lies about the administration you can go to the radio and explain to the people it isn't true," and he added that he expected that watchdog group to seek an injunction against the city to keep it off the air. In the autumn of 1925, Citizens' Union of New York did indeed bring suit against the city, claiming that WNYC was a propaganda organ and that its establishment exceeded the authority of the municipal government. The New York State Supreme Court found for the city.

The federal government—especially Republican Commerce Secretary Herbert Hoover—was also skeptical about New York City owning its own station. But while critics decried the creation of a government-run station from their political perspectives, controversy also raged over the role of AT&T in the new radio industry. City officials believed that AT&T was reluctant to sell transmission equipment for a municipal station and complained to the Federal Trade Commission that AT&T was trying to establish a monopoly through its patent rights and through ownership of WEAF in New York (others had already filed complaints with the FTC). Grover Whalen, the city's commissioner of plants and structures, and the man in charge of getting the new station on the air, complained that WEAF "had taken complete control of the air." He asserted in March 1924 that a city-owned station "means that we will not have to take our religion, our education or our politics from the radio trust. It means the broadcasting station we erect will be as powerful as WEAF … the people of the city and the country at large will be able to listen in to a station that is not operated for commercial gain."

In response, William Harkness of AT&T denied that his company had refused to sell equipment to the city and said that it had even offered advice based on its own experience with WBAY and WEAF. "Mr. Whalen wanted to [transmit] from the top of the Municipal Building," Harkness explained. "We told him that was impractical. Then he would put [WNYC's antenna] on top of the Brooklyn Bridge. We advised against that too." AT&T suggested that the municipal government purchase time on WEAF but did sell it a used transmitter that had just been shipped back from Brazil where it had seen service at that country's Centennial Exhibition. On 15 April 1924, the *New York Times* wrote:

CITY TO BROADCAST
FROM STATION CONY

CONY will be the designation of the municipal radio broadcasting station, if the United States Department of Commerce, which issues the broadcasting license, approves the application of Grover A. Whalen, Commissioner of Plants and Structures…. It is not for Coney Island but for the City of New York that CONY stands…. Mr. Whalen said he had been searching for weeks for a "catchy" series of letters by which to christen the city's broadcasting station and he was on the point of announcing a prize contest for the best description. "I want a designation that will also suggest the name of the City of New

York—something, for instance, that might include the letters C-O-N-Y," he said yesterday afternoon. "Well, what better designation than CONY do you hope to get," his hearer replied. The commissioner scratched his head a moment, and said he believed he would not announce the prize contest.

Whalen stated that the city would not broadcast meetings of the Board of Estimate or the Board of Aldermen, and that it would give "the right-of-way" to police and fire bulletins, which would interrupt other programs in case of an emergency. The station also planned to broadcast concerts in the parks, not only to the home audience but also, through loudspeakers, to other parks.

WNYC (Whalen learned that radio stations beginning with "CO" had to be located in Cuba) raised the curtain at 8:40 P.M. on 2 July 1924 with appropriate pageantry. Eight-foot call letters were spotlighted on the west side of the Municipal Building and illuminated fountains gushed beneath the rooftop antenna. Mayor Hylan led the official party. Vincent Lopez and his orchestra serenaded listeners to the inaugural broadcast. The station's first announcer was Thomas Cowan, who had put WJZ on the air. Unfortunately, the outdoor ceremony was interrupted by a sudden thunderstorm, which drenched the mayor and his fellow dignitaries and flooded the bass horns of the fire department band.

The inaugural broadcast continued inside the station's twenty-fourth-floor studio. The studios were to have been state-of-the-art for the time, including "soundproof wallpaper." The previous day, however, someone noticed that the wallpaper did not match the decorative scheme elsewhere in the building and it was painted, thereby destroying its sound-absorbing qualities. So the room was hung with draperies, "which made the room virtually air tight as well as sound-proof. Some of the more corpulent members of the Police and Firemen's Band suffered in the heat."

At 526 meters wavelength (570kc), WNYC caused interference to AT&T's WEAF at 610kc (some considered this an act of revenge). But WNYC's signal also suffered from interference by ship radios on the maritime frequencies below it, many of which were still using spark-gap transmitters. These technical problems were not the only shortcomings of the municipal station. In *This Fascinating Radio Business* (1946), Robert J. Landry refers to WNYC's "strangely uneven course" as "not the least of New York's radio oddities."

The city government established WNYC in 1924 but little seems to have been done during the first decade. WNYC had two small studios under a blind monitoring system. Microphone rehearsals were unknown and sound "levels" could not be taken before programs were actually on the air. Red tape, politics, no funds, disinterest—whatever the proper explanation, WNYC was incredibly crude prior to 1933…. The station had the reputation of being excessively timid and was far more severe in censorship of talks than most commercial managements. WNYC would not allow the city's own Department of Health to mention the term "social diseases." The program schedule prior to 1933 was heavy with build-ups for Tammany Hall Democrats. To fill in time when nothing else was available announcers would read again and again a series of stale mimeographed talks which were kept in the files for that purpose.

Among WNYC's harshest critics was the popular monthly *Radio Broadcast*. In January 1925 it attacked the station for "propaganda of the most biased sort" that gave the mayor and his supporters greater access to its microphones than his opponents could muster. Two years later the same magazine commented, "Station WNYC should be discontinued because its program standards are hopelessly below par." The magazine complained that the station was spending too much time airing police and fire alarms. Early in 1927, radios were installed in police stations throughout the city with dials locked to WNYC to discourage any officer who might be tempted to tune to something more entertaining. An official history of WNYC even stated that the station "functioned primarily as a bulletin board."

By 1926 WNYC's annual $37,000 payroll was seen as exorbitant, and despite supportive statements by Mayor Walker, the feeling was growing within the city administration that WNYC was a waste of money, an impression that would dawn on every future administration. Walker's commissioner of plants and structures, Albert Goldman, wanted to poll radio listeners to determine if they wanted the station on the air. Among the options explored was limiting WNYC to just one or two nights a week.

Amid these political disputes, WNYC began to present some of the best hours of music to be heard in the city. Without funds to build up a record library, WNYC borrowed albums from record stores around City Hall Park (the stores asked that the records be returned before noon). Finally, a listener began loaning classical records. These favors helped to develop "The Masterwork Hour" in 1929, which would eventually become known as "radio's oldest recorded program of fine music."

The FRC did renew the license of the municipal station in 1927, but on Sunday, 11 November 1928 WMCA moved from the 810 frequency to a time-sharing arrangement with WNYC at 570kc. WNYC was angry about this politically influenced switch, even though it had not been using the full time at its disposal. In July 1929, WMCA complained to the FRC that WNYC frequently delayed "signing off, thus destroying the promptness and regularity of WMCA's broadcasting schedule." The commission asked to see the time schedules of the two stations. WMCA indicated ninety-four "trespasses" in 180 days.

Friday, 14 October 1927

12:00 noon	Distribution of Fire Prevention Essays by Mayor Walker
1:15	Bronx traffic installation luncheon; speakers: Mayor Walker, Joseph V.

	McKee, Henry Bruckner, Joseph A. Warren, and Albert Goldman
6:00	Herman Neuman, piano
6:10	Market high spots
6:20	Piano selections
6:30	French, V. H. Berlitz
7:30	Police alarms, tide, ferries
7:35	Billie King, songs
7:45	John Rogers, bass
8:00	H. Cusenza, mandolin
8:30	Making of a Newspaper—H. V. Kaltenborn
9:00	Rudolph Joskowitz, violin
9:30	Hayes and Mohr, songs
10:00	Government talk
10:10	Bernard Baslow, piano
10:30	Police alarms; weather
10:35	W. S. Jones, ballads
10:50	Military Tournament and its Purposes

Marion K. Gilliam, manager of WMCA, asserted, "WNYC has run over our broadcasting time, causing us concern and annoyance, once every two days." He added that these incursions lasted from a few to fifteen minutes. The municipal station never asked permission to stay on late, and WMCA always stood by waiting for it to go off. WNYC denied the charge, though it admitted that some broadcasts of city functions may have caused it to run over "perhaps a minute to a minute and a half." Gilliam also complained that WNYC was devoting its time to "such program features as sopranos, bell-ringers, pianists and other entertainers, concerning whom the question might be raised if their broadcasting is vital to the city's continued welfare." Commissioner Goldman responded that WNYC would continue with its programming, bell-ringers and all. A 1930 city law established WNYC as "an adjunct of the police and fire departments."

In 1931 WNYC lost its 570kc frequency and was forced to settle down on WMCA's old 810 spot. This left it not only technically inferior but also without a public relations and psychological advantage among New York broadcasters, since many newspapers began their radio listings with the first station on the dial. On its new frequency, WNYC had to sign off at sunset to avoid interfering with the nighttime signal of WCCO, the 50,000-watt CBS station in Minneapolis. (WNYC moved to 830kc in 1941, but so did WCCO. WNYC was later allowed to remain on the air till 10:00 P.M. New York time year-round. This early sign-off continued until 1987, when WNYC moved to 820kHz). The limited hours were a constant frustration to WNYC staff, who often complained that New York City was sacrificing a unique service "for a few farmers in Minnesota." The sign-off announcement once began with the words, "The sun has set in Minneapolis...."

In 1934, Mayor Fiorello La Guardia's reform administration—which had also thought about shutting down WNYC—appointed a citizens' committee to examine the future prospects for the city station. The group, composed of CBS's William Paley, Richard Patterson of NBC, and WOR manager Al McCosker, recommended that the station accept commercial advertising (WNYC had always been licensed as a commercial station). Instead, La Guardia appointed Seymour N. Siegel to program WNYC and conduct it as a public service. New, air-conditioned studios were built in the Municipal Building, allowing announcers to close the windows. Till then, sounds from the streets and harbor were heard so consistently in the background that these noises of New York were considered a trademark of WNYC. In 1936 the transmitter was moved from the roof of the Municipal Building to a better location on city property along the East River in Greenpoint.

In 1937 a revised city charter created the Municipal Broadcasting System. WEVD executive Morris Novik was hired to manage WNYC, reporting directly to Mayor La Guardia. His charge was simply to "serve the people," and WNYC could enter maturity. On 23 October 1937, WNYC opened a new suite of seven studios in the Municipal Building with a play entitled WNYC: *The Voice of the People.* One of the characters was a boy who complained: "They never have anything good. No movie stars or nothin'." His father patiently pointed out the excitement inherent in the daily "Missing Persons Report" direct from police headquarters and in fire department bulletins, which even the mayor listened to. La Guardia played himself on the show, as did manager Sy Siegel. The young skeptic was finally won over when he learned that he could become a member of the Junior Inspector's Club of the Department of Sanitation, which met on the radio every afternoon at 5:15. Series like that did have a following: there were over 100,000 junior sanitation inspectors and even more members of the Police Athletic League, whose activities also included a WNYC program.

Despite the rough criticism, WNYC's programming—even in its early days—could be quite good. Broadcasts of municipal events may have been tedious and politically motivated, but they were probably no drier than the talks and banquet speeches that filled the air. On most days, one or two WNYC programs could be found among the highlights and suggestions on the radio pages.

Tommy Cowan remained with WNYC until 1961, when failing eyesight forced him to retire; he died in 1969 at the age of 85. Over the years listeners heard the voices of announcers Andre Bernard, Bill Slater, Jack Lazare, Lloyd Moss, David Allen, Kevin Kennedy, Tom Terrisi, and Steve Post. For many years, however, the city station had trouble finding and keeping good announcers, who had to apply through the civil service system. The WNYC announcers' written examination lasted six hours, and only those who passed could go on to a formal audition. The following are three of the questions from the 1938 exam:

- State the nature of three amendments to the New York State Constitution which were approved in the recent election.
- List the methods of scoring used and the parts or intervals into which each of the following is divided: Football; hockey; basketball.
- Write a fifty-word announcement on Liszt suitable in introduction to the radio presentation of the Hungarian Rhapsody No. 2.

WNYC built up an excellent library of its own classical records and instituted a fine series of live concerts from around the city, including the famous Goldman Band concerts in the parks. Under music director Herman Neuman—who served WNYC for forty-five years—the station launched its American Music Festival in 1940 to spotlight many neglected contemporary artists. "The Voice of New York" also developed a card of unique public services, from live hearings of the Board of Estimate (despite Grover Whalen's promise, they were an annual event and attracted a concerned audience) to scheduled reports on waiting times at municipal golf courses. Tammany Hall was shown the studio door, and Mayor La Guardia was heard every Sunday at noon, most notably during the 1945 newspaper strike when he read the funnies for the kids, mixed with political points for the grown-ups.

When Morris Novik left in 1946 to run WLIB, Seymour N. Siegel became director of broadcasting, a position that required him also to be protector of this city service. He remained through the next four administrations but resigned in 1971 to protest budget cuts that had forced the layoff of fifty-five employees. A "Save WNYC Committee" was organized by Novik and Mayor La Guardia's widow, Marie, and part of the budget was restored.

Since 1979, WNYC's membership in National Public Radio gave it the status of a "flagship" for a national network. The "Voice of the City" now called itself "New York Public Radio." In 1985 the studios were upgraded and renamed the Fiorello H. La Guardia Telecommunications Center. In the spring of 1989, WNYC moved its transmitter out of the city to the WMCA site in Kearney, N.J., amicably sharing a tower with the station that had dislodged it from 570kc nearly six decades earlier. But political interference did not disappear completely: Mayor Ed Koch tried to control prostitution in the city by having WNYC read the names of "johns" arrested for soliciting. Station management balked, announcers threatened a walkout, and the idea was dropped after one broadcast.

After seventy years on the air, WNYC found itself under threat as a municipal broadcaster one more time. The administration of Mayor Rudolph Giuliani, facing enormous budget deficits, looked at selling WNYC AM, FM, and TV, which could have brought in nearly $40 million as well as eliminated the need for the city to cover the $4 million in operating expenses each year. Since the early 1980s, most funding had come through the independent WNYC Foundation. In

The original WNYC transmitter at its first installation, in Brazil.

March 1995, Mayor Giuliani put the city stations up for sale but agreed to sell WNYC AM and FM to its foundation for $20 million. The foundation would have six years to pay. Station management took to the air to thank the mayor for his generosity. The transfer to foundation ownership took place on 1 July 1996.

WNYC was once a model for municipally operated radio and a prototype for public broadcasting. Under ownership of the WNYC Foundation, it retained its long-standing identity. The city administration allowed WNYC to remain rent-free in the Municipal Building, so WNYC was still under the same roof where it was founded on that muggy evening in 1924. But with the sale, a significant chapter in radio history came to an end: of all the stations that went on the air in the New York metropolitan area in the 1920s, WNYC was the last one owned by its original licensee.

See also WLAW, WMCA.

WNYM

(JULY 1981–AUGUST 1989)

| 1981 | 1330kc s/t WPOW | 5,000w. |

WEVD's owners were striving to keep the Yiddish-language newspaper *Forward* in operation as its readership aged and subscriptions declined. The Forward Association held onto its FM station and sold off the 1330kHz AM frequency that it shared with WPOW. The call letters became WNYM, for New York Ministry, and the new owner was Salem Media, a religious broadcaster who was able to publicize 1330 as "Christian Radio." WNYM and WPOW even issued a joint program guide. At the time WNYM was founded, WPOW gained an option to buy the station within three years.

The sale price of WEVD was $1,033,000 and didn't include studio facilities, since they would still be used by

WEVD-FM. Nor did WNYM receive the WEVD transmitter in Maspeth, which was shut down. WNYM and WPOW operated through the same transmitter till WNYM purchased its own unit, which was installed in WPOW's building.

Studios were established in a renovated recreation building at 7 Smyrna Avenue in Staten Island. Station manager Jimmy DeYoung conducted a daily interview program, and most of the day was filled with paid religious broadcasts, including the controversial Rev. Jerry Falwell and programs from his organization, the Moral Majority. WNYM signed on at 8:30 each weekday morning, there was then some foreign-language programming in the afternoon, a 4:30 sign-off, and then a return to the air after WPOW said goodnight at 10:30 P.M.

In 1983, Radio Vision Christiana, a non-profit Hispanic Pentecostal society, began to lease time on WNYM. The next year Salem Media and WPOW reached a sales agreement that would allow WNYM to become a full-time broadcaster. The studio-transmitter site at 1111 Woodrow Road in the Rossville section of Staten Island was sold for $4 million, and early in 1985 WNYM moved from the recreation center to renovated facilities in Rossville. Spanish Pentecostal programming was expanded, and there were several hours of Jewish-oriented programs in the evening.

Salem Media had indicated that it would sell WNYM to Radio Vision if it could find a more powerful AM outlet in the city; after failing in an effort to buy WHN or WNEW, in 1989 it purchased WMCA. In September 1989, the 1330 spot got its fifth occupant in thirty-two years when WNYM became WWRV.

See also WBBR(I), WEVD, WPOW, WWRV.

WODA

(10 APRIL 1925–11 FEBRUARY 1934)

1925	1340kc	25w.
1926	various frequencies	500w.
1927	780kc s/t WLWL	500w.
1927	1020kc s/t WGL	500w.
1928	1250kc s/t WAAM, WGCP	500w.

In the sometimes rough and radical mill town of Paterson, N.J., community institutions brought order and refinement to life in the early years of the twentieth century. In 1897, the O'Dea family established a music store, somewhat pretentiously named the O'Dea Temple of Music. Patersonians went there for music lessons or to purchase instruments, piano rolls, victrolas, records, and in the early 1920s, radio receivers. In the spring of 1925, owner Richard

O'Dea bought a 25-watt transmitter and set up a station to replace Paterson's defunct WBAN. The O'Dea Radio and Victrola Shop in the Exchange Building at 115 Ellington Street became "The Voice of the Silk City."

Every broadcaster at the time spoke of radio's potential to bring education and public service to the populace, but WODA actually developed worthwhile programming. WODA was one of the first truly educational stations. Richard O'Dea was Paterson's commissioner of education, and his brother Patrick later served as the New Jersey state education commissioner. They established the WODA Free Grammar and High School of the Air in 1927. Working closely with local educators, WODA aired lessons in a dozen subjects from arithmetic to social science.

Friday, 9 March 1928

9:00 A.M.	Morning Glory Hour
9:50	Police alarms
10:00	Telechron Time
	Off the air
12:00 noon	Luncheon music
12:20	News; songs
12:45	Luncheon music
1:00	Police alarms
1:10	Merchants' programs
1:58	Telechron time
	Off the air
5:30	Sport talk
5:55	Police alarms
6:00	Pagan Californians
7:00	Our New Jersey
7:15	Sunshine Boys
7:45	WODA History Class
8:00	Corn Husker Entertainers
8:15	Charles Schular, zither
8:30	Devotional service

There were courses in Americanization targeted at the large immigrant community. Enrollment reached above one thousand, and hundreds of diplomas were handed out each year, in formal commencement exercises broadcast over WODA. Musical broadcasts were above average in both quality and variety. The "Silk City Night Owls on Parade" regularly ran till 2:00 A.M. and gave listeners a reason to stay up late. WODA also acted as the police radio for northern New Jersey in the mid–1920s, airing two minutes of official bulletins ten times a day.

During a time when some New York area stations were obligated to share time on their frequency—and many did so uncomfortably—WODA arranged a schedule on 780kc with the Paulist Fathers' WLWL after only ten minutes of discussion. And during the time when radio stations often drifted from assigned frequencies, causing ear-piercing howls, WODA installed equipment to "zero beat" an offender and clean up the sound.

In 1928, the Federal Radio Commission reassigned many stations, and WODA protested that cutting back its hours would interfere with the education of its listeners. Richard O'Dea pointed out that WODA had "frequently refused commercial contracts because they would curtail our school broadcasts." During a hearing before the FRC in November 1928, O'Dea revealed that some high school lessons had been dropped because there wasn't sufficient airtime. In his appeal, O'Dea won the backing of some of the nation's leading educators, including the presidents of Princeton and Rutgers Universities.

Nonetheless, WODA was assigned to share 1250kc with WAAM in Newark, and those two stations together protested the inclusion of WGCP in Newark as a third partner. The three-way share on 1250 remained in place until 1933, when WODA and WAAM were merged through the efforts of Manhattan advertising executive Milton Biow. For four months the two stations operated under the combined call letters WODA-WAAM while a new corporate entity was created. In the second week of February 1934, the WODAAM Corporation's call letters were changed to WNEW. Soon Count Basie, Frank Sinatra, Dinah Shore, Ella Fitzgerald, the Dorseys, and other giants of the swing era would earn a place in what had once been the O'Dea Temple of Music.

See also WAAM, WBAN, WNEW, WPAT.

WOKO

(14 JUNE 1924–1946)

1924	1290kc	50w.
1927	1390kc	50w.
1928	1440kc	500w.

Station WDBX, operated by the Dyckman Radio Shop in upper Manhattan, held a secondary license for a station called WOKO. In 1925, owners Max Jacobson and Ed Wilbur shut down WDBX and sold WOKO to a fellow radio entrepreneur, Otto Baur, who continued to operate this station from Dyckman Street and then from his shop in Peekskill. With its catchy call letters, WOKO was a lively station with some imaginative programming. It aired a genealogy series that included names of individuals who weren't aware that they were being sought by lawyers to claim a portion of an estate.

In April 1927, "The Pioneer Radio Service Station" became an affiliate of a small network established by WMCA. Much of WOKO's evening schedule came from the New York City station.

Friday, 15 June 1928

10:00 A.M.	Sunshine Hour
11:00	News items
12:00	Luncheon Hour of Music
1:00	Farm Flashes
	Off the air
5:00	Merchants' program
6:00	News items
	Off the air
7:45	Uncle John
8:00	News items; baseball scores
8:25	H. E. Smith, violin; J. Campbell, tenor
9:15	Mabel Storm, mandolin
9:30	Mildred Southwick, piano
9:45	Ocean Life (WMCA)
10:00	Rainbow Orchestra (WMCA)
10:30	Columbia Park Orchestra (WMCA)
11:00	McAlpin Orchestra (WMCA)

In April 1928, WOKO—then owned by engineer and musician Harold E. Smith—moved from Peekskill to the Hotel Windsor in Poughkeepsie and installed a new 500-watt transmitter atop Mount Beacon. From the 1,500-foot mountain, "The Voice from the Clouds" had excellent coverage of the mid Hudson Valley and, starting in July 1929, even ventured some experimental television broadcasts on W2XBU. In February 1931—in a move unique in the history of New York radio—WOKO made one more journey up the river and was established at Albany, where Harold Smith continued to manage it.

WOKO remained for many years the CBS affiliate in the state capital. CBS Vice-President and former FRC Commissioner Sam Pickard was secretly awarded part-ownership of WOKO for bringing it into the network. This transaction led to forfeiture of the station's license in 1946 after WOKO and the FCC appealed all the way to the U.S. Supreme Court. The station is now WGNA.

See also WDBX.

WOR

(22 FEBRUARY 1922–)

1922	360m (833.3kc) s/t WDT,WJY	500w.
1924	740kc s/t WJY	500w.
1927	710kc	5,000w.
1935	710kc	50,000w.

On Wednesday, 2/22/22—Washington's Birthday—engineers Orville Orvis and Jack Poppele powered up a

De Forest transmitter on the sixth floor of Bamberger's Department Store at 131 Market Street in Newark and played Al Jolson's record of "April Showers" into a carbon microphone with a megaphone horn attached. The furniture department had added a line of radio gear, and Bam's opened its own station as a way to stimulate sales. A 15 square foot cubicle held both studio and equipment, and rugs were borrowed from the carpet department to deaden the sound. The antenna was a wire strung between two poles on the roof. Between broadcast times, staffers went back out front and sold radios. That was the start of one of America's outstanding, and most enduring, broadcast operations.

Poppele had gone to Washington two days earlier to personally fetch a license from the Commerce Department. Louis Bamberger wanted his station to be called WLB, but that call had just been assigned, and so his store received a reissued ship's call, WOR. (The ship was the S.S. *California*, owned by Orient Lines.) This was so early in the history of American radio that there was only one wavelength assigned for broadcasting, and WOR had to share time with all other stations.

Jessie E. Koewing became station manager, one of the first women to hold such a position. A concert violinist and imaginative programmer, "JEK" once filled ten minutes that had opened up between programs by leading studio guests in a community sing. WOR was the only station to broadcast on Christmas Day in 1922, and thus was the first sound heard by those who found a crystal set under the tree. It described its schedule as "Not on Sunday but every holiday." The Bamberger station fulfilled its retailing purpose so well ("No records to buy. No upkeep. A lifetime of entertainment—free.") that after one year, the store considered shutting it down. Poppele and others persuaded Louis Bamberger to give WOR a chance to be a player in the new broadcasting industry and not simply a store's merchandising gimmick.

By 1924 policies and personalities were developed that would be part of WOR for decades to come. In December of that year, the Newark station added a studio in Manhattan, on the ninth floor of Chickering Hall at 27 W. Fifty-seventh Street. Morning exercise sessions–New York's first wake-up show—originated from there, conducted by publisher and physical culturist Bernarr Macfadden ("Hands on hips, now 1-2-3-4…") The control operator at Chickering was an English-born engineer named John B. Gambling, who was soon given announcing duties as well. When Macfadden called in sick one morning, Gambling took over the whole program; he later turned it into the "Sun Up Society," "Musical Clock," and "Rambling with Gambling" and established a dynasty of Gamblings who would awaken WOR listeners for the rest of the twentieth century.

Celebrities like Paul Whiteman, Harry Houdini, and Charlie Chaplin came to the WOR microphones, appearances arranged by publicist Alfred "Hollywood" McCosker. In 1926, McCosker became WOR's managing director.

WOR had been sharing the 405-meter wavelength, and when RCA shut down its station WJY in July 1926, Bamberger's was clear to operate full-time. It even added a Sunday schedule. Perhaps the most important development of 1926 was moving the New York studios and establishing the main office on the top floors of a new building at 1440 Broadway, two blocks below Times Square. In June 1927, WOR moved its transmitter from Bamberger's roof to a more effective site in Kearney, N.J., and on the fifteenth of that month it was assigned to 710 kilocycles. That fall the Newark studios were moved from the store to 147 Market Street. Now WOR was a clear, stable, dependable station, a standard of the industry. Bamberger's estimated in 1928 that it had received literally one million dollars worth of publicity value from WOR in the previous four years, double its operating expense.

WOR was the first New York station to carry programming of the Columbia Broadcasting System, originating CBS's premiere broadcast on 18 September 1927. It alternated with the Atlantic Broadcasting Company's WABC as the CBS outlet in New York, and after William S. Paley became head of the struggling network in 1928, he offered to buy either of the local affiliates as the New York flagship. Bamberger was willing to sell WOR to Paley, but WABC was cheaper, and in September 1929 WOR and CBS parted. Severing its ties with CBS was a positive decision for WOR. Despite a "Quality Group" relationship with WLW/Cincinnati and WGN/Chicago, it preferred to continue as an independent station.

In 1929, Bamberger's was bought by R. H. Macy and Company, with WOR in the package. Even though the Newark studios were enlarged and the corporate name was changed to Bamberger Broadcasting Service, some Jerseyites protested that WOR had become a New York station. McCosker replied, "Although most of our programs go on the air from the Broadway site Newark is WOR's home."

In 1931, when a new trade magazine called *Broadcasting* appeared, the cover of its first edition was a full-page ad from station WOR. WOR was solid enough to stand up to New York Mayor Jimmy Walker, who threatened to bar the station from covering any municipal event in retaliation for critical commentaries by H. V. Kaltenborn. (Al McCosker's friendship with Mayor Walker may also have helped calm the situation.) In 1934, during an era when newspapers were able to restrict access to news by radio stations, WOR helped to form the Transradio wire service and aired five fifteen-minute newscasts a day. Newspapers wanted to retaliate by dropping free daily program listings, but the popularity of WOR and the potential loss of print advertising from Macy's and Bamberger's neutralized the threat and opened the way for wider news coverage.

One reason WOR could hold a loyal audience for so long was because it began to attract listeners at a very young age. "Sky Pictures by Mr. Radiobug" was one of radio's earliest children's shows. During the autumn of 1932, "Chandu, the Magician" had WOR's biggest mail pull, drawing eight thousand letters a week. An article in the New York edition of *Radio Guide* in December 1931 stated that most children would rather see "Uncle Don" than Santa Claus at Christmas. Don Carney—the stage name of Howard Rice—had come to WOR in 1927 and was its biggest star during the 1930s. He was cheery and correct and a super-salesman. He sang songs, told stories, and gave sound advice as well as distributed birthday gifts, Santa-like, to the unseen audience. ("Richard in St. Albans, you'll find your present behind the radio where I am." How many kids first peered into the innards of a radio hoping to glimpse Uncle Don?)

Uncle Don was such a wholesome and beloved figure that people were shocked to learn that after one of his avuncular broadcasts, thinking the microphone was off, he muttered something like, "That ought to hold the little bastards for another day." Whether this incident really occurred has been a matter of dispute since the day it happened, or didn't happen. Jack Poppele always denied it, though he may have been protecting his engineers, whose job it was to cut off the microphone. Don's defenders also pointed out that there were usually a few children in the sponsor's booth and that he didn't consider the program over until a curtain in front of the window was drawn.

The earliest newspaper account of Uncle Don cussing the kids was from a newspaper in Baltimore, where "Uncle Don" wasn't heard locally (though WOR could be received there). Accusers may also have confused Uncle Don's alleged gaffe with an earlier incident in Philadelphia. In his 1935 book *Ten Years before the Mike*, announcer Ted Husing stated that he had heard the story repeatedly for five or six years and quipped, "Uncle Don must sign off with the line." Uncle Don's publicist Bill Treadwell rejected the accusation in his otherwise tell-all 1958 biography, *Head, Heart, and Heel.* But veteran WOR sound-effects artist Barney Beck believed it did happen. Radio historian Lee Munsick told of meeting Uncle Don after his WOR days had ended and he was working as a circus organist. Munsick, then in his teens, brought up the cursing incident and asked the former radio star, "Is it true?" Uncle Don responded sheepishly, "Yeah, it's true." That should be direct testimony.

Or maybe Uncle Don was telling a lie. What is certain is that in real life, Don Carney wasn't always a nice man but was a hard-drinking womanizer whose reputation was protected by a New York press corps that believed the truth could be devastating to countless youngsters—an ironic tribute to WOR's power.

By the mid–1930s WOR was literally more powerful. A new transmitting station was built alongside the Arthur Kill at Carteret, N.J., to direct a full 50,000 watts up and down the Eastern Seaboard. This was not the first directional antenna, but it did require careful work with a new technology, and McCosker warned Jack Poppele that the chief engineer's job was on the line if it didn't work. On Monday, 4 March 1935, at 8:00 P.M. President Roosevelt pressed a but-

ton at the White House, and WOR went to 50kw with a gala program from Carnegie Hall.

The Carteret transmitter also was among the first to be modulated 100 percent, which meant that WOR could send out the full range of AM audio and call itself "high fidelity." The site also housed a 30-watt aviation radio beacon. A year later, WOR applied to the FCC for a power increase to 500,000 watts, which was denied.

In the autumn of 1934, WOR joined with some of its Quality Group partners to form the Mutual Broadcasting System. Unlike NBC and CBS, Mutual was a cooperative that owned no stations and that shared facilities and personnel. For WOR it meant becoming a "flagship" and clearly in a class with WEAF, WJZ, and WABC. Additional studios were built at the New Amsterdam Theatre and the converted Guild and Longacre Theatres in the Times Square theatre district. Programs were relayed on shortwave by its station W2XAQ at 65.4 megacycles. WOR even tried to push into the future when it began facsimile transmission in 1938, utilizing overnight hours to experimentally deliver a morning newspaper and other printed matter by radio. The effort never met with public favor, though it can be seen as a forerunner of the on-line services of the computer age.

Conductors Morton Gould and Alfred Wallenstein led house orchestras that, though not the caliber of Toscanini and the NBC Symphony, were respectable musical ensembles. Some of the most wonderful dramatic programs of radio's "golden age" originated in the WOR studios; the best remembered (and highest rated) was "The Shadow," a fixture of Mutual's Sunday afternoon mystery block, which also included "Nick Carter, Master Detective" and "True Detective Mysteries." Knowing it could not match the entertainment resources of NBC or CBS, WOR/Mutual often scheduled its most potent programs for the daytime hours.

At the heart of the WOR daytime schedule, however, was literally a family of broadcasters that had enormous appeal to the families in the audience. Ed and Pegeen Fitzgerald, Dorothy Kilgallen and Dick Kollmar, and Alfred and Dora McCann were married couples heard daily in thousands of households. The Fitzgeralds were a team on WOR for forty-four years (leaving briefly for a stint on WJZ). Sports director Stan Lomax was a regular for over forty years. Patricia McCann took over her parents' program in 1975.

WOR's local programming was often the testing ground for shows that would turn into network features. "Can You Top This," a gagfest created by Roger Bower, became a national favorite in 1942.

A mainstay of the WOR schedule through the 1940s was the low-budget quiz and audience-participation program, including "Twenty Questions," "True or False," the whodunit "Quick as a Flash," and even impromptu quiz sessions from the sidewalk in front of 1440 Broadway. Twice each day from 1937 to 1952, "The Answer Man," Albert Mitchell, responded to listeners' questions. ("What makes bubble gum bubble?")

The 1940s show "Breakfast with Dorothy and Dick," featuring husband and wife Dorothy Kilgallen and Dick Kollmar, was the prototype for hundreds of similar spousal talk shows. The reason the Kollmars were always so charming and urbane in the morning is that the program was generally recorded the afternoon before.

The Gambling family was a morning staple on WOR since the station's beginnings. John B. Gambling, founder of the dynasty, sleeps on the piano while his son, John A., displays a little more effort looking into an unconnected microphone.

"How tall was Jesus?" "When people kiss, should they tilt their heads to the right or the left?" Answers: latex; average height; to the right, since previously the couple had been shaking hands. The last answer was reportedly checked by several staff members in the WOR offices.) It wasn't even necessary for your question to be on the air. Each program ended with the offer, "Ask any question you wish, and provided it has a definite answer that is not of a personal nature and does not violate professional ethics, you will get the answer by mail and free of charge." "The Answer Man" turned WOR into everybody's research department of last resort.

On 1 February 1941, the Bamberger station officially departed Newark and became "WOR, New York" in name as well as fact. WOR was able to spend most of the 1940s and 1950s on a par with its network neighbors. With the advent of WOR-TV in October 1949, the Bamberger station had designs on becoming the flagship of a Mutual TV Network. Big-time radio would soon be on the wane, but not big-time WOR.

In December 1952, the Bamberger Broadcasting Service transferred WOR to General Teleradio, a subsidiary of the General Tire and Rubber Company, and when General Tire acquired RKO, the corporate name became RKO-General. (This followed a brief period when the license of the Mutual flagship was held by the Don Lee Broadcasting System, the MBS West Coast affiliate that had also been purchased by General Tire.) In 1959 WOR left the Mutual network to again become an independent station in the nation's largest market. Mutual generally had the weakest program lineup of all networks, and WOR had built a strong local personality, so the transition did not leave it unsure of its future.

Under the leadership of news director Dave Driscoll, the station's news coverage was among the city's most solid, announced by some of radio's best voices including Henry Gladstone, John Scott, Prescott Robinson, and Harry Hennessey. Through the 1950s Lyle Van's 6:00 P.M. newscast concluded with a fatherly "good night, little redheads," featured a Wednesday "midweek moment of meditation," and even originated occasionally from a WOR auditorium studio so that faithful listeners could come watch Van read the news, responding with applause such as no other newscaster ever heard.

WOR continued to be a technical trailblazer. In 1956 it cleared out its evening schedule and created "Music from Studio X" (letter X, not numeral 10). It was simply continuous pop music, but it originated from a special high-fidelity studio, and each clean new record was touched by a needle only one time. The host was John A. Gambling (whose father was still doing the wake-up show); the program was fed to Mutual, and it put WOR on top of the ratings in the New York market.

On Wednesday, 17 March 1958, the WOR stations broadcast the first stereophonic recording heard on New York radio, but not from Studio X. The Audio Fidelity discs were heard on 710kc on John Scott's news and information program "Radio New York," with the other channel as part of the "Ted Steele Show" on WOR-TV, channel 9. This was five and a half years after the start of WQXR's live AM/FM "binaural" service, but three years before FM multiplex stereo.

Since 1957 WOR had been adjusting to the TV age (and the growth of the music-and-news formula on competing stations) by building on its strength in "talk radio." Arlene Francis, nutritional guru Carlton Fredericks, financial adviser Bernard Meltzer, and one more husband-and-wife team, Tex McCrary and Jinx Falkenberg, helped keep WOR consistently near the top of the ratings.

Storyteller Jean Shepherd developed a following with monologues that rambled on for hours. WOR's own publicity spoke of "reminiscences of his rural childhood roots", disregarding the fact that Shep's hometown of Hammond, Ind. bears the same relation to Chicago that Yonkers does to New York City. If he ran low on words, the audience could be entertained by performances on the nose flute or even the amazingly resonant percussion created by Shep tapping on his head. Jean Shepherd's programs were bounced around the schedule from the 1950s through the 1970s, from Saturday afternoons to Sunday evenings, overnight, Saturday morning, and even a weekday-afternoon show called "Drive East."

His cult doggedly stayed by the radio as if dependent on an intimate relationship, causing Shep to repine years later, "I had five million listeners and each thought he was the only one." One evening, Shepherd asked his listeners to leave their radios and go to West Ninth Street between Fifth and Sixth in Greenwich Village—which happened to be where Shep lived—and mill around. Thousands of people responded, as did the New York Police Department when suddenly faced with reports of a mob in the streets. But the WOR listeners had been advised to merely "mill," keep quiet, and then go home. There was no disturbance. The cult and the legend grew. A staffer remarked of Jean Shepherd, "Nobody at WOR worked with him, instead they tried to work around him."

"Long John" Nebel began his all-night talkfest on WOR in the mid–1950s, specializing in the offbeat and occult. (Guests often had to go out of their way, for the program sometimes originated from a tiny studio at the Carteret transmitter.) Working with engineer Russ Tinklepaugh, Nebel devised the tape-delay system that allowed broadcasters to confidently put listeners on the air and thus made free-wheeling talk shows possible. He left for WNBC in 1966.

In 1968, WOR shut down the historic Carteret facility and moved to a new transmitter site at a former landfill in Lyndhurst, N.J.

Hourly fifteen-minute newscasts and a two-hour news block from 6:00 to 8:00 P.M. made WOR "Your Station for News," with the city's most extensive coverage in the days before the start of all-news radio. There was even an attempt to rekindle daytime radio drama in the 1970s, and it became

WOR's all-star lineup in the early 1960s.

home to the great comedy team Bob and Ray. Staff, audience and sponsors remained faithful over the years, but in the mid–1980s WOR's quest for a younger (and more male) listenership led station manager Rick Devlin to retire some of the most durable personalities in American radio. Existing audiences were outraged. Pegeen Fitzgerald refused to prerecord her farewell program and walked out. Her fans followed her to WNYC. John A. Gambling stayed at WOR, and his son John R. officially took over the morning show on Saturday, 15 December 1990. "Rambling with Gambling" was responsible for over 40 percent of the station's income. Joan Hamburg's and Bernard Meltzer's advice programs were also safe.

In 1987, the FCC forced RKO-General to divest itself of its stations due to misconduct by the parent firm. The next year WOR was sold to S/G Communications, which in 1989 sold it to Buckley Broadcasting for $25 million. By 1996 WOR's ratings placed it third among New York AM stations, a strong and steady voice that still sought to appeal to a mature audience.

WOV

(16 SEPTEMBER 1928–31 OCTOBER 1959)

Sept. 28, 1928	1020kc	1,000w.
Nov. 1928	1130kc	1,000w.
Dec. 1941	1280kc s/t WHBI	5,000w.

WOV entered the New York scene at a pivotal moment in radio history. The Federal Radio Commission had approved the sale of WGL to Sicilian-born importer John Iraci at the same time that it was ordering all stations to update their equipment. WGL/WOV was off the air for a month while engineers installed "the newest appliances known to radio science." When WOV finally signed on, to offer "the highest type of radio entertainment," it remained on its original 1020kc frequency for less than two months before moving up the dial to 1130 as part of the national 1928 reallocations (the imminent switch was even noted in WOV's original publicity).

WGL's impressive corporate name, "International Broadcasting Company," was retained after the sale and soon gained some significance. At first, WOV's programming was aimed at a general audience; there was even a daily astrological forecast. But by the mid–1930s, with radio competition growing stronger and the economy growing weaker, WOV strengthened its ethnic ties and expanded its Italian-language programming to fill the daytime hours. WOV soon became the dominant Italian voice in the Northeast through

its affiliation with WBIL—with which it shared New York studios and management—and Iraci's WPEN in Philadelphia. It also fed Italian programs to a dozen other stations as far away as Montreal and was one of the first foreign-language broadcasters to attract major national advertisers.

WOV gained its "sister station" in 1937 when Iraci and watchmaker Arde Bulova (of "B-U-L-O-V-A, Bulova Watch Time" fame) established WBIL. Bulova was also part-owner of WNEW, and he and Iraci swapped stock to buy into each other's stations. In November 1937, Iraci died suddenly, and management of WOV and WBIL was assumed by his long-time assistant, Hyla Kiczales.

The Iraci stations weren't simply sisters but also neighbors: WOV operated during daytime hours on 1130kc, WBIL was at 1100 in the evening as well as Fridays and Sundays, when WOV was silent. WPG in Atlantic City also occupied 1100, sharing time with WBIL. This cumbersome arrangement ended in 1940 in a complicated series of events when Arde Bulova's Greater New York Broadcasting Corporation (1) bought WPG and absorbed it into WOV, (2) shut down both WOV and WPG on 2 January 1940 because they interfered with WBIL, (3) asked the FCC to cancel WOV's license and move WBIL to 1130kc, and (4) immediately changed WBIL's call letters to WOV. (Three-letter calls hadn't been assigned for a decade, but the FCC recognized the "goodwill value" in this case.)

By 1941, WNEW enjoyed enormous popularity despite a weak 1,000-watt signal on the 1280 frequency it shared on Sundays and Mondays with WHBI. WOV—5,000 watts at 1130—had a large and loyal listenership among the two million members of the Italian community, but the growth potential was obviously to be found at WNEW. So Bulova applied for a swap of frequencies that would open the way for WNEW to become a 50,000-watt clear channel station—a possibility foreseen when WOV began its series of changes.

The request for a switch in frequencies was simply an application for WNEW and WOV to exchange call letters. The FCC was willing to grant this, and since the government doesn't dictate what kind of programs a station should broadcast the lines were rearranged to feed programs of the "new" WOV into the old WNEW transmitter and vice versa. On 1 December 1941 WNEW moved to 1130 and WOV appeared at 1280 on the dial five and a half days a week, now sharing time with WHBI. Listeners followed their favorite shows up or down the dial. There were protests, however, from the engineers' union, for some technicians were unsure of which station they were working for.

WOV's original studios were at 16 E. Forty-second Street, and in 1935 it moved to 132 W. Forth-third Street. In the early 1940s Arde Bulova established a sumptuous new facility in the Heckscher Building at 730 Fifth Avenue (across the street from Tiffany's). The station occupied the entire twelfth floor, and in this showplace the four studios with their RCA equipment were almost an afterthought. Noted interior designer Dorothy Draper created an elegant and

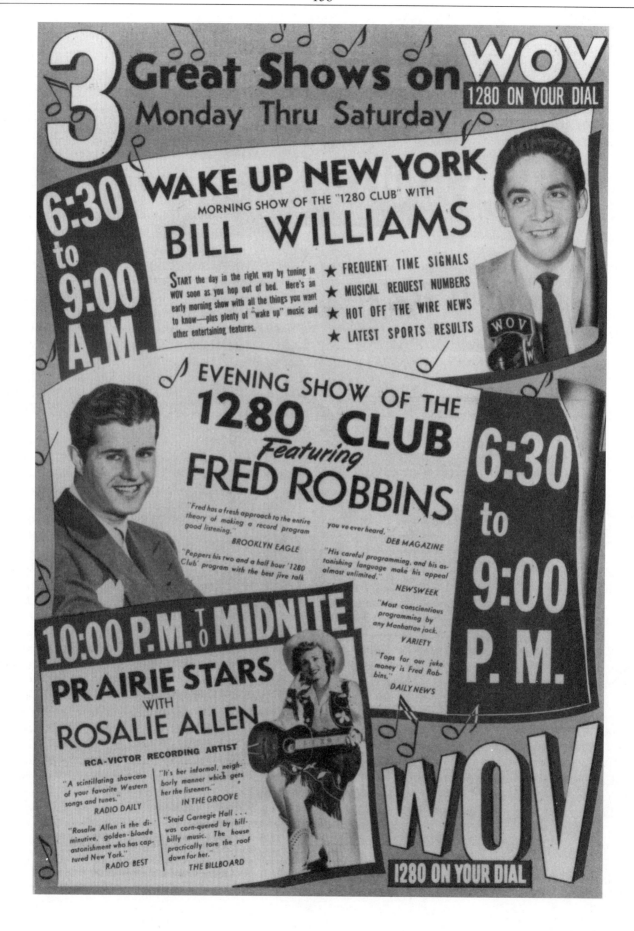

enormous lobby. The second-largest space was the corner office of general manager Ralph Weil, overlooking Fifth Avenue and Fifty-seventh Street. There was also a "clients' room," which Draper bedecked with imported Persian wallpaper. Observed program director Arnold Hartley, "It was the fanciest setup in New York radio at the time, bar none."

Bulova planned to make WOV the key station of a projected Atlantic Coast Network with extended English-language programming, an intention that was carried out by WNEW.

An October 1940 study by the American Council on Foreign Affairs asserted that WOV was selling time to Fascist speakers and canceling speeches by democratic organizations, a charge Bulova rejected. During the war WOV was outspokenly American ("This is W-O-V for Victory") and presented a series of anti-Fascist broadcasts that won a Peabody Award. Each day WOV continued to air live soap operas performed in New York by a some of the world's best Italian radio actors. There were many musical programs even

when it wasn't easy to get the latest Italian recordings; for years WOV's best source was a tiny record shop in the subway arcade at Eighth Avenue and Forty-second Street.

Station WOV developed an appeal that crossed language and racial lines. Starting in 1943, Weil and Hartley maintained a durable format of "Italian all day, jazz all night." When the station resumed English-language broadcasting each evening, there was a solid hour of news and commentary followed at 7:00 by an hour of country music with Rosalie Allen, the "Queen of the Yodelers." There was also an hour of classical music before the midnight sign-off, and the series "America in Music" featured many seldom-heard native composers.

The nighttime schedule featured some of the nation's best disc jockeys, including at one time or another Art Ford, Martin Block, William B. Williams, and Allen Courtney, who combined interviews and liberal political commentary with the hippest sounds of the day. In the early 1940s Courtney welcomed some of the biggest swing bands to the WOV studios, including the Glenn Miller and Charlie Barnet organizations. On "The 1280 Club" and "Robbins Nest," Fred Robbins ("Hepwise Professor of Thermodynamics") presented classic blues and boogie-woogie. Listeners didn't merely send in record requests; one night a week they were invited to bring in their own discs to spin on WOV. Singer/songwriter Mel Torme referred to Robbins as "the most influential disc jockey in New York" during his WOV years. It was Robbins who first called Torme "the Velvet Fog."

The jazz programs featured many new and off-beat performers of the 1930s and 1940s and attracted a strong following among African-Americans. This gave WOV a reputation to build on when it instituted its first gospel programming in the mid-1950s, two hours each evening hosted by Thermon Ruth. WOV also redirected its established early-morning program "Wake Up, New York" at the black audience. ("Good morning, Harlem! Wake up, New York.")

But each day at 9:00 A.M., a bird would chirp (WOV's echo of the famous "uccellino" call signal of Italy's RAI), and the city's most extensive Italian schedule would return, including live variety shows and quiz programs. WOV maintained a shortwave listening post where John Peyroleri monitored transmissions from Italy and relayed news by private teletype line to the studios. Interception of a Morse code signal from Naples allowed WOV to scoop the world's press and report the abandonment of the sinking luxury liner *Andrea Doria* in July 1956.

Opposite and above: WOV made strong inroads in the local market in the late 1940s and early 1950s with Fred Robbins, Rosalie Allen, and a very young William B. Williams (here with George Shearing.) *Collection of Jeff Williams.*

One acclaimed series was "La Grande Famiglia," a postwar request hour that brought not songs but the speaking voices of family and friends in Italy to listeners in America. Italian-language newspapers in New York published family names to alert friends and relatives. In 1946 WOV established a studio on the Via di Porta Pinciana in Rome—it was virtually the only foreign-language station in the United States with a permanent facility in the "mother country"—and sent itinerant reporters around the country to seek out ordinary Italians and tape their messages.

In the 1950s the Italian schedule was extended to 8:00 P.M. and the early-morning and evening hours were increasingly occupied by black-oriented rhythm-and-blues and gospel music. Programming was inspired by the nation's space program: the day began with the "Gospel Rocket," Maurice "Hot Rod" Hulbert rode the "Blue Rocket," and Jocko Henderson took off in "Jocko's Rocketship." Daddy Dee, Joe Crane, and Cleo Rowe were also on WOV, and Thurmon Ruth played inspirational music on "The Old Ship of Zion." Meanwhile, the Italian schedule remained strong thanks to the work of producer-announcers like Aldo Aldi, Giorgio Padovani and Renzo Sacerdoti.

In 1955, the WODAAM Corporation sold WOV to a group headed by Morris Novik, who had run WNYC and WLIB, and including Arnold Hartley and Ralph Weil. WOV tried mightily to develop its black and Italian-language audience, even issuing rate cards with combination rates for both ethnic groups. It promoted itself more aggressively, nicknaming its listeners "WOVbugs" and trying to excite them with contests and giveaways. WOV would hand out bucks to listeners who answered their phones by repeating such doggerel as "Whenever I'm asked I always say I listen to WOV night and day."

Different people may have listened to WOV night and day, but they all heard a consistently high quality of production and performance. In August 1959 the WOV Broadcasting Corporation sold the station to Bartell Broadcasters, which changed the call letters to WADO. As part of the sales agreement, many of the Italian features continued until their contract period expired.

See also WBIL, WHBI, WNEW, WADO.

W P A C

(1 DECEMBER 1951–1973)

1951	1580kc (daytime)	1,000w.
1956	1580kc (daytime)	5,000w.

The first station on Suffolk County's south shore since the 1930s was established by Getschell Broadcasting Com-

pany. WPAC had coverage and programming comparable to that of its local competitor WALK but seldom bettered the latter in the ratings. The studios were in the Mills Building in downtown Patchogue until an overnight fire on 10 February 1956. The station signed on the next morning at 6:45 from a department store across the street and station manager Stan Allen gave listeners an account of firefighters at work hosing down the cinders of his station. WPAC rebuilt and expanded; at the time of the fire it had already been authorized to boost power to 5,000 watts.

In 1973, WPAC became country music station WSUF. *See also* WALK, WLIM.

W P A P

(21 JUNE 1926–9 JANUARY 1934)

1926	830kc s/t WHN, WQAO	500w.
1927	760kc st/ WHN, WQAO	500w.
1928	1010kc s/t WHN, WQAO, WRNY	500w.

Street railways were among the first large-scale users of electric power. To stimulate ridership on days when most businesses were closed, transit companies supported the construction of large amusement parks, which also used a lot of electricity. Palisades Amusement Park was developed by the Bergen Traction Company at the end of the nineteenth century; games and rides were added in 1908, and in 1910 it was sold to Nicholas and Joseph Schenck, who were connected with Marcus Loew's organization and would later control Metro-Goldwyn-Mayer. Palisades was in a prime location across the Hudson from 125th Street and employed a large staff of electricians; it was an attractive prospect for the park to spread some fun onto the radio.

Some of the first broadcasts from Palisades Amusement Park were heard over WHN in 1924, featuring Charles Strickland's dance orchestra. When WPAP took to the air, it shared its frequency with WHN, at Loew's State Theatre, and WQAO, the station of the Calvary Baptist Church on Fifty-seventh Street. For a while, all three stations transmitted from the WPAP site at the amusement park, using a 500-watt Western Electric transmitter that WHN had donated to the church (the same transmitter that had been cause for AT&T's lawsuit against WHN).

Thursday, 16 August 1928

11:00 A.M.	Tune Inn
11:30	Woman's Hour
12:30	Studio presentation
1:00	News flashes

	Off for WHN
6:30	Journal period
7:00	Ruby Van Howe, soprano
7:15	Joe Anderson, tenor
7:30	Eve Rothenberg, piano
7:45	Dr. George Walton King
8:00	Oakland's Terrace
8:30	At the Park Studio
9:00	Christian's Orchestra
9:30	At the Park Studio

Among the most popular of WPAP's programs was "Uncle Robert's Radio Pals," an afternoon children's show from a studio at 18 E. Fifteenth Street, that was decorated like a child's playroom. WPAP also broadcast the "Woman's Hour," sponsored by the *New York Evening Journal*. The program occasionally originated from the Sutton Place apartment of Mrs. William Vanderbilt and featured many noted performers and speakers of the day.

WPAP's studios at the south end of Palisades Park resembled an oversized radio set, with round knob-like windows and a giant "speaker grille." You could imagine the twin towers supporting the transmitting antenna to be a receiving aerial.

On 11 November 1928, WPAP moved to 1010kc, along with WHN and WQAO. Calvary Baptist Church took over WPAP in 1931, and for three years the church and the amusement park operated in tandem with the dual call letters WQAO-WPAP. Gradually, operations of the hyphenated station were moved to WHN; starting in 1932, the programs originated from the WHN studios, and the unique Palisades transmitter was shut down in 1933. Finally, in January 1934, WHN bought WQAO-WPAP. Calvary Baptist Church services continued to be heard on WHN, and over the years there were also pickups from Palisades Amusement Park. In the 1950s, after WHN had become WMGM, deejay Bill Silbert conducted a daily show from the park. Palisades Amusement Park closed in 1970.

See also WHN, WQAO.

WPAT

(3 MAY 1941–)

1941	930kc (daytime)	1,000w.
1949	930kc	5,000w.

WPAT was first heard in 1941, at about the time that hundreds of stations in North America were required by the North American Regional Broadcasting Agreement to change frequency. The Paterson, N.J., station did not need to move but was reassigned from 900 kilocycles and so began operation as a daytime broadcaster at 930 on the dial.

The principal backer of WPAT was engineer James Cosman, soon joined by Donald Flamm, who had recently sold WMCA. The first studios were in the Exchange Building at 115 Ellison Street, a landmark that had been the home of the O'Dea Temple of Music and WODA. "North Jersey's Own Station" saw itself as a regional broadcaster. Among its first programs was "Radio Gravure", a weekly dramatization of stories from the picture pages of the *Newark Sunday Call,* which also provided local newscasts. A year after its first sign-on, WPAT added studios at 1060 Broad Street in Newark (the former WAAM and WNEW address). In 1943 WPAT moved out of the old Temple of Music to new studios at 7 Church Street in Paterson.

WPAT had a varied schedule in its first days. Among its announcers were John Bartholomew Tucker and Joe Franklin, both of whom went on to become notable talk-show hosts. In 1948, Dave Miller came over from WAAT and brought with him WPAT's first country-music program.

Wednesday, 1 March 1950

6:00 A.M.	Hi, Neighbor
7:15	Inspirations
7:30	Hi, Neighbor
9:00	Dave Miller
11:00	Milo Bolton
3:00	Dave Miller
6:00	Revue
7:00	Gaslight
9:00	Favorites
10:00	Waltz Time
10:30	Highways to Safety
12:30	Jamboree (to 6:00 A.M.)

news on the hour, headlines on the half hour

In 1948, the North Jersey Broadcasting Company, a subsidiary of the *Passaic Herald-News*, bought WPAT, and in 1949 the station was granted full-time status and moved to 66 Hamilton Street. Country music continued for three-quarters of its broadcast day; the evening was continuous "easy listening" music. In March 1951 a new evening program premiered that would become the hallmark of WPAT and one of the most-copied formats in radio. It was called "Gaslight Revue," and it caused *New York Times* radio-TV columnist Jack Gould to effuse, "For a little bit of heaven, try tuning to 930 kilocycles."

Arthur Godfrey once even purred about "Gaslight Revue" on his CBS Network program, confessing that it was all he listened to after 7:00 P.M. "Gaslight" was more than just "audible wallpaper." Melodies had to flow gracefully into one another, and WPAT's programmers arranged subtle switches in song tempos; Perry Como singing "Body and Soul" could be followed by Percy Faith's orchestra playing the same melody. At listeners' insistence, titles were never announced. For several years WPAT published a monthly program guide for the benefit of those who listened closely. Most restful of all, commercials were confined to breaks every half hour.

"Gaslight Revue" had such a faithful audience that albums of its music were put on the market. The melodies were recorded and then transmitted back to the recording studio with a distinctly mellow WPAT pace and sound. The philosophy of station president Dickens Wright—who became general manager in 1950 and bought WPAT from the *Herald-News* in 1955—was that "Gaslight" fans would stay tuned to "the center of the dial, at 93" during the daytime when commercials came closer together.

WPAT was one of the first stations to seek a place on the FM band; it put an FM station on the air on 1 February 1948 at 103.5Mc, first called WNNJ and then WPAT-FM. There were so few listeners to FM at the time that when the antenna was blown down in a windstorm, WPAT didn't even bother to get the station back on the air. A new WPAT-FM returned in March 1957 at 93.1Mc. This was the spot previously occupied by Major Edwin Armstrong's pioneering station KE2XCC; more important, WPAT could now identify itself simply as 93 on both AM and FM dials.

The transmitter site at Broad Street and Hepburn Road in Clifton became the studio site as well in 1957, and in 1959 the combined facilities moved into a new building constructed there. Over the years WPAT also maintained studios and offices in Manhattan.

Also in 1959 WPAT took "News around the Clock" from the *New York Daily News* after it was dropped by WNEW, before going to the *Herald Tribune* for its news. Newscasters included Ken Roberts and Charles F. McCarthy, and commentary was heard from humorist Goodman Ace, drama critic Martin Gottfried, and authors Cleveland Amory and William Rusher. But 85 percent of the time, WPAT was playing quiet music.

In 1961, Dickens Wright sold WPAT to Capital Cities Broadcasting Corporation for $5 million. When FCC regulations required AM/FM pairs to operate separately, WPAT merely staggered the tapes that were used for each "Gaslight Revue." The station seized the middle ground of radio listeners; by 1969 WPAT's Arbitron rating was a healthy 16, half of market-leading rocker WABC but double the numbers for classical WQXR.

By the 1970s WPAT had mostly dropped program titles and added a few vocal selections to develop a "soft contemporary" format. It even began to play Frank Sinatra records on Saturday nights. In May 1980, WPAT program director Don LeBrecht declared: "Survey after survey has been done asking people why they did or did not listen to our kind of station and what it would take to get them to listen. One word came out over and over: relaxation."

WPAT became the first AM stereo station in New Jersey in 1984. In 1986, following Cap Cities purchase of ABC,

WPAT was sold to Park Communications. By then, WPAT-FM had become the top-rated station in what must have been a very relaxed metropolitan area. On the AM side, WPAT began to allow more talk into its schedule.

The biggest change to one of the New York area's more consistent stations happened in March 1996 when WPAT was sold to Heftel (which was itself then purchased by media giant Clear Channel Communications) and 930 was converted to a Spanish-speaking station. WPAT even began carrying Knicks basketball in Spanish. But there was still a link to the past. The musical sound embraced Spanish love songs and Latin jazz, a middle-of-the-road approach delivered in uninterrupted fifteen- or thirty-minute segments. It could be "foreground" or "background" music, appealing to a cosmopolitan and metropolitan listenership. There was still a glow of gaslight.

See also WODA.

WPCH

(6 November 1926–4 June 1933)

1926	1100kc	1500w.
1927	970kc	1500w.
1927	920kc s/t WRNY	500w.
1928	810kc	500w.

WPCH came into existence through the merger of two time-sharing stations, WRW in Tarrytown and the ill-fated WFBH in Manhattan's Hotel Majestic. Its creation was described by announcer Norman Brokenshire in his autobiography:

Finally the veil was lifted on the inner doings of WFBH, with the sudden announcement that the call letters would be changed to WPCH, which could mean only one thing, Park Central Hotel, a great structure nearing completion, on top of which could plainly be seen two slender radio spires pointing into the sky—incidentally, standing useless to this day [1954]. We found out also that WPCH was going to be known as the American Bond and Mortgage Station of the Park Central Hotel, owned and operated by the Peoples Broadcasting Corporation. We found out that salesmen were going from door to door, to all the friends of radio who had written in fan letters of any kind, trying to sell them stock in the Peoples Broadcasting Corporation. In short, George F. George [the professional alias of George Sultzbach, a clothing store owner] was battening on the popularity of radio and the "names" he had caught with large salaries and a salesman's build-up.... Our offices were moved from the Majestic Hotel to a large floor of an office building at 119 W. 57th Street, a temporary location until the Park Central Building was completed.

Joining Brokenshire on the announcing staff were two more of the era's best voices, Alois Havrilla and Lewis Reed. Eunice Brokenshire, Norman's wife, was program director. WPCH soon became one of the city's most popular stations and early in 1927 even launched a small metropolitan network, feeding its programs to WDWM in Newark and WARS in Brooklyn.

For a while it looked as if WFBH's poor relationship with its hotel host would be repeated between WPCH and the Park Central. The new antenna atop the hotel went into operation on 6 December 1926. Its signal spread effectively across the city until the Park Central, on the northwestern corner of Seventh Avenue and Fifty-fifth Street, erected a large electric sign to display its name. The sign was so close to the antenna that it absorbed much of the radiated energy, and on 5 May 1927 WPCH sued the Park Central for damages. The matter was not fully resolved until WPCH's transmitter was moved to the Lackawanna Railroad yard in Hoboken in the autumn of 1927. At the same time the station was sold to WMCA, and for a while the station named for the Park Central Hotel was operating from the Hotel McAlpin.

After several shifts in frequency, usually sharing time with WRNY, WPCH was sent to daytime operation at 810kc in the fall of 1928 and expressed satisfaction at the assignment. Shortly thereafter, WPCH and WMCA both moved to new studios at 1697 Broadway.

Thursday, 17 December 1931

9:00 A.M.	Down Reminiscence Road
9:15	Fitzpatrick Brothers
9:30	Retail Grocers' Program
9:45	Mose Sigler
10:00	Talk—Children's Home
10:15	Monsieur Sakele
10:30	Ivriah Program
11:00	The Cherrup Girl
11:15	Hoover Medical Group
11:30	Real Radio Service Program
11:45	The Female Baritone, Charlotte Comer
12:00 Noon	Maritime News
12:15	Musical Travelogue
12:30	The Lydian Trio
12:45	Crooning the Blues Away
1:00	Luncheon Music
1:30	Sunshine Vocal Trio
1:45	Highlights of Sports
2:00	Sweethearts of Radio Land
2:15	Hernan Rodriguez, the Columbian Troubador
2:30	Popular Songs
2:45	On a Coral Strand
3:00	Blind George Russell
3:15	Frank McCabe and Mitchie Lake
4:00	Ann LaPorte, musical
4:30	Harlem Hot Stuff, "Uke" Joyner
4:45	The Sunshine Trio
5:15	Captain Joe's Stories

In August 1932, the twin stations moved their transmitters to a site in Flushing. Call letters WMCA and WPCH flanked the door of the modernistic building. But by then WPCH had become something of a pawn between WMCA and WNYC. To obtain full time on 570kc, which it shared with WNYC, the Knickerbocker Broadcasting Company offered to relinquish WPCH's 810 frequency to the municipal station. In June 1933 WNYC made the change, under protest, and WPCH went silent, its staff and some programs transferred to WMCA.

One of the "slender radio spires" and the superstructure of the sign that blocked its signal stood useless but picturesque atop the Park Central Hotel until 1995.

See also WMCA, WNYC.

WPG

(3 JANUARY 1925–JULY 1938)

1925	1100kc	500w.
1926	1000kc	1,000w.
1928	1100kc s/t WLWL (later WBIL)	5,000w.

For most of the twentieth century, New Yorkers happily journeyed a hundred miles down the coast to enjoy the attractions of Atlantic City. An Atlantic City radio station could easily have a world of talent available to it, as well as strong appeal for both residents and tourists. Although the city was already home to privately owned station WHAR, the municipal government of Atlantic City founded its own outlet, WPG—"the Voice of the World's Play Ground." Unlike New York City's municipal station WNYC, WPG would be an entertainer as well as an information source, boosting the local economy. After all, music by the Hotel Shelburne Concert Orchestra in your living room could easily entice visitors and boost business. Despite the distance from New York, WPG turned out to have a physical impact on stations in the metropolitan area, hence its inclusion in this volume.

The municipality had no trouble finding public property to house its radio station—studios were located at Atlantic City High School, with the transmitter at the local airport. Its station cost the city $13,000, but since as it promised millions of dollars in publicity, the management felt comfortable exaggerating the figure to $50,000.

During the summer of 1927, WPG hired popular announcer Norman Brokenshire, who quickly became a local celebrity tooling around the World's Playground in a blue-and-orange Packard. He broadcast from a glass-enclosed "Marine Studio" at the Steel Pier, and in a throwback to the desperate moment when he thrust a WJZ microphone out the window to present the sounds of the city, Brokenshire once lowered a mike from the booth to allow the world to hear the ocean waves (in this case, it was actually the normal hiss of the carbon mike with the gain raised and lowered). On 19 October 1927, aviator Charles Lindbergh flew the *Spirit of St. Louis* into Atlantic City on his victorious circuit of the nation; the visit was covered by WPG.

Beginning in its days as an independent station, WPG impressed listeners and the radio industry itself with a good variety of music, comedy, and locally produced drama by groups like the Duo-Drama Players and the Toy Theatre Players, the latter show originating on Monday nights from a boathouse. Among its advertisers were Chevrolet and IBM. Its powerful 5,000-watt signal easily made it dominant in southern New Jersey, and with the demise of WHAR in 1928, WPG had the market to itself.

Almost every club and hotel provided a venue for WPG's broadcasts, and in 1929 the station was granted permission to sell commercial time. In May 1929, the facilities were moved to the newly opened Convention Hall. The Neptune and Marine Studios—no plain "studio A" or "studio B" for WPG—and a listening room were open to the public.

In 1931, with the depression putting the World's Playground beyond the reach of many potential visitors, WPG alleviated its own economic difficulties by joining the Columbia Network. This wasn't simply an affiliation with CBS. The network leased the station, assumed the operating costs and shared the profits with Atlantic City.

Tuesday, 28 May 1929

12:55 P.M.	Daily Produce Quotations
1:00	Hotel Morton Luncheon Music
4:00	World Book Man and "Our Gang"
4:30	Closing Market Quotations
4:45	The Hokum Exchange
5:15	Theatrical Review and Playground Highlights
5:30	Twilight Organ Recital
5:45	Last Minute News Flashes and Early Baseball Scores. Press-Union Publishing Co.
6:00	Off for WLWL
8:00	Final Baseball Scores
8:05	Studio musical program
8:30	The Tuneful Tuners
9:00	Special Weekly Request Concert
10:00	Convention Hall Events
10:10	Oriole Glee Club
10:30	Colton Manor Hotel Ensemble
11:00	Harry Dobkin's Orchestra, Million Dollar Pier
11:30	Silver Slipper Club Orchestra

On its inaugural network show, WPG serenaded the national audience with the mighty sound of the Convention Hall theatre organ. There was clearly a mutual benefit in bringing Atlantic City into the Columbia chain.

The CBS lease-affiliation lasted from 1931 to 1935 and yielded no profit. It appears that the network made little effort to do anything beyond routine maintenance. A 1938 account in the *Press-Union* stated, "What Atlantic City has left today of WPG is antiquated, worn and practically useless."

Trouble came from outside in a time-sharing arrangement on 1100 kilocycles with WLWL in New York. The Paulist Fathers' station was on the air only from 6:00 to 8:00 P.M. on most weekdays but sought full time. In July 1931 the Federal Radio Commission cited WPG and WLWL for their failure to reach an agreement on time sharing and granted only temporary license renewal to both.

The Atlantic City administration stated that if WPG received a permanent license, it would again lease the facilities. It especially coveted WLWL's two hours from 6:00 to 8:00 P.M. The FRC, and later the Federal Communications Commission, might be expected to rule favorably on WPG, since the New York metropolitan area was seen as already having too many radio stations, but the larger city ultimately won the spot on the dial.

In June 1937 WLWL was sold to John Iraci and Arde Bulova, New Yorkers whose broadcast interests included stations WNEW and WOV. WLWL became WBIL. In a strategy to give WOV full time on 1130kc—a frequency assignment that set the two New York stations much too close on the dial—Iraci and Bulova made Atlantic City a generous offer. WPG had become a burden to a city government already in the red, with the radio station adding $10,000 to its annual debt. Despite protest from the Atlantic City business community, the station was sold for $275,000. The hours of WPG were taken by WBIL, but that station was soon absorbed into WOV.

See also WOV, WBIL, WLWL.

Department of Public Safety
William S. Cuthbert
Commissioner

Department of Ra
Edwin M. Spenc
Director

Atlantic City Municipal Radio Station
W P G
World's Play Ground

Atlantic City, New Jersey

Wave Length 272.6 Meters

1100 Kilocycles

Power 5000 Wi

My dear Radio Friend:

It is always a great pleasure to realize that W. P. G. radio activities mean enough in the lives of our listeners to inspire interesting messages like the one you favored us with, and I assure you the preference of our audiences are vital to us as there is always an extra thrill in knowing that a special program is being tuned in by those who are in friendly contact with our broadcasters.

We are planning to move, in the very near future, in to our palatial new headquarters in the new $15,000,000 Convention Hall which occupies seven acres along the famous boardwalk. There our facilities to entertain you will be improved and we trust we may soon welcome you to our Spanish Patio where the general public will be welcome to glimpse behind the scenes into our Gold and Silver studios as the loud speakers bring to them the varied activities before W. P. G. microphones.

Future programs give promise of great interest to you and if you cannot arrange to be present at the dedication of the largest building in the world which will welcome leading national conventions, athletic, social and theatrical events; do make it a point to tune in for the special features relative to the inaugural ceremonies beginning May 31st. Send us your request for the schedule listing these events or tune in W. P. G. Tuesday nights at 10:00 P. M. and hear about the ambitious program in store for you.

Thanking you for your hearty cooperation which has been an incentive to better effort to spread the Health and Pleasure gospel of our great City, I am

Cordially yours,
MUNICIPAL RADIO STATION WPG

Ethel Rattay,

Publicity Director

P. S.   _____ (You receipt
of 10, _____

WPG's publicity director said it all.

WPOE

(15 April 1928–1932)

1928	1290kc	30w.
1928	1420kc	30w.

Joseph Lombardi's WLBH was based in Farmingdale, Long Island, but sometimes operated as a portable station, so it was probably not a big problem for him to move it to Patchogue. It was a major change, however, because the South Shore community was to be a permanent home and the station would have a new identity. In April 1928 the Nassau Broadcasting Corporation changed call letters to WPOE and became the station of the Patchogue Order of Elks.

WPOE was installed in a bungalow behind the Elks Club, and a pair of 75-foot towers were erected for the antenna. The *Patchogue Advance* stated, "The lease between the Elks and the broadcasting company is a reciprocal one, the Elks securing considerable time on the air and the call letters in return for the use of the property."

Some of the programs heard on WLBH were continued on WPOE, including a series on animal care from the Black Cat Club of Long Island. The station left the air in the early 1930s.

WPOW

(1 May 1957–31 December 1984)

1957	1330kc s/t WEVD, WHAZ	5,000w.

After thirty-three years on the air, the Jehovah's Witnesses station WBBR in Brooklyn was sold for $133,000 to Tele-Broadcasters of New York, headed by H. Scott Killgore. The call letters were changed to WPOW, the religious talks and placid string and organ music disappeared, and the new station embarked on a series of changes that would repeatedly make it something of a pioneer in New York area radio.

Killgore had purchased a part-time operation, splitting 1330kc with WEVD as well as the venerable WHAZ at Rensselaer Polytechnic Institute upstate in Troy. WPOW also inherited WBBR's transmitter at 1111 Woodrow Road in the Rossville section of Staten Island. Killgore established offices and a closet-sized studio for WPOW at 41 E. Forty-second Street in Manhattan but most of the broadcast operation remained at the Staten Island transmitter.

On the morning of Thursday, 5 September 1957, WPOW became the first New York station to play a form of rock music during most of its daily schedule (a shortened schedule to be sure, but two weeks ahead of WINS). "Rhythm Ranch" was heavily into rockabilly, a blending of country and western and rhythm and blues. It was hosted by WPOW program director Mel Miller and Dave Pryce, who was the station's chief engineer. The show was heard for one hour six mornings a week, for two and a half hours most weeknights, and on Sunday afternoons. Five minutes of UP news was read every half hour. The remainder of WPOW's thirty-five and one-half weekly hours was filled with easy-listening music, paid religion (including "Glad Tidings Tabernacle" and "The Hebrew Christian Hour"), and a Sunday-evening taped description of a Saturday-afternoon Staten Island high school football game.

The anachronistic conditions under which WPOW labored resulted in its occasionally signing on at 3:00 A.M. and leaving the air while the morning drive-time audience was at its peak. By 1959, WPOW's schedule looked like this:

Tuesday–Friday   5:30–8:00 A.M., 5:00–8:00 P.M.
Monday, Saturday   5:30–8:00 A.M.
Sunday   6:00–11:00 A.M., 4:00–8:00 P.M.

Despite the slogan that "WPOW brings more POW-er to New York," the signal was weak in the northern reaches of the Five Boroughs, and the Staten Island location discouraged a lucrative local presence. In February 1958, "Rhythm Ranch" was canceled and the station moved to foreign-language programming, mostly Spanish but including some Polish, French, Armenian, and Byelorussian. There were also a couple of popular Sunday programs for the Irish-American audience: Harry McGuirk's "Shamrock Time" and the "Irish Showboat" with Peter McNulty and John Rooney.

In July 1959, Scott Killgore sold WPOW for $250,000 to John M. Camp, an Illinois-based advertising agent and broker of religious broadcast time. WPOW was to be the showcase for his agency. Camp moved the Manhattan studio and offices to the Roosevelt Hotel on Madison Avenue and Forty-fifth Street (the 1920-era home of WRNY). Naturally, paid religion began to take more time on the WPOW schedule, and ethnic programming also increased. Some holdovers from Tele-Broadcasters days remained, including Jack Smith's "Voices of Staten Island" and "Jazz 'n' Things," produced by Erwin ("Ratings Be Damned") Frankel from 6:00 to 7:15 A.M. Monday through Saturday. Cool and mellow early-morning jazz was punctuated by Frankel's editorializing on events of the day, and his comments finally caused the management to dismiss him from WPOW.

Monday, 7 July 1975

| 3:00 A.M. | News and weather |

3:05	Nightwatch
3:35	Pause for Good News
3:40	Our Daily Bread
3:50	Commentary on Living
3:55	New and weather
4:00	Nightsounds—Bill Pearce
4:30	Life Line
4:45	The King's Hour
5:00	Morning Chapel Hour
5:30	The Campmeeting Hour
5:45	Grace Memorial Hour
6:00	World Missionary Evangelism
6:15	Heaven and Home Hour
6:30	Back to the Bible
7:00	The King's Hour
7:15	Inspiration Time
7:30	Morning Chapel Hour
8:00	A Look at the Book
8:15	American Indian Hour
8:20	News report and weather
8:30	Off for WEVD

Operating as WPOW Inc. Camp's station turned heavily to inspirational and religiously oriented public-affairs programs ("POWer of the Word"), with foreign-language broadcasts largely confined to late-afternoon and evening hours. In 1964, studios moved to 305 E. Fortieth Street. In 1973, Camp purchased WHAZ to operate the Troy station as a daytimer, finally opening Monday nights for New York City on 1330kHz.

In 1979, WEVD-AM was sold to Salem Media and became WNYM. The two stations sharing 1330 on the dial were now broadcasting similar Christian programming (they even issued a joint program guide). Salem later bought out WPOW for $4 million, most of that sum simply for the Staten Island real estate. At 7:59 P.M. on the last day of 1984, WPOW signed off without ceremony, and the last time-sharing arrangement in New York AM radio came to an end.

See also WEVD, WBBR(I).

WPUB *see* WMSG

WPUT

(JUNE 1968–)

1963 (WBRW)	1510kc (daytime)	1,000w.
1992	1510kc (full time)	1,000w.

Putnam County certainly qualifies as part of the New York metropolitan area, although this small slice of hills and lakes between the Hudson River and the Connecticut line feels like a quiet corner of New England or Minnesota. Putnam's first radio station was WBRW, established by Taconic Broadcasters at a transmitter-studio site on Prospect Hill Road in Brewster. J. S. Ogsbury was the original president, general manager, and program director. Most broadcast time was filled with easy listening music, with some fifteen hours of country-and-western music each week. One of the first announcers at WBRW was Marty Wayne, who went on to WNYC.

In October 1968 WBRW was sold to Brewster Broadcasting; among the new owners was Morris Novik, former manager of WNYC and then owner of WLIB. Brewster Broadcasting changed WBRW's call letters to WPUT and hired away staff from neighboring stations: program director and morning deejay John Yottes from WFAS and news director Jim Grehan of WLNA in Peekskill. WPUT adopted an adult contemporary music format and in 1972 affiliated with the ABC Entertainment Network. When the Novik family sold WLIB in 1971, Richard Novik, Morris's nephew and partner in Brewster Broadcasting, became owner and president of the renamed Putnam Broadcasting Corporation. WPUT changed its news affiliation to CNN Radio and began to specialize in big-band and middle-of-the road music. It seemed to fit Putnam County very well, although WPUT was strongly rivaled by WVIP in Mount Kisco for the local audience.

In 1982, WPUT gained an FM affiliate when it put WMJV on the air at 105.5MHz. The FM station was located in Patterson, N.Y., and the studios and transmitter were just across the county line in Dutchess County. Three years later, WPUT and WMJV were sold to Tri-Valley Broadcasting. The new president, Ron Graiff, moved the AM studios out to the FM site in 1987. WPUT's transmitter remained in Brewster, and in 1992, following the sale of the station to Hudson Valley LLP, the station went to full-time operation. Through the 1990s, WPUT specialized in country and western music, not a new departure for a station country and eastern.

(4 MARCH 1923–7 JANUARY 1934)

1923	830kc	250w.
1926	760kc s/t WHN, WPAP	250w.
1928	1010kc s/t WHN, WPAP	500w.

The Calvary Baptist Church at 123 W. Fifty-seventh Street in midtown Manhattan was one of the earliest religious broadcasters in the New York area. WQAO took to the air during the same month that the federal government authorized a band of frequencies for broadcasting; its first spot on the dial was the original broadcast frequency of 830kc. The station cost $1,500 to build, and installation was directed by chief engineer George F. Koster, who was also the church sexton.

WQAO was clear about its mission. Rev. John Roach Straton explained, "I am hopeful that the wider use of radio will tend to break up the dominating influence of commercialized amusements." He envisioned a service that would keep the family gathered by the hearth and loudspeaker. WQAO "would be so efficient that when I twist the devil's tail here in New York his squawk will be heard across the continent."

Dr. Straton was accustomed to taking his message directly to the populace. Since 1918 he had traveled the city streets with a portable pulpit mounted over the hood of a car, preaching the gospel and denouncing evolution, divorce, Ouija boards, and all forms of "modernism." Loew's station WHN broadcast Calvary Baptist services during the period when WQAO was under construction and later shared dial space through several changes in frequency.

In 1927, WPAP at Palisades Amusement Park was added to the WQAO/WHN frequency of 760. This must have given Straton some discomfort, since he often decried the jazz and worldly entertainment that could come into homes on radios already tuned in good faith to WQAO. Nonetheless, WQAO joined with the other two stations in June 1927 to protest an FRC plan to add a fourth station, WBRS, to their shared frequency and later held off a request from WRNY for half-time on 1010kc.

Calvary Baptist Church had stood at 123 W. Fifty-seventh since 1882, and in 1929 the original edifice was demolished and a new high-rise church building—the one still standing, once nicknamed "Straton's tomb"—was constructed in its place. Modern broadcasting facilities were planned, but the station had limited airtime: 11:00 A.M. to 12:30 P.M. and 7:30 to 9:30 P.M. Sundays, as well as an hour from 7:30 to 8:30 P.M. on Wednesdays. The church also shared WQAO with other religious institutions, as in the broadcast of Salvation Army services.

WQAO continued to attract a faithful audience, but the era drew to an end in which churches strived to be heard from their own transmitters. For the final months of its life, WQAO operated in tandem with the secular voices of Loew's Theatres and Palisades Amusement Park. In 1933 Loew's bought out the other three stations on its frequency. As part of the purchase agreement, Calvary Baptist Church was granted time on WHN (later WMGM). Broadcasts continued from the church for another four decades both locally and through international short-wave stations, produced at facilities installed for WQAO. The church later sponsored "The Calvary Hour" over WMCA.

See also WHN, WPAP, WMGM.

WQEW

(DECEMBER 1992–)

| 1992 | 1560kHz | 50,000w. |

The passing of WNEW gave the *New York Times* an opening to rescue WQXR, whose 1560kHz AM frequency had long been bypassed by classical music lovers tuned to FM. During its final week, WNEW rebroadcast several hours of the newer station each day. Blending call letters, WQEW premiered with a program guaranteed to draw the formerly faithful listeners: a live studio performance by singer Tony Bennett.

In addition to the swing, ballads, and big bands, WQEW also brought over some of the voices from WNEW, including Les Davis, Mark Simone (who had hosted the very last record session at eleven-three-oh), and Jonathan Schwartz. Schwartz himself had been trying to start a new station to take the place of WNEW and had been so upset over the demise of the great old station that he had left just weeks before it was shut down. He was a little uncertain about WQEW's intentions until reassured by program director Stan Martin. Rich Conaty, who'd begun presenting pop classics on Fordham's WFUV-FM, brought his knowledge and his record collection to WQEW, playing original vintage recordings from the swing era on "Big Band Saturday Night" and from even earlier on "The Big Broadcast" on Sunday nights.

WQEW also launched a series of live cabaret, jazz, and big-band programs such as had not been heard on any New York station for many years. This included the first weekly pickups from the Rainbow Room, high atop the erstwhile RCA Building in Radio City.

At first, "The Home of American Popular Standards" duplicated WQXR for a few of the nighttime hours; it soon took over all twenty-four hours and even dropped the *Times* news summaries. Initial ratings revealed that 80 percent of former WNEW listeners had followed their favorites up the dial, and soon WQEW could boast that it had more listeners than any other station in the country with a similar format and the largest increase in audience of all broadcasters in the nation. WQEW also became the sanctuary for some of New York City's most experienced announcers, including Del DeMontreux, Lee Arnold and Chuck Leonard. The ratings were nowhere near what WNEW had commanded when it had been the most listened to station in the New York market, but WQEW preserved the music and some of the mood of its ancestor as well as the respectability of its parent.

See also WQXR, WNEW.

W Q X R

(W2XR, 26 March 1929–6 December 1936)
(WQXR, 6 December 1936–December 1992)

1929	2100kc and 1550kc (W2XR)	50w.
1934	1550kc	250w.
1936	1550kc (WQXR)	1,000w.
1941	1560kc	10,000w.
1956	1560kc	50,000w.

Of the many individuals who labored to develop radio, one in particular had a decisive impact on both technology and programming—that is, on both the science and the art of broadcasting. John V. L. Hogan began his career as a teenage assistant to Dr. Lee De Forest. Hogan's father was one of De Forest's backers; young Jack got a job in return for the financial support and thus had a hand in radiotelephone experiments as early as 1908. Another of Hogan's tasks in 1908 was the installation of a receiving station atop the *New York Times* building. In 1910 Hogan managed the experimental transatlantic station built by wireless telephony pioneer Reginald Fessenden at Brant Rock, Mass.

Hogan's most important technical innovation was combining variable capacitors on a shaft to create "single-dial control," freeing listeners from the need to adjust each stage of tuning. Hogan also invented the detector-heterodyne circuit and an improved antenna, all of which made radio easy to use and enjoy.

He pursued many experiments in his Radio Inventions Laboratory at 140 Nassau Street in Manhattan and later at 31-04 Northern Boulevard, above a Ford garage in Long Island City—people using the wrong door often walked in looking for the parts department. By the late 1920s, Hogan

had joined the parade of technical experts and tinkerers trying to send mechanically scanned images through the air. Radio Pictures Inc. received a license in 1929 for an experimental "visual broadcasting station" with the call sign W2XR, the number signifying the Second Call Zone (New York and New Jersey) and the letter X indicating an experimental transmitter.

Hogan's television and facsimile pictures were broadcast at frequencies of 2100kc and above. In 1933, the Radio Commission authorized double-wide 20kc channels at 1530, 1550, and 1570 kilocycles, just past the top of the broadcast band at that time. Hogan decided to accompany his television pictures with classical records on 1550kc. Classical music, live and recorded, was already heard on the radio, but W2XR seemed to have a broader selection as well as superior audio. Many of the better radios could tune the frequency, and Hogan began to win an audience unaware of, or uninterested in, video. The fruitless TV experiments were soon abandoned in favor of achieving high-fidelity audio transmission. This would evolve into one of the nation's premier classical music stations, and make WQXR the only radio station in New York to have begun life on television.

Hogan and engineer Al Barber got special transcriptions from Western Electric and World Broadcasting Company. Each transcription disk carried an indication of which filter to use, so two "extended range" turntables were modified with equalizing filters. A small studio was equipped with Brush crystal microphones. Hogan's secretary, Arthur Huntington, was the first announcer and pianist.

Starting in July 1934, W2XR was on the air a few hours each day. The antenna was on the roof of the Ford garage. Even during its experimental period, the "Scientific Broadcasting Station" took itself seriously. W2XR published a program guide and solicited listeners' reports on its technical tests, including such details as the proper balance between a speaker's voice and the background music. Hogan even designed a special radio to receive W2XR, though few were manufactured.

W2XR—Friday, 11 September 1936

10:00 A.M.	Morning Musicale
10:45	Press Radio News
10:50	Behind the Front Page
11:15	Musical Varieties
	Off at 12:00 noon
5:00 P.M.	Dance Music
5:30	The Monitor Views the News
5:45	Light Classics
6:45	Press Radio News
6:50	Piano Classics
7:00	Haydn—Symphony No. 4, Glazounov—Violin Concerto
8:00	Chamber Music: Dvořák, Mendelssohn, Brahms

In 1936, Hogan joined with publicist Elliott Sanger to form the Interstate Broadcasting Company and turn W2XR into a commercial operation. At that time the organization had only six employees. Their hope was to attract advertisers to a "quality audience," delivering messages consistent with the sound of Bach or Schubert. This required the station to be selective in its choice of sponsors—a curious commercial twist. On Thursday, 3 December 1936, W2XR became WQXR, the new call letters chosen to resemble the old. The station succeeded. Yet Elliott Sanger wrote in his book *Rebel in Radio*, "It is literally true that we rejected enough advertising to run another station profitably." Making a serious effort to avoid the obnoxious, WQXR earned a niche as "the radio station for people who hate radio" (a slogan others in the industry found offensive).

Since WQXR was a commercial venture beyond the range of many radio receivers, early in 1937 Hogan sent engineers Russell Valentine and Bob Cobaugh to visit businesses in the Long Island City area and charge a dollar to adjust sets whose dials stopped short of 1550 kilocycles.

With its new upscale commercial status, WQXR moved its studio from Long Island City to 730 Fifth Avenue in Manhattan. But the lab remained busy, working to extend radio's audio range to 30–16,000 cycles (double the capability of most transmitters of the time) and improving on such devices as the phonograph pickup. On 1 September 1938, WQXR broadcast the first tape-recorded program heard in American radio, act one of *Carmen*, recorded in London. The "Millerfilm" process had been used in Europe and utilized 7-mm. tape engraved by a sapphire stylus. The device never caught on but did demonstrate WQXR's openness to technical innovation.

Nearly all the equipment at WQXR during its first decade and a half, including the transmitters that progressed from 50 to 10,000 watts, was built in the Long Island City shop by "Val" Valentine, working for Hogan's firm, Radio Inventions Inc. With each advance in output quality, Valentine would look over the rest of the station to see what could still be improved, down to the switches on the audio-control board. So it was obvious to WQXR staff and listeners that "standard broadcast" sound had physical limitations. When an amazing new form of radio transmission was demonstrated to the press and public on 18 July 1939, it was fitting that Edwin Howard Armstrong's frequency modulation was modulating WQXR's audio.

On 26 November 1939, W2XQR began broadcasting on FM at 42.3 megacycles. The next day it presented a special concert by the NBC Symphony. It then became W59NY at 45.9Mc. The transmitter was moved from Long Island City in December 1941 to the fifty-fourth floor of the Chanin Building at Lexington and Forty-second streets. W59NY was changed to WQXQ and in 1945 made the switch to the new FM band at 97.7Mc.

WQXR's schedule also embraced a number of nonmusical programs, including "Author Meets the Critics" and regular poetry broadcasts. The great radio writer Norman Corwin produced his first work in New York on WQXR, a 1937–38 series called "Poetic License." Some of the earliest news programs were prepared by the respected *Christian Science Monitor*. In the package with the *Monitor* broadcasts was Rex Keith Benware, an early WHN announcer who had had a brief career in western movies and became one of the most familiar voices on WQXR.

In the early 1940s, the *New York Post* negotiated to buy WQXR, an offer Elliott Sanger said he wished had come from the *Times*. As a result of his offhand lament the *Times* soon made a $1 million offer to Hogan and Sanger, and on 25 July 1944 the city's most prestigious paper took control of the Interstate Broadcasting Company, keeping the existing staff and management. It seemed like a natural arrangement, although some staffers would miss the days when Elliot and Eleanor Sanger had run WQXR as a "mom and pop" operation. There was also one immediate and serious complication. Since December 1941, the *Times* had been providing news to WMCA, which refused to terminate the contract. So "The Radio Station of the New York Times" did not begin to broadcast *Times* news bulletins until 1 July 1946. And it was not until Sunday, 16 April 1950, that WQXR moved from Fifty-seventh Street to studios on the ninth and tenth floors of the Times Building at 229 W. Forty-third Street. *Times* newscasts were fired from the city desk to the WQXR news studio by pneumatic tube, and listeners could tell from the swoosh and clunk when a late bulletin arrived (a noise no less intrusive than the clanging chime that opened each hour's news).

WQXR's live studio concerts were of higher quality and remained longer on the schedule than those of any other New York station. Violinist Eddy Brown formed the first string ensemble for WQXR during the 1930s, and pianist Abram Chasins joined the WQXR staff in 1943 as music director. Dual pianists Leonid Hambro and Jascha Zayde were staff artists. Concerts took place in WQXR's four-hundred-seat auditorium, and it was from this studio that one of radio's most far-reaching experiments began, on Thursday, 30 October 1952. The idea was simple enough: a concert was broadcast into two microphones, one feeding the AM transmitter (usually the right channel), the other FM, to be picked up on two radios about six feet apart. Tests of stereophonic radio actually date from the early 1920s, but WQXR's "binaural sound" can be seen as the immediate forerunner of stereo programming. It was enthusiastically received by the critical WQXR audience, though a careful listener could discern the difference between AM and FM audio more clearly than ever.

As basic to the WQXR sound as Bruno Walter, Vladimir Horowitz, or Marian Anderson were the voices of the announcers. The first full-time announcer to be hired by W2XR was Bill Strauss, who believed he passed the audition because he could announce with two different voices. He remained with the station for over thirty years. Among those

The WQXR master control room in the New York Times Building with Bob Cobaugh on duty, 1975.

WQXR auditorium, with Jascha Zayde at the piano.

WQXR general manager Warren Bodow points out new compact-disc equipment to two visitors from Sweden.

who balanced intimacy and formality to perpetuate a distinct WQXR announcing style were Melvin Elliott, Lloyd Moss, Peter Allen, Frank Waldecker, Chet Santon, Bob Lewis, June Labelle, Hugh Morgan, and Ed Stanton. Program director Martin Bookspan announced the New York Philharmonic concerts. Morning man George Edwards and cocktail-hour host Duncan Pirnie had bouncy, individualistic delivery. On a station that forbade "raucous shouting" and singing commercials as undignified (there were complaints when a string quartet played a seven-second version of the Barney's clothing store jingle), WQXR announcers authoritatively delivered sponsors' messages with graceful vocal gymnastics.

A New York paper (not the *Times*) once surveyed some local disc jockeys about the most exciting thing that ever happened to them in radio. George Edwards' response was, "Nothing exciting ever happens to people at WQXR." With tongue out of cheek, Edwards might have told about the time Melvin Elliott was introducing Wagner's "Damnation of Faust" and fellow staffers lowered a rubber black widow spider into the booth through an air duct. Elliott was surprised but went on reading without even a gasp. Edwards might also have told of announcers exercising by holding fencing matches in the hallways while the symphonies played.

At the beginning of 1953, WQXR expanded its FM coverage through the "WQXR Network," an off-air link that hopped as far west as Buffalo, north to Boston, and south to Washington. On 19 March 1956, WQXR-AM boosted its power to 50,000 watts; a special survey later that year revealed that slightly more than half the audience was still listening on FM. Finally, on Thursday, 7 September 1961, WQXR-FM initiated FM multiplex service and dropped the old "binaural" programs.

By the mid–1960s, this most stable of radio stations realized it had to make some changes. The QXR Network shut down in 1963 as affiliates saw that there was more money in strictly local programming. New FCC regulations concerning duplication of AM and FM, as well as changes in public taste, led WQXR itself to retool the AM channel with light classics, show tunes, and jazz. On New Year's Day 1967, WQXR AM and FM split their operations in what the station publicized as a "divorce," with the FM side considerably "heavier" than the AM. Eight months later—after listeners' grumbling was confirmed by a formal survey—the plan was scrapped. But in 1969, trying to shake an image that station manager Walter Nieman described as "the old lady of Threadneedle Street," WQXR-AM began several non-QXRish programs, including a postmidnight pop-and-rock show featuring songwriter Gene Lees. This concept was also short-lived. WQXR's greatest successes remained such solid classical offerings as "The Vocal Scene" with George Jellinek, "The Listening Room" with Robert Sherman, and "First Hearing," on which Lloyd Moss' expert guests critiqued new recordings without knowing who was performing.

In 1971, the *Times* put the WQXR stations up for sale and found buyers clamoring for 96.3 FM but keeping their distance from 1560 AM. The FCC's nonduplication rule was waived for WQXR, and the stations were taken off the sales block. In June 1989, WQXR moved out of the Times Building and downtown to 122 Fifth Avenue. Still, the AM station remained something of a white elephant for the *Times*, and in 1992 the demise of WNEW gave WQXR president and general manager Warren Bodow a respectable alternative. Classical music—at least of the Beethoven, Rachmaninoff, Verdi type—disappeared from the spot on the dial that John Hogan had opened in 1934. WQXR brought over the sound and some of the personalities of WNEW, and in December 1992 it became WQEW, "the home of American popular standards." The call letters WQXR continued on the FM band, which the station had helped to pioneer.

See also WLIB, WQEW.

WRAN

(19 AUGUST 1964–18 MARCH 1987)

1964	1510kc (daytime)	1,000w.
1968	1510kc	1,000w. day / 500 w. night
1974	1510kc	10,000w. day / 500 w. night

WRAN was established by Lion Broadcasting Company, a subsidiary of *Esquire* magazine. The studios and transmitter were at Route 10 and Millbrook Avenue in Randolph Township, N.J. Sam Kravitz was the first station manager. Dave Holmund was news director and, along with reporter Steve Baltin, brought listeners some of New Jersey's most energetic news coverage (Holmund and Baltin both moved on to WCBS Newsradio 88). Disc jockeys included Al Wunder, Dick Miller, and John Bennett.

The station soon expanded to full-time operation and in December 1968 it was sold to Jersey Horizons, part of the national chain that also owned WGNY in Newburg, N.Y. and WALK in Patchogue, Long Island. By the mid–1970s the adult contemporary music policy, guided by program director Rich Phoenix, and the work of news reporters Frank Anthony and Ann Williams were highlights of a radio station growing in both power and popularity. In 1980 WRAN was again sold, this time to New Jersey 1510 Radio Associates, a group headed by veteran New York deejay "Cousin Brucie" Morrow and radio executive Robert F. X. Silliman. The owners also took over stations WALL in Middletown and WHVW in Hyde Park, N.Y., switched to a rock-oldies format, and proudly presented the great Cousin Brucie himself with a weekly record show on his exurban network.

WRAN went through several changes of ownership in the late 1980s. First it was acquired from the Silliman-Morrow group in 1986 by Bell Broadcasting and a year later was sold to Atlantic-Morris Holdings, a division of Orange and Rockland Utilities. The oldies programming was revived, and on 18 March 1987 the call letters were changed to WMHQ. But the broadcast property was actually declining in value, hurt by its poor coverage and inferior audio. In 1988, the former WRAN fell victim to a trend in AM radio and went off the air forever.

WRAZ see WNJ

WRKL

(4 JULY 1964–)

1964	910kc (daytime)	1,000w.

Rockland County's first radio station was born on the fourth of July in 1964, licensed to the county seat of New City, and housed in a trailer in swampland beside the Palisades Parkway in the hamlet of Mount Ivy. The original owner was Rockland Broadcasters, founded by former WNEW engineer Al Spiro and Keith Connes. The scenic suburb was ready for a radio station of its own, and WRKL brought a thorough news service with two five-minute newscasts each hour—one national, the other local—and three expanded, fifteen-minute news programs a day. Music was middle-of-the-road.

WRKL's main feature and community service was "Hotline," hosted by Al Spiro from noon to 1:30 P.M., Monday through Saturday. Listeners were welcome to comment on matters from the cosmic to the trivial and to use WRKL as a sounding board for opinions on the news. Spiro's philosophy was that radio should be simply one person talking to another.

On 24 July 1967, during a time of racial tension, a "Hotline" caller who identified himself as African-American delivered comments condemning whites. The remarks were the roughest yet heard on Rockland radio and may have been literally incendiary. After sign-off that evening, the WRKL house trailers were gutted by fire. There was an outpouring of help, with other stations lending equipment and with listeners donating records. WRKL was back on the air the next week. (Two men were charged with arson. Both were white, and both were members of a volunteer fire department.)

In 1969 WRKL moved from the patched-up trailers in the swamp to a permanent home. Among those who worked at WRKL were news director Art Athens, who later joined WCBS, and WNEW deejay Bob Fitzsimmons. Rockland County agricultural extension agent Ralph Snodsmith had a weekly farm-and-garden report on WRKL and went on to host WOR's "Garden Hotline."

WRKL was sold in 1985 to Rockland Communications and then in 1995 was acquired by Odyssey Communications, headed by Infinity Broadcasting executive Michael Kakoyannis. The station expanded to twenty-four-hour operation and an all-talk format. Always serious about its news coverage, WRKL was one of the most thorough stations in New York State in its coverage of affairs in Albany.

WRNY

(12 JUNE 1925–10 JANUARY 1934)

1925	1160kc	500w.
1926	800kc, variable	500w.
1927	1070, 970, 920kc s/t WPCH	500w.
1928	1010kc s/t WHN, WQAO, WPAP	500w.

If the early twentieth century with its energetic belief in progress could be called a renaissance, Hugo Gernsback was a renaissance man. He was a clumsy but imaginative writer of science fiction (a term he coined—the Hugo Award for the year's best science fiction publication is named in his honor) and an entrepreneur who was one of the first dealers of wireless equipment as well as the publisher of books and magazines that brought radio to countless experimenters. The Luxembourg-born Gernsback was a scientific seer (he described, in detail, advances from radar to holography long before they were invented), and when radio broadcasting became a reality, his station sought novelty and moved in ways that were literally visionary.

WRNY was licensed to Gernsback's Experimenter Publishing Company. The 500-watt Western Electric transmitter, the antennae on 125-foot towers atop the Roosevelt Hotel at Forty-fifth Street and Madison, and the "radio station in a hotel room" on the eighteenth floor were all state-of-the-art for 1925. The Roosevelt became one of the first hotels to provide radios in its rooms. Initially, sets were not permanently installed, but guests could request a radio from room service.

Among the speakers on WRNY's first broadcast day was the "father of radio," Dr. Lee De Forest. Gernsback's *Radio News* magazine carried the WRNY logo on its cover and the listing "Mr. Hugo Gernsback speaks every Tuesday at 9:30 P.M. from Stations WRNY (297 meters) and W2XAL (30.91 meters) on various radio and scientific subjects," among them a speculative talk on whether there was life on other planets and a prediction that coal would eventually be delivered by radio. The call letters were said to stand for both "Radio News, New York" and "Roosevelt New York."

WRNY's program director was Dr. Charles Isaacson, a concert impresario who enlivened the airwaves with opera, poetry, lectures on sculpture, and literature. His schedules included not only amateur performers but also one of radio's first playwriting contests.

WRNY broadcast live remotes from the Bavarian Restaurant in the heart of New York City's German neighborhood.

In April 1926, "The Radio News Magazine Station" aired a "synchronized" concert with the Hotel Roosevelt orchestra accompanied by an organist four miles away at the West Side Unitarian Church. Two months later, the station presented a recital on the "Pianorad," a forerunner to the synthesizer with eighty-eight oscillating tubes in place of strings. Another technical curiosity was the sound of goldfish swimming in a bowl, amplified ten million times.

But the most notable WRNY broadcasts began on 13 August 1928 when it initiated a regular schedule of "radio television" experiments. The first audience consisted of five hundred students at New York University. In cooperation with John Geloso's Pilot Electric Company, Gernsback presented daily five-minute programs via forty-eight-line mechanical scanners set up at the WRNY transmitter on Hudson Terrace in Coytesville, N.J., since pictures could not be properly synchronized through the Hotel Roosevelt studios. Gernsback admitted when TV programming began that it would probably appeal mostly to experimenters who could build their own receivers from plans in his *Television News*. Reception required a 24-inch scanning disc rotating at 240 rpm. Among the pioneering TV broadcasts were cooking lessons, physical fitness instruction, concerts, and calendars of events. Of course, Hugo Gernsback was one of the stars.

Friday, 19 October 1928

11:00 A.M.	Television broadcast
11:05	Talk—Keeping Fit
11:30	Aching Hearts Club
11:45	Heart talks
12:00 noon	Television broadcast
12:05	Dish-a-Day, Broccoli
12:15	Farm flashes
12:30	Radio farm flashes
12:35	Eddie Wood, songs
12:45	Fashion talk
1:00	Off for WPCH
3:00	Television broadcast
3:05	Winifred Carroll, soprano
3:20	Artie Newborn, songs
3:30	California Vocal Trio
4:00	Television broadcast
4:05	Bob McDonald, ukelele
4:15	Edwin Howard, violin
4:30	Vocal trio
4:45	Marie Fluegel, soprano
5:00	Television broadcast
5:05	Holst's Orchestra
5:25	Temple Emanu-El services
6:10	Television broadcast
6:15	Jewish hour
6:45	Radio Bluebird
7:00	Television broadcast
7:05	Roosevelt news
7:07	Hollywood news
7:35	Larney Young, contralto
7:59	Sawyer Frog talk

Gernsback went bankrupt in 1929 (prior to the Wall Street crash). In April of that year he sold WRNY and W2XAL for $100,000 to the Aviation Radio Station Inc., a company associated with the Curtiss Aircraft Corporation. WRNY would still be a station with a mission to disseminate information about new technology and would provide weather reports and other services to aviators. But it also canceled fifteen hours of jazz programs left over from the free-wheeling Gernsback era. The new owners tried to advance plans for commercial international short-wave broadcasting. In September 1929 WRNY moved from the Hotel Roosevelt to 27 W. Fifty-seventh Street.

A more conservative management, pressures of the depression, and a cumbersome time-sharing schedule with WHN, WPAP, and WQAO drained much of the experimentation and excitement from WRNY. A 1930 brokering arrangement with the Harlem Broadcasting Corporation was terminated when the company was determined to be "unethical." The station expanded into foreign-language programming, including shows for Swedish, Mexican, and Argentinean listeners.

In early 1933, WHN began to buy out its time-share partners on 1010kc and operated WRNY for three hours a day from its own studios in the Loew's State Theatre. By the end of the year the historic *Radio News* station had been absorbed into WHN.

Hugo Gernsback retained his interest in science and prophesied 60-mile-wide TV pictures projected onto clouds. In the 1950s and 1960s he was a regular guest on Jack Paar's *Tonight Show* on NBC-TV. He died in April 1967.

See also WHN, WPAP, WQAO.

WRRC

(15 SEPTEMBER 1965–1968)

1965	1300kc	500w.

One year after WRKL put Rockland County on the air, it gained a bit of local competition from WRRC. Rockland Radio Corporation established its station at Broadcast House, a multi-story building on Route 59 in Nanuet. Its coverage area included Suffern, Hillburn, and Sloatsburg as well as the "city of license," Spring Valley. The programming was intended to complement the exurban life: uninterrupted quarter-hour blocks of music with five minutes of UPI news at five before the hour. News director Bob Davidson was heard in the morning, Dom Allagi in the afternoon. Most of the commercials were delivered by sales manager Frank A. Seitz, the founder of White Plains station WFAS.

WRRC proved to be both too low-key and too low-power. A change in signal pattern extended the coverage area to the east, and the music moved to the middle of the road. But after just three years on the air it changed its call letters to WKQW and began to specialize in rock and roll. Even this wasn't successful and the station shut down briefly until a new owner, WKQW Incorporated, put it back on the air with adult contemporary music and local news coverage. The owner also moved the studios out of Broadcast House to 25 Church Street.

In the late 1970s, WKQW was sold to real estate executive Herbert Greene, who changed the call letters to WGRC. This time the music was "Mellow Gold"—mostly million-seller sides from the 1950s through the 1970s News coverage was expanded, and there was Little League baseball on Saturdays. Programs for the Hispanic, African-American, and Jewish communities began to be heard, a sign that Rockland County was growing larger and more diverse. But WGRC's operation deteriorated; it moved to a trailer with no lock on the door, and the transmitter was so unreliable that its carrier wave was never turned off. Finally, the station was shut down.

In 1984, Greene sold WGRC to Rockland Media Corporation, and the station became WLIR.

See also WRKL, WFAS, WLIR.

W R S T

(14 SEPTEMBER 1925–15 APRIL 1928)

1925	1390kc	250w.
1927	1480kc	150w.
1927	1420kc	150w.

The first broadcasting station in Suffolk County, Long Island, was founded at Bay Shore by the Radiotel Manufacturing Company and quickly established itself as one of the important outlets in the metropolitan area.

WRST presented varied programming with the express purpose of expanding the radio audience. Every day at noon, the Jedlicka Brothers radio store presented the "Jedlicka Music Hour," and the evening schedule that began at 5:00 P.M. usually featured a children's show, financial news, and community-based programs. Musical broadcasts over WRST ranged from sessions with the Oh Boy Juvenile Orchestra and the orchestra from Central Islip State Hospital. Local news was provided by the *Bay Shore Press*.

The manager of WRST was Charles Gregson, assisted by engineers Fred Given and Garo Ray. The engineering staff spent almost as much time on the air as they did tending the equipment—Given presented a regular program on aviation, and Ray answered listeners' questions about radio and even taught Morse code.

Tuesday, 10 April 1928

12:00 noon	Jedlicka Music Hour
5:00	Tea Dance
8:00	Matilda Oberd, soprano; Ethel Perkal, soprano, Natalie Greenhaigh, pianist
8:30	Charles C. Gregson
8:35	Bay Shore, L.I., Hour
9:10	Bay Shore Jubileers
9:40	Warren Howell, piano recital
10:00	Southampton, L.I., Hour
11:00	D.X. Club Hour; Bendave Allen and Gang

"The Radiotel of the Sunrise Trail" had studios at 5 First Avenue in Bayshore before moving to expanded facilities above Freedman's Department Store at 62 East Main Street. During a time when around fifty stations were crowding the local airwaves, WRST was one of some ten stations whose program listings were included in New York's weekly *Radiogram and Guide* magazine.

But WRST had a problem. Some of its listeners liked to refer to the station as "the WoRST," and this bothered Charles Gregson so much that in April 1928 he requested a change of call letters to WINR, which, he explained, "is pronounced 'winner,' and the new letters stand for 'improved new radio.'"

Then WINR fell into one of the worst situations a broadcaster can face. On 23 July 1929 the Bay Shore station applied to the Federal Radio Commission for a renewal of its license, confessing that it had been operating without one for three months and had also moved its transmitter without permission. On 31 July the license was reactivated and extended for three months. Despite its optimistic name, WINR left the air in 1931.

WRW

(16 MARCH 1922–30 JUNE 1926)

1922	360m (833 kc)	40w.
1923	1100kc s/t WEBJ, WBBR, WFBH	150w.

WRW was one of the first stations on the air, the seventy-third broadcaster to be licensed by the Commerce Department. It was built by radio experimenter and ham operator Fred Koenig Sr., who had used his station 2BAK to welcome in the New Year 1922. The program featured the pastor and choir of the Second Reformed Church of Tarrytown as well as violin solos by the Koenig sons.

When WRW premiered three months later it operated on 360 meters, the only wavelength then authorized for broadcasting. As with many other early stations, the "studio" was located in a garage—the Old Post Road Garage at 21 North Broadway in Tarrytown. Fred and Nick Koenig expanded into sales and service of radio equipment and took the name Tarrytown Radio Research Laboratory. Power was increased from the original 40 watts to 150 watts in 1923, which helped make WRW both a widely heard station and a major source of interference to other broadcasters in the New York area.

Friday, 22 May 1925

9:00 P.M.	Police alarms, music
9:20	Baseball scores
9:30	Almo Entertainers
10:00	Radio talk; prize contest
10:15	Irving Grove Orchestra
10:45	Almo Entertainers

As early as 1922, Fred Koenig had tried to interest local police forces in radio, even demonstrating a portable set that could be carried by officers wearing headphones. It would be several years before police cars and motorcycles would commonly be on "radio patrol," but WRW convinced Westchester police and the public of its value by airing crime bulletins every evening. A newspaper item in September 1925 said that WRW was helping to capture "automobile thieves, porch climbers and motorists who leave the scene of an accident" and added, "Persons in localities where the police have no receiving set are requested to notify their police headquarters of any information affecting their territory."

WRW boasted that it presented "Everything on Radio" and wanted to air better musical programs, but it had trouble covering the licensing fees that would soon be required by the American Society of Composers, Authors and Publishers. In the days before radio became a strong commercial medium, Fred Koenig considered public fund-raising,

explaining in September 1925, "If the WRW Radio Music Fund could be created, this [ASCAP] license could be then taken out and other expenses could be met."

In May 1926, WRW was planning to move to Yonkers. It was thwarted by both the city of Yonkers, which would not donate property for studios and transmitter, and by a challenge to its license from the Yonkers Radio Club. In June 1926 Koenig sold out to George Sulzbach, the new owner of WFBH in Manhattan, with which WRW had shared time. The station operation was absorbed into WFBH, which soon became WPCH.

See also WFBH, WCOH.

WSAP *see* WSDA

WSDA

(23 MARCH 1923–27 DECEMBER 1930)

1923 (WSAP)	360m (833.3kc)	250w.
Mar. 1924 (WSAP)	1140kc s/t WAAM	250w.
June 1927	1320kc s/t WARS, WBBC	500w.
Nov. 1928	1400kc s/t WSGH, WBBC, WLTH, WCGU	500w.

The Seventh Day Adventist Church instituted its broadcast operations in 1923 with a station called WSAP, located in The City Temple at 120th Street and Lenox Avenue in Harlem. Minister Louis K. Dickson served as station manager. On 3 June 1925 the call letters were changed to WSDA. Later that year the church building was sold, and the Adventists moved both congregation and radio station to 122 W. Seventy-sixth Street.

Twice in its short history the Adventists' station left the air, but it was back in the spring of 1926 with a regular schedule. By the end of that year the station described its program schedule as "irregular operation"; it had fallen victim to the general chaos on the then-unregulated airwaves. On 15 June 1927 the new Federal Radio Commission assigned WSDA to share 1320kc with two Brooklyn stations, WBBC and WARS.

A plan to move the WSDA transmitter to a site on City Island was scrapped when the station was bought by the Amateur Radio Specialty Company, owner of WARS. In September 1927 WARS took over operation of the station, which continued to broadcast as WSDA. The facilities of both were moved to the St. George Hotel and WARS became WSGH in February 1928. WSDA remained in irregular operation as one of five broadcasters on 1400kc until 1930, when the Amateur Radio Specialty Company sold its stations to the Paramount Broadcasting Corporation. For the final months on the air, WSDA and WSGH operated in tandem with a hyphenated call sign until the call letters were changed to WFOX.

In 1971 Adventist World Radio was founded. Its network of short-wave stations around the globe made it one of the world's major religious broadcasters. By then, WSDA had been forgotten.

WSGH

(FEBRUARY 1928–27 DECEMBER 1930)

Mar. 1928	1320kc. s/t WBBC	500w.
Nov. 1928	1400kc. s/t WBBC, WCGU, WLTH, WSDA	500w.

The St. George Hotel in Brooklyn Heights was one of the grand landmarks of that fashionable old neighborhood. It was founded in 1885 and by the turn of the century had expanded to become reputedly the biggest hotel in the United States. A thirty-one-story addition in 1929 brought the room count to 2,632. The building at Clark and Henry Streets included a rooftop restaurant and a swimming pool in the basement. For a couple of years in the late 1920s, in keeping with a trend among New York hotels, it also housed its own radio station.

At the end of 1927, WARS was about to lose its studio site with the demolition of the Hotel Shelburne in Brighton Beach and opened a studio at the St. George. Two months later the call letters were changed to WSGH and the station moved to Brooklyn Heights.

Thursday, 16 August 1928

12:01 P.M.	Luncheon Music
12:30	Charlotte Palmer, contralto
12:45	Luncheon Music
1:15	Jean Right, monologues
1:30	Radio news
1:37	Musical comedy tunes
2:00	Charlotte Palmer, contralto
2:15	Helen Leonard, pianist
2:30	Advice to parents
2:45	Tea melodies
3:30	Saunter Around Orchestra
4:00	Off for WBBC
6:00	Nat Feinger's Studio
6:15	Bessie Gutkin, pianist
6:30	Ruth Lifschitz, pianist
6:45	Children's joy
7:00	Off for WBBC
10:00	Half Moon Orchestra
11:00	Joy of Living, sketch
11:15	Herbert Procter, tenor
11:30	Teddy Kayne and Betty Reilly
11:45	The Sunburst Trio

The station at the St. George was able to attract a good group of cabaret and concert artists, who performed in the hotel lounges and ballrooms. It also took over the programming of the Seventh Day Adventists' station WSDA, which had been operated by WARS since 1927.

On 11 November 1928 WSGH was one of hundreds of stations in the country to change frequency and one of five ordered to share 1400kc in Brooklyn. Its broadcast hours were greatly reduced, and early in 1929 the studios were moved out of the St. George to 135 Eastern Parkway. By the end of the year Salvatore D'Angelo had moved to take over the station, and for a while it operated with the dual call letters WSGH-WSDA. The station was moved to the Fox Theatre on Nevins Street, where it became WFOX.

See also WARS, WSDA, WFOX.

WSKQ

(OCTOBER, 1983–1995)

1983	620kHz	5,000w.

During most of its thirty-five years, WVNJ appealed to an upscale audience with middle-of-the-road music, jazz, and show tunes. Its final sign-off in the autumn of 1983 signaled a major change in metropolitan New York radio and in the makeup of the region's population. The station was sold to the Spanish Broadcasting System, a company led by Raul Alarcon Jr. and other Cubans whose broadcasting experience had begun in the days before the Castro revolution. Their Miami outlet, WCMQ, displayed the call letters of Cuba's biggest radio station. For nearly sixty years before the first sign-on of WSKQ, the city's foreign-language broadcasters were all crowded into the upper end of the dial. WSKQ made its appearance right next door to WNBC.

In 1985, the "Super KQ" moved its studios from the Livingston, N.J. transmitter to 1500 Broadway, at Times Square. Five years later it relocated to a townhouse at 26 W. Fifty-sixth Street, the corporate headquarters of the Spanish Broadcasting System. At the end of 1995 the call letters were changed to WXLX.

See also WXLX.

WSOM

(19 FEBRUARY 1927–19 OCTOBER 1927)

Feb. 1927	1040kc s/t WAAT, WGBB	500w.
Apr. 1927	1040kc s/t WKBQ	250w.
June 1927	1020kc s/t WAAT, WGBB	500w.

In early 1927, the Hotel Somerset at 150 W. Forty-seventh Street leased the six-month-old WJBV from George Cook's Union Course Laboratories in Woodhaven, Queens. WSOM became one of a dozen radio stations operating from a New York hotel.

Thursday, 5 May 1927

6:00 P.M.	Skeet's Orchestra
7:00	James Wallace, bass
7:15	Health talk
7:30	Carl Smith, tenor
7:45	Helen Lucia, soprano
8:15	Banjo Buddy, songs
8:30	Bob Schaffer, songs
8:45	Peggy Gilroy, ukelele
9:00	Instrumental trio
9:30	Jack Davis, baritone
9:45	Gladys Walton, songs
10:00	Organ and choral program
10:30	Mac Ohman, minstrels
11:30	Concert ensemble

WSOM kept one of the more continuous schedules during a time when many broadcasters operated intermittently. It was on the air from 6:00 P.M. to midnight on weekdays, 4:00 P.M. to midnight on Saturdays, and on Sunday mornings to broadcast services from the Bedford Park Congregational Church.

After only eight months on the air, the facilities of WSOM were sold to the Debs Memorial Radio Fund which changed the call letters to WEVD.

See also WJBV, WEVD.

WSRR *see* WSTC

WSTC

(18 SEPTEMBER 1941–)

1941	1400kc (WSRR)	250w.
19??	1400kc	1,000w.

The Connecticut panhandle got its second radio station in 1941, eighteen years after the demise of Greenwich's WAAQ. Originally called WSRR, it was owned by Stephen R. Rintoul and had studios at 270 Atlantic Street in Stamford. In 1946, the station was sold to the Western Connecticut Broadcasting Company, a subsidiary of the Stamford *Advocate*, and the call letters were changed to WSTC. At about that time, WSTC joined the Connecticut State Network as well as ABC—nearly the only instance from the heyday of network radio of a suburban New York City outlet affiliating with one of the major chains. Its FM station went on the air at 96.7Mc in October 1947.

The mainstay of WSTC's schedule was local variety, including "The Old Commuter" and "Track No. 4" in the morning and evening drive times. Beulah Bestor shared "Luncheon at the Prime Rib" every weekday at one o'clock.

In one of its most venturesome community-service efforts, on Wednesday, 10 May 1950—following months of careful preparation and rehearsal, and under the close eye of both teachers and WSTC staff—the station was operated for its entire broadcast day by students at Stamford High School. This developed into a regular series of teen-produced broadcasts, which allowed WSTC to step away from its usual middle-of-the-road music format and also gave young people their own, sometimes controversial voice. In 1969, a student announcer protested WSTC's policy against editorializing and remarked, "We'll now have a moment of silence for an editorial that I'm not allowed to say."

Even while the teenagers were both pleasing and provoking their elders, the professionals triggered an incident that would ultimately cost the Western Connecticut Broadcasting Company its license. During the 1969 Stamford mayoral race, scripted remarks by the Democratic and Independent Fusion candidates were censored by WSTC whereas the Republican candidate, who was supported editorially by the *Advocate*, was allowed on the air without review. The matter came to a head in 1971—at the height of the next mayoral campaign—when WSTC owner Kingsley Gillespie agreed to pay a $10,000 fine. He blamed the problem on the poor judgment of WSTC's longtime station manager, Julian Schwartz, who was then under medical care for several physical and emotional maladies. Schwartz had been demoted in 1970 after twenty-four years at the helm of WSTC. In 1977, a federal judge found that WSTC had violated the First Amendment rights of the losing candidates and could be held liable for damages. Central to the judge's ruling was the monopoly that WSTC and the *Advocate* held in the local media.

Much of the broadcasting industry rushed to the station's defense, with all the networks and the Radio-Television News Directors' Association protesting that such action could inhibit robust discussion. Meanwhile, Radio Stamford Inc.—a local group headed by Textron executive Al Donahue and including CBS commentator Andy Rooney—challenged the licenses of WSTC and its FM half, by then known as WYRS. The sale was approved in 1981 for $1.8 million. In 1985, Radio Stamford sold WSTC and WYRS to Chase Broadcasting for $4 million. Four years later, Chase sold both stations—WYRS became WJAZ and played jazz all day—to the Forrest-Brody Group for about $8 million.

WTHE

(1 JANUARY 1965–)

| 1965 | 1520kc (daytime) | 10,000w. |
| 1969 | 1520kHz (daytime) | 1,000w. |

Hoping to be *the* station serving Long Island, WTHE replaced the Herald-Tribune Radio Network's WFYI at the start of 1965. The previous owner had tried to make it a source for classical music; the new station looked in the opposite direction and became the first station on the island to specialize in the country-and-western sound.

Facilities were moved to the old WKBS transmitter site on Maple Place in Mineola, a small building where disc jockeys complained or boasted that they could reach any of the thousands of country-and-western discs in the library without getting up from their seat. In 1969, station manager Richard Winslow and his partners formed Bursam Communications Corporation and bought WTHE. The biggest change made by the new owners was to request a reduction in the station's power—a wise move that allowed them to replace the old high-power directional signal with less wattage but a nondirectional pattern that extended into New York City. When WJRZ dropped its country-music format in 1971, and until WHN became a country-and-western sta-

tion in 1973, WTHE was the only place on AM to turn for country music in the nation's biggest urban area. It was soon presenting live country music broadcasts from around Nassau and Queens.

Even during WTHE's country phase there were programs especially for Long Island's black audience—Tommy Brown presented a soul music show every day at noon—and with the sale to Universal Broadcasting Corporation, the emphasis changed to serve the minority community. Gospel music and religious programs were heard through much of the day, and there were shows especially for Haitian, Guyanese, and even Scandinavian listeners. The studios were moved out of the transmitter building to a location with a little more elbow room, at 260 East Second Street.

WTRC

(25 SEPTEMBER 1926–15 AUGUST 1927)

| 1926 | 1250kc | 50w. |
| 1927 | 1470kc s/t WIBS, WMBQ, WLBX | 50w. |

New York City has long had a majority composed of many minorities, and most of those groups found a radio voice. One of the city's smallest radio stations was briefly operated in the 1920s by a small, potent, and often overlooked group of citizens: Brooklyn Republicans.

WTRC was licensed to the Twentieth Assembly District Republican Club—a district based in the Park Slope neighborhood—and was one of the stations that took to the air during the regulatory limbo of 1926.

Thursday, 2 June 1927

6:15 P.M.	Dinner Music
8:00	Tyle and Tyle, songs
8:15	H. Dods, songs
8:30	Anna Wirth, soprano
8:45	Martha Gorst, piano
9:00	Irish Music
9:30	Music; humor and songs
10:15	Century Orchestra

Whatever political connections the Twentieth District Republicans may have wielded didn't help them much following passage of the Radio Act of 1927. The FRC allowed WTRC 50 watts in a four-way split at 1470kc.

For a station with a political mission, WTRC seems to have spent little of its airtime addressing the issues of the day. Its schedules emphasized light classical and popular music, children's shows, and other entertainment.

The most remarkable fact about WTRC is its progeny. In August 1927 WTRC was sold to the Independent Publishing Company of Washington, D.C., which published the *Fellowship Forum*, a weekly magazine supporting the Ku Klux Klan. The sale covered only WTRC's equipment and initially didn't include a transfer of license, but the commission approved the property changing hands and granted a new permit to broadcast. WTRC's equipment was set up at Mount Vernon Hills, Va., and in November the station returned to the air as WTFF. At that time, Fellowship Forum publisher James S. Vance said he intended to eventually be allowed 50,000 watts of power.

WTFF was soon moved to Washington, Vance changed the call letters to WJSV and later sold the station to the Columbia Broadcasting System, which operated it as WJSV until the call letters became WTOP in 1943. So today's 50,000-watt CBS station in the nation's capital had its genesis in 1926 Brooklyn Republicans through the Ku Klux Klan.

WTRL

(18 DECEMBER 1926–1 SEPTEMBER 1928)

1926	1450kc	15w.
1927	930kc (s/t WODA)	15w.

Radio entrepreneur Donald W. May established the Technical Radio Laboratory at Midland Park, N.J., about five miles north of Paterson, and began operating WTRL three weeks after his WDWM went on the air from Newark. In April 1927 the Federal Radio Commission ordered it to share time with WODA/Paterson on 930kc. That summer, May moved WDWM (which had taken over 930kc) to Asbury Park and apparently paid little attention to WTRL, whose license the FRC soon moved to revoke.

May told a U.S. Senate committee in February 1928 that the FRC had treated him unfairly when it had refused to grant WTRL a power increase. In June, New York area radio inspector Arthur Batcheller reported to the FRC that the station had been partly dismantled and had been out of operation for some time. WTRL gained some brief notoriety when radio inspectors reported that its transmitter was located in a barn and that "the transmitter room indicated its use for the housing of innumerable puppies."

In a letter to the commission, Senator James Watson of Indiana wrote that the dogs "may account for some of the 'howls' that we hear about radio.... Also these yelps and snarls and growls going out on the night air may be accepted by some people as an inferior grade of grand opera or by others as high-class jazz.... The gentleman who operates

that station evidently has an eye for thrift if not an ear for harmony, for in all this broad land there probably is not another individual to whom it ever occurred to hitch a dog kennel to a radio station. Inasmuch as you have no jurisdiction over the kennel, but have over the station, it is probably wise for you to demand a separation of the two industries by stopping the station." Despite May's legal appeals, the "dog station" was shut down.

See also WDWM.

WVFW

(25 OCTOBER 1933–1 MAY 1941)

1935	1400kc s/t WBBC, WLTH, WARD	500w.
1941	1430kc	500w.

The Paramount Broadcasting Corporation's WFOX, bearing a prestigious name and studios in the Fox Theatre building in Brooklyn, was still unable to break out of the pack of small Brooklyn stations sharing 1400kc. Operation of the station was largely in the hands of Salvatore D'Angelo, who was not only a veteran radioman but also a veteran of World War I. In 1933 he had the call letters changed, initially to WFWV and then, at the suggestion of the Veterans of Foreign Wars, to WVFW. He brought members of the veterans' organization into the operation of the station, and for the next seven and one half years WVFW operated for the benefit, and sometimes under the protection, of the veterans' group, which then had five thousand members in Brooklyn. Studios were at 49 Fourth Avenue.

In 1934, ownership was formally transferred by Salvatore D'Angelo to his brother Anthony, a stevedore with no broadcasting experience. During a time when federal regulators sought to revoke the license of WVFW and the three stations with which it shared time, the "official Voice of the Veterans of Foreign Wars" drew even closer to its namesake, and in January 1936 complete control of the station was transferred to the VFW. Past County Commander Harold Burke became president of the station, with Sal D'Angelo continuing as managing director. Studios remained in the Fox Theatre Building, and the station was run on a commercial basis, with part of its income dedicated to the support of veterans' relief activities.

A year later, with its license under challenge by WEVD, WVFW was defended in an FCC hearing by a past national commander of the VFW, who stated that the station was part of the organization's Americanism campaigns. At the same hearing, however, it was revealed that Anthony D'Angelo was still the sole stockholder in WVFW, that he had taken control during his brother's illness in 1933, and that his role was limited to signing a few papers.

WVFW shared time with three other Brooklyn stations at 1400kc and, like them, directed its programs to the borough's ethnic audiences. Much of the airtime was in Yiddish or Italian. Its license was nearly canceled in January, 1936 when the Federal Communications Commission sought to untangle the "Brooklyn radio fight" and grant 1400kc to the proposed *Brooklyn Daily Eagle* station. But the FCC reversed itself, and the VFW had another victory ribbon.

With the establishment of WBYN in 1941, WVFW was merged into the new full-time station and Salvatore D'Angelo became one of the partners in the Unified Broadcasting Co.

See also WFOX, WBYN.

W V I P

(27 OCTOBER 1957–14 SEPTEMBER 1997)

1957   1310kc   500w.

Mount Kisco, in the forested, rolling hills of northeastern Westchester, is home to a radio station that was quite literally designed to enhance the village's reputation. In the mid-1950s some former farmland was converted to an industrial and office park. Developer Monroe O'Flyn was joined by Martin Stone, a lawyer who had entered the broadcasting industry in the 1940s as creator of the network series "Author Meets the Critics." The commercial development was called Radio Circle, and at its outer loop was a station originally to be named WWES. O'Flyn and Stone felt that merely getting Mount Kisco's name on the air regularly would draw attention to the exurban village and to Radio Circle.

The studios of WVIP were designed by Edward Larrabee Barnes, then a young architect with no previous experience with broadcast facilities. (His later work would include the IBM Building in New York and the campus of SUNY-Purchase.) Barnes figured that radio signals spiral out from the source—technically they don't but the image is apt—and built a compact circular structure housing a spiral of spaces rotating out from a round master control room that looked into four studios. Barnes even asked a composer friend to create a spiraling musical signature, which was never used. But his work made WVIP nearly the only radio station in the New York metropolitan area that is of architectural interest. As the first occupant of Radio Circle, WVIP would also serve to attract new businesses. Early staffers referred to the still-unpaved circle as the "Burma Road."

The premiere of WVIP on a Sunday in October 1957

featured a four-hour benefit broadcast in support of a local hospital and recounted episodes of Westchester history. For this curtain-raiser, Stone solicited the participation of several community residents, including publisher Bennett Cerf, CBS newsman Alan Jackson, and ABC sportscaster Howard Cosell.

WVIP's first news director was Richard K. Doan, who went on to become the TV critic of the *New York Herald-Tribune* and a columnist for *TV Guide*. On Doan's staff was young Morton Dean, later an anchorman for CBS and ABC News. Musician Winston Sharples created a fresh jingle package for the new station, including a tune whose lyric named fifty-seven towns in the WVIP listening area.

In 1957, financier John Hay "Jock" Whitney (brother-in-law of CBS chairman William Paley) bought the *Herald-Tribune* and set out to expand the newspaper's suburban readership. The *Trib* was one of the city's most authoritative dailies (to its many faithful readers, it was the *Times* with a funnies page). The paper printed some of the city's best radio coverage and supplied newscasts over the years to WMCA, WOR, and WPAT. The newspaper even had a claim to being a radio pioneer: the publicity-minded *Herald* brought Marconi to America to transmit results of the 1899 America's Cup yacht race. Sixty years later its successor would enter the radio business itself.

Whitney brought Martin Stone into his new venture. An offer was made to buy WPAT in Paterson, N.J., which would give the *Trib*'s network a foothold in the New Jersey suburbs and good metropolitan coverage. That offer was rejected, so Stone and Whitney set about to create a chain unique in the history of New York radio.

On Monday morning, 2 March 1959, WVIP became flagship of the Herald Tribune Radio Network. It soon added three other outlets: WNRC in New Rochelle (which became WVOX), WKIT in Mineola, Long Island (renamed WFYI), and WSKL, up the Hudson Valley in Saugerties (which moved to Kingston and became WGHQ). So with a coverage area that swept the eastern and northern suburbs almost to the Capital District, the respected metropolitan newspaper began to reach deeper into the daily lives of an affluent suburban populace.

Initially the network fed all its programs from WVIP with only cutaways for local announcements. The day began with a packed three hours of news, sports, and weather as well as feature stories and commentaries from that day's *Trib*. If this didn't make the morning paper redundant, it at least saved time for the busy commuter.

Monday, 2 March 1959

6:00 A.M.	Operation Early Bird
9:00	Studio in the Round
11:00	Stars and Strings
12:00 Noon	Communique
1:00	Keyboard
2:00	Box Office
3:00	Studio in the Round

5:00   Communique
6:00   Sign Off

Musical programs each had a distinct theme or mood, and the entire operation was clean and low-key. Morton Dean was sent out to train news personnel at the other three stations. Among the alumni of WVIP were newscasters Julie Vaughn and Cameron Swayze. Several staffers went on to run other New York area stations, including WOR's Bob Bruno, Ken Harris, who managed WHLI, and William O'Shaughnessy, who bought WVOX when the *Herald-Tribune* and its radio network went out of existence.

The *Trib* folded in 1966, and its experiment in suburban radio came to an end. Martin Stone became sole owner of WVIP and continued to run it for more than thirty years as a community-minded station with a sophisticated sound. The station's qualities were recognized far beyond its coverage area: in a survey of American radio, the British Broadcasting Corporation called WVIP the outstanding small station in the United States.

In 1974 WVIP took a step that enhanced its unique status in the radio industry when it added cable television to its radio operations. Part of Edward Larrabee Barnes' spiral was made into a small TV studio, and the VIP cable channel carried the audio from WVIP AM and FM as well as local video programming.

During the overnight hours of Wednesday, 10 September 1997, a fire destroyed WVIP. The studio building was unoccupied at the time, and when Martin Stone came to view the destruction he was so shocked that he needed to be hospitalized. Other stations offered equipment and records and the station was back on the air from the adjacent transmitter building by 9:00 AM. Despite an outpouring of community and industry support, on Saturday, 14 September, Martin Stone phoned the station and told listeners that WVIP would go silent.

WVNJ[1]

(7 DECEMBER 1948–1 OCTOBER 1983)

1948   620kc   5,000w.

The Griffith Piano Corporation's experience with radio began in 1921 when it supplied the first pianos to WJZ. The radio industry had grown up when Griffith founded the Newark Broadcasting Corporation and put its own station on the air as an adjunct to the music business. WVNJ bowed in without fanfare at noon on 7 December 1948, but on the nineteenth of that month it held a gala dedication from the Griffith Auditorium honoring contralto Marian Anderson

WVIP's studio-in-the-round. It burned down in September 1997.

and featuring stars of the opera and concert world. With 5,000 watts at 620kc, WVNJ claimed New Jersey's strongest signal. Programs originated from the window of the Griffith store at 45 Central Avenue; the station even planned (and initially abandoned) an FM affiliate.

WVNJ presented a broad range of musical styles, including Latin rhythms in the evening. In November 1953, Griffith sold WVNJ to the Scudder family, owners of the *Newark News,* which gave up WNJR to move down the dial. The *News* brought over general manager Harry Goodwin from WNJR and hired a new chief engineer with a long resumé: Peter Testan, once the owner of Brooklyn's WBBC and a partner in the ill-fated WBYN, which became WNJR. WVNJ even moved to the old WNJR studios at 91 Halsey Street.

Tuesday, 8 December 1953

6:00 A.M.	Wake with Music
7:05	Meditations
7:10	Learn to Live
7:15	Unity Viewpoint
7:30	News; Weather
7:40	Gospel Tabernacle
7:55	Goodwill Mission
8:00	Percy Crawford
8:30	News; Music
9:00	Music Hall
11:00	Harmonies
12:00 Noon	Club 620
1:00	Varieties
2:00	New Records
3:00	Rendezvous
5:00	Through the Years
5:30	News; Cavalcade of Music
7:00	Rendezvous
9:00	Pops Concert
9:30	News; Gospel Ambassadors
10:00	Baritones
11:00	Hal Tunis—talk show
1:00 A.M.	Big Joe's Happiness Exchange

(hourly news at :30 all day)

Accompanying the changes in ownership was a music format that would challenge WVNJ's North Jersey competitor, WPAT. "Great Albums of Music," vocal and instrumental standards and show tunes, were heard throughout the broadcast day. Classical music was part of the weekend schedule, with a complete opera on Sunday nights. There were even simulated variety shows, complete with recorded applause, emceed by announcers Ted Johnson, Alan Saunders, Gary Lesters, and Bob Harris, who would sometimes flip over a record and call the artist back for an encore. (Bob Harris had lost a leg in World War II and wore an artificial limb, whose joint would squeak loudly. It was an odd sight to see Harris seated before the WVNJ microphone, speaking in his smooth and precise baritone, as he lubricated his leg with 3-in-1 Oil.)

"The Best of Broadway" gave WVNJ an unmatched appeal to fans of American musical theatre in the metropolitan area. The station even published its own monthly program guide, a sure sign it had found a selective and faithful audience. Advertising in the trade papers in 1967, WVNJ

WVNJ featured "Great Albums of Music" in this 1965 program guide.

boasted that "hippies hate us" and called itself "the grown-up sound of today."

In 1970, the Scudder family, which had founded the *Newark News* in 1883, sold the paper to Media General Inc. The deal did not include WVNJ, but in 1978 the Scudders sold the radio station to Herb Saltzman's Sabre Broadcasting Corp. The new owners repositioned WVNJ from "beautiful music" to a big-band and nostalgia format. The station had joined the ABC Information Network in 1968, but in the early 1980s it affiliated with both the ABC Entertainment Network and TalkNet, a program service by its neighbor on the New York radio dial, NBC. In October, 1981 jazz deejay Les Davis came to WVNJ-FM with a nightly program from the Greene Street Club, aired live from 8:00 P.M. till 1:00 A.M. and then replayed on tape till 6:00 A.M. In June 1983, WVNJ sold its FM outlet and moved its evening jazz programs to the AM side during its remaining months on the air.

In its last years, "WVNJoy" returned to an easy-listening format. In October 1983 the Spanish Broadcasting System bought the Newark station for $3.2 million, and it became WSKQ.

WVNJ II

(13 DECEMBER 1993–)

1994   1160kHz   10,000w. day /
                                   2,500w. night

A decade after the demise of Newark's WVNJ, the call letters were again heard, from a new station with studios in Teaneck and a transmitter in Oakland, N.J., the official city of license. The construction permit for WVNJ was issued to Rama Communications, but even before the station went on the air it was sold to Bursam Communications, which also owned WTHE in Mineola. The original schedule included some rock oldies, paid religious programs, and talk shows, including the controversial G. Gordon Liddy. This wasn't exactly "Great Albums of Music," but many fans of the original WVNJ must have come back on 6 January 1996 when the Oakland station began to send out some familiar sounds and equally familiar voices.

WVNJ not only switched to a big-band and nostalgia format, but its deejays also brought back some memories. Former WNEW announcers Jim Lowe and Mike Prelee hosted regular programs, as did Ted Brown, Del Dixon, and Bill Owen, one of WABC's original "Swingin' 7." Program director Bill Gaghan did the evening show.

Overnight listeners could again listen to the "Milkman's Matinee," with George Tucker. Bill Owen's midday program

was entitled "The Make Believe Ballroom," a title that had been part of New York radio for over fifty years. At the same time, WJUX-FM ("Jukebox Radio") was also airing a "Make Believe Ballroom." In July 1996 WJUX went into court to stop WVNJ from using the title (which earlier in its history had been the object of dispute between Martin Block in New York and Al Jarvis in Los Angeles) and to cease calling itself "your hometown radio station."

WVNJ protested to the FCC that WJUX, a noncommercial FM station based in Paramus, was illegally bringing its signal into the New York area through low-power "translator" stations in northern New Jersey. Audiences remained unmoved by the legal dispute. WJUX was using the familiar old WNEW jingle package, but for fans who remembered the swing era, there was a special attraction in hearing WVNJ at almost the same location as WNEW on the AM dial.

WVOX

(2 MARCH 1959–)

1959   1460kc (daytime)   500w.

New Rochelle's WNRC was on the skids when it was purchased by VIP Radio Inc. and was brought into the new suburban network organized by the *New York Herald-Tribune*. Between the end of the WNRC era and the advent of the *Trib* network, the station was known as WWES. The network was set up to cover mostly Long Island, Westchester, and the lower Hudson Valley, but WVOX, on both AM and FM, gave it some coverage into the Bronx, Manhattan, and Queens and attracted listeners inside the city, especially since the *Trib* squeezed its network's schedule onto the daily radio-TV page.

Most programming was fed to WVOX from the network base in Mount Kisco until both the *Herald-Tribune* and its broadcast operation went out of business in 1966. Whitney Communications, which the year before had written off the station as a $372,000 tax loss, sold WVOX to the Hudson-Westchester Radio Company headed by Harry Thayer and general manager William O'Shaughnessy. The FM operation was split off to become WRTN ("Return Radio," a big-band and nostalgia format), and WVOX continued heavily committed to local public service, a commitment that wasn't easy.

Facilities on the lower level of the Pershing Building in New Rochelle were described by O'Shaughnessy as an "upholstered sewer." In 1975, O'Shaughnessy assumed complete ownership of WVOX and personally led it to a new popularity. Since the demise of the Herald-Tribune Network, the station had had no clear community identity. Ethnic appeal was a challenge, given the melting-pot population of New Rochelle. The station instituted a long-form musical program called "Music from the Forum" and scattered news reports throughout the day from towns around its coverage area. There was even a "Co-op City Report" from the high-rise community in the Bronx.

WVOX moved into improved studios at One Broadcast Forum and continued to emphasize its news and information services to southern Westchester and nearby Connecticut.

See also WNRC, WVIP.

WVOX's general manager William O'Shaughnessy reports from the station's news car in 1965.

WVP

(1920–1922)

| 1920? | 1,450m (206.8kc) | 3,000w. |

WVP was owned by the U.S. Army Signal Corps and was operated by volunteers in the Amateur Radio Reserve, Second Corps. It was located on Bedloe's Island, home of the Statue of Liberty and one of the favorite sites for early radio. The antenna was just behind the statue, and with 3,000 watts, it was one of the more powerful stations in the area.

Although it operated on a military wavelength below the frequencies assigned to broadcasters—it would today be considered a "long wave" station—it could be received on many of the radio sets then in use. But WVP was as much a broadcaster as anyone else at the time, promising that "programs of educational and amusement value will be rendered," and it played an important role in the development of the medium. Programs were provided by a range of institutions, from the *Brooklyn Daily Eagle* and the *Evening Mail* to veterans' associations and Scout troops.

Hardly anyone who came to sing, play, or speak over WVP had ever experienced radio before, on either side of the microphone. (At least they gave the lie to the old notion that New Yorkers never visit the Statue of Liberty.) During an era before the time when broadcasting stations scheduled discretely titled shows, the "program" was usually an extended card of musicians and lecturers. The presentation

would begin at 9:00 P.M., and sign-off came when the performers had used up their repertoire or when the equipment showed signs of instability.

Brooklyn Postmaster W. C. Burton visited the WVP transmitter to observe "Postal Improvement Week." Rose Roden spoke on "The Meaning of Music Week." There were talks on "The Romance of Steam" and "How the Radiophone Will Relieve the Loneliness of Western Ranchers." Ampico lent a player piano, and Okeh Records ferried some of its artists out to the island. Probably the most valuable series of broadcasts by WVP was a five-minute "Instruction in Radio," and there was a regular session of reading and responding to listeners' mail.

See also WYCB.

WWDJ

(17 MAY 1971–)

| 1971 | 970kc | 5,000w. |

The demise of WJRZ and the premiere of WWDJ took place at about the same time that WMCA switched from a rock-music to a talk format, which gave the new station in Hackensack its first niche. WJRZ had been playing country and western and switched to rock even before the sale to Pacific and Southern Broadcasting Company had been approved.

WWDJ was WABC's only real AM competition in the city for a brief time. Unfortunately, the nighttime signal was lost to most listeners.

Former WNEW manager David Croninger came to run the new station. Detroit deejay Bill Bailey, ex–WMCA "Good Guy" Dean Anthony, and a nighttime host called Bwana Johnny were "the screamin' jocks from Hackensack." Don LaVine and Bill Emerson were holdovers from WJRZ; newscasters Steve Hollis and Bob Brown hailed from WAAT days. Engineer Frank McLean had begun in the WAAT mailroom in 1930.

Newscasts were heard at fifteen minutes past every other hour (11:15, 1:15, 3:15, etc.) and ran for ten minutes, except for the morning drive time, when ten minutes of news was heard at a quarter to and quarter after each hour. Sunday mornings were taken up by a three-hour call-in discussion program, "Your County Speaks," conducted by *Bergen Record* reporter Gene Francis.

WWDJ was the voice of New York Mets baseball through the end of the 1971 season, continuing the agreement with WJRZ. News coverage became a bit more conventional, five minutes on the hour and half hour. But the

frantic rock sound continued, Don Cannon replaced Bill Bailey in the morning, music director Mike Phillips took the noontime show, and program director Sean Casey was heard during the afternoon drive time.

The "Wide World of Disc Jockeys" was the only AM competition to WABC's rock format during the early 1970s, and it was obvious by 1974 that the station wasn't attracting a sufficient number of rock fans, most of whom were following their music over to the stereophonic FM band.

By 1974, WWDJ was hurting badly. The station's signal blanketed northern Jersey well enough but didn't penetrate to the corners of the Five Boroughs. The announcers, members of the American Federation of Television and Radio Artists, went on strike. It was all too much. In the wee hours of 1 April 1974, WWDJ played its last rock tune and said goodbye. It returned with "inspirational programming on WWDJ—the new voice of inspiration for the metropolitan area." Since the change took place on April Fool's Day, some listeners thought the hymns and sermons were intended as a joke. They weren't. WWDJ had become the first full-time commercial AM religious station in the New York area. Working with national religious broadcasting sales agents, WWDJ brought the nation's top market such programs as "Back to the Bible" and "Haven of Rest." Jimmy Swaggart's "Campmeeting Hour" was heard every morning at 9:00, and services from the Akron Baptist Temple in Ohio were now available to listeners in metropolitan New York.

A few rock fans with a taste for gospel music stayed tuned, but WWDJ's new audience was mostly drawn from Fundamentalist Christians, some of whom were so grateful that they mailed contributions to the station. The money was sent back, with a suggestion that the listener support the organization whose program they enjoyed. WWDJ had no need for charity; within three months of changing to a religious format, it was back in the black. Pacific and Southern had merged with Combined Communications, one of the nation's largest broadcast owners. "Your County Speaks" was shifted to Saturday night and then to Saturday morning and was finally canceled.

In August 1978, WWDJ was sued by ASCAP for violating the copyright on some thirty songs. The station responded that it should not have to pay the same fees as paid by stations that broadcast music all day.

In 1994, WWDJ was sold to Salem Media and became a sister station of WMCA. Its programming included Andy Andersen's call-in program as well as "Money Matters" with Larry Burkett and such well-established religious programs as Billy Graham's "Hour of Decision."

W W G L *see* W M S G

W W R L

(26 AUGUST 1926–)

1926	1160kc	100w.
1926	1120kc s/t WBBC, WBKN, WBMS, WIBI	100w.
1927	1500kc s/t WGOP, WBMS	100w.
1934	1500kc s/t WMIL, WCNW, WMBQ, WLBX	250w.
1941 (29 Apr.)	1490kc s/t WCNW	250w.
1941	1600kc	250w.
1950	1600kc	5,000w.

The year 1926 was a time of clumsy growth and terrible tantrums for the infant broadcasting industry. Technology was developing too fast for many stations to keep pace. American radio was turning into a booming business, albeit one seriously threatened by its own disorder. In 1926 the federal government was forced to admit that its only legal framework for issuing a broadcasting license was a fourteen-year-old law that required it to allow any citizen to open a station and that made shutting anyone down nearly impossible. Stations metastasized up and down the radio dial.

In the last six months of 1926 no fewer than eighteen stations went on the air in the New York area. Most of these were small operations broadcasting from storerooms, offices, even private homes. This didn't necessarily mean that the people who built them were inexperienced or ignorant of what they were doing. William Reuman had been in radio nearly all his life, receiving his first ham radio license in 1912 at age fifteen, serving as a shipboard wireless operator, and later working as chief engineer of WFBH. When WFBH became WPCH, Reuman left to found Woodside Radio Laboratory, which built and serviced radio sets and was initially the principal source of support for WWRL. WWRL took to the air at midnight on Thursday, 26 August 1926.

Blue burlap was draped over the walls of the Reuman parlor at 41-30 Fifty-eighth Street in Woodside, Queens, and a transmitter and antenna were installed in the backyard. The Reumans continued to live in the house. Friends and neighbors dropped by to sing, play, or announce the programs.

Sunday, 21 November 1926

2:00 P.M.	Dance Orchestra
2:30	Russ and Dixon, songs
3:00	Radio Hour
4:00	Harmony Girls
4:15	Volly Endrias, contralto
4:30	William Muller, pianist
4:45	Ethel Zimmerman, songs
5:00	Templeton's Ramblers

Most of the artists were local amateurs whose appearance on WWRL would be a high spot in their careers, although Ethel Zimmerman, a singer from Astoria, would go on to superstardom as Ethel Merman. Others who got their start in the Reuman parlor included actor Eddie Bracken—who appeared as a boy singing "mother songs"—and announcer Art Ford, who would later host WNEW's "Milkman's Matinee."

Scheduled programming often ran until midnight, at which time Reuman invited performers and friends to hang around for a nightcap and a party, leaving the station on the air. In a day when broadcasters often maintained an unnatural formality, the impromptu performances, conviviality, and small talk after hours on WWRL resulted in some spontaneous and appealing programs.

By 1927, Reuman had begun to explore the commercial possibilities of WWRL and was selling time to local merchants for three dollars a spot. At the same time, the new Federal Radio Commission was attempting to end the disorder on the airwaves and directed WWRL—as well as WBKN, WBMS, and WIBI, with whom it was then sharing the 1120 spot on the dial—to move up to the highest AM frequency at that time, 1500 kilocycles. Reuman protested that if he shifted to a frequency that high (beyond the tuning range of some older radios), "our signals would be practically unheard. It is evident that our commercial contracts, which now amount to sixty hours per week, would suffer greatly." But the station did move, it survived, and in 1929 Reuman incorporated as the Long Island Broadcasting Corporation.

WWRL was one of the first stations in the metropolitan area to gather and report local news. "The Voice of Queens County" played to ethnic groups in at least a dozen languages. Program director Lou Cole personally announced shows in Italian, German, French, Hungarian, Slovak, and Czech, as well as English. From its earliest days, WWRL aired programs for Jewish and black listeners. A regular Saturday-afternoon feature was "Martha's Kiddie Hour," with Martha Wallace presenting talented tots as young as age two.

In 1938, WWRL took over the time of WMBQ, the Williamsburg station that had gone silent. When the North American Regional Broadcast Agreement rearranged the radio dial in 1941, WWRL was reassigned for one day, 29 April, from 1500 to 1490kc and then was moved to the new top of the dial at 1600. With WCNW's departure from 1600

WWRL ad from 1959.

two days before Christmas 1941, WWRL came into full possession of "The High Spot on Your Dial."

Edith Dick, who had started as a stenographer at WWRL when she was nineteen, rose to general manager in 1946 at the age of twenty-nine. She was one of the few female station heads in the country and possibly the youngest. Also in 1946, when the United Nations was temporarily meeting at the former World's Fair site in Flushing Meadow, WWRL carried meetings of the world organization. In 1951, the city of license was officially changed from Woodside to New York.

Ethnic programming was diversified, adding Greek, Syrian, Irish, Ukrainian, Russian, and several Scandanavian tongues, though most programs were intended for Spanish-speaking and African-American audiences. By the late 1950s, WWRL was on the air twenty-four hours a day, most of the time in Spanish. "Noche de Ronda" was the overnight show, and the "Spanish Breakfast Club" began at 5:00 A.M. For the black audience, WWRL featured some of New York's best disc jockeys: Reggie Lavong, Hal Jackson, and Tommy Smalls, known as Dr. Jive. Others whose careers took them to WWRL included Jane Tillman Irving, Chuck Leonard, and sportscaster Art Rust Jr.

William Reuman retired and sold WWRL to a group headed by Egmont Sonderling in January, 1964. The station then concentrated on black-oriented programming, playing rhythm and blues and, for a while in the late 1970s, affiliating with the Mutual Black Network. In 1980, Sonderling merged with Viacom International, and a year later WWRL joined the ill-fated Enterprise Radio Network, an all-sports network. In 1982, Viacom donated WWRL to the United Negro College Fund, which sold the station for $1.5 million to the Unity Broadcasting Network, a subsidiary of the National Black Network. WWRL took its place as a network flagship. The Top 40 music was replaced by contemporary black gospel and reggae music as well as live broadcasts from houses of worship on most evenings and on weekends.

The last station on the dial was also the last in the metropolitan area whose technical conditions required it to keep an engineer at the transmitter at all times; it was allowed to install remote control in 1988. To expand its coverage in the mid–1990s, WWRL applied for a power increase to 25,000 watts and sought to buy WLNG in Sag Harbor, Long Island, also on 1600kHz, and WERA in Plainfield, N.J., close by at 1590.

Through all these developments, one thing was unchanged. Although the transmitter was moved from the backyard to the meadows of Secaucus, N.J., the studios and offices of WWRL remained at 41-30 Fifty-eighth Street in the Woodside section of Queens, the address that performers had sought out in 1926 to be greeted by Bill Reuman welcoming them into his home and his radio station. And of all the stations that took to the air in New York during the lawless era of the mid–1920s, WWRL was the only one still radiating in the late 1990s.

WWRV

(AUGUST 1989)

| 1989 | 1330kc | 5,000w. |

Radio Vision Christiana Management Corporation—a branch of the Hispanic Pentecostal Congregations of New York, New Jersey, and Connecticut—began leasing seven hours a day from religious broadcaster WNYM in 1983. Six years later Salem Media, which owned WNYM, purchased WMCA and, having ensured its place on the New York AM dial, agreed to sell the 1330 outlet to Radio Vision. The sale price was $12 million, which was also the purchase price for WMCA.

WWRV became only the third New York AM station to successfully operate noncommercially (WNYC and the Jehovah's Witnesses' WBBR were the first two). It also became the first Spanish-language religious broadcaster in the city, with inspirational talk and counseling, religious music, and revival meetings.

"World Wide Radio Vision" closed down the old WBBR facilities at Rossville, Staten Island, that it had inherited from WNYM, leaving the city's most outer borough without an AM station. New studios were established at 240 Broadway in Paterson, N.J., and a new transmitter was switched on at a site in Hackensack shared with fellow religious broadcaster WWDJ.

In 1994, Radio Vision Christiana International opened a 100,000-watt station on 535kHz on South Caicos Island in the Caribbean, relaying WWRV programming around the clock. A station whose signal had trouble covering all corners of New York's five boroughs was now reaching a regular audience in South America.

See also WBBR, WNYM.

WWZ

(24 MARCH 1922–5 NOVEMBER 1923)

| 1922 | 360m | 100w. |

Department stores were among the first institutions to enter the broadcasting business. John Wanamaker & Company had involved itself in wireless communications from the days of spark-gap transmitters; a Marconi installation flashed sales information between its stores in New York and

Philadelphia in 1912. (It was at the New York store that young Marconi operator David Sarnoff monitored rescue information—*not* the SOS—when the Titanic sank.)

Wanamaker's put two broadcasting stations on the air at about the same time, WOO in Philadelphia and WWZ in New York. The Philadelphia station operated through the 1920s; the New York outlet lasted little more than a year and a half. WWZ was one of ten New York area radio stations dividing time on the sole broadcasting frequency of 833 kilocycles during radio's first years. Rival Bamberger's had put WOR on the air a month before, and Gimbel's would later launch WGBS. The Wanamaker's studio was the most sumptuous of all, with a chandelier above the grand piano.

Tuesday, 29 August 1922

1:15 P.M.	Excerpts from "Aida," as recorded for the Victrola
1:25	Timely Hints from *House and Garden*; subject, "Making the Kitchen Colorful"
1:35	"Midsummer Music in Lighter Vein," as recorded for the Ampico by the Famous Trio
1:50	Fashion Talks for Men from *Vanity Fair*; subject, "The Latest Word on Men's Fashions from London"
2:00	Excerpts from "Carmen," as recorded for the Victrola
2:15	Off the air
7:30	Children's Hour by Elsie Jean
7:45	"Children's Songs," by Leota E. Fischer, soprano
8:00	Joint recital by T. A. Yagodka, pianist and composer of Hindu and Oriental music; string quartet

Rodman Wanamaker was excited by the possibilities of radio, and his leadership of a special committee appointed by Mayor John Hylan led to the founding of station WNYC. But WWZ was a short-lived merchandising phenomenon of the New York store. Wanamaker's continued to advertise on radio. Its sponsorship of 106 concert programs made it WJZ's biggest customer in 1923.

In the 1940s, the Wanamaker store housed a studio of the DuMont Television Network's WABD, channel 5.

	(1995–)	
1995	620kHz	5,000w.

The Spanish Broadcasting System changed the call letters of its station WSKQ to WXLX in 1995 and brought the Tex-Mex sound to the largely Caribbean Latino audience in metropolitan New York. The music was then enjoying a general surge in popularity, and there were more than a few listeners who tuned in even though they might not understand every word.

The staff brought a depth of experience. Program director Polito Vega was a veteran from the days of WBNX, and newscaster Enrique Girona started in New York radio at WHOM. The news director was Renato Morffi, while Luis Miranda specialized in covering the political scene. Even with the strength of the local news team, many of WXLX's newscasts originated from the SBS newsroom at WCMQ in Miami. Deejays included Carlos Knaugh, Carlos Cabrerra, Manny Santana, and Luisa Martinez. They made WXLX a music-and-news station with a distinct sound in both music and news.

The studios were at 29 W. Fifty-sixth Street in Manhattan; a new transmitter was installed at Lyndhurst, N.J. The city of license was officially Newark—reminder that this spot on the dial was earlier occupied by the original WVNJ. But shortly after it was established, WXLX applied to move its broadcast operation to Jersey City, giving that municipality its first radio station since WHOM had abandoned it for Manhattan in 1946.

WYCB

	(1922)	
1922?	1,450m (206.6kc)	3,000w.

WYCB was a broadcasting station of the U.S. Army Signal Corps. It was situated at one of the city's best locations: Governor's Island, between lower Manhattan and Brooklyn, and was sister station to WVP, which shared Bedloe's Island with the Statue of Liberty. It was operated by the Amateur Radio Reserve, a civilian organization open to anyone sixteen years of age and older with one year of radio experience. The Reserve was composed mostly of ham operators who used the Signal Corps facility to aid in the transfer of wireless messages (a precursor to the Military Affiliate Radio Service later run by hams and the Pentagon).

February, 1922

9:00 P.M.	musical program
9:05	Talk on Amateur Radio Reserve
9:15	Musical program
9:30	A lecture on "Electrode Vacuum Tubes" by C. J. McBrearty

WYCB transmitted on long wave, on a frequency allocated for "government and public broadcasting," and kept a nightly schedule from 9:00 to 9:55. Given the determination of radio buffs and the poor selectivity of early receivers, the station could be picked up easily and had a wide audience.

See also WVP.

(1989–)

1989	1480kHz	5,000w.

The creation of WZRC by Infinity Broadcasting marked a reversal of conventional thinking about programming on the upper end of New York's AM dial. Since

"Z-Rock" bumper sticker.

the late 1920s, the frequencies above 1200 in the city were regarded as best left for the enjoyment of ethnic and specialized audiences. WZRC's predecessor was WJIT (and before that, WHOM), a stalwart of the "Spanish Main"— the stations at 1280/1380/1480, which were well-established with Hispanic listeners. But WZRC believed that it could attract a wide audience of fans of heavy-metal rock music.

"Z-Rock" was a service of the Dallas-based Satellite Music Network, which was so anxious to enter the New York market that it negotiated a deal with Infinity for the time of WJIT. Z-Rock was poorly promoted, it had a harsh edge (commercials sometimes contained profanity), and the WZRC signal was weak in the suburbs and the outer boroughs.

So in December 1992, WZRC switched to country music—another oddity on the upper end of the AM band. But a year later the 1480 spot returned to more traditional ways, recognizing changes in the city's ethnic makeup. In 1993, Infinity signed a lease agreement with a Korean programming service making WZRC the first full-time Korean-language station in New York.

APPENDIX

NEW YORK SPORTS ON THE RADIO

Baseball

Brooklyn Dodgers	1939–42	WOR	Red Barber, Bill Slater, Stan Lomax
	1943–57	WHN/WMGM	Barber, Connie Desmond, Vin Scully ('48) Scully and Desmond ('51)
New York Giants	1946–57	WMCA	Russ Hodges and Mel Allen, Ernie Harwell ('51)
New York Yankees	1943–45	WOR	Bill Slater, Stan Lomax, Connie Desmond ('45)
	1946–57	WINS	Mel Allen, Red Barber ('51), Jim Woods
	1958–59	WMGM	Allen, Barber, Phil Rizzuto ('58)
	1960–66	WCBS	Allen, Rizzuto, Jerry Coleman ('61), Joe Garagiola ('64)
	1967–71	WHN	
	1972–76	WMCA	
	1977–81	WINS	
	1982–	WABC	
New York Mets	1961–63	WABC	
	1964–66	WHN	
	1967–71	WJRZ/WWDJ	
	1972–74	WHN	
	1975–77	WNEW	
	1978–86	WMCA	
	1986–	WFAN	

Football

Brooklyn Dodgers	1939–42	WHN	Red Barber, Bill Slater

New York Giants	1943–57	WHN/WMGM	Red Barber, Marty Glickman ('49)
	1958–60	WCBS	
	1961–91	WNEW	Kyle Rote, Al De Rogatis
	1992–	WOR	
New York Jets	1962	WABC	
	1963	WHN	
	1964–77	WABC	
	1978–80	WOR	
	1981–83	WCBS	
	1984–89	WABC	
	1990–92	WCBS	
	1993–	WFAN	

Basketball

New York Knicks	1946–54	WHN/WMGM
	1955–59	WINS
	1960–63	no radio or TV
	1964	WOR
	1965	WNBC
	1966–70	WHN
	1971–73	WNBC
	1974–88	WFAN
	1992–94	WEVD
	1995–	WFAN (WEVD if schedules conflict)
		WPAT in Spanish

New York Nets	1977–88	WMCA
	1989–91	WNEW
	1992–94	WFAN
	1995	WPAT
	1996	WOR (WQEW if schedules conflict)

Hockey

New York Rangers	1943–57	WHN/WMGM
	1958–59	WINS
	1960–61	no radio or TV
	1962–66	WCBS
	1967–71	WHN
	1972–74	WNBC
	1975–86	WNEW
	1987–92	WEVD
	1993–	WFAN (WEVD if schedules conflict)

Selected Bibliography

From the CEO positioning a broadcasting company to respond to economic and demographic changes to the deejay picking the next record, radio people are always thinking about the future. The preservation of broadcasting history has frequently been haphazard, sometimes accidental. There are many, too many, accounts of radio stations discarding or abandoning files, photos, business records, tapes, and transcriptions of historical value. The authors of this book have sometimes literally salvaged such material, and in kindness we shall not credit all those sources.

At the same time, where records exist (the historical kind, as well as those with a hole in the center), they can overwhelm with minutiae. In crossing the historical landscape, we passed through many deserts and a few dense jungles of information.

We read thousands of newspaper and magazine articles. Jan Lowry's *Broadcast Pro-Files* were very helpful in tracing licensing history and the "genealogy" of many stations. Program listings in this book were taken from many newspapers and magazines, as well as from schedules and publicity material that had been issued by the stations.

Books

Anderson, Arthur. *Let's Pretend: A History of Radio's Best Loved Children's Show by a Longtime Cast Member*. Jefferson, NC: McFarland, 1994. An account of the CBS children's series; also a fine account of network activity in New York.

Bain, Donald. *Long John Nebel*. New York: Macmillan, 1974.

Banning, William Peck. *Commercial Broadcasting Pioneer: The WEAF Experiment*. Cambridge: Harvard University Press, 1946.

Barnouw, Erik. *A Tower in Babel*. New York: Oxford University Press, 1966.

_____. *The Golden Web*. New York: Oxford University Press, 1968.

_____. *The Image Empire*. New York: Oxford University Press, 1970.

Biow, Milton. *Butting In: An Adman Speaks Out*. New York: Doubleday, 1964. Memoir of the founder of WNEW.

Brokenshire, Norman. *This Is Norman Brokenshire*. New York: McKay, 1954.

Buxton, Frank, and Bill Owen. *The Big Broadcast*. New York: Viking Press, 1966.

De Forest, Lee. *Father of Radio*. Chicago: Wilcox and Follett, 1950.

Dreher, Carl. *Sarnoff: An American Success*. New York: Quadrangle, 1977.

Gambling, John A. *Rambling with Gambling*. Englewood Cliffs, NJ: Prentice-Hall, 1974. The recollections of the longtime morning man; a thorough history of the Gambling radio family and of station WOR.

Goldsmith, Alfred N., and Austin C. Lescarboura. *This Thing Called Broadcasting*. New York: Holt, 1930.

Granlund, Nils T. *Blondes, Brunettes, and Bullets*. New York: McKay, 1957.

Gray, Barry. *My Night People*. New York: Simon and Schuster, 1975.

Gross, Ben. *I Looked and I Listened*. New York: Random House, 1954.

Grudens, Richard. *The Best Damn Trumpet Player*. Stony Brook: Celebrity Profiles, 1997.

Husing, Ted. *Ten Years before the Mike.* New York: Farrar and Rinehart, 1935.

Landry, Robert J. *This Fascinating Radio Business.* Indianapolis: Bobbs-Merrill, 1946. Includes a section on network and local radio in New York; a good overview of the scene in the mid–1940s.

Leonard, Bill. *In the Storm of the Eye.* New York: Putnam, 1987.

McNamee, Graham. *You're on the Air.* New York: Harper, 1926.

Passman, Arnold. *The Deejays.* New York: Macmillan, 1971.

Sanger, Elliott M. *Rebel in Radio: The Story of WQXR.* New York: Hastings House, 1973. Reprinted in 1986 for WQXR's fiftieth anniversary.

Sklar, Rick. *Rocking America: How the All-Hit Radio Stations Took Over.* New York: St. Martin's, 1974.

Slate, Sam J., and Joe Cook. *It Sounds Impossible.* New York: Macmillan, 1963. Reminiscences by the general manager and program director of WCBS.

Treadwell, Bill. *Head, Heart, and Heel.* New York: Mayfair, 1958. Biography of "Uncle Don" Carney by his scriptwriter and publicist.

INDEX